The Political Economy of Indigo in India, 1580–1930

European Expansion and Indigenous Response

VOLUME 22

The titles published in this series are listed at *brill.com/euro*

The Political Economy of Indigo in India, 1580–1930

A Global Perspective

By

Ghulam A. Nadri

BRILL

LEIDEN | BOSTON

Cover illustration: "Indigo Manufacture in India", in: *The Graphic*, September 3rd 1887, p. 253. From Brill's own collection.

Library of Congress Cataloging-in-Publication Data

Names: Nadri, Ghulam A., author.
Title: The political economy of indigo in India, 1580-1930 : a global perspective / by Ghulam A. Nadri (Georgia State University).
Description: Boston : Brill, 2016. | Series: European expansion and indigenous response, ISSN 1873-8974 ; 22 | Includes bibliographical references and index.
Identifiers: LCCN 2016015288 (print) | LCCN 2016016816 (ebook) | ISBN 9789004311541 (hardback : alk. paper) | ISBN 9789004311558 (E-book)
Subjects: LCSH: Indigo industry--India--History. | Dyes and dyeing--India--History. | India--Politics and government.
Classification: LCC HD9019.I3 N33 2016 (print) | LCC HD9019.I3 (ebook) | DDC 338.4/766726--dc23
LC record available at https://lccn.loc.gov/2016015288

Typeface for the Latin, Greek, and Cyrillic scripts: "Brill". See and download: brill.com/brill-typeface.

ISSN 1873-8974
ISBN 978-90-04-31154-1 (hardback)
ISBN 978-90-04-31155-8 (e-book)

This book is printed on acid-free paper and produced in a sustainable manner.

Contents

General Editor's Foreword VII
Acknowledgements X
List of Illustrations XII
List of Abbreviations and Short Titles XIV
Currency, Weights, and Measures XVI
Glossary XVII

Introduction 1

1 The Making of Indigo: Cultivation and Manufacture 12

2 From Manufactory to Market: Logistics and Commerce 61

3 The Indigo Trade: Local and Global Demand 85

4 The Making of the World Market: Indigo Commodity Chains 124

5 The Political Economy of Indigo: States, Merchants, and Producers 154

Conclusions 192

Appendices

1 Annual Volumes (in Dutch pounds) and Values (in guilders) of the VOC's Indigo Exports from Surat, 1619–1742 197

2 Quantities and Values of Annual Indigo Sales by the VOC, 1642–1765 200

3 Indigo Sale Prices (stivers/pound) in Amsterdam, 1695–1760 206

4 Quantities (in lb.) of Indigo Exported by the EIC from Surat/Bombay, 1615–1729 208

5 Values (in rupees) of Annual Indigo Exports from India, 1795/96–1933/34 211

6 Quantities (in Dutch pounds) and Values (in guilders) of VOC's Exports of Java Indigo to the Dutch Republic, 1704–1781 216

7 Values (in guilder) and Volumes (in kilogram) of Indigo Exports from Java, 1824–1873 217

8 Indigo Prices (rupees per *man* and stivers per Dutch pound) in India, 1609–1757 219

9 Indigo Prices in Calcutta (rupees/factory *man*) and London (pence/lb.), 1843–1921 221

Bibliography 223
Index 240

General Editor's Foreword

Over the past half millennium, from ca. 1450 until the last third or so of the twentieth century, much of the world's history has been influenced in great part by one general dynamic and complex historical process known as European expansion. Defined as the opening up, unfolding, or increasing the extent, number, volumes or scope of the space, size, or participants belonging to a defined people or group, location or geographical region, Europe's expansion initially emerged and emanated physically, intellectually, and politically in general in southern Europe and specifically on the Iberian peninsula in the fifteenth century and developed rapidly to include all of Europe's maritime and, subsequently, most of its continental states and peoples. Most commonly associated with events described as the discovery of America and of a passage to the East Indies (Asia) by rounding the Cape of Good Hope (Africa), during the early modern and modern periods, European expansion and encounters with the rest of the world multiplied and morphed into several ancillary historical processes including colonization, imperialism, capitalism, and globalization and dealt with themes, amongst others, that relate to contacts, … 'connections and exchanges peoples, ideas and products, especially through the medium of trading companies; the exchange of religions and traditions; the transfer of technologies; and the development of new forms of political, social and economic policy, as well as identity formation'. (from the series' original objectives and mission statement) In consequence of its intrinsic importance, extensive research has been performed and much has been written about this field and the diverse topics that embody this subject over this entire period.

With the first volume published in 2009, Brill launched the European Expansion and Indigenous Response book series at the initiative of a well-known scholar and respected historian, Glenn J. Ames, who prior to his untimely passing was the founding editor and guided the first seven volumes of the series to publication. George Bryan Souza, who was one of the early members of the series' editorial board, was appointed the series' second General Editor. The series' founding objectives were and are to focus on publications 'that understand and deal with the process of European expansion, interchange and connectivity in a global context in the early modern and modern period' and to 'provide a forum for a variety of types of scholarly work with a wider disciplinary approach that moves beyond the traditional isolated and nation bound historiographical emphases of this field, encouraging whenever possible non-European perspectives'… 'that seek to understand this indigenous transformative process and period in autonomous as well as inter-related cultural, economic, social, and ideological terms'. (from the series' original objectives and mission statement)

The history of European expansion is a field that is challenging and interest in it, which is high is likely to continue, if not grow, in spite or perhaps, because of it being so polemical. The heightened dispute about the field has centered primarily on tropes conceived and written in the past by Europeans, primarily, concerning their early reflections, claims, and contestation about the transcendental historical nature of this process and its emergence and importance in the creation of an early modern global economy and society.

One of the most persistent complaints about the field is that it is 'Eurocentric', which is a complaint about the perennial difficulty in introducing and balancing different historical perspectives, when one of the actors to some degree is neither European nor Europeanized—a conundrum that is alluded to in an African proverb, which states: 'Until the lion tells his tale the hunt will always glorify the hunter'. Another and, perhaps, an even more important and growing historiographical issue is that with the re-emergence of historical millennial societies (China and India, for example) and the emergence of other non-Western European societies successfully competing competitively politically, economically and intellectually on the global scene vis-à-vis Europe, the seminal nature of European expansion is being subjected to greater scrutiny, debate, and comparison with other historical alternatives.

Despite and, perhaps, because of these new directions and stimulating sources of existing and emerging debating points or lines of dispute about the field of history of European expansion, Souza and the editorial board of the series will continue with the original objectives and mission statement of the series and vigorously '... seek out studies that employ diverse forms of analysis from all scholarly disciplines, including anthropology, archaeology, art history, history, (including the history of science), linguistics, literature, music, philosophy, and religious studies'. In addition, we shall seek to stimulate, locate, incorporate, and publish the most important and exciting scholarship in the field.

Towards that purpose, I am pleased to introduce volume 22 of Brill's EURO series, entitled: *The Political Economy of Indigo in India, 1580–1930: A Global Perspective*, which is a well-researched and well-written, detailed history of indigo trade and production in South Asia for over four centuries. Incorporating a commodity chain approach, its author, Ghulam A. Nadri, has taken an inanimate object and explained how it was produced, went through significant expansion, fostered cross-cultural transactions, and transformation on the Indian subcontinent in the early modern period. He has taken one commodity, a plant that naturally makes a blue dye, and presents its production, trade, enterprise, and politics in one narrative. He also demonstrates how a thing, so suggestively insignificant, could and did become entangled and embroiled in the history of European expansion to the degree that it did and significantly contributed to the historical process of globalization. Based upon extensive archival research, primarily in Dutch and English materials, this is evidence-based historical scholarship at its best. Nadri has succeeded in offering a connected narrative that links the history of agricultural development, technology, and imperial expansion in north, west, south and eastern India with that of the rest of Asia, the New World and Europe. The readers of this series should warmly welcome this work!

George Bryan Souza

Acknowledgements

This book comes out after about twenty years of my first academic interest in the subject. That was in 1996, when I wrote my M. Phil thesis on Sarkhej indigo. Since then, it has kept me intrigued even when I was working on other research projects. I am happy that I finally returned to it and was able to pursue its fascinating historical trajectory and write this book. In the process of doing this, I have immensely benefited from many scholars, authorities and staff of archives, libraries, universities, and other institutions, colleagues, friends, and family. I take this opportunity to thank them all for their contribution to this project. Over the last couple of years, I have had the opportunity to interact with scholars whose insightful comments and suggestions have helped me to develop ideas and engage with issues and interpretations presented in the book. I am particularly thankful to Tirthankar Roy and Dirk H. A. Kolff for commenting on an earlier draft of the chapters. I am grateful to Leonard Blussé, Michael Pearson, Maxine Berg, Giorgio Riello, Philippe Minard, Christelle Rabier, David McCreery, Makrand Mehta, Patrick O'Brien, Om Prakash, and Irfan Habib for their encouragement and for sharing their thoughts on my work. I presented drafts of some chapters at workshops and seminars at the University of Warwick, University of Paris, London School of Economics and Political Science, Ecole des Haute Etudes de Sciences Sociale, Paris and Marseilles, and Georgia State University and I thank the participants for their comments and feedback. I also benefited from several of my colleagues and friends who showed keen interest in my research and shared their knowledge of indigo in this part of the world. I am particularly thankful to Glen Skew, Richard Laub, Mary Rolinson, Katheryn Wilson, Ian Fletcher, Hugh Hudson, and Douglas Reynolds. I am indebted to Marguerite Martin for drawing my attention to some useful documents in the Marseille Chamber of Commerce archives, and to Denise Davidson, Yael Fletcher, and Christelle Rabier for their help in reading some documents in French. My friends, Irma Roefs and Cynthia Viallé, have always shown interest in my work and helped me decipher some difficult texts from the Dutch archives. Thanks to both of them that I always felt at home whenever I was in Leiden. I am grateful to the two anonymous reviewers of the book manuscript and to George Bryan Souza for their generous comments and insights. I am thankful to Lincoln Paine for copyediting the manuscript and for his helpful suggestions.

I am thankful to the staff and authorities of the British Library, the National Archives in Kew, London, het Nationaal Archief, The Hague, Bibliothèque Nationale, Paris, West Bengal State Archives, Kolkata, Maharashtra State Archives, Mumbai, Bihar State Archives, Patna, the Archives of the Chamber of

Commerce and the *Archives Départementales* in Marseille and the libraries of the London School of Economics and Political Science, Georgia State University, the University System of Georgia, Leiden University, Cambridge University, Oxford University (Bodleian Library), and the School of Oriental and African Studies, University of London. The staff was very helpful and responsive to my enquiries and requisitions.

Major funding for this project came from the Royal Society and the British Academy, UK, which generously supported my two-year stay as a Newton International Fellow at the Economic History department, London School of Economics and Political Science, in 2011–2012. I thank their staff and the Newton Fellowship team for their support. Previous funding from Georgia State University (Research Initiation Grant, 2008 and the Ellen L. Evans History Faculty Enrichment Endowment, 2009) and the NWO (Netherlandse Wetenschappelijk Onderzoek or Dutch Scientific Research) Visiting Fellowship (fall 2010), the Netherland, facilitated my preliminary archival research in Europe and India. I thank the staff and authorities of these institutions. I thank the director and staff of the International Institute for Asian Studies (IIAS), Leiden, especially Sandra van der Horst, for welcoming me as a fellow at the institute during my research visits to the Netherlands. I am grateful to Paula Sorrell and Carolyn Whiters (History Department, GSU) and Linda Sampson and Tracy Keef (Economic History Department, LSE) for being supportive and for taking care of funds and logistics. I thank Caroline Evans for drawing the maps.

I am indebted to my friends and their families who have always stood by me and supported my research in innumerable ways. I would like to thank Mr. Hasan Kamal, Abeer and Shahab Shamsi, Urmila Staudacher, Uma Shankar and Hiramani Gupta, Mohammad Parwez, Syed Jabir Raza, Syed Zaheer H. Jafri and Faiz Habib. My special thanks to my friends Devendra K. Singh, Mohammad Nizamuddin, M. Mallikarjun, and Enayatullah Khan for their help during my field surveys in India. I am greatly indebted to my father, Dr. Mohammad Abdul Quadir Ahqur, whose vast knowledge about the indigo manufactories (*neel kothis*) in Bihar made it possible for me to survey some of them during my field trip. I am indebted to my family for their love, care, and support.

In all these years, my wife has been a great companion and a source of inspiration. Her encouragement and support, frank opinion and useful comments on my draft chapters, as well as her forbearance during my long absences when I traveled abroad, contributed a lot to the fruition of this research project and I am forever grateful to her. In the last two years, our son has provided the necessary digression and cheered me up, which added to the pleasantness of research and writing. To them I present this book as a token of appreciation of what they have done for me.

List of Illustrations

Maps

1.1 Map of India: major indigo production areas 14
4.1 World Map: major production and distribution areas 125

Images

1.1 Indigo vats, Jalali, c. early 17th century 19
1.2 Lower circular vat with a receptacle, Jalali, c. 17th century 21
1.3 Indigo vats, Shahpur, Aligarh, c. 19th century 43
1.4 Lower circular vat with a receptacle, Jalali, c. 17th century 58
1.5 Lower circular vat with a receptacle, Shahpur, Aligarh, c. 17th century 59
1.6 Furrowed steeping vat, Kowahi, Bihar, c. 19th century 60

Tables

3.1 Ten-yearly average annual exports of indigo by the EIC (in lb.) and the VOC (in Dutch pounds) from Surat, 1615–1729 102
3.2 Ten-yearly average annual quantities (in Dutch pounds) and values (in guilders) of indigo from India sold by the VOC in the Dutch Republic, 1642–1760 106
3.3 Ten-yearly average annual indigo exports (in lb.) from India to Great Britain, 1782–1898 115
3.4 Ten-yearly average annual values (in rupees) of indigo exports from India, 1796/97–1933/34 116
3.5 Ten-yearly average annual quantities (in cwt of 112 lb.) and values (in pound sterling) of indigo imports from Bengal, Madras, and Bombay into Great Britain, 1861–1898 117
4.1 Five-yearly average annual imports (in Dutch pounds) of Java indigo into the Dutch Republic, 1831–1913 130
4.2 Ten-yearly average annual imports (in lb.) of American indigo into Great Britain, 1701–1780 132
4.3 Five-yearly average annual imports (in lb.) of indigo into Great Britain, 1782–1796 133
4.4 Sale prices (per lb.) of Bayana and Sarkhej indigo in London 149

Figures

3.1 Ten-yearly average annual exports of indigo by the EIC (in lb.) and the VOC (in Dutch pounds) from Surat, 1615–1729 102
3.2 Ten-yearly average annual quantities (in Dutch pounds) and values (in guilders) of indigo from India sold by the VOC in the Dutch Republic, 1642–1760 106
3.3 Five-yearly average annual imports (in lb.) of indigo into Great Britain, 1782–1796 114
3.4 Ten-yearly average annual exports (in lb.) of indigo from India to Great Britain, 1782–1898 114
3.5 Ten-yearly average annual values (in rupees) of indigo exports from India, 1796/97–1933/34 116
3.6 Ten-yearly average annual imports (in cwt of 112 lb.) of indigo from Bengal, Madras, and Bombay into Great Britain, 1861–1898 117
4.1 Five-yearly average annual values (in guilders) of indigo exports from Java, 1825–1873 130
4.2 Five-yearly average annual exports (in lb.) of Guatemala indigo to Europe, 1772–1818 141
4.3 Sale prices of Bayana and Sarkhej indigo in London (pence/lb.) 149
4.4 Average annual prices (stivers/Dutch pound) of indigo in India, 1610–1742 149
4.5 Ten-yearly average annual indigo prices (Rs/factory *man*) in Calcutta, 1843–1921 151
4.6 Ten-yearly average annual prices (pence/lb.) of Bengal indigo in London, 1873–1921 151

List of Abbreviations and Short Titles

BCP	Bombay Commercial Proceedings of the East India Company
BL	British Library, London
CUP	Cambridge University Press
DFI	*The Dutch Factories in India*
EFI	*The English Factories in India*
EIC	the [English] East India Company
FRS	Factory Records Surat
GG&R	Gouverneur Generaal en Raad [Governor-General and Council] at Batavia
MSA	Maharashtra State Archives, Mumbai, India
NA	*Het Nationaal Archief*, The Hague, The Netherlands
NA, Kew	The National Archives, Kew, UK
OUP	Oxford University Press
Rs	Rupees
VOC	De Verenigde Oost-Indische Compagnie [the Dutch East India Company]
WBSA	West Bengal State Archives, Kolkata, India
WCA	Western Cape Archives, Cape Town, South Africa

Generale Missiven — *Generale Missiven van Gounerveurs-Generaal en Raden aan Heren XVII der Verenigde Oostindische Compagnie,* [*General missives of the governors-general and councilors to the Gentlemen XVII of the Dutch East India Company*]
Vol. I, 1610–1638, ed., W.Ph. Coolhaas ('s-Gravenhage: Martinus Nijhoff, 1960).
Vol. II, 1639–1655, ed., W.Ph. Coolhaas ('s-Gravenhage: Martinus Nijhoff, 1964).
Vol. III: 1655–1674, ed., W.Ph. Coolhaas ('s-Gravenhage: Martinus Nijhoff, 1968).
Vol. IV: 1675–1685, ed., W.Ph. Coolhaas ('s-Gravenhage: Martinus Nijhoff, 1971).
Vol V: 1686–1697, ed., W.Ph. Coolhaas ('s-Gravenhage: Martinus Nijhoff, 1975).

Dagh-Register — *Dagh-Register gehouden in't Casteel Batvia van't passerende daer ter plaetse als over geheel Nederlandts-India* [Daily register kept in Batavia Castle of events taking place there and in the entire Dutch East-Indies]

1631–1634, H.T. Colenbrander ('s-Gravenhage: Martinus Nijhoff, 1898).
1636 (ed.), J.A. van der Chijs ('s-Gravenhage: Martinus Nijhoff, 1899).
1637 (ed.), H.T. Colenbrander ('s-Gravenhage: Martinus Nijhoff, 1899).
1640–1641 (ed.), J.A. van der Chijs ('s-Gravenhage: Martinus Nijhoff, 1887).
1643–1644 (ed.), H.T. Colenbrander ('s-Gravenhage: Martinus Nijhoff, 1903).
1644–1645, (ed.), J.A. van der Chijs ('s-Gravenhage: Martinus Nijhoff, 1903).
1661 (ed.), J.A. van der Chijs ('s-Gravenhage: Martinus Nijhoff, 1889).
1682, part II (ed.), W. Fruin-Mees (Batavia, G Kolff & Co., 1931).

Currency, Weights, and Measures

Currency

1 rupee (Surat)	=	16 annas; 1 ½ guilders
1 rupee (Bengal)	=	1–2 shillings
1 *anna*	=	one-sixteenth of a rupee; 1 pence; 4 pice or *paisa*
1 *xeraphin*	=	40 *stivers* (2 guilders)
1 cruzado	=	1.3 *xeraphins*
1 pound sterling	=	20 shillings
1 shilling (s.)	=	16 pence (d.)
1 guilder (*f.*)	=	20 stivers
1 stiver	=	16 penningen or pennies

Weights

1 *man* (Surat)	=	30–36 Dutch pounds; 34.5-36 lb.
1 *man* (Agra)	=	50–53 lb.
1 *man* (Bombay)	=	41 ½ lb.
1 factory *man* (Bengal)	=	74.5-75 lb.
1 *man-i Shahjahani*	=	40 seer
1 Dutch pound	=	1.09 lb. avoirdupois
1 *bahar*	=	480 Dutch pounds
1 *fardel*	=	usually 4 *man* in Surat
1 pack (Surat)	=	usually 4 *man* (of 36 lb.)
1 pack (Agra)	=	usually 4 *man* (of 53 lb.)
1 *churl*	=	4 *man* in Surat
1 bale	=	120 lb. (Coromandel) half of a *candy* (784 lb.) in western India
1 hundredweight (cwt)	=	112 lb.

Measures

1 *bigha* (Bengal)	=	one-third of an acre
1 *bigha* (Bihar)	=	about an acre; equal to 3 Bengal *bighas*
1 acre	=	4,046.85 square metres
1 *cobido*	=	53.67 centimetres

Glossary

anna	A money of account, one-sixteenth (1/16) of a rupee.
assamiwar	See *raiyyati* below.
arroba	A measure of weight equal to about 32 lb. used in Portuguese Brazil.
bahar	A measure of weight equal to about 480 lb.
Bania	A term used for a number of Hindu and Jain merchant castes of Gujarat.
bigha	A land measure with considerable regional variation. In Bengal, it was one-third of an acre.
caravan	An overland (and also waterborne) transportation of merchandise on carts and camels and accompanied by large number of people.
churl	A measure of weight, equal to 4 *man* in Surat.
cobido (or *cavado*)	A measure equal to 53.67 centimetres.
diwani	Right to collect land revenue; a right that the EIC obtained from the Mughals to collect revenue in Bengal, Bihar, and Orissa in 1765.
Faraizi	An agrarian socio-economic movement against landlords in Bengal in the nineteenth century.
fardle	A measure of weight, usually a pack of 4 Surat *man*.
farman	An imperial decree or order issued by Mughal emperors to provincial governors and subordinate officials of the empire.
khud-kasht	Lit., self-cultivation; a system of agricultural production in which peasants cultivated plots of land on their own.
khushki	A system of agricultural production by which peasants voluntarily cultivated indigo on their own land and sold the crop to indigo planters.
lathials	Group of men with sticks (*lathi*) attached to some indigo manufactories in Bengal in the nineteenth century mainly to look after indigo cultivation and force peasants to grow indigo.
man	A common unit of weight in early modern and colonial north and western India with considerable regional variation. In Surat/Gujarat in the seventeenth century, it weighed from 34 to 38 lb. and in Agra 50–53 lb. In Bengal in the nineteenth century a factory *man* weighed 75 lb.
nij or *zera'ati*	A system of agricultural production in which a person could obtain land on lease for a certain period of time and cultivate it with the help of wage labourers. Many indigo planters in Bengal and Bihar obtained teneurial rights through leases and employed wage labourers to work on fields to grow indigo.

ocques	A measure of weight used in Europe; 44–45 *ocques* were equal to one quintal.
Opperkoopman	Chief merchant; a VOC official in-charge of commercial transaction at the company's factories.
pargana	An administrative sub-division in the Mughal Empire.
rahdari	An internal transit duty or local toll in the Mughal Empire.
raiyyat/ryot	A peasant; a cultivator.
raiyyati	(or *assamiwar*) A system of agricultural production in which peasants cultivated indigo on their own land under contract and upon taking monetary advance from an indigo planter.
Rajput	A class of Hindu warriors and rulers mostly in Rajasthan and Gujarat.
rupee	A silver coin current in entire northern India since the sixteenth century whose exchange values changed from one place to another and from one period to another.
theeka	Lit. a contract; a system of land tenure in which land was leased by indigo planters for some years from the local *zamindar*, common in Bengal and Bihar in the nineteenth century.
voorkoper	An intermediary merchants, a merchandise dealer or supplier.
zamindar	Lit. a landholder; in Mughal India, a *zamindar* was a person who held hereditary rights to collect revenue from a tract of land not under direct imperial administration. In colonial India, he was a landlord whose right to collect revenue was conditional and transferable to another person.

Introduction

This book explores the history of indigo production and trade in India between the late sixteenth and early twentieth centuries. It studies indigo as a global commodity from a long-term perspective and underscores continuities and changes in the ways and means of production and patterns of trade and consumption. It examines the local and global forces that affected the potentialities of production in India and elsewhere and caused periods of boom and slump in the industry. It uses the conceptual framework of commodity chains to examine the dynamic trajectory of indigo involving a chain of processes: cultivation of the plant, manufacturing of the dye, marketing and transportation, distribution, and consumption. The book aims to achieve two main objectives, namely, to write the history of indigo in early modern and colonial India in a global context, that is as a part of the global processes of indigo production, trade, and consumption; and to present this history in a commodity chains framework by examining the processes and trajectories of production and exchange and their connections to other commodity chains and embeddedness in the politics of empire and colonial expansion.

India has been the home of commercial indigo production since antiquity, and there were periods when the blue dye produced in some parts of India dominated the world market.[1] During this period, the region produced natural blue dye (extracted from the plant species *Indigofera tinctoria*) on a large scale for local consumption and for export to Asian, European, and American markets. In the late sixteenth century, Indian indigo began to gain popularity in European markets at the expense of locally produced blue dye (woad indigo extracted from the plant species *Isatis tinctoria*) despite opposition to and restrictions on its use by some European states such as England, France, and many German and Italian city states. By the early seventeenth century, a world market developed, and indigo from competing production regimes in Asia and the Americas sought to capture an ever-large share of the market in Europe and West Asia. From the mid-seventeenth century, the monopoly of Indian indigo was seriously challenged by indigo produced in Europe's transatlantic colonies. Consequently, the European demand for Indian indigo declined and over the next hundred and forty years (from the late 1640s to the 1780s) only a little of it was exported to Europe. At the end of the eighteenth

1 I use the term world market as a collective noun to refer to regions where commercial indigo was produced and/or used on a large scale for the purposes of dyeing cotton, woollen, and silk textiles.

 | DOI 10.1163/9789004311558_002

century, however, Indian indigo once again dominated the market in Britain and Europe, and it continued to do so through the nineteenth and early twentieth centuries. By the end of the First World War, synthetic indigo produced in Germany began to replace natural indigo in the world market. Indigo production in India rapidly declined and, by the early 1930s the industry was almost completely dismantled. This book is a detailed study of this convoluted trajectory of indigo and its global context.

Indigo is a unique commodity in many respects. It is one of the oldest commodities still known and used by some in its pristine form. It was, for long, a globally traded commodity that from production to consumption involved people and resources from five continents—Asia, Europe, Africa, and North and South America. Indigo was one of the most widespread plants in the world and its cultivation and processing encompassed all forms of labour: free peasants, slaves, wage workers, and bonded labourers. It provided livelihoods to millions of peasants and labourers around the world and created commercial opportunities for a multitude of merchants, manufacturers, European companies,[2] brokers, bankers, and a host of intermediaries. It generated enormous revenues for many states and their rulers and inspired them to intervene in the economy and, occasionally, to create monopolies. In early nineteenth-century India, indigo was the first commodity to undergo a major transformation from small-scale peasant production to large-scale capitalist production using wage labour and salaried professional managers and agents. Perhaps more than any other commodity, it sparked revolts and rebellions and prompted governments to frame laws that would regulate production and govern labour relations. Thanks to these various attributes, indigo has attracted wide scholarly attention and generated a body of literature that investigates some of the aforementioned characteristics of indigo.[3] This book draws upon

2 I use the term European companies mainly to refer to the English East India Company (EIC) and the Dutch East India Company (*Vereenigde Oost-Indische Compagnie* or VOC) and it does not include the Danish or the French East India Company.

3 B.B. Chowdhury, *Growth of Commercial Agriculture in Bengal, 1757–1900* (Calcutta: R.K. Maitra, 1964); Jenny Balfour-Paul, *Indigo* (London: British Museum, 1998); Blair B. Kling, *The Blue Mutiny: The Indigo Disturbances in Bengal, 1859–1862* (Philadelphia: University of Pennsylvania Press, 1966); S.K. Mittal, *Peasant Uprisings and Mahatma Gandhi in North Bihar: A Politico-Economic Study of Indigo Industry, 1817–1917 with special reference to Champaran* (Meerut: Anu Prakashan, 1978); Prabhat Kumar Shukla, *Indigo and the Raj: Peasant Protests in Bihar, 1780–1917* (Delhi: Pragati Publications, 1993); Indrajit Ray, 'The indigo dye industry in colonial Bengal: A re-examination', *Indian Economic and Social History Review*, vol. 41, no. 2 (2004), 199–224; Jacques Pouchepadass, *Champaran and Gandhi: Planter, Peasants and Gandhian Politics* (New Delhi: OUP, 1999). On the Mughal-period indigo industry, Van Santen's PhD

and critiques this existing literature, and introduces new perspectives on indigo production and trade and state-economy relationships in early modern and colonial India.

Indigo in Indian Historiography

The literature mentioned above has illuminated many important aspects of indigo production and trade in India. Many contributors to it were pioneers who introduced the commodity into the historical narrative and laid the foundation for later research on commodity history. There are, nevertheless, some major gaps in the study of indigo, particularly in the pre-colonial period. While this study attempts to fill some of these holes, what distinguishes this work from the existing literature is its attempt to make major conceptual advances in three areas.

First, the scholarship on indigo has generally maintained the disjunction between the pre-colonial and colonial eras, with most of the research concentrated on the latter period. Scholars writing on Mughal-period indigo, including my own study of Sarkhej indigo in the seventeenth century, have generally confined their focus to that period, and those writing on colonial-period indigo

dissertation on Mughal India is the first major attempt to examine in some detail the indigo industry and trade in the seventeenth century using the Dutch sources. H.W. van Santen, 'De Vereenigde Oost-Indische Compagnie in Gujarat en Hindustan, 1620–1660' (PhD. dissertation, Leiden University, 1982). My MPhil thesis on Sarkhej indigo was based primarily on published English sources. Ghulam A. Nadri, 'Indigo Industry and Trade in Gujarat in the Seventeenth Century' (MPhil thesis, Aligarh Muslim University, 1996). Other studies of indigo production or trade in Mughal India are mainly descriptive and some are focused on the methods and technology of indigo processing. Jagdish Narayan Sarkar, *Studies in Economic Life in Mughal India* (Delhi, 1975); Iqtidar Alam Khan, 'Pre-Modern Indigo Vats of Bayana', in Attilio Petrucioli (ed.), *Environmental Design, Journal of the Islamic Environmental Research Centre* (Rome, 1989), 92–8; K.K. Trivedi, 'Innovation and Change in Indigo Production in Bayana, Eastern Rajasthan', *Studies in History*, vol. 10, no. 1 (1994), 53–80; Ishrat Alam, 'New Light on Indigo Production Technology during the Sixteenth and Seventeenth Centuries', in A.J. Qaisar and S.P. Verma (eds.), *Art and Culture: Felicitation Volume in the Honour of Professor S. Nurul Hasan* (Jaipur: Publication Scheme, 1993), 119–26; Syed Ali Nadeem Rezavi, 'The Design of Pre-Modern Indigo Vats in North India: A Study of Seventeenth and Eighteenth Century Indigo Vats of Bayana and Kol Indigo Tracts', *Journal of the Asiatic Society*, vol. 61, no. 3 (2009), 71–92. Ghulam A. Nadri, 'Indigo Processing in Mughal India: 16th–17th Centuries', in Harbans Mukhiya (ed.), *History of Technology in India vol. II* (New Delhi: Indian National Science Academy, 2012), 355–66; Ishrat Alam, 'Indigo production Technology in Medieval India', in Mukhiya (ed.), *History of Technology in India*, 367–80.

have seldom engaged seriously with its pre-colonial antecedents.[4] Consequently, an adequate comparative study of the indigo industry in Mughal India and that of colonial India has not yet been undertaken.[5] The binary between the two periods is reinforced by yet another distinction, between the European and the indigenous methods of indigo manufacturing. Many nineteenth-century European authors of treatises and essays on indigo production claimed that the indigenous mode of production was traditional or primitive, and paid little or no attention to the scientific and technological aspects of production processes or product quality. In contrast, they characterised European method of manufacturing as modern, scientific, and technologically advanced. In 1828, for example, John Crawfurd wrote,

> Europeans first began the culture and manufacture of indigo about forty-five years ago. What was manufactured by the natives of India prior to that time was trash unfit for the European market, then almost wholly supplied by America. There are at present in Bengal 309 manufactories of indigo for exportation, of which thirty-seven only are conducted by natives, and these in imitation of the European process. The Indians cannot even imitate us to any advantage with so many examples before them, for the indigo thus prepared is full fifteen per cent. lower in value than that manufactured by Europeans: and as to indigo made by the old native process, it is still wholly unfit for the foreign market.[6]

4 The division mainly emanates from the convoluted historical trajectory of indigo trade, in which the two periods of large-scale exports to Europe, one in the early seventeenth and the other in the nineteenth century, were separated by a long interregnum in which little or no indigo was exported to Europe. The dominant trend in South Asian historiography of treating the EIC's political conquests and the colonial state formation in the second half of the eighteenth century as a major break in the political and economic history of the region has also shaped this division between pre-colonial and colonial periods. Seema Alavi (ed.), *The Eighteenth Century in India: Debates in Indian History and Society* (New Delhi: OUP, 2002); P.J. Marshall (ed.), *The Eighteenth Century in Indian History: Evolution or Revolution?* (New Delhi: OUP, 2003).

5 Some attempts at comparison in the past have yielded contradictory interpretations. Trivedi, 'Innovation and Change in Indigo Production in Bayana'; Raaj Sah, 'Features of British Indigo in India', *Social Scientist*, vol. 9, nos. 2–3 (1980), 67–79; P.J. Marshall, *East India Fortunes: The British in Bengal in the Eighteenth Century* (Oxford: Clarendon Press, 1976), 157.

6 John Crawfurd, *A View of the Present State and Future Prospects of the Free Trade and Colonisation of India* (London: Ridgway, 1828), 8.

Modern scholarship on indigo is so focused on agrarian relations, the conditions of the peasantry, and the colonial state's manipulation of the economy that it has not been able to engage with the binaries constructed on the basis of assumptions regarding technology and scientific expertise between the Mughal and colonial periods or between European and indigenous methods of manufacture. It has generally attributed the large-scale production of good quality indigo in the nineteenth century and India's success in the world indigo market to new technologies and skills developed by European manufacturers.[7]

This study critically engages with these dichotomies and shows that, throughout this period, indigo production techniques and technology underwent continuous improvisation as a result of the industry's response to the changing dynamics of the world market. A critical analysis of the development of production and regional variations in the practice of this craft and in the application of knowledge and technology by indigo manufacturers reveals that a richer history lies beyond the simplistic binaries so often promulgated in the historiography of early modern and colonial India. This book argues that there were remarkable similarities in some basic features of the indigo industry between the Mughal and the colonial periods. It identifies patterns of development over a long period and reveals pre-colonial precedents for many features that are generally attributed to the colonial period. For example, it has been argued that the indigo industry in colonial India was based on a new European model of capitalist production. It is evident, however, that many features of the organisation of indigo production in this period were already present during the Mughal period. This book adds to the literature that traces the pervasiveness of some pre- or proto-capitalistic features in the indigo economy of colonial India.[8] It also underlines major changes in indigo's varied fortunes over time and explicates the local and global circumstances affecting those changes.

Second, this book puts indigo at the centre of the narrative and explores the fluctuations in its production and trade from long-term and comparative perspectives. Such an approach allows us to understand the nuances of the rural economy, Mughal and colonial governments' economic and commercial measures and policies, and local and metropolitan responses to economic

7 P.J. Marshall and, more recently, Prakash Kumar have argued that new European technologies and managerial skills contributed to the large-scale indigo production in British India. Marshall, *East India Fortunes*, 157; Prakash Kumar, *Indigo Plantations and Science in Colonial India* (Cambridge: CUP, 2012), 5–8, 99–110.

8 Peter Robb, 'Peasants' choices? Indian Agriculture and the Limits of Commercialization in Nineteenth-Century Bihar', *Economic History Review*, vol. 45, no. 1 (1992), 97–119; Kumar, *Indigo Plantations and Science in Colonial India*, 303–7.

opportunities. Past scholarship has not recognised indigo as a topic in its own right. Instead, it has generally been treated as a part of peasant history or the history of trade. As a result, there is little in the literature on Mughal-period indigo, even though it was a major commodity exported from Agra and Ahmadabad. The indigo industry in the colonial period, likewise, is generally understood in terms of a colonial economic enterprise undertaken by British and other European entrepreneurs and the colonial state. In the literature on colonial-period indigo, the dominant analytical framework is colonialism and its ambitions to make the colony economically beneficial for the metropolis by appropriating vast agrarian surpluses and remitting them to Britain. Thus, indigo is either conspicuously absent from or only marginally alluded to in the narrative of Bengal's transition to a colonial economy.[9] Scholars who have studied the agrarian transformation and the potential for growth in the economy have generally examined indigo and the development of commercial agriculture as an example to substantiate their views on colonial manipulation of the economy.[10] Prakash Kumar's recent book, *Indigo Plantations and Science in Colonial India*, is an exception as it is the first major work on indigo in colonial Bengal that treats the subject on its own and studies the role of practical and scientific knowledge in the industry.[11]

The development of the indigo industry in colonial Bengal was very much embedded in the politics of empire and colonial expansion. For the English East India Company (EIC), the promotion of the indigo industry in Bengal in the late eighteenth century was 'an object of the highest importance', and in 1790 the Privy Council in London even considered it as 'a national object likely in time to afford such a supply of indigo to Great Britain as to render any importation of that article from foreign countries unnecessary'.[12] At that

9 The transition is primarily understood in terms of a displacement by the EIC and British private traders of Indian merchants, bankers, and brokers who had until then dominated the economy and trade of South Asia. Sushil Chaudhury, *From Prosperity to Decline: Eighteenth Century Bengal* (New Delhi: Manohar, 1999); Marshall, *East India Fortunes*.

10 H.R. Ghosal, *Economic Transition in the Bengal Presidency (1793–1833)* (Calcutta: Firma K.L. Mukhopadhyay, 1950); Chowdhury, *Growth of Commercial Agriculture in Bengal*; Amales Tripathi, *Trade and Finance in the Bengal Presidency, 1793–1833* (rev. ed., Calcutta: OUP, 1979); Sunil Sen, *Agrarian Relations in India (1793–1947)* (New Delhi: People's Publishing House, 1979).

11 See my review of Prakash Kumar's *Indigo Plantations and Science in Colonial India* in *Studies in History*, vol. 31, no. 2 (2015), 249–52.

12 BL, Home Miscellaneous 434, Short Sketch of the measures adopted for the introduction of indigo and the promotion of agriculture in Bengal between the years 1779–1790, Bengal (Hugli), 30 Dec. 1790, p. 599.

time, the EIC's colonial state was restructuring the agrarian economy of northern India, which had recently come under its political control. Soon, indigo emerged as one of the most important commodities exported from the colony to the metropolis. By 1800, indigo produced in the Bengal Presidency had come to cater, almost entirely, to the rapidly expanding European demand.[13] The coincidence of the EIC's political conquests and colonisation in India and the growth of the indigo industry, in which the British and other European planters-manufacturers played a key role, has given rise to a tendency among historians to view the industry as an economic enterprise run by a government-planter nexus, in which peasants and labourers were completely subordinated to European capital and subjected to violence and excessive exploitation.

Such an understanding of the rise and growth of the indigo industry is rather simplistic. It glosses over several important and dynamic processes that contributed to the pre-eminence of Bengal indigo in the world market. This book uncovers those processes and analyses the anxieties, contestations, and compromises that characterised the relationship between the EIC and indigo planters and between them and peasants. It examines the objectives, strategies, constraints, and failures of the Mughal and colonial states in promoting and controlling the indigo industry and trade. While this study recognises the role that states played in the development of the indigo industry especially in the colonial period, it argues that the state-economy relationship was a two-way street in which indigo could potentially affect the attitudes of states or even reshape their political authority.[14]

Finally, this book studies Indian indigo in the broader context of global production and trade and explores the role it played in early modern globalisation. Most studies on indigo are India-centred and generally written from a nationalist viewpoint, especially those on colonial Bengal and Bihar. Only recently have some scholars begun to emphasize a global context to study the rise of Bengal indigo in the colonial period.[15] The growth of the indigo industry

---

13 In the late 1820s, British India supplied three-fourths of all indigo brought into European markets. Charles H. Weston, 'Observations on the Manner of Manufacturing Indigo in the Southern Provinces of India', *Journal of the Franklin Institute*, vol. 8, no. 4 (1829), 233.

14 In a recent study, Tirthankar Roy has reminded us of the unfeasibility of decoupling 'development and government' or 'quiet purging of the state from economic history'. Tirthankar Roy, *An Economic History of Early Modern India* (London/New York: Routledge, 2013), 5.

15 The history of indigo is generally told, as Willem van Schendel has recently pointed out, in the form of 'fragmented, unconnected, local histories' and mainly from an anti-colonial nationalist perspective. He emphasized the need for a broader and a more global perspective on the history of indigo. Pierre-Paul Darrac and Willem van Schendel, *Global Blue: Indigo and Espionage in Colonial Bengal* (Dhaka: The University Press Limited, 2006), 4–5;

in Bengal, according to this view, was an outcome of Britain's loss of indigo-producing American colonies and the decline of indigo production in Central America and the West Indies. Undoubtedly, the patterns of global production and exchange impinged upon the indigo industry in India, and adequate attention must be paid to this. But attributing the rise of Bengal indigo and its success in European markets to a shortage of supplies from Britain's former transatlantic colonies ignores several other dynamics underlying the substitution of American indigo in European markets with indigo from colonial India. Local political circumstances, European commercial rivalries, and Britain's desire to dominate the European indigo trade played a significant role in the development of the indigo industry in Bengal. This study uses an approach that integrates the local colonial and global commercial perspectives. The success of Bengal indigo in European markets in the nineteenth century reveals that the growth of the industry in Bengal had more to do with Britain's desire to substitute imports of French and Spanish colonial indigo than with making up for shortages of indigo arising from the loss of its transatlantic colonies.

A global context is equally relevant for any analysis of the indigo industry in Mughal India. In the sixteenth and seventeenth centuries, too, the fate of the commodity was shaped as much by global political and economic forces as by local circumstances. Large-scale exports of Bayana and Sarkhej indigo to West Asia and Europe in the early seventeenth century and their subsequent mid-century decline can only be understood if we take into account global and local political and economic forces that gave rise to competing chains of indigo supplies. As this study shows, Europe's difficulties in obtaining good-quality indigo at low prices in India, its colonial conquests across the Atlantic Ocean, and the desire to dominate intra-continental trade played a significant role in the proliferation of competing indigo chains in Asia and the Americas.

Willem van Schendel, 'The Asianization of Indigo: Rapid Change in a Global Trade around 1800', in Peter Boomgaard, Dick Kooiman, and Henk Schulte-Nordholt (eds.), *Linking Destinies: Trade, Towns and Kin in Asian History* (Leiden: KITLV Press, 2008), 41–6. More recently, Prakash Kumar has underlined the globality of the indigo knowledge and of the circumstances that went into the making of the indigo industry in colonial Bengal. Prakash Kumar, 'Planters and Naturalists: Transnational Knowledge on Colonial Indigo Plantations in South Asia', *Modern Asian Studies*, vol. 48, no. 3 (2014), 720–53; idem, *Indigo Plantations and Science in Colonial India*.

Indigo and the Global Commodity Chains Framework

This study benefits from the literature on global commodity chains to explore the processes involved in the making and marketing of indigo. With the recent emergence of the global commodity chains framework, a new literature is addressing the history of commodities from a variety of perspectives.[16] Indigo, however, has been less visible generally, and Indian indigo of the pre-colonial period does not figure at all.[17] This book is an attempt to study indigo using the global commodity chains framework. It examines indigo's course of development from plant to dye and from manufactories to markets in a wider set of global political and economic contexts. It explores the roles played by peasants, merchants, European companies and private entrepreneurs, local intermediaries, and states and their rulers, as well as the complexities of their mutual relationships, at various stages in the indigo commodity chain as well

16 The socio-cultural, economic, and political dimensions of commodities like cotton, sugar, textiles, and coffee are fairly well explored. See, Giorgio Riello, *Cotton: The Fabric that Made the Modern World* (Cambridge: CUP, 2013); G. Roger Knight, *Commodities and Colonialism: The Story of Big Sugar in Indonesia, 1880–1942* (Leiden/Boston: Brill, 2013); Giorgio Riello and Tirthankar Roy (eds.), *How India Clothed the World: The World of South Asian Textiles, 1500–1850* (Leiden/Boston: Brill, 2009); Giorgio Riello and Prasannan Parthasarathi (eds.), *The Spinning World: A Global History of Cotton Textiles, 1200–1850* (Oxford: OUP, 2009); Steven Topik, Carlos Marichal, and Zephyr Frank (eds.), *From Silver to Cocaine: Latin American Commodity Chains and the Building of the World Economy, 1500–2000* (Durham: Duke University Press, 2006), introduction; William Clarence-Smith and Steven Topik (eds.), *The Global Coffee Economy in Africa, Asia and Latin America, 1500–1989* (New York: CUP, 2003). For a discussion of various dimensions of the global commodity chains framework, see Gary Gereffi and Miguel Korzeniewicz (eds.), *Commodity Chains and Global Capitalism* (Westport, Greenwood Press, 1994); Jennifer Bair (ed.), *Frontiers of Commodity Chain Research* (Stanford: Stanford University Press, 2009). Recently, George Souza has applied the commodity chain framework using sugar production and trade in East Asia as a case study. George Bryan Souza, 'Hinderlands, Commodity Chains, and Circuits in Early Modern Asian History: Sugar in Qing China and Tokugawa Japan', in Tsukasa Mizushima, George Souza, and Dennis Flynn (eds.), *Hinterlands and Commodities: Place, Space, Time and the Political Economic Development of Asia over the Long Eighteenth Century* (Leiden/Boston: Brill, 2014), 15–47.

17 David McCreery, 'Indigo Commodity Chains in the Spanish and British Empires, 1560–1860' in Topik, et al., *From Silver to Cocaine*, 53–75; Darrac and Van Schendel, *Global Blue*, Chapters 2–6. A recent addition to the literature is Andrea Feeser, *Red, White, and Black Make Blue: Indigo in the Fabric of Colonial South Carolina Life* (Athens: University of Georgia Press, 2013).

as among competing chains.[18] This study follows indigo from production to trade or export up to its final destination in Europe, West Asia, or America, where indigo was sold and distributed among textile dyers, painters and printers, and other consumers. How indigo was distributed, who consumed it, and its impact on markets, societies, and economies are important problems, but they are only partly explored in this book.[19]

Structure of the Book

The next five chapters examine in detail the local and global dimensions of indigo production, trade, production relations in Mughal and colonial India, and competing indigo commodity chains. This study is based on evidence culled primarily from English and Dutch primary sources, but also from some Persian chronicles and records as well as from archaeological surveys of the remains of pre-colonial and colonial-period indigo vats in northern India. The book examines the imperatives and implications of European commercial and colonial expansion in early modern and colonial India as well as local responses and initiatives, hence its place in Brill's European Expansion and Indigenous Response series.

Chapter 1 discusses how indigo was produced in India and evaluates the role of labour, capital, technology, and institutions in the indigo industry in Mughal and colonial India. Chapter 2 focuses on the nature of the market and its organizational specifics, and on the practices of sale and export of indigo to overseas markets. Chapter 3 investigates the local and global demand for indigo by looking at the volume and value of indigo exports from India since the late sixteenth century. It explicates the endogenous and exogenous circumstances

18 The world-systems framework treats commodity trade as necessarily between a core and a periphery, as monopolistic, and as an exchange in which profit is always concentrated in the core. Immanuel Wallerstein, *The Modern World-System: Capitalist Agriculture and the European World-Economy in the Sixteenth Century* (New York: Academic Press, 1974); Terence K. Hopkins and Immanuel Wallerstein, 'Commodity Chains in the World-Economy Prior to 1800', *Review* (Fernand Braudel Center), vol. x, no. 1 (1986), 157–70; Gereffi and Korzeniewicz (eds.), *Commodity Chains and Global Capitalism*; Topik, et al., *From Silver to Cocaine*, 14–5.

19 For a preliminary analysis of the impact of indigo imports from India on the market in London in the seventeenth century, see Ghulam A. Nadri, 'The Indigo Trade of the English East India Company in the Seventeenth Century: Challenges and Opportunities', in Maxine Berg, et al. (eds.), *Goods from the East, 1600–1830: Trading Eurasia* (Palgrave Macmillan, 2015), 61–76.

that caused fluctuation in trade and evaluates merchants' and the companies' responses to it. Chapter 4 moves on to discuss how and why Europe looked for alternative sources of indigo supplies and what the implications were. It examines the development of the world indigo market and explains why Indian indigo failed to respond to the expanding European demand for this dye in the mid-seventeenth century. Chapter 5 examines the political economy of the indigo industry, evaluating the role of the state in indigo production and trade and the dynamics of production relations among peasants, merchants, planters and manufacturers in Mughal and colonial India. The conclusion sums up the findings of this study and recapitulates some major interpretations and issues surrounding the history of Indian indigo.

CHAPTER 1

The Making of Indigo: Cultivation and Manufacture

> [N]either the variety of the plant, nor the locality where it grows, influences the quality of the dye offered in the market. The excellency or inferiority of the Indigo depends solely on the care and intelligence exercised in its manufacture.
>
> F.E.C. LINDE, *Indigo: A short sketch of the Cultivation, Manufacture & Trade of Indigo*, 1882, P. 8

A primary factor in the success of an indigo commodity chain was the ability to produce large quantities of indigo of a relatively good quality and to put it on the market at competitive prices. This in turn depended on advantages in terms of natural and human resources that a producing region was endowed with in relation to potential competitors. The presence of suitable land, water, and climate in some parts of India gave it an advantage over other indigo producing regions of the world. India also had the advantage of being commercially well-connected with Europe, the Mediterranean world, and West Asia through both overland and maritime routes. Most important, however, was the availability of skilled manufacturers and cheap labour, which contributed to Indian indigo's competitiveness in the market. These factors, together with the capital coming from merchants, peasants, and producers, played an important role in making India a major producer and supplier of indigo. Such advantages were, however, relative, and other regions could produce indigo of better quality and secure European consumers' preference over Indian indigo. There were two other significant factors, namely the distribution costs (distance and transportation) and political intervention in the market, both of which played an important role in the success or failure of an indigo chain. Under certain political and economic circumstances, as during the mid-seventeenth and late eighteenth centuries, these factors could offset the relative advantages that India had over its competitors and that had contributed to its success in the world market during the sixteenth and seventeenth centuries and would again in the late eighteenth and nineteenth centuries.

During the sixteenth and seventeenth centuries, commercial indigo was produced in various parts of India. Of all places, the Bayana and Sarkhej tracts (in Rajasthan and Gujarat, respectively) were known for producing

 | DOI 10.1163/9789004311558_003

the best-quality indigo on a large scale.[1] Indigo was also produced at various places on the Coromandel Coast, mainly in the villages around Masulipatnam, Nagapatnam, and Pulicat.[2] Some villages in the province of Sind were also known for producing good indigo on a modest scale. Indigo of an ordinary sort was also produced at some other places, such as Khurja, Mewat, Jalali, Hindaun, Basawar, and many other villages in the *doab* region (tracts of land between the Ganges and Yamuna Rivers), and Dholka, Jambusar, Broach, Cambay, and Nadiad in Gujarat (Map 1.1).[3] European and Asian merchants knew very well that Bayana and Sarkhej produced the best indigo and strove to procure these varieties. They bought other varieties only when supplies of these indigo were insufficient. Indigo from places other than Bayana and Sarkhej was mainly for local consumption, although some of it was exported to West Asia and, occasionally, Europe.

While some of these places continued to produce indigo in the colonial period, a major shift certainly occurred in the location of the industry.[4] In the last quarter of the eighteenth century, some districts of Bengal, Bihar, Banaras, Awadh, Agra, and parts of the Madras Presidency produced indigo on a much larger scale than in previous centuries (Map 1.1). In the nineteenth century, Bengal indigo reigned supreme in the world market. The rapid growth of European demand for the blue dye triggered by the rapid expansion in textile production in Europe led to a major restructuring in global indigo production and trade. Certain political developments, such as British colonial conquests

1 It transpires from European records that the best indigo in India was produced in the Bayana tract (Bayana and villages around it are located at an aerial distance of about 45 miles southwest of Agra). Pelsaert has listed the villages in the Bayana tract that produced indigo. Francisco Pelsaert, *De Geschriften van Francisco Pelsaert over Mughal Indië, 1627: Kroniek en Remonstrantie* [The writings of Francisco Pelsaert about Mughal India: chronicle and remonstrance], (eds.), D.H.A. Kolff and H.W. van Santen ('s-Gravenhage: Martinus Nijhoff, 1979), 259–60. The second best variety came from Sarkhej (a village near Ahmadabad, capital of the Mughal province of Gujarat) and areas adjacent to it.

2 Pieter Van Dam, *Beschryvinge van de Oostindische Compagnie,* vol. 2 part 2 (ed.), F.W. Stapel ('s-Gravenhage: Martinus Nijhoff, 1932), pp. 192–205. *Generale Missiven,* vol. I, 1610–1638, p. 204.

3 Contemporary authors have mentioned these places as producing indigo of an inferior quality. BL, East India Company Correspondence with the East, 1602–1753 (E/3) 1, Original Correspondence with India, 1609, doc. no. 11; Pieter van den Broecke, *Pieter van den Broecke in Azië,* ed., W. Ph. Coolhaas, vol. II ('s-Gravenhage: Martinus Nijhof, 1963), 380–2.

4 Sind, for example, continued to produce indigo in the colonial period. In the first quarter of the nineteenth century, a good proportion of indigo exported from Bombay came from this region. MSA, Returns and Statements: External and Internal Commerce, 1801–02 to 1826–27, vols. 3, 4/5, 5/6, 8–16, 20–6.

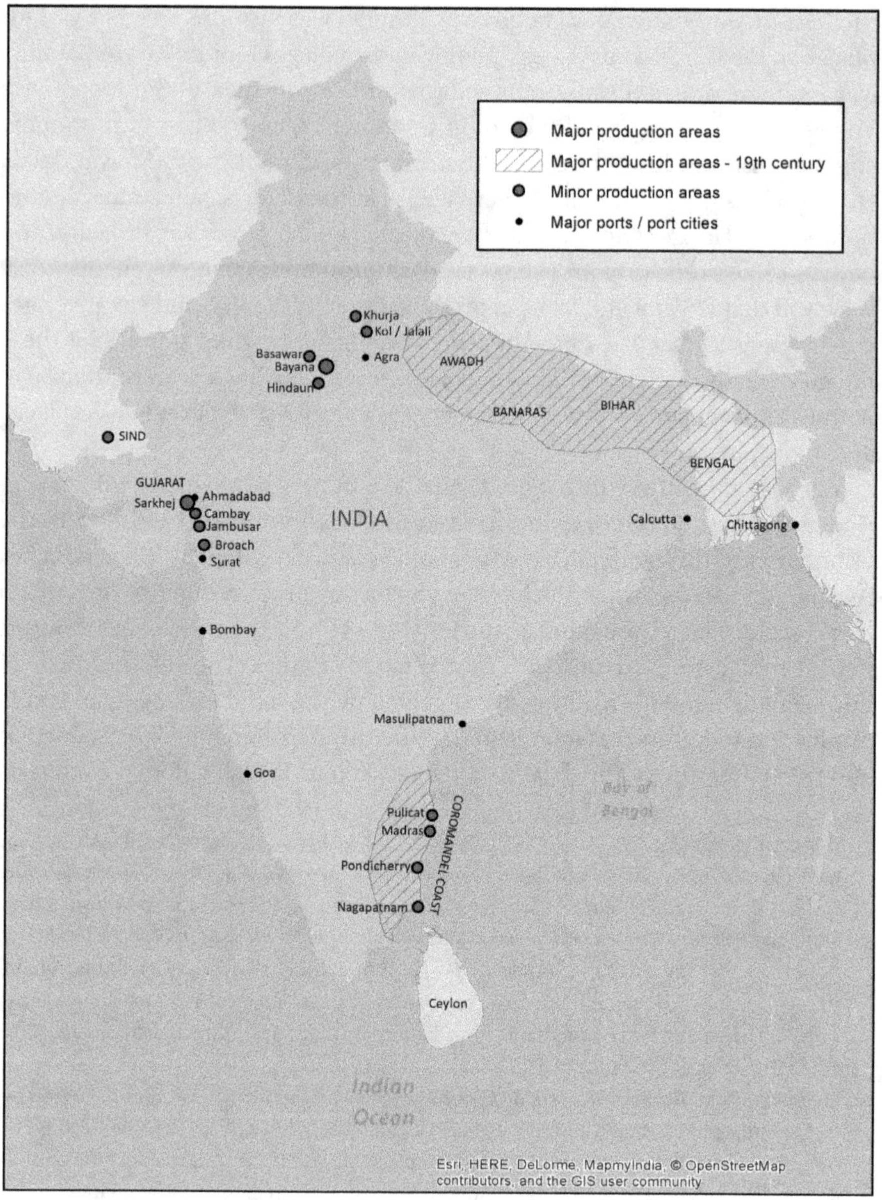

MAP 1.1 *Map of India: major indigo production areas*

in the Indian subcontinent and the almost simultaneous loss of the colonies that became the United States precipitated this transformation.

In the literature on indigo, the success or failure of Indian indigo is generally attributed to improvements to or a deterioration in its quality resulting from changes in technology and manufacturers' proficiency. The loss of European demand for Indian indigo in the mid-seventeenth century, thus, is attributed to adulteration.[5] Similarly, the success of Bengal indigo in the world market in the nineteenth century is attributed to the novelty of the colonial production system, the adoption of new technology, and improvements in manufacturers' expertise. Thus, the rise and fall of competing chains of indigo production and supplies are explained in terms of their relative advantages in technology, skills, and the industry's organisational structure. What follows below is an analysis, in a long-term perspective, of the technical, technological, financial, and organisational dynamics of indigo production in Mughal and colonial India.

Indigo Production in the Seventeenth Century

Cultivation of the Plant

Indigo dye was extracted from the plant species known as *Indigofera tinctoria*, which grew in different parts of India and other tropical regions.[6] It could be grown on any type of land, but black, sandy soil, and land with a mixture of clay and sand were highly suitable for its cultivation.[7] The leaves of the plant

5 'The quality of Gujarat indigo deteriorated steeply in the second half of the seventeenth century resulting in virtual stoppage of its export to Europe' Surendra Gopal, *Commerce and Crafts in Gujarat, 16th and 17th Centuries: A Study in the Impact of European Expansion on Precapitalist Economy* (New Delhi: People's Publishing House, 1975), 72.

6 The genus *indigofera* alone was reported to have about 69 species of which *tinctoria* was the most remarkable and produced the best dye. John Phipps, *A Series of Treatise on the Principal Products of Bengal: 1 Indigo* (Calcutta: Baptist Mission, 1832), p. 69. According to Linde, there were 150 species of *indigofera* grown in tropical countries and according to Martin-Leake, there were 350 species of which more than 40 were indigenous to India. F.E.C. Linde, *Indigo: a Short Sketch of the Cultivation, Manufacture & Trade of Indigo* (Calcutta: Central Press, 1882), pp. 1–2; Hugh Martin-Leake, 'A Historical Memoir of the Indigo Industry of Bihar', *Economic Botany*, 29 (1975), 361–2. For a description of various species of indigo around the world, see George Watt, *The Commercial Products of India: being an abridgment of The Dictionary of the Economic Products of India* (London: John Murray, 1908), 660–72. A recent study puts the number of *indigofera* species at 800. Margriet van Eikema Hommes, *Changing Pictures: Discolouration in 15th–17th-Century Oil Paintings* (London: Archetype, 2004), 111.

7 Contemporary Dutch sources point out that sandy (*santachtig*) soil was the best for indigo. NA, Collectie Geleynssen de Jongh [Geleynssen de Jongh collection], 14, Bewindhebberen aan GG&R [Directors to Governor-General and Council], Amsterdam, 20 Dec. 1622, f. 50^v; Pelsaert, *De Geschriften van Francisco Pelsaert over Mughal Indië*; Geleynssen de Jongh mentions that in Sarkhej indigo was grown on black sandy soil (*swarte santachtige aerde*) and red sandy soil (*rootachtige zant*). Geleynssen de Jongh, *De Remonstrantie van W. Geleynssen de Jongh* [the remonstrance of W. Geleynssen de Jongh], (ed.) W. Caland (s'Gravenhage: Martinus Nijhoff, 1929), p. 46. The best and the most appropriate land for indigo is the one

grown on sandy soil were more substantial and yielded more indigo than those of plants grown on other soil.[8] Being a tropical plant, indigo required sufficient rainwater but excessive water in flooded fields was injurious to the plant.[9] Indigo growers ploughed the land usually after the rainy season and prepared it for sowing. The number of times that land had to be ploughed differed from one type of land to another depending upon its elevation.[10] The advantage of frequent ploughing was that large quantities of weeds were uprooted before indigo was sown. The indigo plant grown on such fields was reportedly luxuriant and required less rigorous weeding.

In the Agra and Sarkhej tracts, the seed was sown usually in June and July either by broadcasting or the drill method.[11] After broadcasting the seed, the field was harrowed so that the seeds were buried under the soil. The moisture in the soil or a short rain shower helped the seeds to germinate in about a week's time. Cultivators had to make sure that the growth of young indigo plants was not impeded by unwanted shrubs or even by indigo plants planted too close to each

---

that is two-thirds sand and one-third clay. Daniel Havart, *Op-En Ondergang van Cormandel* [Rise and decline of Coromandel], (Amsterdam: Jan ten Hoorn, 1693), p. 19; Van Dam, *Beschryvinge van de Oostindische Compagnie,* vol. 2 part 2, p. 192; H.W. van Santen, 'De Verenigde Oost-Indische Compagnie in Gujarat en Hindustan, 1620–1660' (PhD dissertation, Leiden University, 1982).

8 Van Dam, *Beschryvinge van de Oostindische Compagnie*, vol. 2 part 2, pp. 192–3.

9 In 1621, EIC authorities in Surat anticipated that indigo will rise in price because the indigo fields in the countryside had been inundated by excessive rain, not seen in the last hundred years, causing much damage to the crop. *EFI 1618–21*, Agra to Surat, 22 Aug. 1621, p. 260; ibid., Agra to Surat, 8 Sept. 1621, p. 268.

10 Ploughing the land several times is reported by many contemporary accounts of indigo cultivation in India. A Dutch account of indigo production in Coromandel shows that the land was ploughed one or two times in September and ploughed again in December before the seeds were sown. VOC 4886, not foliated. A later report too mentions three or four ploughings. VOC 1472, Report on indigo cultivation, Datcheron, 31 Aug. 1689, f. 1111r.

11 It could be sown at any time of the year, but it gave the best and the richest harvest when sown after the rainy season (during June–July in the Agra and Sarkhej tracts and in December and January in Coromandel). *De Geschriften van Francisco Pelsaert*. In Sarkhej, sowing took place in early September and October and was harvested in November and December. *Remonstrantie van Geleynssen de Jongh*, p. 46. November–December was the harvest time for Sarkhej indigo as this was the time when indigo makers bought indigo leaves in the villages. VOC 1571, Memorandum on indigo cultivation and manufacture in Sarkhej by Matheus van Heck, Surat, 1687, f. 24r; VOC 4886, not foliated or dated; Van Dam, *Beschryvinge van de Oostindische Compagnie*, vol. 2 part 2, pp. 193, 202. A 1689 report, however, shows that in Coromandel, indigo was sown after the hot and rainy summer in June and July. VOC 1472, Report on indigo cultivation, Datcheron, 31 Aug. 1689, f. 1111r.

other. A second or third weeding was required if weed continued to grow. Sometimes when the rainfall was scanty and irregular, the fields had to be irrigated. However, it seems that most peasants depended for their indigo crops almost entirely on rainwater and seldom irrigated their fields.[12] In about three months from the sowing time, indigo fields were ready for the first harvest. The plant was cut about six inches to a foot from the ground. Stalks left on the land sprouted branches that matured quickly for subsequent cuttings. Indigo plant had the characteristic of yielding two, three, and sometimes four harvests in a year and the plant stood on the land for three years. The dye-yielding substance of the leaves gathered from the same plant varied from one year to another and from one cutting to another. The best indigo was grown in the second year, and in both Bayana and Sarkhej regions, the leaves harvested from the second cutting (known as *jari* in Bayana and *sien* in Gujarat) yielded the best indigo.[13] Leaves from the first year produced indigo of an inferior quality and a still poorer sort was obtained from the third year's harvest. In the second or third year, some cultivators left the plant on the ground to bear seeds because these were needed for sowing in the next cycle. After three years, the land was left fallow for a year to regain fertility, ploughed a couple of times, and also possibly fertilised.[14]

There were variations in the timing and duration of agricultural chores in the cultivation of indigo. The length of time between sowing and the first harvest as well as between the successive harvests varied according to the type of land, the moisture retained by the soil, rainfall, and overall climatic conditions. There was, therefore, no fixed timing of ploughing, sowing, weeding, and harvesting, and these processes were not carried out simultaneously in

12 This is evident from numerous references in our sources to crop failure due to scanty rainfall or a complete lack of it. In northern India, wells were not uncommon and peasants used various devices such as the *arhat* (Persian wheel), *charas* (leather bucket), and *dhenkli* (bucket) to draw water from wells and irrigate their fields. Irfan Habib, *The Agrarian System of Mughal India, 1557–1705* (New Delhi: OUP, 1999), 28–30.

13 William Finch, *Early Travels in India, 1583–1619*, (ed.) William Foster (London: OUP, 1921), 152; *De Geschriften van Francisco Pelsaert*, 255–8; VOC 1575, Resoluties [Proceedings], Batavia, 15 Jan. 1697, ff. 1645r–v. The British indigo planters too were aware of this and where possible, as in the Upper Provinces especially on high lands not inundated by rivers, a second crop was preferred since it gave the best indigo. It was called *khoonti* or *assaroo* crop and the best quality indigo was produced from this. Phipps, *A Series of Treatises on the Principal Products of Bengal*, 104–5.

14 Regarding Coromandel indigo, it was noted in 1622 that indigo exhausted the soil so much that the land needed to be left fallow for a year before the next round of crops could be grown. Collectie Geleynssen de Jongh, 14, Bewindhebberen aan GG&R, Amsterdam, 20 Dec. 1622, f. 50v.

all indigo-producing regions.[15] Indigo cultivators applied their discretion and carried out these processes as and when appropriate according to their experience and on-site observation. Their practical knowledge of indigo cultivation when combined with suitable land and supported by timely and appropriate rain produced a successful crop on which depended the quality and volume of the blue dye. Once harvested, the plant was either immediately processed at the manufactories or was left to dry to be processed later. Extracting the indigo dye from leaves involved a chain of complex processes carried out by skilled and experienced indigo manufacturers.

Manufacturing of the Dye

Indigo leaf that contained the blue dye-yielding substance dissolved in water when steeped in it. This also initiated a series of changes in the chemical properties of the liquescent indigo leaves. After fermentation had taken place, the water was oxygenated by stirring and beating which also caused indigo granules to form. Being heavier than water, these granules precipitated to the

15 Contemporary accounts give different timings for sowing and harvesting and provide details about patterns of sowing and harvesting that are often mutually incompatible. A 1622 Dutch description of indigo production on the Coromandel Coast shows that the plant gave three cuttings in the first year (in August, October, and January) and that it stood on the soil for three years (second crop was cut in October–November in the following year). Collectie Geleynssen de Jongh, 14, Bewindhebberen aan GG&R, Amsterdam, 20 Dec. 1622, f. 50v. Writing about the Bayana tract, Pelsaert (c. 1626) mentions that in the second year, the crop was sometimes so plentiful that it gave three cuttings. *De Geschriften van Francisco Pelsaert*, p. 256. A later description of indigo production in south and north Coromandel (in the regions of Nagapatnam and Pulicat respectively) shows that indigo was sown in January and gave four harvests in a year in March and early April, May and early June, July and early August, and the beginning of September and early October. Van Dam, *Beschryvinge van de Oostindische Compagnie*, vol. 2 part 2, pp. 193, 202. French traveller Tavernier testifies to the practice of three cuttings from the same plant in the Bayana and Sarkhej tracts. He writes that the first cutting was the richest and yielded the best indigo. Jean-Baptiste Tavernier, *The Six Voyages of John Baptista Tavernier through Turkey into Persia and the East Indies* (London, 1678), p. 60. Another Dutch description of indigo cultivation on the Coromandel Coast (c. 1689) shows that indigo was sown in June or July after the summer and rainy season and it stood on the ground for two years. Each year, it gave two cuttings first in September and October and then in November and December. VOC 1472, A report on indigo cultivation, Datcheron, 31 August 1689, ff. 1111r–v. Inconsistencies aside, these accounts certainly help us to get an idea of the plant and the processes of indigo cultivation.

IMAGE 1.1 *Indigo vats, Jalali, c. early 17th century*
SOURCE: PHOTO BY THE AUTHOR.

bottom of the vat once stirring stopped. The clear water on top was then carefully drained off through an outlet provided for that purpose or scooped out manually. The thick substance was removed in a piece of textile, dried in the sun, given the form of a small ball (as in the Bayana tract) or a flat cake (as in the Sarkhej and Coromandel tracts), and dried again. In general, this is how indigo dye was extracted from the plant, whether in India or elsewhere; yet, the output and quality of indigo differed from one region or sub-region to another. This was mainly because the way in which indigo processing activities were carried out differed somewhat from place to place.

A typical indigo manufacturing unit in northern and western India consisted of a well, sometimes a water tank, and multiple pairs of upper and lower vats made of brick and lime mortar and plastered on the inside (Image 1.1). The number of such pairs in a unit and the size of the vats varied from one place to another depending on the volume of indigo leaves to be treated in a season. The upper, or steeping, vat was rectangular or square in shape and was usually built on a raised platform so that its lower base was level with the top of the lower, or beating, vat. This beating vat was circular in shape and was large enough to take in the fermented water from the upper vat. An outlet consisting of a single hole in the base of the steeping vat opened into the beating vat.

A similar outlet was sometimes found at the bottom surface of the beating vat from where the receptacle descended to drain off the clear water from it after precipitation. This was common in the Bayana tract where the vats were generally built on a raised platform that made it possible to drain off the water from lower vats through an outlet. Where the lower vat was sunk into the ground an outlet was not possible and the clear water had to be taken out manually with the help of buckets.[16] Beating vats contained a small receptacle in the centre in which the indigo granules would settle down.[17] At some places, a small bowl-like cavity was made inside the receptacle to facilitate scooping of indigo granules.[18]

Some early European travellers noted that in Sarkhej and some other places, a single vat was used for both steeping and beating purposes.[19] This could have been possible because producers in Sarkhej used the dry-leaf method (described below), which meant that the dry leaves were steeped in water after being pounded and stripped from their branches. The leaves would dissolve in water rather quickly and the contents of the vat could be stirred for oxidation purposes. This was not unique to Gujarat or even India; the single-vat system

16 The lower circular beating vats at most of the indigo production units in the Aligarh tract were sunk in the ground, hence they were not provided with an outlet for draining off the water. My findings from the survey of some indigo production sites in Aligarh and Jalali confirm this. In the Bayana tract, both steeping and beating vats were generally built on a raised platform and the latter had an outlet. Iqtidar Alam Khan, 'Pre-Modern Indigo Vats of Bayana', in Attilio Petrucioli (ed.), *Environmental Design, Journal of the Islamic Environmental Research Centre*, Rome, 1989, 92–8; K.K. Trivedi, 'Innovation and Change in Indigo Production in Bayana, Eastern Rajasthan', *Studies in History*, vol. 10, no. 1 (1994), 53–80; Syed Ali Nadeem Rezavi, 'The Design of Pre-Modern Indigo Vats in North India: A Study of Seventeenth and Eighteenth Century Indigo Vats of Bayana and Kol Indigo Tracts', *Journal of the Asiatic Society*, 61/3 (2009), 71–92. At some places in the Bayana tract, the lower circular vats were sunk in the ground and had no outlet for draining water from it. The remains of the lower circular vats of an indigo manufactory in Weer, near Bayana, shows that they were sunk in the ground.

17 *De Geschriften van Francisco Pelsaert*, 255–6; Khan, 'Pre-Modern Indigo Vats of Bayana', 92–8; Trivedi, 'Innovation and Change in Indigo Production in Bayana'; Rezavi, 'The Design of Pre-Modern Indigo Vats in North India', 71–92.

18 Some lower circular vats in Jalali have this bowl-like small cavity inside the receptacle (see Image 1.2).

19 Pelsaert mentions that in Mewat a single vat was used for both steeping and beating processes as was the practice in Sarkhej. *De Geschriften van Francisco Pelsaert*, pp. 260–1; Jean-Baptiste Tavernier, *Travels in India, 1640–67*, (tr.) V. Ball, (ed.) W. Crook, vol. 2 (New Delhi, 1977), pp. 8–9; Rezavi, 'The Design of Pre-Modern Indigo Vats'.

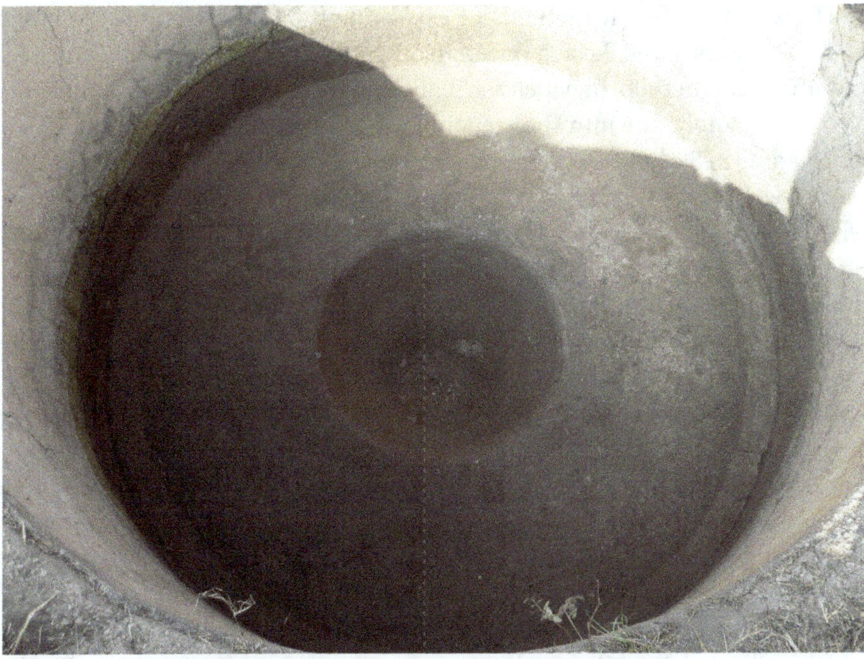

IMAGE 1.2 *Lower circular vat with a receptacle, Jalali, c. 17th century*
SOURCE: PHOTO BY THE AUTHOR.

of indigo production was also practiced in Spanish Guatemala.[20] In a description of indigo manufacture in Sarkhej written in 1696, Matheus van Heck reported that the manufacturing unit consisted of a well, water tank, and separate vats for steeping and beating purposes (known as *ner*, or male, and *madah*, or female, respectively).[21] Unlike in the Bayana and Sarkhej tracts, the indigo processing unit in Coromandel comprised a number of earthen pots and possibly a well and a water reservoir. The fermentation and oxidation processes were carried out in steeping pots (*weeck-potten*) and collecting pots (*verzamel-potten*) respectively.[22] The variety in the number, size, and shape of vats testify to the numerous ways indigo was manufactured in different parts of India.

20 Robert S. Smith, 'Indigo Production and Trade in Spanish Guatemala', *Hispanic American Historical Review*, 39/2 (1959), 185.

21 VOC 1575, Resoluties, Batavia, 15 Jan. 1697, ff. 1649ʳ–1650ʳ.

22 Collectie Geleynssen de Jongh, 14, Bewindhebberen aan GG&R, Amsterdam, 20 December 1622, ff. 51ᵛ–52ʳ; VOC 4886, not dated, not foliated; Van Dam, *Beschryvinge van de Oostindische Compagnie*, vol. 2 part 2, pp. 194–5, 202–3; VOC 1474, Description of indigo cultivation, Datcheron, 31 Aug. 1689, ff. 1112ʳ⁻ᵛ.

There were different methods of extracting the blue dye from the indigo plants. Growers in the Bayana tract and other parts of northern India practiced the green-leaf method, in which the plant was cut, brought to the manufactory, and immediately put into the steeping vat. Where the dry-leaf method was followed, as in Sarkhej and Coromandel, the cut plant was allowed to dry until the leaves fell off the stalks. About twenty to twenty-five days after the harvest when they were completely dry, the leaves were steeped in water. Depending on the weather conditions, fermentation took about a day or a day-and-a-half during which time the leaves dissolved and the water assumed a green tint and began to release a kind of odour. The liquid was then drawn into the beating vat by opening the plughole in the steeping vat. In the beating vat, the liquid was exposed to oxygen through vigorous stirring and beating. This was done by a group of labourers who stood inside the vat and agitated the liquid with their arms or with wooden staves or bats.[23] According to Van Heck, this was done by a group of labourers consisting of four men and four women who stood in the vat and stirred the liquid in such a way that it created a rhythm that was a pleasure to watch.[24] In the process of oxidation, indigo granules were formed and separated from water. The colour of the water changed from green to blue, which indicated that the oxidation process was complete and the beating could stop. The indigo granules at the bottom of the vat were scooped out by hand after the clear water above was carefully drained off.

In south-eastern India, the manufacturing method was somewhat different. It transpires from several early seventeenth-century reports on indigo production on the Coromandel Coast that manufacturing indigo from dry leaves was more common than from green leaves. There were two things—use of earthen pots for steeping and beating purposes and cooking or boiling of the leaves in the steeping pot or of the granules in the beating pot—that distinguished Coromandel from other indigo production areas such as Bayana and Sarkhej.[25] Small earthen pots set in a row, sometimes about 100 in number, were packed with dry indigo leaves until the pot was about 90 percent full. The pots were then filled with clear sweet or brackish water. In some places, especially where

23 *De Geschriften van Francisco Pelsaert*, pp. 255–6.

24 VOC 1575, Resoluties, Batavia, 15 Jan. 1697, f. 1657r; Ashin Das Gupta, *Indian Merchants and the Decline of Surat, 1700–1750* (Wiesbaden: Franz Steiner, 1979), 60.

25 There are several seventeenth-century Dutch reports on the cultivation and manufacture of indigo on the Coromandel Coast that describe in detail how the plant was sown and harvested and how the dye was manufactured. Collectie Geleynssen de Jongh, 14, Bewindhebberen aan GG&R, 20 Dec. 1622, ff. 50v–54v; VOC 4886, not foliated; VOC 1472, Report on indigo cultivation, Datcheron, 16 Aug. 1689, ff. 1111r–1113v. The most detailed is the one that was written in about 1688 and that describes the processes in north and south Coromandel. Van Dam, *Beschryvinge van de Oostindische Compagnie*, vol. 2 part 2, pp. 192–205.

the water was sweet, fermentation was facilitated by boiling or cooking the contents of the steeping pots. Cooking continued for about three hours or until the water had assumed a dark green colour. After cooking had stopped, the pots were left to cool down. Overcooking turned the leaves white and the water assumed a purple colour, and it adversely affected the quantity and quality of the dye. The liquid from eight steeping pots was then emptied into a beating pot. Four of the emptied pots were again filled with fresh cold water and stirred so that the thick substance sticking at the bottom would mix with it. This water was then emptied into the remaining four pots for the same purpose, and when these were rinsed, they were emptied into the beating pot. This was done slowly and carefully so that no unwanted leaf or shrub would go into the beating pot.[26] According to one report, this was done by covering the mouth of the collecting pot with a thick cloth into which the water from the steeping pots was transferred with a small earthen scoop. The leaf particles collected on top of the textile was then pressed with hands, squeezed, and put back in the same pot to be steeped again in cold water. The process was repeated in order to make sure that the leaves had released all the indigo substances into water and that the pots were emptied into the collecting pot.[27]

Beating or collecting pots were provided with a small plughole at about a quarter of its height from the bottom. The liquid in the collecting pot was stirred or churned with a two-meter-long bamboo or wooden stick that was split on one end and fitted with a round crown made of straw.[28] The stirring or churning of the liquid continued until the dark green water turned dark blue and white froth appeared on the surface. In some cases, the juice of a tree known in the local language as *tamohago* or *nagamarram* (in Portuguese, *jamblion*), was added to the liquid at this time. The sap was diluted in water for one-and-a-half to two hours before it was poured into the liquid in the beating pot. Some manufacturers added the juice of another tree called *merusa* or *merula* (in Portuguese, *jacca*), but this rendered the dye hard and heavy.[29] This was done mainly to facilitate the separation of indigo granules from water.

26 VOC 1472, Description of indigo cultivation, Datcheron, 16 Aug. 1689, f. 1112^v.

27 VOC 4668, not dated.

28 In a description of indigo production in southern Coromandel, this instrument is specified as a bamboo stick of about 4 *cobidos* (one *cobido* or *cavado* was equal to 53.67 centimetres) long that was split on one end with a round crown made of straw and wound with a straw thread. Van Dam, *Beschryvinge van de Oostindische Compagnie*, vol. 2 part 2, p. 195. Another source describes it as a wood split into 4 or 6 parts as a round crown or also provided with a carved and holed flat board. VOC 1472, Description of indigo cultivation, Datcheron, 16 Aug. 1689, f. 1112^v.

29 Collectie Geleynssen de Jongh, 14, Bewindhebberen aan GG&R, Amsterdam, 20 Dec. 1622, f. 51^v.

When the right amount of sap was added, the liquid assumed a brown-blue colour and yielded a good-quality indigo. If too much was added, it rendered the liquid heavy and brown.

Within a few hours after the beating or churning had stopped, granules settled down at the bottom of the vat or pot and the clear water above it was drained off. The granules were then collected in a piece of cloth spread over a bed of sand made in such a way that it was high on the four sides and low in the centre. In this way, the remaining water filtered through and drained into the sand underneath. In a semi-solid state, the substance was converted into small balls or cakes that were left to dry in the sun. Before too long, however, they were removed from the sun and kept in a shaded place to be dried by wind. This process of drying partly in the sun and partly in the wind was repeated for two or three days so that the cakes were completely dry and light in weight.[30] Once completely dry, the indigo was stored in a wind-free room built for the purpose.

The variety of ways in which indigo was manufactured in seventeenth-century India reveals regional diversity in production techniques and technology. At the same time, this also shows how people devised techniques that befitted the environmental and climatic conditions in their geographical areas. We get hardly any clue in the sources that help us explain why technologies and processing methods in Coromandel were so different from those of the Agra and Gujarat regions. In the hot and humid climate of southern India, it may not have been feasible to produce indigo in large open vats. Further, it was more convenient to use small earthen vessels if the liquid had to be boiled or cooked either in the steeping or collecting pots. It is highly unlikely that indigo producers in Coromandel were unaware of the manufacturing techniques and methods used in Bayana and Sarkhej. The sources indicate that technical and technological knowledge was shared among indigo-producing regions. The practice of extracting indigo from green leaves in Gujarat and Coromandel in the Bayana fashion points to this. We begin to have references to Gujarati manufacturers applying the green-leaf method of producing indigo in the Bayana fashion as early as the 1630s. They also gave their indigo a globular shape (instead of making it into flat cakes), as was done in Bayana. Subsequently, round indigo from Sarkhej became a part of the EIC's and VOC's indigo consignments

30 Van Dam, *Beschryvinge van de Oostindische Compagnie*, vol. 2 part 2, pp. 195–6; VOC 4668, not foliated. In Coromandel, indigo cakes were sometimes placed on a piece of textile spread on a flat bed of ashes (obtained from burning cow-dung) or baked in an oven. *Generale Missiven*, vol. I, 1610–1638, Memorie van 1617 en 1619, pp. 120–1. The VOC officials complained that this practice of baking rendered the indigo cakes so hard that one required a hammer to break them. Ibid.

to Europe.[31] Van Heck mentions that Gujarati manufacturers extracted indigo from dry and green leaves (known in Gujarati as *sukhaponka* and *silaponka* indigo respectively).[32]

Output and Quality

Some contemporary estimates of indigo production are available for Bayana and Sarkhej. The earliest estimate comes from an EIC official who noted in 1614 that Sarkhej produced about 3,000 *churls* (12,000 *man*) of indigo.[33] For the Bayana tract, we have the first estimate from Pelsaert, who puts the total indigo production of that region at 4,000 packs (16,000 *man*) in the period preceding 1621.[34] At its peak in the late 1630s, the total production of Bayana indigo was reported to be between 25,000 and 30,000 *man* (1.25 to 1.50 million Dutch pounds) and of Sarkhej indigo between 20,000 and 25,000 *man* (690,000 to 862,500 Dutch pounds).[35] Irfan Habib puts the average production of Bayana, Sarkhej, and Sind indigo at 1.8 million pounds avoirdupois.[36] Contemporary authors distinguished Bayana or Sarkhej indigo from varieties produced elsewhere. These quantities, therefore, do not include indigo produced at places like Kol, Khurja, Hindaun, Mewat, and others. If we include the output from these regions, the total indigo production in northern India would go up substantially. Despite their shortcomings, these estimates are helpful in calculating the total acreage of land occupied by indigo in the Bayana and Sarkhej tracts. Since the cultivation of indigo was concentrated in some villages, the proportion of land occupied by indigo in those villages may have been high.

---

31 *Dagh-Register, 1644–1645*, pp. 231–2.

32 VOC 1575, Resoluties, Batavia, 15 Jan. 1697, ff. 1646[v]–1647[r]; VOC 4886, not foliated. Ishrat Alam, 'New Light on Indigo Production Technology during the Sixteenth and Seventeenth Centuries', in A.J. Qaisar and S.P. Verma (eds.), *Art and Culture: Felicitation Volume in the Honour of Professor S. Nurul Hasan* (Jaipur: Publication Scheme, 1993).

33 BL, East India Company Correspondence with the East, 2, Original Correspondence from India with Collateral Documents, Vol. II, Anno 1614, Consultations, Surat, 1614, f. 242[a].

34 Pelsaert gives 4,000 packs (each equal to 4 *man*) as the total production in the Bayana tract. *De Geschriften van Francisco Pelsaert*, p. 259; Van Santen, 'De Verenigde Oost-Indische Compagnie in Gujarat en Hindustan'; Habib, *Agrarian System of Mughal India*, 48.

35 *Generale Missiven*, vol. I, 1610–1638, p. 620. The Agra *man* is taken here as equal to 50 Dutch pounds and that of Sarkhej 34.5 Dutch pounds. In 1630, EIC officials in Surat noted that indigo production in Sarkhej suffered due to excessive drought and the total produce was not more than two or three hundred *fardles* (800 or 1,200 *man*) whereas formerly it was not less than 4,000 to 5,000 *fardles* (about 16,000 to 20,000 *man*). *EFI 1630–33*, Surat to London, 31 Dec. 1630, p. 125.

36 Habib, *Agrarian System of Mughal India*, 48.

Assuming that the Bayana tract produced about 30,000 *man* of indigo in the mid-1630s, this would have required about 600,000 *man* of indigo leaves produced on some 33,000 to 35,000 *bighas* of land.[37] The estimated production also implies that a large amount of money (exceeding a million rupees) circulated in the village economy of Bayana and its surrounding areas. W.H. Moreland has rightly observed that the Dutch and the English purchases must have increased the income of the indigo producers by about three lakhs of rupees, which was a very substantial sum for the limited areas in which it was expended.[38]

Indigo production fluctuated heavily from one year to another. Several factors including external demand for indigo and its relative market value vis-à-vis other crops, especially food grain, determined the total acreage of cultivable land indigo would occupy in a year. These factors, in combination with natural and man-made calamities, could contribute to sudden fluctuations in the annual production of Bayana and Sarkhej indigo and, consequently, in the annual purchases of the EIC and the VOC between the 1620s and 1660s.

Despite all efforts and care to produce as much pure indigo as possible, the end product did not always meet the expectations of buyers and dyers. The quality of the dye was compromised sometimes and it became a real challenge for merchants, especially the Europeans, to ensure that the indigo they bought was of a good quality. They followed certain methods that, to some extent, helped them to ascertain the quality and to differentiate pure indigo from bad or adulterated types. Nothing, however, could help them overcome this problem completely, one result of which is that the decline in the European demand for Indian indigo that began in the mid-seventeenth century came to be attributed to its deteriorating quality.[39] Even if we keep this in perspective, the role that quality had come to play in the emerging world indigo market in this period can hardly be overlooked.

The quality of processed indigo depended on many factors, the most important of which were the quality of water and the producer's care in carrying out manufacturing processes. Contemporary observers pointed out that the water

---

37 In a good season, a *bigha* of land produced about 18 *man* of plants and 20 man plants were needed to obtain a *man* of indigo dye. Thus, to produce 30,000 *man* indigo, about 600,000 *man* of plants were required that could have been produced on land measuring about 33,000 *bighas*. A variation in these figures may be allowed because the dye-output of the plant varied according to the luxuriance of the leaves.

38 W.H. Moreland, *From Akbar to Aurangzeb: A Study of Indian Economic History* (London: Macmillan Press, 1923), 118; M.S. Commissariat, *A History of Gujarat, 1573–1758*, vol. II (Bombay: Orient Longmans, 1957), 304.

39 Gopal, *Commerce and Crafts in Gujarat*, 72.

used in manufacturing indigo had a major impact on the quality of the dye. Pelsaert attributes the superior quality of Bayana indigo to the brackish water found in that region.[40] Manufacturers were aware of the ill-effects of sweet water on indigo and as mentioned above they sometimes added the juice of a tree to the liquid in order to facilitate the formation of indigo granules and precipitation. Most producers, it seems, knew the plant and the properties of water very well, and were familiar with the technical aspects of indigo production. The quality also depended on the degree of precision with which such knowledge was applied. There were some standard procedures based on the changing colour of the liquid during the process that certainly helped manufacturers to determine how long to steep or beat the leaves. But a margin of error was unavoidable. If steeping or beating continued for a slightly shorter or longer time than required, it had adverse effects on the quality and quantity of the finished product. The difference in the precision with which indigo producers applied their knowledge was reflected in the wide range of quality of indigo produced in India. A knowledgeable producer was to be careful at all stages of manufacturing activities. If not, unwanted substances like sand, ashes, and plant particles got mixed with the indigo, rendering it poor in quality. European buyers sometimes complained about adulteration and the poor quality of indigo and often attributed this to manufacturers' carelessness.

Producers had no control over natural forces that affected indigo production such as rain, temperature, sunlight, and wind. A primary determinant of output and quality was the indigo leaves the dye was extracted from. As already mentioned, some plants produced more indigo of a superior quality than others, depending on where and when they were grown and harvested. Clearly, peasants and manufacturers depended on nature and its bounties for a desirable harvest and dye output. But sometimes, they manipulated the manufacturing processes in a way that compromised the quality. This had to do with the nature of the indigo plant and the enterprise. If the leaves harvested from the first or third cuttings were by nature inferior and yielded poor indigo, no producer could afford to process them and obtain indigo of the poorest sort. To avoid this, they mixed leaves from the first or third year with the best harvests of the second year. This was the most common form of adulteration in all indigo-producing tracts. From peasants' and manufacturers' perspectives, this

40 *De Geschriften van Francisco Pelsaert*, p. 259. The water used in indigo manufacture was drawn from wells. Most indigo production units of the Bayana and Sarkhej tracts included a well. Each set of premodern indigo vats that I surveyed in the districts of Agra, and Aligarh, contained a well located close to the vats.

was a logical strategy to avoid a situation in which they would have ended up producing the poorest sort of indigo for which there was hardly any demand.

Indigo was also adulterated when manufacturers were not careful enough to prevent the leaf particles, sand, or dirt from mixing with indigo granules. In Coromandel, some manufacturers were keen on producing pure indigo and, as we have seen, they used textiles to strain the liquid when transferring the mixture from steeping to beating pots.[41] Others, possibly deliberately, mixed in foreign matter to increase the weight of their indigo.[42] Similarly, adding tree sap to the liquid, as was commonly done in Coromandel, could adversely affect the colour and quality of the indigo, while making the end product heavier. This was more so when a disproportionate amount of tree sap was added to the liquid. Sometimes, soggy indigo cakes or balls were left to dry directly on a bed of sand and ashes instead of spreading them on a piece of textile.[43] In this way, sand and ashes got stuck to indigo making it heavy and poor in quality. The best indigo was very light and dry and one could easily break it by hand, as was the good-quality indigo that the Spaniards brought from Guatemala.[44] Several European reports on indigo production in India allude to the mixing of sand, ashes, oil, and clay with indigo and other practices that rendered the dye poor in quality.[45] Such practices brought disrepute to the industry and may have adversely affected the European demand for it. It is interesting to note, however, that such complaints became frequent starting in the 1640s, and these increased so much that one is led to believe that manufacturers were totally unconcerned about the quality of their product. The alleged apathy of indigo producers may be attributed to the nature of the indigo market in India and to the non-elasticity of demand in Europe.

---

41 Van Dam, *Beschryvinge van de Oostindische Compagnie*, vol. 2 part 2, pp. 194–5.

42 Ibid., pp. 198–9.

43 In a French memoir written in the late 1670s and 1680s, George Roques warns merchants to be watchful in buying indigo because the manufacturers in Sarkhej mixed sand in indigo and dried it on sandy grounds as a consequence of which indigo was much adulterated. Indrani Ray, 'Of Trade and Traders in Seventeenth-Century India: An Unpublished French Memoir by George Roques', in *The French East India Company and the Trade of the Indian Ocean, A collection of Essays by Indrani Ray*, (ed.), Lakshmi Subramanian (New Delhi: Munshiram Manoharlal, 1999), 57.

44 *Generale Missiven*, vol. I, 1610–1638, pp. 120, 124–5.

45 Ibid., pp. 120–3, 192–205; Collectie Geleynssen de Jongh, 14, Bewindhebberen aan GG&R, Amsterdam, 20 Dec. 1622; VOC 4886, not foliated; VOC 1472, Report on indigo cultivation, Datcheron, 16 April 1686. The Coromandel indigo was sometimes hard and unbreakable by hand. The VOC officials attributed this to the practice of drying or baking it in oven. *Generale Missiven*, vol. I, 1610–1638, pp. 120–1.

As it was for textiles, the indigo market in early modern India was a seller's market. Indigo producers took full advantage of the competition among buyers, especially between the EIC and VOC, who were constrained by their circumstances to secure the desired quantities rather hastily in order not to miss the caravan and the season when the homeward-bound ships would depart from Surat.[46] Pelsaert's description of merchants' behaviour in the indigo market of Agra testifies to the competition and buyers' desperation to procure indigo even if it was not of the best quality.[47] Those who had advanced money to peasants and manufacturers were sometimes at a disadvantage. They had to accept what was offered to them because the recovery of the loaned money was not easy. Uncertainty regarding output and prices forced the companies to secure supplies of indigo by advancing money to producers and suppliers. Producers were sure to find buyers for their indigo even if it was of an inferior sort. European preference for the best indigo and rejection of poor sorts should have induced manufacturers to produce good-quality indigo, but competition among buyers tempted the indigo producers to enhance the output rather than improve the quality. Even imperial intervention and occasional prohibitions on adulteration issued by some Mughal governors failed to have the desired effect on the industry.[48]

In the 1640s, Europeans were worried and grew increasingly impatient whenever they discovered adulterated indigo among imports from India. In 1646, the EIC went so far as to declare Sarkhej indigo unworthy of bringing home.[49] The average annual exports of indigo from Surat to Europe fell sharply from the late 1640s a phenomenon that is generally attributed to adulteration and poor quality of the dye. Yet, the decline in indigo exports from India to Europe seems to have been precipitated not so much by adulteration and poor quality as by the changing dynamics of the indigo market in Europe and the European incapacity to absorb any supplies from India that would top up the amount it received from the New World.

In earlier times, too, the Europeans had compared the quality of Indian indigo with the variety from Guatemala. But European merchants and dyers

46 Cf., Commissariat, *A History of Gujarat*, vol. 2, 120–1, 303.

47 *De Geschriften van Francisco Pelsaert*, pp. 261–2.

48 In 1640, the governor of Gujarat, Azam Khan, summoned a number of indigo makers from the area and 'after discharging a whole volley of revilings' on them for their base methods, 'he threatened to punish with death anyone who should thereafter dare to mix oil or sand or any other substance than what nature gave to indigo'. *EFI 1637–41*, Surat to London, 29 Dec. 1640, p. 274; Commissariat, *A History of Gujarat*, vol. 2, 121, 303.

49 *EFI 1646–50*, London to Surat, 26 March 1646, p. 32

perhaps became more quality-conscious after the supplies of American indigo into Europe resumed and expanded rapidly after the Eighty Years' War between the Netherlands and Spain ended in 1648.[50] The influx of indigo from the Spanish colonies in America into European markets reduced the sale prices of the commodity. Indian indigo, consequently, lost the premium it had enjoyed before. Moreover, multiple sources of indigo created market conditions in which the buyers came to have a wide range of options with regard to quality and prices. Naturally, the companies that supplied Indian indigo into Europe became particularly attentive to the quality of indigo they procured in India.[51] The failure of the Indian indigo industry to respond to the challenges of growing competition from Europe's transatlantic colonies in the following century-and-a-half may not be attributed to producers' apathy or indifference towards quality and marketability of indigo. The loss of European markets for Indian indigo was due to a combination of factors, including Mughal intervention in the trade, the nature of the agrarian economy and uncertainties of supplies that prompted the European search for alternative sources of supplies, rising purchase prices in India and falling sale prices in Europe, and, more importantly perhaps, the European preference for American indigo.

Organisation of Production: Land and Labour

Agriculture in precolonial India was a free household enterprise. While most agricultural tasks were typically carried out by members of the household, hiring wage labour was not uncommon for large-scale undertakings. The peasantry in India was highly stratified and there existed in villages a pool of landless labourers. It was not uncommon for *khud-kasht* (self-cultivating) peasants to use wage labourers.[52] Indigo as a commercial crop was sown usually in large fields, and farmers required both human labour and capital sufficient to buy seeds and

---

50 Jonathan Israel, *Dutch Primacy in World Trade, 1585–1740* (Oxford: Clarendon Press, 1989), 177–8; idem, *Dutch Republic and the Hispanic World, 1606–1661* (Oxford: Clarendon Press, 1982), 296, 432. The war had choked the Atlantic supply channels in the last three decades prior to 1648. Ibid.

51 The Gentlemen XVII and the Court of Directors issued instructions to their officials in India to buy only the best indigo otherwise not to buy at all. Subsequently, the companies' annual orders for indigo to be supplied from India, even though substantially slashed, were often conditional. The officials were directed to buy certain quantities only if it was of a good quality and if procurable at or below the prices limited by the home authorities. BL, Court Minutes (IOR/B), 29, pp. 130, 169–70, 173.

52 For a discussion on peasantry in Mughal India, see Habib, *The Agrarian System of Mughal India*, Chapter 4; idem, 'Peasants in Indian History', in Irfan Habib, *Essays in Indian History: Towards a Marxist Perception* (London: Anthem, 2002).

bear the expenses of agricultural operations. Growing indigo was also a risky enterprise as there were impending perils of natural and man-made calamities such as floods, torrential rain, drought, locusts, warfare, and the uncertainty of demand for the dye and thereby of its prices. Naturally, not every peasant could afford to grow indigo plants and certainly not those whose landholdings were not large enough to grow as much as to attract prospective manufacturers.

Those who cultivated indigo were, it seems, rich peasants with a landholding of their own and, perhaps, the resources to hire labour.[53] Indigo cultivation was a labour-intensive enterprise especially when it was carried out on a large scale. It required three-times as much labour as any other crop.[54] A complete cycle from sowing to harvesting involved several tasks that required labour to work in indigo fields. The land had to be ploughed, fertilised, levelled, and prepared; the seed had to be sown; unwanted grass had to be frequently weeded out; the plant had to be irrigated if necessary; and it had to be cut, stacked, and taken to the nearby manufactory or dried and readied for processing. Thus, even for large households with several members, it might not have been possible to undertake indigo cultivation without the help of wage labourers.

Some agricultural tasks such as weeding and harvesting had to be carried out within a day or two and required a number of labourers working together. We do not have contemporary estimates of the size of the labour force used in indigo cultivation, though it seems that labour costs accounted for a fairly large proportion of the expenses incurred in indigo cultivation. In 1731, when the VOC cultivated and manufactured indigo in two villages in Coromandel, the company paid for 1,512 days of 'coolie' labour employed in cutting, handling, and processing leaves.[55] More than 47 percent of the total production costs was on wages paid to labourers excluding the wages paid to indigo-makers.[56]

---

53 In the Mughal Indian system of land tenure the proprietary rights over land were vested in peasants. These rights remained inalienable as long as they cultivated the land and paid revenue to the state. The rulers' claim of a share in the produce did not take these rights away from primary producers. The system of land grants and the superior fiscal rights it bestowed on the recipients also did not undermine peasants' proprietary rights over the land they cultivated. Most peasants who cultivated indigo during this period, it may be argued, did it on the land over which they exercised proprietary control.

54 Tobacco and sugarcane cultivation required 100 and 80 labourers per acre of land respectively. Prakash Kumar, 'Scientific Experiments in British India: Scientists, Indigo Planters and the State, 1890–1930', *The Indian Economic and Social History Review*, vol. 38, no. 3 (2001), 256.

55 The total harvest was 840 units that produced 471 lb. of cooked indigo. VOC 8854, Resolutities, Coromandel, 7 Sept. 1731, pp. 979–80.

56 Ibid.

Most peasants who grew indigo on their fields, it seems, sold the crop to prospective manufacturers. Frequent references in the sources to the sale and purchase of indigo leaves in the Bayana and Sarkhej tracts indicate that indigo cultivation was a free-peasant undertaking. However, some resourceful farmers also owned a set of indigo vats and manufactured the dye themselves.[57] They carried out this activity as an adjunct to their agricultural activities. The enterprise required some capital for the construction of vats (or for buying earthen pots, as in Coromandel) and a storehouse, for buying leaves from peasants, and above all for hiring labourers to carry out steeping and beating processes and to assist with drying, storing, and packing the indigo. Money was also needed to purchase wood for boiling indigo, and to buy tools and manufacturing kit that included, among other things, some pieces of textiles, wooden staves and beams, earthen and copper pots and buckets, and gunny bags for packing.[58] Rich peasants alone could undertake this enterprise, and cash advances from prospective indigo buyers may have served as the operating capital and also enabled them to secure supplies of indigo leaves from peasant cultivators as well as to pay for the labour costs incurred in production. Indigo cultivation and manufacture were, and remained until the late eighteenth century, a peasant undertaking in which merchant capital played a significant supporting role.

There was not yet any separation between the agricultural enterprise of growing indigo plants and the industrial undertaking of extracting the dye.[59] This was primarily due to the nature of the plant, for unlike other agricultural crops, indigo leaves were a final product in and of themselves and had no use except as a source of blue dye to be extracted from it. No peasant would cultivate it unless he himself processed the leaves or he was sure that other manufacturers would buy his crop. In northern India where the dye was extracted through the green-leaf process, the harvested leaves had to be processed immediately. A close coordination between cutting and processing indigo was

57 In 1687, Van Heck noted that many indigo peasants in Sarkhej had their own vats, mostly a set of two, three, and four vats, located in nearby fields. VOC 1575, Resoluties, Batavia, 15 Jan. 1697, f. 1648r.

58 In his description of indigo production in Sarkhej in 1696, Matheus van Heck has listed about 15 accessories that were required for indigo production. VOC 1575, Resoluties, Batavia, 15 Jan. 1697, ff. 1651v–1652r; Alam, 'New Light on Indigo Production Technology', 120–1.

59 In the textiles sector, peasants who grew cotton and weavers who produced textiles were separated both in time and space. Cotton grown in Gujarat and the Deccan, for instance, was exported all the way to Bengal and China or Europe to be spun and woven. That was not the case with indigo. The plant once harvested had to be processed either immediately or after no later than a month (in places where the dye was extracted through the dry-leaf process). Many peasants who grew indigo leaves also manufactured the dye.

therefore vital for the industry. This continued to be, as we will see below, a fundamental feature of the industry as it developed in the Bengal Presidency in the late eighteenth and nineteenth centuries. A major change then was that the industry came to be increasingly dominated and controlled by European indigo planters, who invested their capital and undertook indigo cultivation and manufacture while divesting peasant-cultivators of their role and primacy of place in the industry.

Merchant Capital and Organisation of Production

In the seventeenth century, considerable merchant capital was involved in the indigo industry. Prospective buyers of indigo, including European companies, extended monetary advances to peasants and manufacturers. By doing so, they induced producers to undertake indigo production on the one hand and on the other secured for themselves the delivery of indigo so produced. Advance buying was a common feature of the commodity market in India. In an early seventeenth-century description of the Bayana indigo market, Pelsaert mentions that intermediary buyers (*voorcopers*) extended monetary advances to indigo growers binding them to deliver their crop to them and to none else.[60] The Portuguese, the EIC, the VOC, private European traders, and a number of Asian merchants competed with each other to secure indigo. Under such circumstances, advancing money to producers was a strategy to which most large-scale buyers had recourse. Such an arrangement also worked for producers. They received the money they needed to undertake indigo production and they also stood assured that their produce would not be left unsold. Generally, the VOC and the EIC advanced money to indigo producers in the villages in and around Bayana and Sarkhej to ensure that the receivers deliver their indigo to the company.[61] On the Coromandel Coast, too, the VOC extended loans to producers in order to encourage them to undertake indigo cultivation and production. In 1636, the VOC officials in Masulipatnam proposed to send the chief merchant (*Opperkoopman*), Gijsbert Pelle, to villages to procure indigo and advance money to producers as a measure to encourage them to produce

60 *De Geschriften van Francisco Pelsaert*, p. 261.

61 For a detailed study of the VOC's involvement in the rural credit system, see Van Santen, 'De Verenigde Oost-Indische Compagnie in Gujarat en Hindustan', 153–62. The Dutch participation in the rural credit system needs to be kept in perspective. The Dutch capital in the indigo production system was neither enormous nor it was unique and this may not have provoked the Mughals to monopolise the indigo trade in the empire as Van Santen and George Winius and Markus Vink have suggested. George Winius and Markus Vink, *The Merchant-Warrior Pacified: The VOC and its changing political economy in India* (Delhi: OUP, 1991), 62.

more in the next season.[62] Evidence is not conclusive on whether these advances legally bound the receiver to sell his indigo to the creditor, but most producers, it seems, generally abided by the terms of this arrangement and delivered indigo to their creditors. However, they could also sell their produce to anyone who paid higher prices even if they had received money in advance from others. In that case, they had to return the money to creditors with interest at the rate stipulated in the contract. This was an accepted mode of business. A letter written by VOC officials in Surat to Batavia in 1636 says,

> Rs 15,000 or more is given to indigo producers under surety [*cautie*] that they [the receivers] had to deliver their indigo to us at the market price (and not to sell it to others), so they are bound to us, but if someone else offers a higher price and if we are not willing to pay the same or a higher price, they will sell it to him, they will have to return our money (with interest for the period they had kept it).[63]

The VOC charged interest of 1½ percent per month if the receiving peasants failed to deliver indigo to the company. In 1637, the indigo producers of Bayana, who had received money in advance from John Tack, a VOC official, were reluctant to deliver their indigo to him at the price stipulated in the contract and demanded Rs 44 or Rs 45 per *man*. The VOC officials had to let them sell their indigo to others and return the money to the company with interest.[64] Intense competition among indigo buyers rendered this otherwise useful method of advance buying somewhat unworkable for the companies. The VOC officials complained that other buyers paid higher prices than the Dutch were willing to pay, which induced the producers to sell their indigo to others.[65] Thus, it would seem that monetary advances in the seventeenth century were not much different from interest-bearing loans. Advancing money may have been

62 *Dagh-Register, 1636*, Resoluties, Masulipatnam, 9 Oct. 1636, p. 242.

63 VOC 1122, Directeur en Raad van Surat aan GG&R, 2 Dec. 1636, f. 519v.

64 VOC 1122, Directeur en Raad van Surat aan GG&R, 8 April 1637, f. 560r. Van Santen, 'De Verenigde Oost-Indische Compagnie in Gujarat en Hindustan', 153–62. This aspect is much discussed in the context of advance buying of textiles and weavers' freedom to sell their produce to anyone paying the highest prices. See, K.N. Chaudhuri, *The Trading World of Asia and the English East India Company, 1660–1760* (Cambridge: CUP, 1978), 141–5; Prasannan Parthasarathi, *The Transition to a Colonial Economy: Weavers, Merchants and Kings in South India, 1720–1800* (Cambridge: CUP, 2001), chapters 1 and 3; Ghulam A. Nadri, *Eighteenth-Century Gujarat: The Dynamics of Its Political Economy, 1750–1800* (Leiden: Brill, 2009), 145–7.

65 VOC 1122, Directeur en Raad van Surat aan GG&R, 5 May 1637, f. 560r.

an instrument for merchants to control the indigo market, but the producer-recipients often used it to their advantage by securing a buyer for their produce while at the same time exercising the freedom to sell it to the highest bidder. Merchants and their capital undoubtedly facilitated indigo production, but the primary producers remained in control of their produce and were free to sell it to any merchants or companies at market prices.

Occasionally, attempts were also made by some European individuals and the EIC and VOC in India to manufacture indigo on their own account. In 1636–37, for instance, Simon Janssen, a Dutch official in Agra, cultivated indigo on a piece of land in the village of Renier and got 2 ½ *man* (about 132 Dutch pounds) indigo manufactured. But this was his private initiative and came as something of a surprise to the high officials in Surat and Batavia.[66] The VOC carried out experiments with indigo production on the Coromandel Coast with the help of hired labourers and indigo-makers.[67] This was possible because of the distinct nature of the political economy in Coromandel, which enabled the VOC to acquire control over several villages where the company promoted indigo production.[68] Such attempts, however, could not help the company to produce as much indigo as Amsterdam required from India. The VOC continued buying indigo from local peasants and producers. The EIC also tried to manufacture indigo on its own account in Sarkhej. It bought indigo leaves and employed local people to carry out the manufacturing. The company did not succeed in this enterprise and lost about Rs 20,000.[69] Such European attempts to produce indigo in India on their own remained unsuccessful, probably due to their lack of expertise in the art of indigo making and their inability to compete with local manufacturers, who seem to have jealously guarded their professional interests. In view of the risks involved in this enterprise and an almost total dependence on local labour and expertise, the European companies and private entrepreneurs did not make determined efforts to produce indigo on their own accounts. This would change, as we will see below, once Bengal and some other parts of the subcontinent came under the political control of the EIC in the second half of the eighteenth century.

---

66 VOC 1122, Directeur en Raad van Surat aan GG&R, 8 April 1637, f. 559^{r}.

67 Van Dam, *Beschryvinge van de Oostindische Compagnie*, vol. 2 part 2, pp. 204–5; VOC 1522, Extracts from J. Bacherus's letter to Bewindhebberen, Datcheron, 25 July 1692, ff. 1057^{r}–1059^{r}; VOC 8854, Resoluties, Coromandel, 7 Sept. 1731, pp. 979–80.

68 The enterprise was also facilitated by the availability of relatively cheap labour in south-eastern India. *The Dutch Factories in India, 1617–1623: A Collection of Dutch East India Company Documents Pertaining to India* (hereafter DFI) (ed.), Om Prakash (New Delhi: Munshiram Manoharlal, 1984), p. 269.

69 Ray, 'Of Trade and Traders in Seventeenth-Century India', 57.

Indigo Production in the Late 18th and 19th Centuries: Continuity and Change

Cultivation of the Plant

Indigo production in colonial India was based on a combination of local modes of cultivation and manufacture and methods borrowed from indigo plantations in the West Indies and Caribbean. While indigo production retained fundamental features such as the double vat system and the processes of fermentation, agitation, precipitation, and drying, some improvements certainly took place during this period. The changes may be noticed in the shape and dimension of indigo vats, the degree of precision in carrying out the procedures, application of the knowledge derived from transatlantic indigo plantations, and in the use of technological devices not known in the earlier period. These developments contributed to its production on a large scale and also to an improvement in its quality. By the early 1790s in Europe, Bengal indigo had come to be considered equal to, and even better than, the best indigo imported from Guatemala, the West Indies, and South Carolina. On 30 May 1792, the Court of Directors noted, 'the article [indigo] as to quality is still increasing in reputation. It has already surpassed the American & French, and there is no doubt but by perseverance and attention on the part of the planters, it will effectually rival the Spanish. A parcel of 5 chests belonging to Gilchrist & Charters was declared to be superior to Spanish & sold at higher rate'.[70] This was the reason why the blue dye produced in the EIC's Bengal Presidency had, in the early nineteenth century, largely replaced American indigo in the markets of Britain and continental Europe.

When the Court of Directors in London instructed the company's officials in Bengal to encourage indigo production in the company's territories in India and its exports to Britain in the 1770s, the commodity was then mainly produced in the erstwhile Mughal provinces of Awadh, Agra, and Delhi. Soon thereafter, however, indigo cultivation rapidly spread in Bengal and Bihar where the river deltas with their vast tracts of fertile alluvial soil were highly suitable for indigo cultivation. The annual swelling of rivers inundated vast tracts of land that were to be sown with indigo soon after the water receded leaving behind deposits of mud and sand very useful for plantation.[71] Thus, the geo-ecological conditions in the Bengal Presidency were favourable for indigo cultivation.

---

70 BL, Board's Collections, 60, Extract Court's commercial letter to Bengal, 30 May 1792, p. 3.

71 In was reported in 1831 that about nine-tenths of all land under indigo culture in Bengal was more or less under water by the end of July. BL, Board's Collections, 1504 (no. 58997),

For the EIC, however, promoting indigo culture was not without challenges. Although, indigo was not completely unknown in Bengal, the region had never before produced indigo on a scale that would attract European companies or other merchants. The region, instead, was known for its production of silk, sugar, rice, and later in the eighteenth century, cotton. The vast tracts of alluvial land that indigo would occupy in the 1780s and after were primarily used for paddy cultivation. The challenge for the EIC was to convince peasants within the Presidency to grow indigo. Peasants in general were reluctant to grow indigo because of the precariousness of the plant, which was liable to be completely lost if early inundation occurred. Moreover, their primary occupation in growing rice and other food grains left them with no inclination to try a new crop. As late as 1831, it was reported that peasants in Bengal considered indigo a secondary product and never gave their best land to it unless circumstances prevented them from sowing it with grain.[72] Even when the company and indigo manufacturers could persuade peasants, there was yet another challenge: how to protect the nascent indigo industry that was still threatened by large-scale production in the rival Awadh and Agra regions. By initiating certain institutional changes that seemingly restructured agrarian relations in Bengal and by adopting commercial measures favourable to indigo produced within the Presidency, the company succeeded in taking the indigo culture in Bengal to such a height that it soon stood unrivalled by any other country or region in output and quality.[73] The average annual value of indigo exports from Bengal to Britain rose from an insignificant amount in the late 1770s to more than 4.1 million *sikka* rupees (hereafter Rs) between 1795–96 and 1799–1800; this was about 21 percent of the average annual value of all exports during those years.[74] How was this sudden upsurge in the production of indigo in the Presidency possible?

Peasants, it seems, were initially enticed to undertake indigo cultivation by monetary advances extended to them by indigo manufacturers. On contract, peasants undertook to cultivate indigo on their lands and supply the plant to manufacturers at mutually agreed prices. This was known as the *assamiwar* or *raiyyati* system. For indigo manufacturers, this was the most preferred mode of obtaining indigo plant. There were different forms in which this system was

Agriculture and Horticulture Society, Calcutta, Extract from the proceedings of Government in the Revenue Department, 8 Nov. 1831, p. 105.

72 Ibid.

73 Indrajit Ray, 'The Indigo Dye Industry in Colonial Bengal: A Re-Examination', *Indian Economic and Social History Review*, vol. 41, no. 2 (2004), 199–224.

74 BL, Home Miscellaneous, 406, Appendices, Value of indigo exported from Bengal.

practiced. In Bengal, for instance, peasants on receiving Rs 2 per *bigha* in advance, contracted to grow indigo on their lands and deliver the crop to the lender-manufacturer at the specified price per bundle (usually 6–9 bundles per rupee).[75] In Bihar (Tirhoot), peasants generally signed a written contract by which they agreed to cultivate indigo on their lands upon a payment of Rs 6 per *bigha* and deliver the crop to the creditors. The contract remained valid for five years. The manufacturers kept for themselves the privilege of selecting the land for indigo cultivation, supervising the production processes, and instructing peasants to carry out the tasks in a way that would ensure the best results. Peasants were sure to receive up to Rs 3 in case of crop failure due to natural calamity. A penalty of Rs 12, however, was imposed on peasants for each *bigha* that was short of the agreement.[76]

Where peasants could not be persuaded to raise indigo, as in Banaras and Bihar, manufacturers leased land from local landlords for that purpose.[77] The manufacturers, anticipating the ever-expanding demand from Europe, erected large manufactories that could process massive amounts of leaves.[78] To ensure regular supplies of indigo leaves that these factories would process, manufacturers sought permission of the company's government to obtain leases to or ownership of land on which factories could be erected and indigo could be cultivated. The government issued licenses to those European entrepreneurs who undertook to supply indigo to the company for export to Great Britain. It also granted them the right to secure land leases from local landlords or *zamindars* against an annual rent payable to the latter.[79] Cultivation on such lands was

75 BL, Board's Collections, 1504 (no. 58997), Agriculture and Horticulture Society, Calcutta, Extract from the proceedings of Government in the Revenue Department, 8 Nov. 1831, pp. 108–9.

76 Ibid.

77 Ibid., 87–8.

78 The processing units were in general large in dimension and the number of vats in one unit was usually 6 or more. In 1793, a British indigo planter, Mr Becher, erected several factories with a total of 120 vats and dug 300 wells for indigo production in Awadh. BL, Board's Collections, 471 (11338), Concerning the claims of Robert Becher's indigo farm and its forcible possession by Almas Ali Khan, 1796, pp. 3–4. A factory with twelve pairs of vats was considered a good one while some large ones had sixteenth to twenty pairs of vats. Phipps, *A Series of Treatises on the Principal Products of Bengal*, 120–1. Of the seven factories in Jessore and Kishangarh, one had 20 sets of vats, another had 14, yet another had 12, the remaining four had 9, 8, and 5 sets of vats. Ibid., 154.

79 This also worked for the *zamindars*, who were hard-pressed under high fiscal obligations to leave their land under 'better resourced managers' that included European indigo planters. Peter Robb, *Peasants, Political Economy, and Law* (Oxford: OUP, 2007), 17.

carried out by hired labourers. This was known as the *nij* or *zera'ati* system in which the manufacturers were also planters. From the planters' point of view, this was not a preferred mode since it was more expensive than ordinary peasant cultivation (the *raiyyati* system) because of the high costs of overseeing and management and also because the entire tract of land under a planter's proprietorship was not necessarily suitable for indigo.[80]

The ratio of total lands cultivated under the *zera'at* and *raiyyati* systems was 1:2. But by 1830, the *nij* system was increasingly given up in favour of the *raiyyati,* due mainly to the higher costs of cultivation of the former system. Around 1830, the cost of *nij* cultivation in Bengal was about Rs 4 per *bigha*. Under the *raiyyati* system, manufacturers obtained the produce of a *bigha* for just Rs 2. In Bihar, the cost of cultivation of a *bigha* of *zera'at* land was estimated at Rs 16, while the cost at which indigo was obtained from the *raiyyati* land was 25 percent less.[81] By then, the practice of leasing land was becoming prevalent and manufacturers preferred this over the *nij* system. In a report on indigo production published in 1882, the planters were spoken of as landowners or *zamindars* holding large estates either in perpetual lease or leasing the land for a number of years on payment of a nominal rent to the government. The land was divided among *raiyyats* in small lots of three to seven acres either permanently or for some years, and the holdings were assessed according to their comparative values. These *raiyyats* were required to set aside a portion of land (usually the best and most productive part of the holding) and were forced to grow indigo on that. The planter provided the seeds and the *raiyyats* supplied the crop to the factory.[82] Some manufacturers contracted with the *raiyyats* of other *zamindars* binding them to undertake indigo cultivation against an advance payment of Rs 2 to Rs 4 per *bigha* of land. Upon delivery of the plant to the factory, they were paid at the rate of three to eight bundles per rupee as per the current price.[83]

Some peasants cultivated indigo on their own and sold their crop to manufacturers at the market price. This was known as *khushki* system. Peasants'

80 *Nij* cultivation was two times as expensive as the *raiyyati* system. Phipps, *A Series of Treatises on the Principal Products of Bengal*, 76, 79; BL, Board's Collections, 1504 (no. 58997), Agriculture and Horticulture Society, Calcutta, Extract from the proceedings of Government in the Revenue Department, 8 Nov. 1831, pp. 105–6; see Prabhat Kumar Shukla, *Indigo and the Raj: Peasant Protests in Bihar, 1780–1917* (Delhi: Pragati Publications, 1993).

81 BL, Board's Collections, 1504 (no. 58997), Agriculture and Horticulture Society, Calcutta, Extract from the proceedings of Government in the Revenue Department, 8 Nov. 1831, Indigo culture in Tirhoot, pp. 113–4.

82 Linde, *Indigo: A Short Sketch*, 2.

83 Ibid., 3–4.

loss of independent control over land in the nineteenth century left them with no incentive to undertake indigo cultivation on their own. Attempts by some indigo-makers to promote *khushki* cultivation in Bihar failed because such an arrangement worked neither for peasants nor for manufacturers.[84] Thus, in the nineteenth century traditional small-scale peasant cultivation continued wherever *raiyyati* system was practiced. The system of large indigo plantations, like those of the transatlantic colonies, was also introduced in India. The difference was that agricultural tasks on such plantations in India were carried out by wage labourers, whereas slave labour was used in most American plantation colonies except in Guatemala, where indigo cultivation was generally carried out by peasants and wage labourers.

The timing and method of sowing indigo varied from one region to another and from one type of land to another, as did the plant yield per unit of land and the dye-yielding qualities of the plant. On low-lying, annually-inundated alluvial soil, sowing generally took place either in October (autumn sowing) or in late February and March (spring sowing).[85] October sowing was preferred because it took place right after the subsiding of flood waters and was done at low cost. But the quality of the plants was poor because of the lack of rain and proper nourishment during the cold months of December and January. Spring sowing, on the other hand, was expensive, as it required careful preparation of the land by frequent ploughing and harrowing, and weeding out weeds and the stubble from the previous crop. Yet the harvest from plants sown in the spring and that had grown fully and quickly due to frequent rain was rich in granules and yielded indigo of good quality.[86] About six *sers* of seed was broadcast on a *bigha* of land in case of October sowing and four *sers* if sown in spring. On an average, a *bigha* produced ten to twelve bundles.[87] The plant matured in three or four months, but sometimes it had to be cut earlier to prevent its being flooded. At most indigo manufactories in Bengal, processing began in June or early July and the activities continued until August. Cultivation at higher elevations beyond the range of inundation required elaborate preparations. This included frequent ploughing (four to eight times) and harrowing of land, manuring the fields, and even turning over the soil with a spade. The preparation

84 Robb, *Peasants, Political Economy, and Law*, 26–31.

85 Pierre-Paul Darrac and Willem van Schendel, *Global Blue: Indigo and Espionage in Colonial Bengal* (Dhaka: The University Press Limited, 2006), 61–2. Throughout northern India, sowing or re-sowing actually continued between September and July depending on the elevation of the fields, rain, drought, and other climatic conditions. Phipps, *A Series of Treatises on the Principal Products of Bengal*, 80–2, 98, 104.

86 Darrac and Van Schendel, *Global Blue*, 56–7.

87 A bundle was measured by rounding a six-foot rope or chain in the middle of it. A bundle took in about a *man* and a half of indigo plant in Awadh.

was necessary for preserving the moisture and to remove weeds.[88] In all cases, nevertheless, frequent weeding was required in the early stages of growing the plant, especially in the first one-and-a-half months.

In the alluvial tracts of Bengal and parts of Bihar, indigo was an annual plant. Once submerged in the rain and river water, the stubble did not grow again. The fields had to be sown afresh with indigo every year. In places where indigo growing fields were not inundated by rivers, taking several cuttings from the same plant for two or three years was not uncommon. Pierre-Paul Darrac wrote in an 1823 report that indigo was an annual plant in Bengal but in Hindustan (the upper or western provinces) it was considered a perennial plant, as it usually persisted for three years.[89] The poor quality of the plant in the third year, however, did not encourage peasants to cultivate it. Instead, they left it on the field if they intended to obtain seeds from it. Indigo seed in itself had become a commodity and in view of the large demand from the Bengal and Bihar tracts, large quantities of it were produced in the western provinces and exported to those areas.[90]

When the plant had matured, it was cut between one and six inches above the ground. A treatise on indigo cultivation and manufacture written by De Cossigny advises manufacturers to avoid a premature or delayed cutting and pointed out that the maturity of the plant could be ascertained from the intensity of the colour and stiffness of the leaves.[91] The leaves in different stages of maturity fermented either too quickly or too late causing much loss of indigo to manufacturers. He also recommended that the plant not be cut early in the morning when the dew had not yet evaporated, or during the heat of the day, and that it should not be allowed to remain piled up for long. Such precautions were necessary to avoid fermentation before the plant was actually conveyed to the steeping vat. After it was cut, the plant was immediately taken to the factory for processing either carried on men's head or in carts and river boats, the last being more common in Bengal. In Bihar and the western provinces, it was more commonly transported on bullock-carts (*hackery*) for which prior arrangements were made through advances to cart owners. In the 1830s, John Phipps noted that advances of Rs 30 were made to each cart holder before the

88 For details on the preparation of indigo fields for sowing, see Martin-Leake, 'A Historical Memoir of the Indigo Industry', 362.

89 Darrac and Van Schendel, *Global Blue*, 61–2.

90 In Bengal, indigo cultivators and planters depended on seeds from the western provinces. In the 1820s and 1830s, manufacturers bought indigo seeds at 7 to 10 Rupees per *man*. Costs of buying seeds constituted a significant portion (more than 10 percent) of the total expenses incurred by manufacturers under both *raiyyati* and *nij* cultivation systems.

91 De Cossigny M. de Palma, *Memoir Containing an Abridged Treatises on the Cultivation and Manufacture of Indigo* (Calcutta: Company's Press, 1789), 19–20.

beginning of the manufacturing season.[92] Upon arrival at the factory, the plant was steeped in water for fermentation, the first of the several stages of indigo manufacture.

Manufacturing of the Indigo Dye

The indigo factory in the nineteenth century typically consisted of several sets of two, and sometimes three, inter-connected vats and a large tank or reservoir for collecting and storing water for steeping purposes. The fundamental principles of extracting indigo from the plant—that is fermentation, oxidation, and precipitation—remained as they were in earlier times, but the shape and size of colonial-period indigo vats were certainly different from those of the Mughal period. Most factories had six or more sets of large steeping and beating vats, and some even had twenty or more. The smaller circular beating vats of the Mughal period were given up for large square or rectangular tanks connected to the upper rectangular steeping vats. Many late-eighteenth- and nineteenth-century descriptions of indigo production and the remains of some nineteenth-century indigo vats in northern and southern India show that both steeping and beating vats were rectangular (Image 1.3).[93] Obviously, the shape and dimension of the vats were of some technical and technological importance and greatly affected the quality and yield of the dye so produced. The number of vats in a unit and the dimension of vats varied from one factory to another, depending on how much indigo was to be manufactured at a particular unit.

Most indigo production sites were located on the riverbanks and possibly used the river water for manufacturing indigo.[94] The river water was thought to be better-suited for indigo processing than the saline water from wells. A late eighteenth-century treatise on indigo recommended that manufacturers

---

92 Phipps, *A Series of Treatises on the Principal Products of Bengal*, 100. Several contemporary representations of indigo factories at work depict bullock carts with indigo plants. Darrac and Van Schendel, *Global Blue*, 68–9; Martin-Leake, 'A Historical Memoir of the Indigo Industry', 366.

93 De Cossigny, *Treatise on the Cultivation and Manufacture of Indigo*; Darrac and Van Schendel, *Global Blue*; Phipps, *A Series of Treatises on the Principal Products of Bengal*; John Shortt, *An Essay on the Culture and Manufacture of Indigo* (Madras: Fort Saint George Gazette Press, 1860).

94 This pattern is clearly seen in the nineteenth-century maps of indigo manufactories in Bengal and Bihar. Linde, *Indigo: A short sketch*. My own survey of some nineteenth-century indigo vats in the Vaishali and Muzaffarpur districts (in the Tirhoot division) supports this. Out of 14 sites I surveyed, 9 are located on riverbanks and possibly used the river water as there are no signs of there being a well nearby.

IMAGE 1.3 *Indigo vats, Shahpur, Aligarh, c. 19th century*
SOURCE: PHOTO BY THE AUTHOR.

should not use saline well water because salt retained and attracted dampness and rendered indigo heavy and unmarketable.[95] This runs contrary to the early seventeenth-century perception that brackish well water was more suitable than sweet water. Rainwater was equally good and some indigo factories even had a large reservoir to collect rainwater to be used in processing the plant. Various methods were used to collect water for steeping the plant depending upon the source and location. In the Lower Bengal region, where most manufactories were located on riverbanks and used river water, China pumps were commonly used.[96] The pumps were sometimes used for irrigating the land

95 *A Treatise on Indigo: containing a succinct account of the proper soil, the culture and preparation of that important article of commerce…*, translated from French by Ricard Nowland (Calcutta: James White, 1794), p. 14.

96 Phipps, *A Series of Treatises on the Principal Products of Bengal*, 121. China pump was a mechanical device using a chain of buckets to draw water from a river or a tank or well and worked by a group of labour. It could be a simple or a complex water-lifting device depending on the source of water and purpose of the pump. For a mid-nineteenth century description of the Chinese pump and drawings of it by an anonymous author see,

as well. Many factories used the more common hand-pumps for lifting water from its source and collecting it into reservoirs. In factories without a reservoir, water from a neighbouring tank or pool was used and probably transferred manually to the vat in buckets. Some factories seemingly continued using well water drawn in buckets through the use of human and animal power.

In the Agra and Awadh regions, indigo factories generally had masonry wells lined with bricks or stones (*pakka* wells) from which water was drawn by a pair of bullocks.[97] A late eighteenth-century sketch of an indigo factory in Cambay (Gujarat) shows a well that supplied water to the vats worked with a pulley and a pair of oxen.[98] Many contemporary observers have noted that the quality of water was an important determinant of the quality of indigo. But in the discourse on indigo production in the colonial period, the emphasis seems to have focused on the precision in the timing and duration of steeping, beating, and drying, and the extraordinary care in carrying out these processes. Most treatises and essays written on indigo production in the late eighteenth and nineteenth centuries warn manufacturers of the adverse consequences of deficient or excessive fermentation and oxidation for the yield and quality of indigo, but say little about the water used per se.[99]

As noted, the green-leaf process was commonly practiced in the indigo tracts of northern and southern India. John Shortt's description of indigo production in the Madras Presidency in 1860 refers to the practice among indigenous manufacturers of extracting indigo from dry leaves, but admits that the green-leaf process was most common even among them.[100] As soon as the plants arrived in the factory, the plants were spread out in the steeping vat with wooden beams placed on top to keep them submerged. Care was taken that the plants were not so compressed as to obstruct fermentation. Several factors, including the quality of the plant, air temperature, and whether the season was dry or rainy influenced the process of fermentation. Despite research and experiments by several European chemists and botanists, no fixed timing (in hours) could be prescribed for indigo manufacturers to follow in carrying out

---

Rural Life in Bengal: Illustrative of Anglo-Indian Suburban Life [Anonymous] (London: W. Thacker & Co., 1860), 123–5.

97 Phipps, *A Series of Treatises on the Principal Products of Bengal*, 122. My survey of two major indigo manufactories in the Aligarh district, shows that water was supplied from a well attached to the unit and the water was drawn through the pulleys by animal power.

98 'Plan and View of the process observed in manufacturing indigo at Cambay, referred to in the Memoir by Mr Mallet from an original drawing by Bramin Sada Nund', 1789, in De Cossigny, *Treatise on the Cultivation and Manufacture of Indigo*, 151–6.

99 De Cossigny, *Treatise on the Cultivation and Manufacture of Indigo*, 2–6, 55–8.

100 Shortt, *An Essay on the Culture and Manufacture of Indigo*, 7.

manufacturing processes. The steps that they recommended, if properly carried out, certainly reduced the margin of error that manufacturers had likely suffered from previously. Colour of the water in the steeping vat continued to be the key indicator of the degree of fermentation. When the water acquired a bright green colour and the proper degree of heat in the water threw up deep violet scum all over the vat, fermentation was thought to be complete.[101] Indigo manufacturers had to closely monitor the colour and chemical properties of the water after the plant had been steeped in it. Contemporary texts recommend testing the fermenting water in a clean silver or crystal cup to see if the exposure to air by shaking it leads to the formation of blue grains.[102] Manufacturers were advised to steep the plant in the evening or early in the night so that they would be able to judge the proper degree of fermentation at dawn the following morning, a procedure that might have been inconvenient to perform in the darkness of the night.[103] As early as 1789, the use of thermometers was recommended to accurately judge the state of fermentation and to prevent the loss of indigo caused by overheating of liquid.[104] In the Madras Presidency, fermentation was affected by boiling the indigo leaves. Plants were stacked in large boilers filled with water and boiled for several hours until the water had absorbed the colouring matter of the plant. The state of fermentation was judged by observing the colour of the water and boiling was discontinued when the water was in a state of agitation.[105]

Once fermentation was complete, the liquid was drawn into the beating vat in which it was subjected to continuous agitation or stirring. Several labourers stood for several hours inside the vats and stirred the water with their hands or with wooden planks.[106] At some manufactories in the Madras Presidency and

---

101 Ibid., 15.

102 To obtain the best result, this experiment was to be made with the water from the top, middle, and bottom of the vat because one level might be in a different state of fermentation than the other. De Cossigny, *Treatise on the Cultivation and Manufacture of Indigo*, 83; Nowland, *A Treatise on Indigo*, 16–17.

103 Nowland, *A Treatise on Indigo*, 13.

104 De Cossigny, *Treatise on the Cultivation and Manufacture of Indigo*, 40–1; *Reports and Documents connected with the Proceedings of the East India Company in regard to the Culture and Manufacture of Cotton-Wool, Raw Silk, and Indigo in India* (London: J.L. Cox and Sons, 1836), Extract letter from the Court of Directors to the Governor-general in Council, 8 April 1789, p. 19.

105 Shortt, *An Essay on the Culture and Manufacture of Indigo*, 18.

106 According to John Phipps, *Chamars* performed this task in the western provinces and they were paid Rs 4 per month. Phipps, *A Series of Treatises on the Principal Products of Bengal*, 105.

elsewhere, this was done with an apparatus with paddles that was rotated by coolies or worked with animal power.[107] As this process continued, the green water turned blue and a thick scum would rise with the movement of water. This scum was sometimes suppressed by mixing fish oil or mustard oil during the beating process. Exposure to air helped the indigo contents (or fecula) to separate from water and concentrate in the form of little blue granules.[108] Indigo-makers ascertained the state of agitation and observed the formation of indigo grains in the beating vat by taking the extract in a clean crystal or silver cup or on a white plate and observing the formation and precipitation of indigo grains.[109] Another mode of ascertaining the state of agitation was by pouring a few drops of the extract from the beating vat into a crystal glass full of clean water. If the extract formed a blackish cloud, the agitation process was thought to be complete. These procedures only indicated the state of agitation and it was up to the discretion of the indigo-makers whether to stop or continue the agitation process. Once the beating stopped, the liquid in the vat was allowed to settle. The blue indigo grains settled to the bottom of the vat in three to four hours. The clear yellow water on top of the thick indigo sediment was then drained off through outlets made for that purpose. Usually, the beating vats were provided with one or more outlets vertically arranged that were unplugged in succession to drain out the clear water.[110]

The thick indigo substance was then drawn off the beating vat and collected into a receptacle (or fecula vat) connected with the beating vat. At this point, manufacturers subjected the fecula to intensive boiling in fresh water for several hours. The fecula was conveyed to the boiler either through pumps attached to the receptacles or with a bucket. This was done primarily to prevent a second fermentation and to extract the air with which the fecula was impregnated.[111] Thereafter, the fecula was transferred to the draining table or strainer, usually a piece of cotton or flannel spread over a wooden frame. It was left to drain for twelve to eighteen hours after which it was taken to a press box

107 Shortt, *An Essay on the Culture and Manufacture of Indigo*, 18.

108 For a scientific explanation of the chemical changes in the fermentation and oxidation processes, see De Cossigny, *Treatise on the Cultivation and Manufacture of Indigo*; Shortt, *An Essay on the Culture and Manufacture of Indigo*, 20–2.

109 De Cossigny, *Treatise on the Cultivation and Manufacture of Indigo*, 57–69.

110 Phipps mentions vats with three or four holes, one on top of the other, in the bottom outer wall of the beating vat. Phipps, *A Series of Treatises on the Principal Products of Bengal*, 120.

111 According to John Shortt, if the fecula was not boiled immediately after the beating had stopped, fermentation began once again, which adversely affected the quality of indigo. Shortt, *An Essay on the Culture and Manufacture of Indigo*, 21–2.

for squeezing and draining of any water left in the fecula. Where a boiler was not used, the fecula was collected in a piece of cotton or a bag to allow further drawing off of any water the indigo still contained.

Indigo-makers followed different modes of drying their indigo and readying it for the market. The simplest method of draining the water from the fecula was to hang the cloth that contained it and squeeze as much water from it as possible. A more elaborate procedure was followed in many parts of India. Draining tables consisting of cisterns with wooden frames were built and these had sheets of cotton cloth spread over in which the fecula was conveyed from the boiler.[112] Large blocks of stone or other weights were placed on top of the table and left for several hours for the water to drain into the cisterns. The remaining paste was then either spread into shallow wooden boxes about 1½ inches deep to dry or was further squeezed by mechanical force applied through a press box.[113] The wooden boxes were then put in sunlight and heat and then taken to a shaded place to dry in air. Too much exposure to sun was not helpful as it dried the surface and caused it to develop cracks. Meanwhile, indigo in the semi-solid state in the boxes was cut into square pieces of not more than 1 ½ or 2 inches and were turned upside down to dry them. The semi-solid cakes from the press boxes were arranged in trays and left to dry in large drying rooms with sufficient light and air. The best results were obtained when indigo was placed air-dried in the shade. The drying process took several days during which the cakes developed a mould that needed to be softly brushed and cleaned. Once completely dry the indigo was ready for the market.

Organisation of Production: Land and Labour

The organisational structure and the relations of production in the indigo industry in colonial India varied from one region to another. While peasants, labourers, and merchants and their capital continued to play a vital role in the industry, the way in which these different actors related with each other and with indigo planters was both dynamic and highly complex. As in earlier times, indigo cultivation in the colonial period was mostly carried out by peasants on their own holdings (*raiyyati* cultivation) or by wage labourers on land over which the planters had secured superior tenurial rights (*nij* cultivation). The former was the most common mode of cultivation and, for indigo planters, a highly preferred mode of securing indigo plants for their manufactories.[114]

112 Ibid., 23.

113 Phipps, *A Series of Treatises on the Principal Products of Bengal*, 124–5.

114 Overwhelming proportions of the total land under indigo cultivation was *raiyyati* and worked by peasants. According to an estimate, 61,000 *bighas* out of the total 75,000 *bighas*

Under the *theeka* system practised mostly in Bihar, peasants cultivated the land assigned to them by farm-holding planters and over which they held temporary or conditional tenure. Since the scale of production was rather large during this period, indigo cultivation was generally undertaken by rich peasants with large landholdings and privileged tenure. During this period, two inter-connected changes that increasingly undermined the position of the peasantry seem to have taken place in the organisation of the industry. First, the peasants' role had become limited to growing the plant and delivering it to manufactories owned by the indigo planters. They were divested of even this role at places where the planters cultivated their land with the help of wage labourers, a kind of American plantation system but without slaves. Second, capital owned by the European merchants and agency houses came to dominate both the agricultural and manufacturing processes.

Due to the nature of the agrarian economy, the complex land tenure system, and the relatively low cost of the *raiyyati* cultivation, European planters eventually came to depend on peasants.[115] The latter, it seems, took advantage of the growth of indigo production by undertaking its cultivation upon monetary advances from the planters. Initially, the enterprise was profitable because cultivating indigo on alluvial land was less expensive and yields were high.[116] But as the industry expanded and required peasants to take their non-alluvial uplands off grain or other cash crops, growing indigo became risky and less remunerative. Under such circumstances, peasants became disinclined to cultivate indigo.[117] The only factor that still induced them to produce indigo

---

of land cultivated under the Bengal Indigo Company in 1860 was the *raiyyati* land. *Report of the Indigo Commission appointed under act XI of 1860* (Calcutta, 1860), Evidence of R.T. Larbour before the commission, 19 June 1860, 118; Sugata Bose, *Peasant Labour and Colonial Capital: Rural Bengal since 1770* (Cambridge: CUP, 1993), 47.

115 For a detailed analysis of the land tenure system in early colonial north and eastern India, see Dharma Kumar, (ed.), *The Cambridge Economic History of India*, vol. 2, c. 1757–2003 (Delhi: CUP, 1983; New edition, Orient Longman, 2008), chapter 2, Parts 1 and 2.

116 Even at a cash advance of Rs 2 per *bigha* peasants may have found indigo cultivation profitable because they grew it on alluvial land, which required no preparation, no ploughing, and less weeding and upon which no staple grain crop could be grown.

117 In the early nineteenth century, peasants sold their indigo plants to the manufacturers at the rate of 6–10 bundles per rupee. At the average rate of 8 bundles per rupee, the cultivators earned Rs 2 or less per *bigha*, which was not even sufficient to cover the costs of growing indigo, which was estimated to be Rs 3 and 3 *ana* per *bigha*. A *bigha* of land yielded about 15–20 bundles (each weighing 3½–4 *man*) of leaves. In the early 1830s, some planters raised the price to 5 bundles a rupee. Even at this price, peasants could not make any profits. Bose, *Peasant Labour and Colonial Capital*, 48.

was the availability of cash advances that came with it, which enabled them to meet other expenses. This was the case in parts of Bengal where an indigo mania led to a proliferation of indigo manufactories and where peasants were stuck in a production relation that was characterised by planters' control and coercion and peasants' resilience and resistance.[118] This was not the case with all peasants at all manufactories and places. According to the author of the *Rural Life in Bengal* (1860), many indigo planters in Bengal treated their peasants well and, in favourable seasons, the latter benefited from indigo cultivation.[119] Indigo-growing peasants of Bihar, Benaras, and Awadh, and in the Madras Presidency produced indigo on better terms than their counterparts in Bengal and shared the benefits accruing from the booming indigo business.[120]

Some peasants had their own production units and manufactured indigo themselves. Many contemporary reports on indigo production in the colonial period have referred to local Indian manufacturers. Such manufactories were the sites where indigo continued to be produced by peasants and where merchant capital was important but not dominant.[121] It is not possible to find data in our sources on small Indian-owned production units that would allow us to examine their organisational structure and production relations. It may nevertheless be argued that while manufactories may have embraced new tools and techniques in the nineteenth century, some retained many features of the precolonial indigo industry. That is why such manufactories elicited European authors' comments and comparison with the production system of the European indigo planters.

The large scale of indigo production entailed deploying a number of wage labourers to carry out agricultural operations. Ploughing the land, harrowing and breaking the clods, weeding, irrigating the fields if necessary, and cutting, stacking, and transporting the plants to factories required cultivators to recruit large numbers of labourers. These tasks were performed by peasants, village

118 In 1859, there were about 900 indigo manufactories in the Bengal presidency. *Rural Life in Bengal*, 81.

119 Ibid., 73–84.

120 Kumar, *The Cambridge Economic History of India*, vol. II, chapter III, Part I, 260–1.

121 There was a sizeable presence of Indian manufacturers in Awadh and its surroundings, who produced indigo for the EIC and other European merchants. In the nineteenth century, the European planters dominated the industry. P.J. Marshall, 'Economic and Political Expansion: The Case of Oudh', *Modern Asian Studies*, vol. 9, no. 4 (1975), 477. In Bengal, too, many Indians, including some *zamindars*, owned indigo factories. See, Blair B. Kling, *Partner in Empire: Dwarkanath Tagore and the Age of Enterprise in Eastern India* (Berkeley: University of California Press, 1976).

labourers, and tribal labourers or hill coolies.[122] Contemporary sources allude to the availability of cheap labour as a factor in the growth and expansion of indigo production in Bengal. The demand for agricultural wage labour was seasonal and labourers were remunerated on a daily basis. In the early 1830s, the daily wages paid to boys, girls, and women who laboured in preparing fields for indigo cultivation or for weeding and irrigation, varied between 1 and 5 *pice* (Rs 0.5–2.3 per month of 30 days) whereas men received 6 *pice* (Rs 2.8 a month).[123] In the Upper Provinces, the labourers employed in agricultural and other chores received wages varying between Rs 2.8 and Rs 3 per month, which were higher than their counterparts in Bengal.[124]

Indigo processing at the manufactory too was labour intensive and during the manufacturing season it generated considerable demand for labour. Phipps estimated that in a season in the 1820s, about 170,500 people were employed in all indigo manufactories in the country, with an average total production of 125,000 *man*.[125] This labour force was chiefly comprised of coolies, but some boys and skilled workers and craftsmen were also included in the pool. These people were employed for the duration of the manufacturing season for which prior contracts and monetary advances were made. Coolies were mainly employed to stir the liquid in the beating vat, to work at pumps and press houses, and to carry out other miscellaneous tasks.[126] Young boys cleaned the vats and worked at press and drying houses. In addition, there were chain-men, cake-cutters, press-*mistiry* [Hindi. mechanic], and carpenters.[127] During the off-season, they were employed by either planters or peasants to carry out agricultural chores. It is interesting to note that the monthly wages of some of these

122 Many tribal people displaced by the penetration of colonial agrarian economy into the hills and mountains joined the pool of agricultural labourers in indigo producing areas.

123 Phipps, *A Series of Treatises on the Principal Products of Bengal*, 100.

124 Ibid., 105.

125 Ibid., 158. According to an estimate made in 1859, the total number of labourers employed during a good manufacturing season at the Mulnath manufactory and its seventeen dependent concerns may have been about 10,000. *Rural Life in Bengal*, 141.

126 In Bengal and Bihar, the colonial agricultural restructuring and the extension of agriculture in tribal areas made a pool of labour available to meet the needs of the indigo industry. 'Hill Coolies' and forest dwellers of Chhota Nagpur were employed in large numbers in the indigo factories in Lower Bengal. Tirthankar Roy, 'Sardars, Jobbers, Kanganies: The Labour Contractor and Indian Economic History', *Modern Asian Studies*, vol. 42, no. 5 (2008), 979–80.

127 Coolies' wages varied from Rs 2 and 8 *annas* to Rs 4 per month, boys received a monthly wage that varied from Rs 1 and 14 *annas* to Rs 2, and skilled workers received Rs 4 per month. Phipps, *A Series of Treatises on the Principal Products of Bengal*, 159. In the 1850s, the Bhuna tribesmen who worked as coolies in the beating vats received Rs 3 per month. *Rural Life in Bengal*, 140.

employees were less than what labourers received in Agra two centuries earlier or what labourers received in Gujarat in the eighteenth century.[128]

In addition to large numbers of wage labourers, indigo planters also employed a permanent staff to look after the activities in the fields and at the manufactories. The staff generally consisted of an Indian overseer, an accountant, a *wakil* (representative) to conduct suits in a court of law, an *amin* (inspector) with assistants to superintend land measurement and cultivation, and a number of watchmen and security personnel who received monthly wages.[129]

Merchant Capital and Indigo Production

Large-scale indigo production in colonial India meant that large investments had to be made in vats, reservoirs, drying room, storehouses, tools and machines such as beating wheels with paddles, boilers, China pumps, press boxes, among others, and in procuring indigo plant and recruiting labour. Indigo manufacturing as an industrial enterprise during this period, therefore, came to depend heavily on European entrepreneurs and their capital.[130] Colonial capital, Prakash Kumar has rightly observed, was the primary driver of the indigo production system in the late eighteenth and nineteenth centuries.[131]

Advance-buying continued to be an important aspect of the commodity market in colonial India. Indigo contracts, that had been earlier negotiable and had allowed a degree of flexibility, acquired a legal status. The receivers of monetary advances were now legally bound to deliver their produce to their creditors on terms and at prices stipulated in the contract, even if the market prices were higher at the time of the delivery. In some cases, the contracts also

128 In Agra in 1637, they received a monthly wages of 3.5 Rupees. Najaf Haider, 'Structure and Movement of Wages in the Mughal Empire, 1500–1700', in Jan Lucassen (ed.), *Wages and Currency: Global Comparisons from Antiquity to the Twentieth Century* (Bern: Peter Lang, 2007), 293–322; Nadri, *Eighteenth-Century Gujarat*, Appendix 2.

129 John Phipps mentions *gomashta* (agent or local overseer, Rs 12–25 per month), *muharrir* (accountant, Rs 6–12 per month), *wakil* (to conduct suits in the court, Rs 6–10 per month), *amin* (to measure land and superintend cultivation, Rs 4 per month), *classies* (assistants to *amin*, Rs 3–4 per month), *jamadar* (Rs 6–8 per month) and *chaukidars* (security men, Rs 4–5 per month), and *barkandaz* (night watchman, Rs 4–5 per month). Phipps, *A Series of Treatises on the Principal Products of Bengal*, 163.

130 Until the end of the eighteenth century, there was a sizeable presence of Indian manufacturers in Awadh and its surroundings who produced indigo for the EIC and other European merchants. Soon, however, the British planters took the industry in their hands and came to dominate the industry. Marshall, 'Economic and Political Expansion: The Case of Oudh', 477. In Bengal too, many Indians, including some *zamindars*, owned indigo factories and supplied indigo to the EIC or private merchants. Kling, *Partner in Empire*.

131 Prakash Kumar, *Indigo Plantations and Science in Colonial India* (Cambridge: CUP, 2012), 5.

stipulated penalties to be imposed on peasants if they failed to keep up the contract. The contracts were irrevocable and the terms could not be changed to account for changed circumstances.[132] The colonial state's legal system and its other institutions contributed to this transformation as much as the emerging social and political structures of power in colonial India.[133]

Initially, the EIC extended loans to prospective indigo-makers. This assured that it would receive indigo of the desired quantity and quality and also induced indigo contractors to undertake production on a larger scale than what their personal financial resources would have permitted. As soon as Bengal indigo gained popularity in Britain and continental Europe and the company began allowing private trade in indigo, a number of agency houses in Calcutta began speculative investments by extending loans to prospective indigo manufacturers.[134] After the company's loss of the trade monopoly in 1813, many European entrepreneurs got involved in indigo production and trade, which was becoming a highly remunerative enterprise because of the rising demand for indigo in the burgeoning textile production in Britain and Europe. The spectacular growth in indigo production in the British-ruled territories in India and its exports to Britain, continental Europe, and the United States in the nineteenth century was made possible by investments made by several of the joint firms or agency houses.[135]

The entire indigo business had come to be based on speculation and was controlled by European mercantile houses based in Calcutta. Some agency houses also owned factories, produced indigo, and exported it to Europe.[136]

132 In the same way as the contracts between the EIC and indigo manufacturers were irrevocable. WBSA, Proceedings of the Board of Trade, Fort William, Calcutta, 6 Dec. 1811, p. 62.

133 For a detailed analysis of these aspects of colonialism's impact on the Indian labour market including indigo workers in Bihar and Bengal, see Robb, *Peasants, Political Economy, and Law*.

134 Since the 1780s, investment in indigo was one of the major activities of the agency houses in the company's three presidencies, especially in Bengal. Anthony Webster, *The Twilight of the East India Company: The Evolution of Anglo-Asian Commerce and Politics, 1790–1860* (Woodbridge: Boydell Press, 2009), 25.

135 B.B. Chowdhury has noted that the entire system of indigo production in India had come to be inextricably linked up with the agency houses. B.B. Chowdhury, *Growth of Commercial Agriculture in Bengal, 1757–1900* (Calcutta: R.K. Maitra, 1964), 84.

136 In 1829, the indigo factories owned by John Palmer and Co. produced 24,665 factory *man* of indigo that amounted to about 16 percent of the total production in north India. Anthony Webster, 'An Early Global Business in a Colonial Context: The Strategies, Management, and Failure of John Palmer and Company of Calcutta, 1780–1830', *Enterprise & Society: The International Journal of Business History*, vol. 6, no. 1 (2005), 115. This agency house was also involved in the indigo enterprise in Java in the early nineteenth century. Elly Marie Corrie van Enk, 'Britse Kooplieden and de Cultures op Java: Harvey Thomson

The fortunes of the agency houses depended so much on indigo that when the European market for indigo collapsed in 1826, almost all major firms in Calcutta went bankrupt.[137] In a study of the commercial enterprises of perhaps the richest and the largest agency house in Calcutta, John Palmer and Co., Anthony Webster has underlined the role of indigo in bringing about the ruin of this agency house.[138] When new agency houses emerged in Calcutta in the late 1830s and 1840s, the nature of Anglo-Indian commercial enterprise underwent some changes. The new firms were now more closely governed by their London headquarters and were less independent than their predecessors.[139] There also occurred a shift in their commercial priorities. Many new firms were primarily interested in importing British cotton manufactures into India. Indigo, nevertheless, continued to be one of their major business concerns in this period.

Indigo Processing in India: A Long-Term View

How does indigo production in the colonial period compare with the precolonial production systems? One obvious difference is in the scale of production that was much larger in the nineteenth century than ever before. Another difference, one may argue, was in the quality of the material produced. The indigo of the colonial period was in general of a good quality and comparable with that from the Americas. The extent to which these differences could be explained in terms of comparative technical and technological knowledge and their application in the respective time frames is a question several scholars have attempted to address. The scholarship has put forward two mutually contradictory views. One holds that large-scale indigo production in the colonial period was possible because of new machines and managerial expertise that the British introduced in India.[140] The other regards the indigo production system in Mughal India as equally advanced both in terms of technology and product

(1790–1837) en Zijn Financiers' (PhD dissertation, Vrije Universiteit, Amsterdam, 1999), 108–10.

137 Chowdhury, *Growth of Commercial Agriculture in Bengal*, 84–111; Kling, *Partner in Empire*; Chaudhuri, *The Economic Development of India under the East India Company 1814–58: a Selection of Contemporary Writings* (Cambridge: CUP, 1971), 21.

138 Anthony Webster, *The Richest East India Merchant: The Life and Business of Johan Palmer of Calcutta, 1767–1836* (Woodbridge: Boydell Press, 2007), 34, 58–60, see especially Chapter 6; idem, *Twilight of the East India Company*, 87–91; idem, 'An Early Global Business in Colonial Context'.

139 Kling, *Partner in Empire*, 4; Webster, 'An Early Global Business in Colonial Context', 129.

140 P.J. Marshall, *East India Fortunes: The British in Bengal in the Eighteenth Century* (Oxford: Clarendon Press, 1976), 157.

quality. This latter view does not credit the colonial-period indigo-makers with any major technological breakthroughs.[141] Many nineteenth-century European authors of treatises, monographs, essays, and reports on indigo production in the colonial period have created a kind of binary between the 'native' and 'British' or 'European' modes of indigo production and proposed that the indigenous production system was traditional and primitive, with little attention paid to scientific and technical aspects of indigo manufacture or the quality of produce.[142] In a memorandum presented to the governor general, several European indigo planters and firms of Bengal and Banaras wrote that 'the quality of indigo natives make in these regions [Agra and Delhi] is inferior to those manufactured in the company's provinces. Native mode of manufacturing indigo will not admit their indigo to be equal in quality and purity to ours, nor have they, we presume, any knowledge of the theory of an art, the perfection of which depends so immediately on science'.[143] Later, in 1832, John Phipps wrote,

> In some small factories, particularly small ones, and those belonging to native manufacturers, reservoirs are seldom if ever built; on account of the expense in erecting them: in such factories water is often supplied from a neighbouring tank, or even a dirty pool, constantly disturbed by cattle going into them; in many cases, when the factory is situated on the bank of a river, the water is obtained from the latter, at a season when it is full of sediments and impurities. To such causes, and to the apathy of these people, may be ascribed the reason indigo manufactured by natives is generally heavier, and less free of sand and other impurities, than that which proceeds from factories under the superintendence of Europeans or their descendants.[144]

While there may be an element of truth in this, the binary created between European and Indian indigo producers is not far from imaginary. This may be seen as a part of the larger metropolis-colony discourse of the nineteenth century, in which the latter was almost always projected as traditional,

141 Trivedi, 'Innovation and Change in Indigo Production in Bayana'; Raaj Sah, 'Features of British Indigo in India', *Social Scientist*, vol. 9, nos. 2–3 (1980), 67–79.

142 In 1829, Charles Weston noted that the 'indigo of the East Indies, which at one time ranked so low in its comparative value, has, by better mode of manufacture, been progressively improving, and, consequently, as gradually making its way into European markets…' Charles H. Weston, 'Observations on the Manner of Manufacturing Indigo in the Southern Provinces of India', *Journal of the Franklin Institute*, vol. 8, no. 4 (1829), 233.

143 BL, Board's Collections, 60 (Doc. no. 1369), Extract proceedings of the Board of Trade in Bengal, 28 Oct. 1796, pp. 54–5.

144 Phipps, *A Series of Treatises on the Principal Products of Bengal*, 121–2.

stagnant, and backward as against modern, dynamic, and technologically and scientifically-advanced Europe.

The quality of Bayana indigo in the early seventeenth century was in general not inferior to the indigo from Europe's transatlantic colonies with the exception of the variety from Guatemala. Manufacturers in seventeenth-century India knew the plant very well and were fully aware of the means and methods of manufacture. Even though they may not have understood the scientific and chemical aspects of it, they had mastered the art of making indigo as a practical craft. Their knowledge was advanced enough to elicit Europeans admiration and stimulate them to learn the craft when it was necessary. Apparently, the Europeans failed to fully acquire the knowledge and skills to be able to produce indigo themselves. Repeated attempts by the EIC and the VOC to manufacture indigo were unsuccessful due to the Europeans' lack of skills and expertise. The companies had to solicit the support of local experts in promoting indigo production in India, Java, and elsewhere in Asia. The VOC officials in Surat even proposed to get some Dutchmen to Bayana or Khurja to learn the art of indigo making and use the skills so acquired in promoting indigo cultivation in Java.

Indigo manufacturers of the nineteenth century followed the same manufacturing procedures, but they were seemingly more informed than their seventeenth-century Indian counterparts about the chemical properties of indigo and also perhaps had acquired a degree of precision in carrying out manufacturing processes. By the 1830s, several scientific studies of indigo plants and the manufacture of indigo dye and manuals on the art of indigo making were published and indigo planters and manufacturers may have benefited from them.[145] Interestingly, the authors of these treatises emphasise precision in carrying out steeping and beating processes as being key to successful production. They accordingly prescribe, as we have seen above, methods and procedures to ascertain the state of the vat and determine when an activity should begin or stop. To what extent these instructions and prescriptions were actually followed by indigo-makers remains uncertain. Most of them, it seems, followed the basic scientific principles of indigo processing and also made use of some modern devices and instruments available to them. A clear example is the replacement

145 See, for instance, *The Complete Indigo-Maker, translated from the French of Elias Monnereau, planter in St. Domingo* (London: P. Elmsly, 1769); De Cossigny, *Treatises on the Cultivation and Manufacture of Indigo;* Nowland, *A Treatise on Indigo*; Pierre-Paul Darrac, 'De la Culture d l'Anil et de la fabricquation de l'Indigo au Bengale' ['The Culture and Manufacture of Indigo in Bengal'], in Darrac and Schendel, *Global Blue*; Phipps, *A Series of Treatises on the Principal Products of Bengal*; William Osborn, *Treatise on the Process and Manufacture of Fine Indigo* (printed in the Indian lithographic press by William Holland), 1832.

of small, deep, and circular beating vats of the earlier period with wider but shallower rectangular vats to facilitate proper oxidation during the beating process.[146] Some indigo factories were also equipped with labour-saving devices such as beating wheels with paddles, to stir the liquid in the beating vat, and they also may have used thermometers to measure the temperature of the liquid in the steeping vats. The procedure of boiling the pulp after precipitation had occurred was yet another improvement in the processing technique because it prevented a second fermentation that would have adversely affected the yield and quality of indigo. Similarly, the use of wooden frames and press boxes to squeeze water from indigo paste must have facilitated faster drying in shady and airy rooms and may also have lowered the labour costs.

Recourse to these methods undoubtedly enabled producers to make indigo on a large scale and it may also have helped them to improve the dye output of the plant and lower the costs of production. Nothing, however, could privilege them to always produce the best and purest indigo. The dye produced in Bengal by the Europeans greatly varied in quality, texture, and colour and the proportion of the best and 'very fine' indigo to the total exports from India to Britain was rather low, and the middling and ordinary sorts occupied the largest share. As Phipps noted in 1832, 'Bengal [indigo] consisted of full three-fourths middling and ordinary qualities, generally imperfect, and more or less mixed; the remainder good with a small proportion of fine'.[147] There were no major breakthroughs in the production technology in the nineteenth century that would have substantially enhanced the product quality and output. Neither were experiments carried out with new indigo plants or with new means and methods of manuring, planting, and cultivation with the same intensity as in the early twentieth century, when the Indian indigo industry was faced with competition from synthetic indigo.[148]

The chemical dye was put on the international market in 1897 by the German chemical firm Badische Anilin und Soda Fabrik (BASF), and it came to consumers as a better, less expensive, and more user-friendly alternative dye. Subsequently, the colonial state in India, indigo planters, and British agricultural scientists joined hands together to rescue natural indigo. Efforts were directed towards enhancing the plant's dye-yield and the quality of indigo

146 Larger the surface of the vat better was the exposure to air and formation of indigo grain during the beating process; hence De Cossigny's advice to erect shallow beating vats to facilitate proper oxidation. De Cossigny, *Treatises on the Cultivation and Manufacture of Indigo*.

147 Phipps, *A Series of Treatises on the Principal Products of Bengal*, 62. See also pages 56–65 for London prices and sales of Indian indigo of different colour and qualities.

148 Kumar, 'Scientific Experiments in British India', 249–70.

so that the product could be marketed at competitive prices.[149] Experiments were carried out with new plants, fertilizers, and various chemical substances, but nothing could save the doomed natural indigo industry.[150] The absence of similar concerted efforts in the nineteenth century leads one to conclude that the European indigo planters and manufacturers in India failed to achieve the level of technical and technological perfection that would have optimised the crop and dye output. It is also important to note that even in the late nineteenth century, European indigo planters were generally reluctant to implement measures recommended by chemists and botanists after their scientific experiments because of the uncertainty of the anticipated outcomes. They depended more on their experience and established practices than on indigo science, which was seemingly very much confined to the domain of pure knowledge and its discourse.

Thus, it would seem that indigo production techniques and technology in India in the colonial period represents a complex mix of continuities from the precolonial past, improvements, and innovations. Throughout the period under consideration, indigo manufacturers displayed their keenness to improve the output and quality of their product. This could be seen in a number of technical and technological innovations and adaptations. Some of these have already been mentioned. Adoption of the green-leaf method of extracting indigo by manufacturers in Gujarat and south-eastern India in the early seventeenth century is one example of their openness to change and improvement and their responsiveness to market demands. The replacement of a single-vat system by separate steeping and beating vats in Sarkhej and other places was undoubtedly a major improvement. The transition may have occurred in the late sixteenth century in response to the growing Portuguese and European demand for indigo. In the seventeenth century, a set of inter-connected upper and lower vats had become a common feature of indigo manufactories in Gujarat and northern India.[151]

Some improvements were also made in the structure of the lower tanks. Two lower circular tanks at a production site in Jalali, of a slightly later period than the other two, had a bowl-like cavity inside the receptacle (compare

149 Kumar, *Indigo Plantations and Science in Colonial India*, chapters 4–5.

150 The responses came rather late. The Java indigo plant that would have doubled the crop output, for instance, was not introduced in India until 1900. Kumar, 'Scientific Experiments in British India', 260–5; idem, *Indigo Plantations and Science in Colonial India*, chapters 4–5.

151 This is evident from the descriptions of indigo manufacture in Sarkhej by Geleynssen de Jongh (1630s) and Matheus van Heck (1697). Geleynssen de Jongh, *Remonstrantie van W. Geleynssen de Jongh*, 47–8; VOC 1575, Resoluties, Batavia, 15 Jan. 1697, ff. 148r–151r.

IMAGE 1.4 *Lower circular vat with a receptacle, Jalali, c. 17th century*
SOURCE: PHOTO BY THE AUTHOR.

Images 1.2 and 1.4). This was an improvement in the structure of the tanks that would have facilitated scooping out of the indigo paste. These vats and the receptacles are also a little larger in dimension and deeper than the other two that already existed there. The circular tanks in Jalali have flat bases without any noticeable slope toward the receptacle in the centre as was generally the case in Bayana.[152] At a seventeenth-century manufactory at Shahpur in Aligarh district, the lower circular vats are shallower and larger in dimension than those in Jalali and they have two-stepped receptacles (Image 1.5). This shows the variation in the structure and design of premodern indigo vats in India.

All nineteenth-century indigo manufactories had large rectangular lower tanks. Large open surface allowed proper oxidation. This was certainly a major improvement in production technique. Large tanks, however, required more labour to agitate the water, and may also have induced some to install beating wheels with paddles. However, not all manufactories at all places had tanks of the same design and dimension. There were some local initiatives and innovations made in the structure of the vats. A unique feature at some

152 Trivedi, 'Innovation and Change in Indigo Production in Bayana', 61–2. According to Matheus van Heck, the bottom of the beating vats in Sarkhej sloped towards the receptacle in the centre. VOC 1575, Resoluties, Batavia, 15 Jan. 1697, ff. 148ʳ–151ʳ.

IMAGE 1.5 *Lower circular vat with a receptacle, Shahpur, Aligarh, c. 17th century*
SOURCE: PHOTO BY THE AUTHOR

manufactories in Bihar was the bowl-like receptacles provided in the steeping vat just below the outlet. This was probably to allow unwanted substances to settle in it and prevent them from being mixed into the lower tank. This may also have facilitated cleaning and removal of plant residues from the steeping vat. To facilitate it further, narrow grooves descending into the receptacle were also sometimes provided in steeping vats. At a manufactory in Kowahi (Bihar), three of the four steeping vats have furrows (Image 1.6). At this site, a deep receptacle is also made in the lower vats, probably to facilitate the scooping and collection of indigo. But unlike the circular tanks of Jalali, a receptacle in a nineteenth-century vat was provided at the outer edge of the vat towards the outlet (Image 1.3). Shallow vats allowed beaters to agitate the liquid with greater ease and vigour and the liquid containing indoxyl—a crystalline compound that is a by-product of indigo manufacture—was exposed to oxygen better than in vats three or more feet deep. Wheel beating, a labour-saving device, was a later addition and that, too, was restricted to a few indigo factories. In general, beating continued to be performed by groups of men and, also occasionally, women. The use of boilers was, likewise, a late development and was confined to some large manufactories.

IMAGE 1.6 *Furrowed steeping vat, Kowahi, Bihar, c. 19th century*
SOURCE: PHOTO BY THE AUTHOR.

Indigo production was the most important stage of the commodity chain. All subsequent activities and stages depended on how much was produced, at what cost, and who owned or controlled the produce. It was here that many older practices showed resilience amidst new and innovative changes both in terms of production methods and technology and in the ways labour related with the capital. The latter was about controlling the processes of production and securing the final product. The analysis above has shown that the indigo industry evolved from small-scale free peasant-household production in the seventeenth century to a merchant-controlled large-scale capitalist enterprise in the nineteenth century. The following chapter analyses how merchants and the trading companies secured supplies of indigo from producers, and what processes, costs, and challenges were involved in getting it to market. Logistics played an important role in the indigo trade and was rather instrumental in determining its price and profitability at the end stage of the commodity chain.

CHAPTER 2

From Manufactory to Market: Logistics and Commerce

In the sixteenth and seventeenth centuries, indigo manufactories were the hub of village economic activities during the annual manufacturing season, when a number of Asian and European merchants, their agents and brokers, and even the European companies' officials gathered there to purchase indigo. Indigo was delivered to the buyers; it was packed and loaded; carts and camels were hired; attendants and security guards were recruited, provisions were gathered; caravans were formed and they departed for Surat or other destinations. This was also the time when large amounts of money were pumped into the rural economy and it circulated and changed hands among merchants, intermediaries, manufacturers, labourers, and the people of the caravan. Indigo had to be transported overland to distant markets or to port cities, such as Surat or Cambay, from where it was then shipped to overseas destinations. In the villages, buyers competed not only for indigo but also for labour, carts, and camels. This was the time when rural labour found employment opportunities and the services they rendered in carrying out various tasks were fairly well rewarded.

Economic life in indigo-producing villages during the manufacturing season was even more vibrant in nineteenth-century Bengal and north India because of the large scale of production and exchange. Nevertheless, two notable changes during this period transformed the role of such villages in the indigo market. First, the villages were no longer the place for negotiations, sales, and purchases. Instead, indigo was simply manufactured and packed for dispatch to Calcutta, where actual business transactions took place. Second, forward buying and contract systems stripped the village industry of commercial spontaneity and agency. Villages simply produced indigo for Calcutta-based entrepreneurs and business houses that financed the industry. Intermediary merchants and dealers no longer played any significant role in the market. These changes notwithstanding, large-scale indigo production employed large numbers of people in manufacturing, sifting, weighing, packing, and transporting indigo. What follows below is an analysis of indigo's path from manufactory to market in a long-term perspective. It examines how indigo was sold and purchased, packed, and transported; the structural dynamics of the commodity

 | DOI 10.1163/9789004311558_004

and labour markets in Mughal India; and how these dynamics changed in the colonial period.

Structure of the Market: *voorkopers* and other Merchants

Merchants could purchase indigo either in the villages where it was produced or in the nearby city, where it was available in large quantities. They generally knew that the best indigo at most favourable prices could be bought only in the villages where it was produced. But not all merchants could afford or cared to go to such production sites and bought indigo in the major urban markets instead. Those who made it to villages could buy either directly from indigo producers or from dealers (*voorkopers*) and suppliers (*leveraars*). *Voorkopers* were intermediary merchants who bought indigo from manufacturers mainly to sell it to Europeans and other merchants either in the village itself or in the marts of Agra, Ahmadabad, and Surat.[1] They anticipated the market and the European demand for indigo and accordingly procured greater or lesser quantities of it. They either advanced money to manufacturers or paid upfront for indigo at the beginning of the season with a view to selling it later at a higher price. Many of them could earn even higher profits by selling their indigo in the marts of Agra, Ahmadabad, Surat, or other major cities. This was a speculative enterprise and these intermediary merchants were always at the risk of losing money whenever the market was unfavourable due to diminished demand. In the early seventeenth century, the European demand for indigo was large and stable and their businesses generally prospered and they could make profits out of this speculative enterprise.

These intermediary merchants played a crucial role in the indigo market. By taking the commodity to those cities where most merchants came to buy indigo every year during the season, they extended the spatial limits of the market. This enabled merchants to buy indigo in the marts of Agra, Ahmadabad, Surat and other cities that served as collection centres for indigo produced in nearby villages. There were a few prominent indigo dealers in Bayana and Agra who feature prominently in the European companies' records. The

1 For a discussion of the organisation of indigo production in the villages of Bayana and the VOC's mode of buying indigo there, see H.W. van Santen, 'De Verenigde Oost-Indische Compagnie in Gujarat en Hindustan, 1620–1660' (PhD dissertation, Leiden University, 1982), 145–62; R.J. Barendse, *The Arabian Seas: The Indian Ocean World of the Seventeenth Century* (New York: M.E. Sharpe, 2002), 234–7.

VOC often obtained a part of its indigo from these intermediary merchants.[2] In Pulicat, on the Coromandel Coast, the VOC entered into a contract with a supplier to buy 50–60 *bahars* (each weighing about 480 Dutch pounds) of indigo at 21 pounds per pagoda.[3] The EIC often bought indigo from merchants and dealers. In 1642, the English president, Fremling, bought Bayana indigo from some Mughal merchants in Surat at Rs 37 per *man* of 34½ pounds.[4] It was this particular structure of the market that seems to have inspired the Mughal imperial indigo monopoly in 1633.

There were different modes of buying indigo no matter who the seller was. Indigo could be bought in advance by extending monetary loans to producers and intermediary merchants before or at the beginning of the production season. It could also be bought on the spot from manufacturers and dealers in the villages or from intermediary merchants at the major cities. In either case, the services of a broker or agent were crucial especially for the European companies and portfolio entrepreneurs who could not always be personally present at the transaction site. Such substantial buyers generally had their brokers or agents go to indigo producers or dealers in the villages to secure deliveries of

2 In 1637, the VOC officials in Agra bought indigo from several merchants such as the ones given below.

Merchants	Indigo (in Dutch pounds)	Value in rupees
Khwaja Ahmad	48,416	45,671
Mirbuland Lala	4,056	3,826
Mulla Abdul Majeed	5,724	1,000
Sultan Mohammed	2,014	1,710
Asoor Beg	1,736	1,638
Abdul Nabi	1,060	980
Rupji Raghav		5,000

SOURCE: COLLECTIE GELEYNSSEN DE JONGH [GELEYNSSEN DE JONGH COLLECTION], 116, AGRA, 12 MARCH 1637. IN 1639, THE DUTCH BOUGHT 44 PACKS (9,328 LB.) OF MEWAT INDIGO FROM A BANIA MERCHANT BHAGWAN AND 17 PACKS (3,604 LB.) OF KHURJA INDIGO FROM A MUGHAL MERCHANT MIRZA MIR ALI IN EXCHANGE FOR SPICES. THEY ALSO BOUGHT 2 PACKS (424 LB.) OF INDIGO FROM MIAN PARVEZ IN EXCHANGE FOR PORCELAIN. COLLECTIE GELEYNSSEN DE JONGH, 117, COPIJ NEGOTIEJOURNALEN VAN HET COMPTOIR AGRA (COPY OF THE TRADE JOURNAL OF THE AGRA FACTORY), 15 AUG. 1639 AND 18 AUG. 1639. THE EIC TOO BOUGHT INDIGO FROM LOCAL MERCHANTS. IN 1646, THE FACTORS IN AHMADABAD BOUGHT A PARCEL OF 'EXCELLENT INDIGO' FROM A MERCHANT ABDUL LATIF. *EFI 1646–50*, AHMADABAD TO SURAT, 19 MARCH 1646, P. 31.

3 *Dagh-Register, 1636*, Resoluties, 9 Oct. 1636, p. 242.

4 Ibid., p. 185.

required quantities. These brokers, who were generally local Banias and also possibly had their trading networks with producers and dealers in the villages, advanced money on behalf of their patrons to manufacturers, and secured the delivery of indigo from them.[5] They usually received a brokerage commission of 1 percent of the total value of the transaction. Our sources refer to brokers servicing the European companies in Agra and Ahmadabad in the seventeenth century. In the 1630s, the VOC had Madari and Wissendas as its brokers in Agra and Ahmadabad, respectively, to assist in the procurement of indigo; and in the 1690s, an Armenian merchant and broker, Agha Piri, assisted the Dutch in the procurement of Bayana indigo in Agra.[6]

Right from the beginning, the European companies and large-scale buyers of indigo were concerned about how to make sure that they obtained the desired quantity of the best-quality indigo at current prices. They soon found that the best way to accomplish this was to purchase indigo in the villages where it was produced. The companies pursued this option vigorously and their officials visited indigo-producing villages every year during the manufacturing season.[7] Brokers assisted them in carrying out transactions. Even if it was an expensive

5 Forward buying through advance cash payments to producers was a common method of securing supplies of textiles, indigo, and other commodities in India. In this respect, it was different from the 'putting out' system of pre-Industrial Revolution Europe in which merchants supplied tools and raw material to weavers and producers to ensure production and delivery of goods. K.N. Chaudhuri, *Trade and Civilisation in the Indian Ocean: An Economic History from the Rise of Islam to 1750* (Cambridge: CUP, 1985), 201–2. In Bengal, the VOC secured supplies of textiles by advancing money to weavers through merchants who also served the European companies as brokers or intermediaries and in that capacity they were known as *paikars* or *gomashtas*. Om Prakash, *The Dutch East India Company and the Economy of Bengal, 1630–1720* (Princeton: Princeton University Press, 1985), 102–12.

6 Collectie Geleynssen de Jongh, 106, Directeur en Raad van Surat aan GG&R, Surat, 30 April 1637, pp. 111–2; *Dagh-Register, 1636*, pp. 51–2; VOC 1127, Directeur en Raad van Surat aan GG&R, Surat, 31 Dec. 1637, f. 39r. In 1695–96, the VOC procured 52,250 Dutch pounds of Bayana indigo through Agha Piri, an Armenian merchant and the company's broker in Agra. *Generale Missiven,* vol. V, 1686–97, p. 770; Bhagwandas was one such broker who procured indigo for his English/Dutch employer in Agra.

7 As early as 1614, an EIC official in Surat, Thomas Kerridge, noted that advance-buying in indigo-producing villages or '*parganas*' near Agra was the established custom and the 'cheapest course' of procuring it. *Letters Received by the East India Company from its servants in the East transcribed from the 'Original Correspondence' series of the India Office records (hereafter Letters Received)*, 6 vols (eds), Frederick Charles Danvers and William Foster (London: Sampson Low, Marston & Company, 1896–1902), vol. II (1897), Thomas Kerridge to the EIC in London, 20 Sept. 1614, p. 106. The VOC officials in Coromandel were directed by their superiors in Amsterdam in 1622 to go to indigo-producing villages and to purchase indigo from

venture, it was worth undertaking because this was the best way to buy indigo of the desired quality and quantity. The VOC and the EIC bought the largest portion of their total indigo in and around the villages of Bayana and Sarkhej.[8]

Having a broker and showing up at the production site were not enough to ensure the best deal. An understanding of the market and a good knowledge of indigo were also important aspects of this enterprise. Indigo greatly varied in quality and it was impossible even for frequent buyers to judge the purity of indigo unless they examined it closely. Expertise and experience were, therefore, required in order for merchants to be able to buy good-quality indigo. The European companies often solicited the services of indigo experts who readily helped the officials in the procurement of indigo.[9] Indigo's quality could be determined by following some standard procedures. The first indicator was colour. The best indigo was dark blue or violet brown in colour.[10] Indigo buyers had to have the ability to judge its quality by looking at the fineness of the grain and colour. There were other ways to check the quality of indigo such as by weighing a cake or ball in hand, breaking it, or by dipping it in water. If light, it broke easily and floated on water. If it was heavy and contained impurities, it sank.

Another procedure that merchants generally followed was to burn a piece of indigo. If it burnt quickly without leaving any sand or dirt in the ash, the indigo was considered good. In 1616, an English factor in Surat referred to clean burning and swimming in water as signs of indigo's purity and lightness.[11] The lighter it was in weight the better it was in quality. If one was not sure of its

---

producers and not from intermediary merchants and dealers. Collectie Geleynssen de Jongh, 14, Bewindhebberen aan GG&R, Amsterdam, 20 Dec. 1622, ff. 53r, 54r.

8 René Barendse has suggested that the companies bought most of their indigo from the 'chief farmers' (*hoofdbouwers*). Barendse, *The Arabian Seas*, 235.

9 Hans Baron in Coromandel and Johannes Baptista are spoken of as indigo experts assisting the VOC in its procurement of indigo. *The Dutch Factories in India* [hereafter *DFI*], *1617–1623 A Collection of Dutch East India Company Documents Pertaining to India*, (ed.), Om Prakash (New Delhi: Munshiram Manoharlal, 1984), pp. 31, 63; *Generale Missiven*, vol. I, 1610–38, pp. 122–3. In 1622, VOC officials in Coromandel were advised to seek assistance in the purchase of indigo of an experienced person who had a good knowledge of indigo. Collectie Geleynssen de Jongh, 14, Bewindhebberen aan GG&R, Amsterdam, 20 Dec. 1622, f. 53v. In 1629, Hendrick de Wit, *Opperkoopman* in Coromandel, was an indigo expert (*indigokenner*) and was sent to Bengal to explore the possibilities of procuring indigo there. *Generale Missiven*, vol. I, 1610–38, Batavia, 7 March 1631, p. 292. In 1637, VOC officials in Coromandel were advised to use the services of an indigo expert (*goed-kender*) in buying indigo. Collecite Geleynssen de Jongh, 108, Masulipatnam to Surat, 23 Sept. 1637.

10 VOC 1055, Masulipatnam to Batavia, 15 June 1610, p. 122; *Generale Missiven*, vol. I, 1610–38, p. 125.

11 BL, Factory Records: Surat [hereafter FRS], 84, Consultations, Surat, 17 May 1616, f. 33b.

heaviness, the cake or ball was cut into pieces. If the indigo was pure, the knife would go through it smoothly and nothing would stick to the knife.[12] These procedures were performed in all major indigo tracts in India. Writing about Sarkhej indigo, George Roques advised merchants to open each pack and collect samples for testing from the middle of it where, according to him, adulterated indigo was generally put in or mixed.[13] Since the cakes or balls were randomly selected, these procedures could not guarantee that each and every piece in a pack was of the best quality. In the EIC and VOC records, there are references to the poor-quality and adulterated indigo found in the packets sent from India.[14] All that merchants could do was be attentive at all times while receiving the deliveries of indigo.

Since many Asian and European merchants and company officials preferred to buy indigo from producers in the villages, the market there was also highly competitive. The manufacturing season was short and indigo destined for overseas markets had to be conveyed to Surat before the end of the sailing season or it had to reach the markets in West Asia before merchants and caravans departed. These constraints added to the dynamism of the indigo market in Bayana, Sarkhej, and other villages. One cannot fail to notice the anxiety that pervaded all buyers, but especially the VOC officials, who were further restricted in their indigo transactions by quality- and price-ceilings imposed by their superiors. Quite often, they attributed the high prices of indigo to the large-scale purchases by the EIC, the Armenians, Persians, and other Asian merchants.[15] The company advanced money to producers and dealers in order to secure deliveries of indigo. In 1636, for example, the VOC officials lent Rs 30,000–35,000 to indigo producers at an interest rate of 1½ percent.[16] The

12 *Generale Missiven,* vol. I, 1610–38, p. 126; Collectie Geleynssen de Jongh, 14, Bewindhebberen aan GG&R, Amsterdam, 20 Dec. 1622, f. 52v.

13 Indrani Ray, 'Of Trade and Traders in Seventeenth-Century India: An Unpublished French Memoir by George Roques', in *The French East India Company and the Trade of the Indian Ocean: a Collection of Essays by Indrani Ray,* ed., Lakshmi Subramanian (New Delhi: Munshiram Manoharlal, 1999), 56–7.

14 In 1639–40, several indigo packs sent in the *Leeuwaerden* were found to be containing clay/earth in place of indigo. *Generale Missiven,* vol. II, 1639–55, Batavia, 30 Nov. 1640, p. 116.

15 VOC 1097, Vertooch op t' stuck van den specerij-handel gedaen aen den E. Heere Generael ende de Raden van India verhoudende op t' Casteel Batavia [Exposition on the subject of the spice trade made to the Honourable Governor-General and Councilors of the Indies at Batavia Castle], Agra, 26 Oct. 1627, ff. 421r–424r; VOC 1112, Directeur en Raad van Surat aan GG&R, Surat, 2 Dec. 1636, ff. 516r–517r, 518r.

16 VOC 1112, ff. 559v–560r.

EIC and other buyers also had recourse to advance buying and consequently advanced large sums of money to indigo manufacturers. In 1614, EIC officials in Surat advanced 500 pounds sterling to indigo producers in the Bayana region before the manufacturing season began.[17] In 1636, it was reported that a number of Armenian and Mughal merchants had advanced about Rs 350,000 to indigo producers.[18] In 1643, VOC officials in Coromandel could buy only a small quantity because local merchants had bought the best indigo from producers early in the season.[19] Merchants continued to compete with each other for indigo even in the second half of the seventeenth century, when the European demand for it had declined considerably. In 1696, VOC officials in Ahmadabad noted that the price of Sarkhej indigo went up by 10¼ percent because of poor harvest and fierce competition among buyers.[20] Competition not only raised indigo prices but also pushed up the demand for camels, carts, and labour, thereby increasing the total cost of inland transportation.

Packing and Transportation: The Caravan System

Indigo was sifted and packed into large gunny bags for transportation. For workers in the indigo trade, the greatest concern was over inhalation of indigo dust. The French traveller Jean Baptiste Tavernier wrote that workers covered their faces with a linen cloth that had two little holes to see through, and that they frequently drank milk that worked as a 'preservative against the piercing quality of the dust'.[21] Despite all care, Tavernier writes, they spit blue for quite some time after they had sifted indigo for nine or ten days. So fine and pervasive was the dust that an egg would turn blue on the inside if kept for a day at the place where sifting was done.[22] Evidence is lacking on whether inhaling indigo dust had any health hazards or whether it had any implications for the life expectancy of the people doing this job. Once indigo was sifted and classified according to their quality, it was then packed in large chests whose size, shape, and contents varied in accordance with the mode and means of transportation.

17 *Letters Received*, vol. II, Thomas Kerridge to the EIC in London, 20 Sept. 1614, p. 106.

18 VOC 1112, Directeur en Raad van Surat aan GG&R, Surat, 2 Dec. 1636, f. 518^r.

19 VOC 1151, Van Masulipatnam aan GG&R, 11 June 1643, ff. 778^v–779^r. These merchants went to villages every year and advanced money to producers, bought indigo, and carried it upwards. Ibid.

20 *Generale Missiven*, vol. V, 1686–97, Batavia, 8 Feb. 1696, p. 771.

21 Jean-Baptiste Tavernier, *The Six Voyages of John Baptista Tavernier through Turkey into Persia and the East Indies* (tr.), John Phillips (London, 1678), p. 60.

22 Ibid.

Indigo had to be carried on pack animals and carts from the villages to port cities or inland destinations. In the case of the European companies, it was taken to their nearest establishment (Agra or Ahmadabad) and then dispatched to Surat. There were different measures in which the volume of indigo was expressed. The standard unit of weight was the *man* (or *maund*), which was the equivalent of about 32–36 Dutch pounds in Surat and about 50–53 Dutch pounds in Agra (*man-e Akbari* or *man-e Shahjahani*).[23] This was the primary unit in which all prices were given and purchases were made. In Coromandel, *bahar* was the standard measure of weight that contained about 480 Dutch pounds. A pack, usually containing about 4 *man* (as in Agra) and sometimes 6 (as in Surat), was the most commonly expressed measure in which indigo was transported from Agra and Ahmadabad to Surat and further on to overseas destinations. The way indigo was packed had some implications for freight, customs duties, tonnage it occupied, and for the protection of the dye from breaking into pieces. Local merchants, it seems, had indigo packed in round *churls,* which was perhaps convenient to carry on camels or other animals. Those who took their indigo to Aleppo carried it in square chests, each of which contained two *churls*. Indigo was packed in calico bags that were then wrapped in leather.[24] This mode was preferred, especially when indigo had to be transported by sea, because this way the dye was protected against dirt, wind, moisture, and water during the journey. This was also the most efficient way of packing indigo because the chests, being cubic in shape, could be stowed close to each other. The sizes and actual weights of all baskets or chests were not uniform.[25]

The EIC and VOC paid considerable attention to this aspect and tried to pack their indigo in a way that was economical and safe for the commodity. In 1616, EIC authorities in London advised their Surat officials to pack indigo in such a way that ships' space could be fully utilized. They thought that packing indigo in square chests, as was done in Gujarat, was the best and most economical way. As against this, round *churls* took more space because they could not be stowed close to each other.[26] In fact, they attributed the waste of space

23 See for more details on *man* and other units of weight used in the sixteenth and seventeenth centuries, Irfan Habib, *The Agrarian System of Mughal India, 1556–1707* (New Delhi: OUP, 1999), Appendix B, 420–31.

24 FRS 84, Consultations, Surat, 1616, f. 90[a].

25 In 1621, EIC officials in Ahmadabad could not specify the weight of each chest and bale and noted that 'squar basketts are not made all of one biggnesse, and moreover all indicoe fills not alike'. *EFI 1618–21*, Ahmadabad to Surat, 6 Oct. 1621, p. 291.

26 Indigo in round *churls* were laden on ships bound to London. *EFI 1618–21*, Surat to London, 7 Nov. 1621, p. 324; *EFI 1618–21*, Ahmadabad to Surat, 13 Nov. 1621, pp. 329–30.

in the *Trope* to the lost space that came of stowing round *churls*.[27] The VOC dispatched its indigo mainly in packs (the standard weight of which was 4 *man*) and some in fardles (bundles) and chests.[28] Indigo was put in linen bags, which were wrapped and stitched in leather cover. Many times, it happened that the packs broke open in the course of being transported from Agra to Surat or during loading and unloading causing spillage and loss of indigo. To avoid this, VOC officials in Agra and Surat were advised to place the leather-clad packages in yet another gunny bag.[29] The accounts of packing and transportation expenses in the subsequent period indicate that leather packs were wrapped in gunny cloth and stitched. The shape, size, and weight of indigo packs/sacks/bags depended on the mode of transportation. Since the European companies shipped their indigo to Europe, they needed a different type of packaging from those who travelled overland to Persia and other places or from those who supplied indigo to domestic users.

In the seventeenth century, Europeans transported indigo that they bought in the Bayana or Sarkhej tracts overland to Surat. In Coromandel, too, indigo was brought overland to Masulipatnam from production areas about 60 miles away from the port.[30] This was done in overland caravans consisting of a large number of carts, camels, and other pack animals, soldiers, peons or coolies, camel drivers, and a number of servants who assisted in provisioning the caravan and looking after the logistics. An English traveller William Symson noted that goods from Agra, Delhi, and Ahmadabad were brought to Surat on camels, dromedaries, and asses and also observed that 'the strength and hardiness of the camels render them most fit for this service; they carry vast burdens and travel with much speed; they can travel longer without food or drink than many other creatures'.[31]

27 FRS 84, Consultations, Surat, 1616, f. 90[a].

28 In 1640, the Chambers of the VOC received Sarkhej indigo in 1078 packs and 4 chests. Collectie Geleynssen de Jongh, 237, Report on merchandise received in 1640. Coromandel indigo was transported in packs, *fardles*, and chests. Collectie Geleynssen de Jongh, 314, Extract uijdt de missive van de Heeren Bewindhebberen der Oost Indische Comp:e ter vergadering van den 17 uijt Amsterdam aen den GG&R [Extract from the missive of Honourable directors of the East India Company at the meeting of the 17th from Amsterdam to governor-general and council], 22 Oct. 1639, not foliated.

29 VOC 1127, Directeur en Raad van Surat aan GG&R, Surat, 31 Dec. 1637, f. 34[r].

30 In 1610, VOC officials in Masulipatnam noted that much indigo was brought overland to the port city from production areas located at a distance of about 60 miles from the port. VOC 1055, Masulipatnam to Batavia, 15 June 1610, pp. 120–1.

31 William Symson, *A New Voyage to the East Indies: viz. I Suratte and the coast of Arabia* (London, 1720), p. 29.

In early modern India, the most common mode of transportation between Agra and Surat was the overland caravan because there was no direct river transportation between the two places. No European contemporary traveller or merchant failed to notice the caravans transporting grain and other commercial goods from one place to another. Many of them have left vivid descriptions of the peripatetic world of the caravanneers as well as the hazards and challenges they came across during the journey. Overland caravans carrying high-value goods such as indigo and textiles were particularly exposed to excessive local tolls (*rahdari*), importunity, theft, plunder, and other exigencies. European records contain references to hazards that befell the caravans carrying the companies' goods including indigo between Agra and Surat. But before discussing these, let us first examine the economic and political aspects of the caravan system and their implications for the indigo market.

In the trajectory of indigo from manufactories to markets, the overland caravan transportation was the most complex of the tasks and a collective exercise carried out by people of different occupational groups. Caravans were the sites where one could locate a division of labour at work and see how each collaborated with or complemented the other during the journey. We know little about the organisational dynamics of the caravans and almost nothing about the actual people involved in making the transportation of commercial goods possible. It was a costly undertaking. In the 1630s, the expense of conveying indigo from Agra to Surat was usually between 6 and 8 percent, and from Ahmadabad to Surat between 5 and 6 percent, of the purchase value of the merchandise.[32] A substantial part of this went towards freight charges (carts and camels) and labour (soldiers, peons, and other employees). Most indigo during this period was conveyed to Surat on camel-drawn carts in small caravans. There were brokers and intermediaries who helped the companies hire carts and camels and recruit soldiers and peons. There are references to brokers of carts and headmen of cart-people who played important roles in the formation of the caravan. The labour market in Agra, it seems, was well organized and, in normal circumstances, the companies had no difficulties in recruiting labourers and hiring carts to transport their merchandise to Surat.

The costs of transportation and other related expenses depended on where indigo was purchased. If purchased in villages, it was brought first to the

32 In 1638, the cost of carriage of 806 packs of indigo from Sarkhej to Ahmadabad and then to Surat was Rs 4,965 that is 5.28 percent of the purchase value (Rs 93,942) whereas the total costs, including transportation, tolls, interests, and remittance charges, amounted to Rs 21,295 or 22.66 percent of the purchase value. VOC 1127, Factoire van indigo Sirchees [An invoice of Sarkhej indigo], Surat, 20 April 1638, not foliated.

companies' warehouses in Agra or Ahmadabad (if bought in Sarkhej and its vicinity). This involved some extra expenses for labour, house rent, and travel costs for the companies' officials. The rates at which carts and camels were hired varied from one caravan to another, depending on the availability of these services. In 1627, VOC officials in Agra had to pay freight charges at the rate of Rs 2½ per *man* of 53 Dutch pounds. They complained that this was rather high and had gone up from Rs 1½ and Rs 1¾ per *man* due to competition.[33] In 1634, the freight rates for carts/camels between Agra and Ahmadabad was reportedly Rs 2¼ per *man*.[34] Later in that decade, it seemingly went up substantially. During 1637–40, carts were hired in Agra for carrying indigo to Surat at rates varying between Rs 19 and Rs 24 per 6 *man*.[35] Caravans departing from Agra for Ahmadabad and Surat may have generated some employment opportunities. Each caravan was accompanied by a number of soldiers, servants, and peons, as well as the company officials' personal servants. Soldiers and peons/coolies accompanying a caravan were employed for two months and were paid a monthly salary of 3¾ or 4 rupees. Those recruited for loading or unloading the carts and in bringing the packs from other places to the companies' warehouses were paid on a daily basis. Sometimes, a person was employed for a longer period to stay in the production areas/villages and help the companies in indigo purchases. One such employee in 1637 was Taradas, who stayed in Bayana for eight months and helped the VOC to procure indigo. Another employee, Gandi, stayed in Bayana for three and a half months and assisted the company. Both of them received a salary of Rs 10 a month.[36] In the absence of a company official, a local employee was in charge of the caravan. He was generally responsible for the payments of tolls and other customary dues. Sukhram and Jan Mohammad accompanied the Surat-bound caravans and rendered these services in the late 1630s.[37]

A caravan could be a risky enterprise too. Even if it was convoyed by a number of European and local soldiers, its safe arrival in Surat was a major concern for all companies and merchants. In the early seventeenth century, caravans carrying indigo and other high-value commercial goods were exposed to

33 VOC 1097, Vertooch op 't stuck van den specerij-handel, Agra, 26 Oct. 1627, f. 422^{r}.

34 The VOC hired 400 camels in Agra to transport indigo to Ahmadabad at Rs 20 per 9 *man*. VOC 1113, Agra to Surat, 18 March 1634.

35 Collectie Geleynssen de Jongh, 113, Register van de facturen der uit Agra naar Suratte en Ahmadabad afgezonden goederen [Register of invoices of goods sent from Agra to Surat and Ahmadabad], 9 April 1637–25 Jan. 1640.

36 Ibid.

37 Ibid.

various hazards.[38] On the way between Agra and Surat, they were subjected to local tolls and official importunities. The companies had to pay numerous inland duties on goods conveyed from the interior to Surat and vice versa. Sometimes, EIC and VOC authorities obtained an imperial farman (an order or edict) from the Mughal emperor that stipulated that the company paid an annual lump sum for the privilege of conveying goods and merchandise between Surat and Agra free of inland duties. Such exemptions did not always work. Local *zamindars* (hereditary chiefs) in the interior between the two places, often, did not honour imperial orders and forced the companies and merchants to pay taxes that they claimed were due to them. Even provincial governors sometimes obstructed caravans to exact revenues from them.[39] Usually, caravans from Agra went to Surat via Ahmadabad and Broach and paid duties at the latter place and in Aklesar. Sometimes, provincial governors, too, imposed higher duties and customs officials assessed indigo and other merchandise at high rates and exacted more from the companies. In 1641, the governor of Gujarat, Mir Musa, had the VOC goods assessed at such exorbitant rates that the company diverted its caravan to a different route. To avoid the unreasonable prices and unbearable extortion (*onreedelijcke prijsen ende onlijdelijcke extorsien*), the director of the company advised that all caravans from Agra should take the Agra–Burhanpur–Surat route.[40]

The company's caravans also suffered under unforeseen circumstances. In 1632, for example, all camels—about 1,000 of them, carrying 1,400 packs indigo and some saltpetre—and other animals from a VOC caravan were confiscated by the Mughal emperor, who was on his way to Agra.[41] The company's goods had to stay in Burhanpur until the next opportunity for their transportation to Surat. In 1634, the EIC officials in Surat noted the scarcity of camels and consequent high costs of carriage from Agra to Surat due to Shahjahan's visit to Lahore and the employment of all camels in his service.[42] Caravans were also exposed to raids and plunder by local chiefs or bands of robbers who thrived on attacking caravans and seizing goods and merchandise. Many times, the EIC and the VOC suffered losses on account of such attacks on the caravans.

38 For a brief description of such hazards befalling the EIC caravans between Agra and Surat in the early years of the seventeenth century see, J.C. De, 'The Earliest Phases of the Company's Indigo Trade', *The Indian Historical Quarterly*, vol. 18, no. 2 (June 1942), 137–55.

39 In 1636, the governor of Gujarat held some 360 *man* Sarkhej indigo from the VOC possibly to exact money from the company. *Dagh-Register, 1636*, Batavia, 22 March 1636, p. 52.

40 *Dagh-Register, 1640–41*, p. 379.

41 VOC 1103, Directeur en Raad van Surat aan de Bewindhebberen, May 1632, f. 188r.

42 *EFI 1634–36*, Surat to London, 21 Feb. 1634, pp. 12–3.

In 1619, EIC officials reported the plunder and taking away of 14 *churls* of indigo from its Agra caravan en-route Surat.[43] In 1621, Deccani raiders attacked an EIC caravan carrying 357 camel loads of merchandise, while in 1636 another caravan was looted and burnt and much indigo and other goods were taken away.[44] In 1637, a VOC caravan carrying 280 packs of indigo laden on 27 carts was blocked by the Rajputs, who demanded a toll from the company.[45] In 1659, the ruler of Sirohi, a semi-autonomous chieftaincy in Gujarat, seized about 400 packs of Bayana indigo from a VOC caravan.[46] Soldiers and guards convoying the caravans fought against the raiders and, sometimes, it resulted in the loss of lives. In 1619, four or five attendants were killed by raiders who attacked the EIC caravan.[47] In 1644, similarly, an attack on an EIC caravan resulted in the loss of seven servants including Ibrahim, the conductor of the caravan, and left twelve seriously wounded.[48] Notwithstanding these hazards, the caravan system worked quite well for all merchants and companies.

The efficient working of the caravan system was an outcome of the stable political regime that the Mughals established in India. The Mughals, to a large extent, were able to ensure safe and secure transportation of commercial goods within the empire. In the late seventeenth, and more so in the early eighteenth century, the routes that connected Gujarat with Delhi and Agra regions became increasingly unsafe and inland transportation became more expensive for merchants and the European companies than before. Consequently, the VOC and the EIC purchased Sarkhej and Bayana indigo in Ahmadabad and Surat from local merchants and intermediary dealers.[49] The VOC withdrew itself from Agra and gave up its establishments there in 1712. Thereafter, it became even more difficult for the Dutch to procure Bayana indigo from Agra. In 1725, VOC officials in Surat had to excuse themselves from procuring 150,000 Dutch pounds of Bayana indigo ordered from home because transportation of

---

43 *EFI 1618–21*, Surat to London, 9 and 15 Feb. 1619, pp. 59–60; ibid., Consultations, Surat, 25 Nov. 1620, p. 210.

44 *Generale Missiven, vol. I, 1610–38*, p. 107; VOC 1122, Governeur en raad van Surat aan GG&R, 5 May 1637, f. 541^{v}.

45 VOC 1122, Governeur en raad van Surat aan GG&R, 5 May 1637, f. 542^{r}.

46 *Generale Missiven, vol. III, 1655–74*, Batavia, 16 Dec. 1659, p. 274.

47 *EFI 1618–21*, Surat to London, 9 and 15 Feb. 1619, p. 59.

48 *EFI 1642–45*, Surat to London, 26 March 1644, p. 163.

49 VOC 1215, Copia Factura der laadinghe inde jachten Naarden ende Goutsbloem uijt Suratta naar Batavia versonden, anno 1656 [Copies of the invoices of the cargoes in the yachts *Naarden* and *Goutsbloem* sent from Surat to Batavia in 1656], f. 642^{r}; VOC 1297, Bevindinge van de Souratse boeken in den jare 1667 en 1668 [Finding of Surat's account books in 1667 and 1668], f. 230^{r}; ibid., 1668–69, f. 232^{r}; ibid., 1669–70, f. 234^{r}.

merchandise from Agra to Surat was extremely difficult on account of troubles in the empire and the resulting insecurity on caravan routes.[50]

The Indigo Market in Colonial India

The structure of the indigo market as it evolved in the colonial period was different from what it was in the seventeenth century. A major change was the centralisation of the indigo market at the presidency headquarters in Calcutta, and later Madras. Prospective merchants and company officials no longer gathered in the villages to purchase indigo as they had in early seventeenth-century Bayana or Sarkhej. Most indigo from village manufactories in the Bengal Presidency was transported to Calcutta either to be auctioned there or straightaway freighted to Europe and other overseas destinations. The second major transformation in the market was the substitution of the native suppliers and *voorkopers* by professional British and European indigo contractors through whom the EIC and other European and American merchants generally made their purchases. A concomitant development was the consolidation of several spheres of economic activity in a single merchant firm or agency house. In the aftermath of the collapse of the indigo market in London and consequently of planter-manufacturers in the early 1830s, some agency houses, like John Palmer and Co., took possession of the manufactories in a bid to recover the capital they had lent to the planter-manufacturers.[51] Such agency houses then came to dominate the indigo commodity chain from cultivation of the plant and manufacturing of the dye to exports and sales. By the 1830s, the line that had formerly separated production from trade became indistinct. Many manufacturers financed and controlled the production of indigo plant, thus changing what had formerly been a free-peasant–owned agrarian enterprise. They leased or acquired ownership of land and cultivated the plant with the help of wage labourers or through the cash-advance system. They came to control this primary link in the commodity chain.

As the new commodity chain came under tighter control of British and European merchants and agency houses, the arena in which local Indian merchants, brokers, and bankers had previously played an important role shrank considerably. Indigo-producing villages lost the autonomy of the marketplace.

50 VOC 9059, Extract uijt den eijsch van retouren uijt India voor den jare 1725 [Extracts from the orders for return goods from India for the year 1725], f. 72v.

51 Anthony Webster, *The Twilight of the East India Company: The Evolution of Anglo-Asian Commerce and Politics, 1790–1860* (Woodbridge: Boydell Press, 2009), 87–8.

As Sudipta Sen has rightly observed, the new distributive and acquisitive modes of capital reduced the autonomy and quality of space associated with exchange.[52] Villages became an integral part of a global indigo chain and their economic fortunes came to depend heavily on the world market, a process that Sugata Bose calls 'dependent commercialisation'.[53] A key figure in this reconstituted village agrarian order was the salaried British/European manager employed by manufactory owners. In supervising indigo production, the managers were assisted by a group of Indian employees and servants. Their services became even more crucial in the second half of the nineteenth century, when some large conglomerates came to own clusters of manufactories.[54]

Merchants could buy indigo through prior contracts with manufacturers or they could buy it at the auctions in Calcutta. Initially, the EIC, being the sole purchaser of indigo for European markets, procured indigo through contracts with merchants and several joint merchant firms.[55] The company advertised the quantity it required in a season and invited proposals from manufacturers who wished to supply the company.[56] The sealed proposals contained the amount of indigo (expressed in factory *man* of 75 pounds) and the prices at which the commodity was to be delivered. The company considered all proposals and accepted them in accordance with their merits. Thus, contracts were made with manufacturers and advance payments were made on the

---

52 Sudipta Sen, *Empire of Free Trade: the East India Company and the Making of the Colonial Marketplace* (Philadelphia: University of Pennsylvania Press, 1998), 154–5.

53 Sugata Bose, *Peasant Labour and Colonial Capital: Rural Bengal since 1770* (Cambridge: CUP, 1993), 41–2.

54 The Ganges Indigo Company (formed in 1852) and the London-based Tirhoot Indigo Association owned many manufactories in Bihar during this period, which were managed by European managers. See for details and names of many of those managers, Minden Wilson, *History of Behar Indigo Factories (also) Reminiscence of Behar, Tirhoot and its Inhabitants of the Past, History of Behar Light Horse Volunteers* (Calcutta: General Printing Company, 1908).

55 Between 1779 and 1784, the EIC bought indigo from John Prinsep and subsequently, from several merchants and mercantile firms. BL, Home Miscellaneous, 434, Memorandum of measures and means to introduce, improve, and enlarge the manufacture of indigo in Bengal and Bahar, Hugli, 30 Dec. 1790, p. 601. In 1790, the company's indigo contractors included Carl Blume, Thomas Harding, Gilchrist and Charters, Perreau and Stephens, James Orr, G.U. Lawtie, Robert Heaven, and Herbert Harris. WBSA, Board of Trade, vol., 85/1, Commercial Proceedings, 2 March 1790, pp. 34–5; ibid., vol. 86, Commercial Proceedings, Fort William, Calcutta, 16 April 1790, pp. 7–8. Mercantile firms, such as Fairlie & Co., Colvins and Bazett, Campbell and Radcliff, supplied indigo to the company. B.B. Chowdhury, *Growth of Commercial Agriculture in Bengal, 1757–1900* (Calcutta: R.K. Maitra, 1964), 76.

56 WBSA, Board of Trade, Proceedings, Fort William, 6 Dec. 1811, p. 36.

promise of a future delivery of indigo and on reliable security given by some other merchants or firms. The persons and firms who gave security were liable to be charged for the sum advanced to manufacturers if the manufacturers failed to deliver the stipulated amount of indigo. Those who stood surety for contractors were mostly Europeans, but there were also some indigenous merchants or bankers who served in the same capacity for European contractors. In 1789, for example, Durgacharan Mukherji and Banarsi Ghose stood surety for Herbert Harris, who contracted to supply indigo to the EIC.[57]

Another major change during this period was that the indigo market in India was no longer a free market in which sellers or buyers competed with each other for a favourable transaction. On account of its trade monopoly, the EIC was, until 1788, the sole purchaser and exporter of indigo to Great Britain.[58] Notwithstanding the monopsony, its indigo trade was unprofitable because of the high purchase prices in India and low sale prices in Europe.[59] For the company, indigo was a means of transmitting revenue surpluses from India to Britain and, therefore, profitability was not a major concern. Peter Marshall has rightly remarked, 'so long as imports from India were regarded as the means of remitting a tribute, the company was bound to maintain them at the highest level without paying overmuch regard to their profitability'.[60] After 1788, the company allowed private indigo exports to Britain, but it controlled the actual transportation from Calcutta to London and sales there. Through a complex contract system, the company exported indigo to Britain and kept the terms of trade in its favour.[61] Under the new system, the contractors submitted a sample of indigo (4 *seers* of equal quality) whose value was then assessed by the company's appraisers and three-fourths of the appraised value of all indigo was advanced to manufacturers. The company withheld one-fourth of the assessed value to meet the costs of freight and home customs duties (5 percent),

57 WBSA, Board of Trade, vol. 86, Commercial Proceedings, Fort William, Calcutta, April 1790, p. 14.

58 This is important because Britain was the main market for indigo in the colonial period. Between 1796–97 and 1825–26, about 82 percent of the total exports of indigo from Bengal was to Britain/London.

59 In 1788–89, for example, the company's average net loss in indigo trade amounted to 33 percent. BL, Home Miscellaneous, 393, Report of Commercial Occurrences, 6 Nov. 1788 and 9 Nov. 1789, pp. 345–7.

60 P.J. Marshall, *Problems of Empire: Britain and India, 1757–1813* (London: Routledge, 1998), 94.

61 The contract stipulated all the terms and conditions, rights and responsibilities, and specified when and how the advances were to be made to the contractors and dates when specified instalments of indigo were to be delivered to the company. WBSA, Board of Trade, vol. 84, Commercial Proceedings, Fort William, Calcutta, 2 Jan. 1789, pp. 2–5.

and warehouse space (2 to 2½ percent).[62] By manipulating the estimation of sale prices in London and the rupee-to-pound sterling exchange value in its favour, the company freed itself from the risks of a poor sale at home.[63] This method, however, was disadvantageous for manufacturers as the terms of the contracts were unfavourable to them.

The indigo market in the early colonial period discriminated against the products of the territories outside the company's rule. Thus, indigo from Banaras, Awadh, Agra, and Delhi paid an extra 15 percent duty in Calcutta. The company framed regulations aimed at promoting indigo culture in the Bengal Presidency. The new scheme presented to the Court of Directors in 1790 proposed that all indigo manufactories in the Presidency be registered and numbered and that only indigo manufactured in those manufactories using plants produced within the company's territory was to be accepted aboard the company's ships.[64] The government would advance money to manufacturers in the Presidency at the rate of 100 rupees per *man* for the total amount of indigo each promised to supply. Each had to give assurances that they would supply the stipulated quantity of indigo, and in the case of a shortage or failure to do so, would return the money to the company on a pro-rated basis. The 5 percent customs duties payable in London were to be abolished, the warehouse charges were to be reduced from 2½ percent to 1 percent, and the freight charges were not to exceed 3 pence per pound. The total money advanced in Bengal plus all the charges were to be deducted from the sale proceeds at the rate of 2 shillings per rupee. The balance was to stay in the company's treasury, for which amount bills were to be issued on the government of Bengal in favour of the proprietors.[65] The company's share of indigo exports from Bengal decreased while that of the European private merchants increased substantially. The colonial attitude of privileging indigo produced within the Presidency would change after the major indigo-producing areas of Delhi, Agra, and Awadh came under British control in the early and mid-nineteenth century.

62 BL, Home Miscellaneous, 434, Memorandum of measures and means to introduce, improve, and enlarge the manufacture of indigo in Bengal and Bahar, Hugli, 30 Dec. 1790, p. 603.

63 The estimated sale price of indigo in London (3 shillings per pound), as arbitrarily determined by the company's appraisers, was usually one-third less than what it would actually sell for in Britain (4 shillings and 6 pence per pound). Similarly, the exchange was fixed at a high rate of 2 shillings and 3 ½ pence per Bengal rupee which was 14 percent more than the usual exchange rate of 2 shillings per rupee. Ibid., p. 602; WBSA, Board of Trade, vol. 84, pp. 2–5.

64 BL, Home Miscellaneous, 434, Memorandum on the manufacture of indigo, Hugli, 30 Dec. 1790, pp. 607–17.

65 Ibid.

Many private traders and, occasionally, the EIC bought indigo in Calcutta at the annual auctions. This mode of buying had some advantages. Buyers did not have to pay several months in advance and, thus, were free from the risks of losing money in bad debts if production failed or if the product quality was not satisfactory. Contrary to the contract system, spot purchases enabled merchants to have up-to-date knowledge of the market at home and buy the sort of indigo they desired at prices that would ensure a profitable transaction. This system had some disadvantages, too. Uncertainties of season and impending shortages of supplies and high prices sometimes left merchants with no indigo at all. In such circumstances, those merchants who had advanced money to manufacturers received indigo on a priority basis and others had to compete for whatever was put on the market through auctions. For large-scale buyers, advance buying through contracts with manufacturers was the preferred mode of procuring indigo. The EIC purchased indigo mostly through contracts and cash advances to manufacturers. In the early nineteenth century, EIC officials deliberated on the company's mode of buying indigo, and some held the view that the company should buy indigo in Calcutta. The experiment, however, was not successful. The EIC failed to procure indigo in 1809–10 and 1810–11 at the auctions in Calcutta.[66] The company had imposed a price ceiling (Rs 110–130 per *man*), which limited the flexibility that the officials on the spot needed to bid for the commodity at the auctions.[67]

Packing and Transportation

No matter how the commodity was purchased and what the contract terms were, indigo from all manufactories had to be transported to Calcutta to be auctioned or loaded on ships bound for either Europe or the Americas.[68] Indigo was packed in large wooden boxes, each of which contained from 3¼ to 3½ or 4 *man* of indigo.[69] Indigo cakes were sifted and packed close to each other in such a way as to minimize the chance that pieces would break during

66 WBSA, Board of Trade, Proceedings, Fort William, Calcutta, 6 Dec. 1811, pp. 39–42.

67 Ibid., pp. 56–7.

68 Some indigo from the North Western provinces went to Karachi from where it was conveyed to Europe.

69 A factory *man* in Bengal was equal to 75 pounds. A box would thus contain indigo from about 245 to 263 pounds. John Phipps, *A Series of Treatises on the Principal Products of Bengal: Indigo* (Calcutta: Baptist Mission Press, 1832), 140; F.E.C. Linde, *Indigo: a Short Sketch of the Cultivation, Manufacture & Trade of Indigo* (Calcutta: Central Press, 1882), 8.

transportation or when inspected at auction. Sorting indigo according to its quality and colour was a priority. Manufacturers were advised not to mix the cakes produced from different vats and different rounds of production because the quality and colour of indigo from one vat were not identical with that of the other vats.[70] The use of cutting machines enabled manufacturers to attain a degree of uniformity in the size of the cakes, which enabled them to pack indigo in a box as closely as possible. If there still remained some gaps, they were filled with cakes of lesser dimension and thickness made especially for that purpose. Indigo boxes were taken to Calcutta mostly in sail- or oar-powered boats and ships until the middle of the century, when steamers and then the railways offered more efficient and faster means of transportation. A labyrinth of small and large rivers crisscrossing the indigo-producing areas of Bengal, Bihar, Awadh, Agra, and Banaras provided a convenient means of conveying goods and merchandise to Calcutta. An eighteenth-century account of the river systems of Bengal by James Rennell testifies to the prevalence of inland river transportation in northern India.[71] Compared with the overland caravan routes from Agra to Surat, the eastward riverine routes were faster, safer, and less vulnerable to attacks and plunder. Boats and vessels required fewer people and provisions than caravans; hence, their manning costs were less expensive too. Fleets carrying commercial goods to or from Calcutta encountered fewer customs and toll barriers than did caravans moving westward from Agra. Moreover, there was a strong maritime tradition in the region, and people in general were accustomed to using this mode of transportation.[72] Conveying indigo to the Calcutta market may have been as much of a consideration in selecting the sites for manufactories as finding sources of water for processing indigo. Contemporaries have noted the use of waterways for carrying indigo to Calcutta. In the second half of the century, steamships navigated the distances rather quickly and facilitated transportation of commodities to Calcutta.[73] Railways may have been a faster means of conveying goods to Calcutta in the late nineteenth century, but it was not competitive with other forms of

70 Phipps, *A Series of Treatises on the Principal Products of Bengal*, 139–40.

71 James Rennell, *An Account of the Ganges and Burrampooter Rivers* (London: J. Nichols, 1781).

72 Sunil Kumar Munsi, *Geography of Transportation in Eastern India under the British Raj* (Calcutta: K.P. Bagchi, 1980), 3, 5, 17, 23; Anand A Yang, *Bazaar India: Markets, Society, and the Colonial State in Gangetic Bihar* (New Delhi: Munshiram Manoharlal, 2000), 27–32.

73 A return journey between Calcutta and Patna took about 38 days of which upward journey took about 27 days. Munsi, *Geography of Transportation in Eastern India*.

transportation. Thus, indigo from Bihar continued to be conveyed to Calcutta mainly via boat.[74]

In Calcutta, descriptive catalogues were printed and handed out to merchants who, after examining the contents of the boxes, could select the type of indigo and the number of boxes they wished to buy.[75] They then offered a price and bid at the auction. Against each lot and variety on the printed list, they wrote the prices they were willing to pay and also indicated the number of boxes they wanted to buy. Once they had collected all the papers, the sellers would know who the highest bidder was and would finalise the deal. To be able to make a reasonable offer, the prospective buyers had to know the indigo markets in India and at home well. They also had to be familiar with indigo and have the ability to judge its quality. Usually, foreign merchants solicited the assistance of native brokers, but large-scale buyers and exporters often employed European experts as a permanent staff to help them procure indigo of the desired quality.[76] Brokers and indigo experts examined the chests and boxes and advised their employers about the quality and prices. Indigo prices depended on the quality, which was measured according to the percentage of dye it contained. Besides quality the manufacturers' mark, colour, shape and appearance, and the overall demand and supply also played a role in determining prices.[77]

In the nineteenth century, as in former times, certain procedures were carried out to test the quality of indigo. Several accounts of indigo production written in the late eighteenth and early nineteenth centuries refer to lightness, feeling dry between fingers, floating in water, and burning like wax without

74 In his account of Bihar indigo, Minden Wilson notes that indigo was carried on boat to the chief factories and then sent down the Ganges to Calcutta. Wilson, *History of Behar Indigo Factory*, 21, 23. Christopher Bayly has observed that on account of high freight charges the railways could not compete with river transportation until the mid-1880s. C.A. Bayly, 'State and Economy in India over Seven Hundred Years', *Economic History Review*, vol. 38, no. 4 (1985), 592.

75 Linde, *Indigo: A Short Sketch*, 9.

76 The experts were men who made the indigo business as their especial vocation and specialized in the technical knowledge of the commodity. Ibid., 10. Many such experts had immigrated to India from Europe's transatlantic colonies where they had worked on indigo plantations.

77 Indigo prices ranged between Rs 100 and Rs 320 per *man* depending on the quality. According to Linde, Bengal indigo was of a superior quality and contained from 40 to 70 percent dye whereas the lot from the Upper Provinces contained only 30 percent. Linde, *Indigo: A Short Sketch*, 10.

leaving any sediment except ashes as signs of its purity.[78] Colour remained, of course, the main identifier. The best indigo from Bengal had a fine, rich blue or deep violet colour. When broken into pieces for inspection, the interior of good-quality indigo was bright purple in colour and of a close and compact texture. Rubbing with a fingernail gave it a shining, copper-like appearance.[79] All merchants, especially those who preferred to buy good-quality indigo, employed these methods of testing the quality on random pieces of indigo cakes chosen from the boxes before committing to buy any. When these procedures were completed, the indigo was finally packed or re-packed according to the shipping specifications, and chests/packs were sealed and marked with the owners' identification. Indigo was then ready to sail to the intended destinations.

From India to Britain

Indigo was shipped to London from Calcutta, and later on from Madras as well. As long as the EIC monopolised the trade, only its ships could carry exports from India to the metropolis. Many private British merchants sent their indigo on Danish ships to Copenhagen and from there to London.[80] On account of the long distance between India and Britain and the large cargo spaces that indigo occupied on homebound ships, the costs of transportation were substantial.[81] This had a huge impact on sales in London and in determining which indigo would sell at competitive prices in Europe. It was, therefore, crucial that merchants keep the transportation costs low. But so long as the EIC held onto its freight monopoly merchants had to acquiesce to the high freight rates it charged. Freight and warehouse charges as well as home duties were included in the contracts under which merchants consigned indigo to London. Attempts to reduce these costs were unsuccessful. In 1792, for example, the committee of warehouse resolved to reduce freight from £25 per ton of 12 hundredweight to £15 per ton of 20 hundredweight, but no tonnage was allowed to merchants.[82]

78 Phipps, *A Series of Treatises on the Principal Products of Bengal*, 70.

79 Ibid.

80 In 1797–98, ships under Danish colour exported goods including indigo worth more than Rs 4 million. BL, Home Miscellaneous, 57, Danish Trade from Bengal, 1797–98, p. 281.

81 In 1800, the company charged £41:13:4 per ton of 20 hundredweight (2,240 pounds) and the total costs including customs and other London charges came to £88:13:4 per ton. BL, Home Miscellaneous, 406, D. Scott's Memorial on India Trade, India House, 10 Sept. 1800, pp. 201–2.

82 Ibid., p. 202.

John Cochrane's memorandum on shipping underlines the exorbitant freight and demurrage charges, as well as the scarcity of tonnage available to merchants.[83] The indigo trade benefited immensely from the withdrawal of the EIC's monopoly on the India trade in 1813 and the rise of private shipping that delivered transportation services at competitive rates. Merchant firms and associations that had taken over the indigo business from the EIC could then consign large volumes of it to their correspondents in London and elsewhere.

Once in London, indigo was sold to dyers and printers, grocers, and merchants who then distributed it to various British and European markets. Indigo brought to London in EIC ships was sold through auctions held at the company's behest. More than the quality, the shortage or abundance of imports determined the sale prices in London. Until the 1830s, there was limited elasticity of demand, and any large supplies adversely affected the price. On several occasions in the nineteenth century, such wide price fluctuation occurred that it depressed the market and led to the collapse and ruin of merchants and agency houses. The volatility of the London market was partly due to indigo's association with the remittance business and partly because the production of textiles in Britain and mainland Europe had not expanded to the extent that it could absorb the rapidly increasing imports. Indigo exports from India were not so much contingent on European demand as on the volume of colonial capital and revenue surpluses to be transferred to Britain.

In the second half of the century, several circumstances—rapid expansion in industrial production of textiles, the development of faster and more reliable transportation between India and Britain, the emergence of large joint firms managing the indigo commodity chain from production in India to sales in London and distribution in Europe, and the relative peace and prosperity in Europe—created conditions in which the indigo trade could flourish and expand. With the coming of steamships and the opening of the Suez Canal in the late 1860s, more cargo space became available and conveying indigo to London became safer, faster, and less expensive. This is evident from a rapid increase in the average annual value of indigo exports between 1866 and 1875.[84] The markets in London and Europe stabilised due to better coordination between demand and supplies under the large indigo conglomerates. Merchants and agents in India sent indigo to their patrons and correspondents in London, who then sold it to others for consumption or distribution elsewhere

83 BL, Home Miscellaneous 406, Memorandum by John Cochrane on India Trade and Shipping (not dated).

84 It went up from less than 20 million rupees during 1856–1865 to more than 28 million rupees during 1865–1775. Appendix 5: Indigo exports from India.

in Europe. This end of the indigo commodity chain has not been explored in detail, and our knowledge of the intra-European merchant networks, the role of indigo firms in the distribution of the commodity in mainland European markets, prices, and consumption culture, must unfortunately remain sketchy until studies of these aspects are undertaken.

In the early seventeenth century, indigo sold by the EIC to London merchants was distributed to other parts of Europe through their trade networks. One such merchant was George Warner, who distributed indigo and other commodities he bought from the company to other parts of Europe through his trade networks.[85] Similarly, we have references of London merchants re-exporting indigo to France and Netherlands during the late 1790s. Merchant such as Robert Pedder and Thomas Baker petitioned to the Privy Council on behalf of other merchants for permission to export indigo to France in 1797.[86] In the late nineteenth and early twentieth centuries, indigo dealers, agents, and brokers in London purchased indigo in India, imported it into London, and supplied it to British and other European consumers. When the supply of synthetic blue dye from Germany was interrupted during the First World War, the British government solicited the services of professional brokers to keep dyers supplied with natural indigo from India. In 1914, for example, the government made arrangements with Lewis and Peat, a London-based brokerage firm, for the purchase of indigo in India and its distribution among Britain's small-scale textile dyers and printers as well as dealers who supplied indigo to consumers in the textile industrial towns of Manchester, Liverpool, Yorkshire, Lancashire, and elsewhere.[87] The distribution networks and the impact of indigo on markets and market relations in Britain, the Netherlands, and elsewhere in Europe need to be explored in order to complete the study of the indigo commodity chain. Elsewhere, I have examined how the indigo trade of the EIC induced

85 This is evident from the collection of his correspondence with his agents and merchants transacting business in his behalf in Hamburg, France, and Livorno. NA, Kew, George Warner Papers, SP 46/84.

86 In several petitions to the Privy Council, Robert Pedder and Thomas Baker & Sons sought permission to export indigo to France. NA, Kew, PC 1/37/111, Diverse petitions to export indigo and other goods to France, 1797. In a petition dated 16 March 1797, Robert Pedder sought permission to export 25 tons of indigo to France. In another petition dated 21 March 1797, Thomas Baker & Sons sought permission to export 25 tons of indigo to Calais, a French port in the Northern Sea.

87 The firm bought indigo in India at the stipulated prices and supplied it to British consumers at the minimum possible rates. NA, Kew, BT 13/60, Minutes and Correspondence between Mr Devitt (of the Lewis & Peat Company) and the Board of Trade and Chancellor of Exchequer, diverse dates 1914.

competition and private trade leading to competing networks and disaffected market relationships in London in the early seventeenth century. For example, Bayana indigo became a brand name in European markets and it encouraged imitation, counterfeiting, and deceitful activities in Britain.[88] One gets a similar impression of the markets in late eighteenth-century London, where merchants were selling Bengal indigo to consumers as indigo from French Saint-Domingue or Spanish Guatemala. These and similar other interesting aspects of the trade await detailed investigation.

---

88 Ghulam A. Nadri, 'The Indigo Trade of the English East India Company in the Seventeenth Century: Challenges and Opportunities', in Maxine Berg and et al. (eds.), *Goods from the East, 1600–1830: Trading Eurasia* (Palgrave Macmillan, 2015), 61–76.

CHAPTER 3

The Indigo Trade: Local and Global Demand

> When we reflect upon the cheapness of labour in Bengal and the favourable climate it enjoys, we cannot harbour a doubt of the possibility of making indigo a most valuable article of importation.
>
> —EXTRACT COURT'S letter to GG, 12 April 1786, p. 5

The indigo trade or transmission of the commodity from the region where it was produced to the people who consumed it was a vital component of the commodity chain. This is also the component about which our sources contain consistent and reliable data. This allows us to work out trade aggregates over a fairly long period, to identify and analyse patterns of growth and decline, and to interpret these phenomena in their local and global contexts. The expansion or contraction in the volume of indigo trade reflects the potentialities of production and supplies in India on the one hand and the dynamics of local and external demand for it on the other. Between the late sixteenth and early twentieth centuries, the indigo trade in India underwent alternating phases of expansion and contraction due to a combination of political and economic circumstances at home and in Europe and the Americas. What follows below is a detailed analysis of the local and global demand for Indian indigo, impediments and challenges in carrying out indigo trade, and their implications for the world indigo market.

A unique feature of the Indian indigo commodity chain in the seventeenth and eighteenth centuries was that it was not totally dependent on European markets.[1] A substantial local demand kept the industry going even when the EIC and VOC stopped exporting it to Europe. The cotton textile-producing areas of Bengal, Sind, Agra and Awadh, Gujarat, the Deccan, and the Coromandel Coast consumed substantial quantities of indigo every year. This domestic demand grew as textile production expanded in the seventeenth and eighteenth centuries. Large quantities of indigo were also exported annually to the markets of the Persian Gulf, the Red Sea, the north-eastern Mediterranean, and Europe. While some indigo was consumed in West Asia and Ottoman Turkey, some was re-exported from there to Europe. Contrary to the substantial and stable domestic consumption, the large European demand for Indian indigo fluctuated widely.

1 Most other indigo producing regions had no significant local demand and, therefore, depended heavily on European and, in some cases, Asian markets.

 | DOI 10.1163/9789004311558_005

From the late sixteenth to the middle of the seventeenth century, indigo was exported in large quantities to Europe by the Portuguese Estado da India,[2] the EIC, and the VOC. By the end of this period, a world market had emerged in which India was no longer an exclusive supplier of this commodity. Indigo became a global commercial commodity and the networks of production and distribution expanded to areas previously unknown for producing commercial indigo. Competing chains of supplies emerged primarily as a consequence of Europe's colonial conquests and a restructuring of the colonial agrarian economy that followed. After the British colonial conquests of Bengal and north India and the restructuring of the region's agrarian economy, the reconstituted indigo commodity chain in India once again dominated the world market.[3] As we will see below, in the nineteenth century the EIC, private European and American merchants, and Indian and Asian traders exported large quantities of indigo to numerous overseas markets.

Local Consumption in Pre-colonial India

As noted, flourishing textile production in many parts of India kept up the demand for indigo throughout this period. For lack of contemporary estimates, it is not possible to quantify local consumption, but given the large size of the textile industry in India, it may be presumed that the market was large and that the producers in some localities targeted this potential demand.

Since antiquity, dyers in India had used indigo to obtain blue, green, and many related shades of colour.[4] During the period of the Delhi Sultanate in the thirteenth and fifteenth centuries, indigo dyeing was an important profession and a source of revenue to the state as well. In 1375, Sultan Firuz Shah (1351–1388) of Delhi abolished taxes on certain professions, including *nilgari* (indigo manufacturing or dyeing).[5] A variety of indigo-dyed clothes were used

2 The Portuguese overseas empire in Asia established in the early sixteenth century after their conquest of some strategic Indian Ocean ports such as Hormuz, Diu, Goa, and Malacca.

3 Throughout the nineteenth century, India catered to the large demand for indigo in the rapidly expanding textile industry of Europe, North America and Asia. While Britain was the largest market, Indian indigo was also exported in large quantities to France and Italy and substantial quantities were also exported to Japan in the early twentieth century.

4 Mira Roy, 'Dyes in Ancient and Medieval India', *Indian Journal of History of Science*, vol. 13, no. 2 (1978), 83–112.

5 *Sirat-i Firuz Shahi*, c. 1370–71 (MS. Persian, Centre of Advanced Study in History Aligarh Muslim University, Aligarh), Rotograph 168, f. 61[a]; Edward Thomas, *The Revenue Resources of the Mughal Empire in India, from A.D. 1593 to A.D. 1707: A Supplement to The Chronicles of the*

in various parts of India and also exported to West and South-east Asia in the fourteenth and fifteenth centuries.[6] References to indigo and the methods and techniques of dyeing get multiplied from the late sixteenth century. Several Mughal and late-Mughal Persian treatises testify to the practice of using indigo for dyeing and printing textiles. A late seventeenth-century Persian text, *Bayaz-i Khusbui*, mentions indigo as an important source of obtaining blue and its various shades.[7] Another Persian treatise, *Nuskha Khulasatul Mujarribat*, refers to the use of different types of indigo by dyers to obtain blue, emerald green, and *Majmu'at* (dark or blackish blue colours).[8] *Majmu'at-us Sanaye* refers to the use of indigo in colouring stone, ivory, textiles, as well as hands, feet, and hair.[9] In the seventeenth century, qualitative evidence on local consumption becomes more frequent as European commercial interest in indigo began to generate documentation on its production, trade, and consumption. The EIC and VOC sources generally allude to local consumption of indigo whenever officials reported on the output and prices of indigo and its availability in the market.

Although indigo production was widespread in India and most textile producing places had their local sources of indigo, large-scale production of textiles for commercial purposes necessitated the use of good-quality indigo from the Bayana and Sarkhej tracts. It transpires from some Persian treatises that the fineness of colours or shades depended much on the quality of indigo used in dyeing the object.[10] Dyers of Bengal and eastern India, thus,

---

Pathan Kings of Dehli (London: Trübner & Co., 1871), 5–6; Moti Chandra, 'Costumes and Textiles in the Sultanate Period', *Journal of Indian Textile History*, vol. 6 (1961), 12.

6 Chandra, 'Costumes and Textiles in the Sultanate Period'.

7 *Bayaz-i Khushbui* [Notebook on Fragrance] (ed.), Mirza Mu'tamid Khan, copied by Muhammad Azam, (Shaban 1109 A.H. 42 RR Aurangzeb Alamgir), c. 1698 (BL, Islamic Manuscript), ff. 114^{a-b}, 116^{b}, 117^{a-b}, 121^{b}, 141^{b}, 150^{a}, 152^{b}–153^{a}.

8 *Nuskha Khulasatul Mujarribat* [Manuscript-copy of the summary of prescriptions] copied by Shaikh Ahmad (*katib*), 1189 AH (c. 1790) (BL, Islamic Manuscript), ff. 113^{a-b}, 116^{b}, 118^{a}, 124^{b}, 134^{a}. See also *Risala mushtamil bar nuskhahai ataria wa talween-i parcha* [Essay based on treatises on perfumes and textile dyeing], copied by Sayed Hussain, *Rajab* 1121 A.H. (c. 1709), (BL, Islamic Manuscript), ff. 12^{a-b}, 15^{a-b}, 22^{a}, 28^{b}–29^{a}; Hamida Khatoon Naqvi, 'Colour Making and Dyeing of Cotton Textiles in Medieval Hindustan', *Indian Journal of History of Science*, vol. 15, no. 1 (1980), 58–70.

9 *Majmu'at-us Sanaye* [A Compendium of Artifices] by an anonymous author from Morocco, (*Hakim Philosoph-i magaribi*), copied by Sayid Ghulam Murtaza Jafri, 22 RY of Aurangzeb Alamgir (c. 1679), (BL, Islamic Manuscript), pp. 29, 32–3, 58, 71, 188, 192–4.

10 *Nuskha Khulasat-ul Majarribat; Risala mushtamil bar nuskhahai ataria wa talween-i parcha; Majmu'at-us Sanaye*. References to *nil khassa* (special or pure indigo), *khum* or *qum nil* [raw or poor-quality indigo], *nil qism-i awwal* (indigo of the first quality), *nil bayabani*

depended mainly on the supplies of Bayana and Sarkhej indigo. Textile producers of north-western India also used Bayana indigo. The EIC officials noted that much Bayana and Khurja indigo was taken to Multan where it was sold at high prices.[11] Even though indigo was produced at some places in Sind (Bubak, Nasarpur, and Sann), local dyers of Thatta and Sind used Bayana and Sarkhej indigo as well. This implied that there was a considerable internal trade in which local merchants actively participated. In European sources, one comes across frequent references to Gujarati Bania and Muslim merchants buying indigo in the Bayana and Sarkhej tracts for local dyers and for export. In the sixteenth century, Francois Pyrard and John Huyghen van Linschoten mention these merchants carrying on a considerable trade in indigo between Gujarat and Goa, which had emerged as a great trade emporium.[12] In 1610, a Muslim merchant in Masulipatnam was observed to be expecting eighteen camel loads of Bayana indigo from Agra.[13] In the 1640s, Indian merchants were reportedly buying Coromandel indigo for the markets of Bijapur and Burhanpur.[14] Bengal and the whole of eastern India were kept supplied with indigo by local merchants and itinerant traders. In 1609, the VOC even contemplated establishing a factory at Chittagong, in the kingdom of Arakan (now south-eastern Bangladesh), mainly for purchasing indigo that Indian merchants brought there from northern India in large quantities.[15] Uncertainties of supply and fluctuating prices sometimes prompted dyers and merchants to explore possibilities of indigo production at the local level and produce it themselves. European capital and demand for indigo also played a supporting role. Indigo growers and

---

(wild indigo) indicate the use of indigo of varying qualities by dyers and the quality of colour they produced.

11 Bayana indigo was sold in Multan at Rs 85 per *man* and Khurja indigo at Rs 80 per *man*. *EFI 1637–41*, Henry Bornford's Account of his Journey from Agra to Tatta [Thatta], March 1639, pp. 135–6.

12 Francois Pyrard, *The Voyage of François Pyrard of Laval to the East Indies, the Maldives, the Moluccas and Brazil*, vol. II, tr., & ed., Albert Gray (London: Hakluyt Society, 1887), p. 247; Jan Huyghen van Linschoten, *The Voyage of John Huyghen van Linschoten to the East Indies*, vol. 1, ed., A.C. Burnell (London: Hakluyt Society, 1885), p. 252; Surendra Gopal, *Commerce and Crafts in Gujarat, 16th and 17th Centuries: A Study in the Impact of European Expansion on Pre-capitalist Economy* (New Delhi: People's Publishing House, 1975), 83–4.

13 VOC 1055, Masulipatnam, 15 June 1610, p. 121

14 Tapan Raychaudhuri, *Jan Company in Coromandel, 1605–1690: A Study in the Interrelations of European Commerce and Traditional Economies* ('s-Gravenhaag: Martinus Nijhoff, 1962), 164.

15 Every year, Bania and Khatri merchants came to Arakan from Hindustan, Lahore, Agra, Delhi, and other places with indigo that the company aspired to obtain in exchange for spices and Chinese goods. VOC 1055, Masulipatnam to Batavia, 25 May 1608, p. 18.

producers in Sind, for example, were greatly encouraged in their craft by the EIC's indigo investments in the 1640s and 1650s.[16]

A considerable part of the indigo produced in Khurja, Mewat, Basawar, Brahmabad, Kol, Jalali, Sarkhej, Broach, Jambusar, Cambay, Baroda, and Sind was locally consumed.[17] Asian merchants and the companies also exported some to West Asia, mainly to Basra and Gombroon on the Persian Gulf. William Finch mentions that indigo produced in Kol was consumed locally and also exported to Samarqand, Kashghar, and other parts of Central Asia.[18] Indigo from most of these places was of an inferior quality and the companies' authorities in London and Amsterdam generally discouraged their import into Europe.[19] Initially, the EIC exported some Coromandel indigo to Europe, but the company gave it up once it began purchasing large quantities of indigo in Bayana and Sarkhej. The VOC exported Coromandel indigo on a fairly large scale in the seventeenth century. In general, however, European dyers preferred Bayana and Sarkhej indigo over any other variety from India. Coromandel indigo was mainly used by local dyers and some was exported to West and Central Asia. There was also a substantial local trade in indigo and the bulk of it was consumed by weavers and dyers on the coast and in the interior.[20]

In the seventeenth century, the European companies got some of their textiles dyed in India. In 1638 and 1639, the VOC procured 165 and 157 *man* of (mostly Khurja) indigo (about 8,250 and 7,850 Dutch pounds), respectively, for dyeing its textiles in Agra.[21] The EIC, too, got some of its textiles dyed in Agra. The companies hired local dyers, provided them with indigo and other ingredients, and put them to work under the supervision of company officials. The demand that such activities generated for indigo may not have been insignificant. With the rising European demand and consequent increase in textile production in the second half of the seventeenth and eighteenth centuries, local consumption of indigo may also have gone up.[22] Among all the textile-producing regions

16 *EFI 1646–50, passim*; *EFI 1651–54, passim*.

17 In the early 1640s, it was estimated that one-sixth of the total produce (about 6,000 *man*) of the Sarkhej tract was consumed by local dyers. *EFI 1642–45*, Surat to London, 26 March 1644, pp. 163–4

18 William Finch, *Early Travels in India, 1583–1619*, (ed.), William Foster (Oxford: OUP, 1921), 179.

19 H.W. van Santen, 'De Vereenigde Oost-Indische Compagnie in Gujarat en Hindustan, 1620–1660' (PhD. dissertation, Leiden University, 1982).

20 Raychaudhuri, *Jan Company in Coromandel*, 162–4.

21 Collectie Geleynssen de Jongh, 117–118, Copie-Negotiejournalen van het comptoir Agra [Copy of the trade journals of the Agra factory], 1 Feb. 1638–31 Jan. 1639 and 1 Feb. 1639–31 Jan. 1640 (not foliated).

22 The average annual value of textiles exported by the VOC from India thus rose from *f.* 0.89 million in 1648–50 to *f.* 3.94 million in 1668–70 and to *f.* 8.20 million in 1698–1700. The

of India, Bengal benefitted the most from the surge in European consumption of cotton and silk textiles or the 'calico craze' of the late seventeenth and eighteenth centuries.[23] Bengal's share in the VOC's average annual value of exports from India went up from ƒ. 0.31 million in 1675–76 to ƒ. 2.40 million in 1698–1700 and rose further to about ƒ. 3.5 million in the 1720s.[24] The percentage of Bengal's share in the EIC's total exports from India similarly went up from about 13 percent in 1668–70 to about 53 percent in 1758–60.[25] By the early eighteenth century, Bengal had emerged as India's most prominent textile-producing region and it had come to cater to the vast European and American demand for cotton and silk clothes. With this, the consumption of indigo also expanded. K.N. Chaudhuri has pointed out that the consumption of indigo expanded in India and the Middle East due to the phenomenal growth in the textile industry in both regions during the century between 1660 and 1760.[26]

Until the end of the eighteenth century, Bengal obtained supplies of indigo mainly from Agra, Awadh, and Delhi. Indigo that had formerly flowed westward from these places to Gujarat, West Asia, and Europe, now began to flow eastward to Bengal for local consumption. This internal demand kept indigo production going. The regions of Agra and Awadh continued to produce indigo on a large scale in the eighteenth century and even later. When the EIC revived its indigo trade in the early 1780s, a large part of its annual exports to London initially came from these regions.

West Asian Demand for Indian Indigo

West Asia was a major market for Indian indigo.[27] Many early Arabic and Persian accounts of the region from the tenth to the fifteenth centuries refer to

value of EIC's average annual exports to England, similarly, grew from about £0.20 million in 1668–70 to £0.85 million in 1698–1700 and to £1.33 million in 1738–40. Om Prakash, *European Commercial Enterprise in Pre-Colonial India* (Cambridge: CUP, 1998), 115, 120 (Tables 4.1 and 4.2), 268.

23 Beverly Lemire, *Fashion's Favourite: The Cotton Trade and the Consumer in Britain, 1660–1800* (Oxford: OUP, 1991), chapter 1.

24 Prakash, *European Commercial Enterprise in Pre-Colonial India*, 203.

25 Ibid., 121.

26 K.N. Chaudhuri, *The Trading World of Asia and the English East India Company, 1660–1760* (Cambridge: CUP, 1978), 334.

27 Indigo was mainly used in dyeing yarn and textiles. It was also considered a valuable cosmetic and was used in a variety of ways by men and women in the Arab-Persian world. Fatema Soudavar Farmanfarmaian, '"Haft Qalam Arayish": Cosmetics in the Iranian World', *Iranian Studies*, vol. 33, nos. 3–4 (2000), 285–326; Willem Floor, *Agriculture*

this commodity as a major import from India. In the tenth century, Kabul annually received large quantities of Indian indigo that was exported to different parts of Central Asia and the Middle East.[28] A part of it was also re-exported to the Mediterranean world, particularly Eastern Europe. In the fourteenth century, Florentine dyers were reportedly using Indian indigo to colour their textiles.[29] In the fifteenth and sixteenth centuries, Persia and Ottoman Turkey consumed large quantities of indigo that Armenian, Indian, and other Asian merchants supplied from India. Indigo was so valuable a commodity in the markets of Mecca and Jeddah that in 1548 Sultan Mahmud III of Gujarat sent 100 *sundas* of Sarkhej indigo to one of his nobles, Asaf Khan, who was in Mecca with the Sultan's harem (probably *hajis*), from the proceeds of which Asaf Khan was to purchase a ship and provide for his return journey to Gujarat.[30] At the end of the sixteenth century, Abul Fazl wrote that much indigo was produced in India and was taken to Turkey.[31] An Arabic history of Gujarat mentions that ships from the Gujarati port of Gogha carried much indigo to Jeddah in the late sixteenth century.[32] These regions were the most important markets for indigo until the late sixteenth century, when the blue dye from India acquired wider acceptability among dyers in Europe.[33] Aleppo was the most important emporium of trade from where much indigo was exported to Europe in the late sixteenth and early seventeenth centuries.[34] English and

---

in Qajar Iran (Washington DC: Mage Publishers, 2003), 512–13; Jenny Balfour-Paul, *Indigo* (London: British Museum, 1998).

28 G. Le Strange, *The Lands of the Eastern Caliphate: Mesopotamia, Persia, and Central Asia from the Moslem Conquest to the time of Timur* (Cambridge: CUP, 1905), 349.

29 In 1338, Florence had over 200 workshops which processed between 70,000 and 80,000 pieces of cloths annually. The dyers used indigo that was brought from India. Ernst Samhaber, *Merchants Make History: How Trade has Influenced the Course of History Throughout the World* (tr.), E. Osers (London: George G. Harrap & Co., 1963), 116.

30 M.S. Commissariat, *A History of Gujarat, 1297–1573*, vol. I (Bombay: Longmans, Green & Co., 1938), 425–6. Indigo was sold at a very high price in Mecca (each *sunda* of indigo being worth 200 pieces of gold) because the Portuguese had stopped importing it from Gujarat. Ibid.

31 Abul Fazl, *Ain-i Akbari*, vol. 2 (tr.), H.S. Jarrett (Calcutta: Baptist Mission Press, 1891), p. 241.

32 Abdullah Muhammad bin Omar al-Makki al-Asafi Ulughkhani, *Zafar ul-Waleh bi Muzaffar ul Alih*, vol. I, (ed.) Sir E. Denison Ross (London: John Murray, 1910), 313.

33 W.H. Moreland, *From Akbar to Aurangzeb: A Study in Indian Economic History* (London: Macmillan Press, 1923), 108; Balfour-Paul, *Indigo*.

34 Venice possibly obtained Indian indigo through its Levantine trade connection. Textile dyers of Venice were using Indian indigo in the 1590s despite the government prohibition. Archivio di Stato di Venezia, Collegio, Risposte di dentro, filza 10: n. 159 [Venetian State Archives, Collegio, Risposta di dentro, volume 10, document 159], Petition by the dyers' guild, 14 November 1597. I am grateful to Luca Mola for drawing my attention to this

French merchants trading in the Levant played an active role in this branch of commerce. The Levantine connection was so strong that the standards of price and quality of indigo in the London market were set by Aleppo rather than Lisbon or Amsterdam, where the Portuguese and the Dutch imported large quantities of indigo from India.[35] In its early years, the EIC itself purchased indigo in Aleppo and Mocha for the London market.[36] Subsequently, however, indigo was mainly taken to Europe via the Cape of Good Hope, first by the Portuguese and then by the EIC and the VOC.

There was a fairly large demand for indigo in Persia itself and, it seems, much of the dye imported from India into Hormuz, Bandar Abbas, and Basra in the sixteenth and seventeenth centuries was used by Iranian yarn and textile dyeing.[37] Iran's flourishing cotton and silk textile manufactures and its well-established carpet weaving industry kept the demand for indigo high into the early twentieth century.[38] Although, some areas in the provinces of Kirman,

information and providing a transcript of this valuable source and to my colleague, Nick Wilding, for translating the document for me.

35 Moreland, *From Akbar to Aurangzeb*, 109. A part of indigo was re-exported from Lisbon to England whose volume and value remain uncertain. K.N. Chaudhuri, *The English East India Company: The Study of an early Joint-Stock Company, 1600–1640* (London: Frank Cass & Co., 1965), 174–5. Indigo imports from Aleppo into the London market and continental Europe were so large that in the first quarter of the seventeenth century it damaged the EIC's indigo trade more than the imports by the Portuguese or the Dutch. Chaudhuri, *The English East India Company*, 174–5.

36 John Jourdain, *The Journal of John Jourdain, 1608–1617*, (ed.), William Foster (Cambridge: Hakluyt Society, 1905), xxv, xliv, 69, 205, 207. In 1616, the company's letter to Surat refers to the practice of buying indigo in Aleppo and re-packing it into square chests for shipment to England. BL, FRS, 84, company's letter from England, Surat, 1616, f. 90[a].

37 Many European travelers and EIC officials of this period have noted that these ports received large imports of indigo from India. Willem Floor, *The Persian Gulf: A Political and Economic History of Five Port Cities, 1500–1730* (Washington: Mage, 2006), 59, 147–8, 508–9. Indigo was also used in book illustrations and paintings as well as for colouring other stuffs. Chemical analysis of several sixteenth-century book illustrations has confirmed the use of indigo together with other colourants by the artists of Persia and Turkey. Alicia Jurado-Lopez, Omela Demko, Robin J.H. Clark, and David Jacobs, 'Analysis of the palette of a precious 16th century illustrated Turkish manuscript by Raman microscopy', *Journal of Raman Spectroscopy*, vol. 35, no. 2 (2004), 119–24; Robin J.H. Clark and Sigrid Mirabaud, 'Identificaion of the pigments on a sixteenth century Persian book of poetry by Raman microscopy', *Journal of Raman Spectroscopy*, vol. 37, nos. 1–3 (2006), 235–39.

38 In the seventeenth century, John Chardin observed that dyeing was more improved in Persia than in Europe and noted that the Persian dyers used Indian indigo to colour their textiles. John Chardin, *The Travels of Sir John Chardin in Persia* (1643–1713), vol. II (tr.) Edm. Lloyd (London: J. Smith, 1720), 303–4. Until the early twentieth century, Persian

Khuzestan, and Bam produced indigo, production was insufficient to meet the local needs, hence large quantities of indigo continued to be imported from India.[39]

By 1600, Mocha had emerged as an emporium of trade in West Asia where merchants flocked from all directions and where goods and merchandise were exchanged and re-exported to various destinations, especially to Aleppo. Much indigo was available in Mocha, where it was annually brought by Indians, Armenians, Persians, and the European companies. Many Asian merchants carried Bayana indigo overland, but some followed the maritime route from Cambay and Surat to the Persian Gulf and the Red Sea. One finds frequent references to Armenian and other merchants buying Bayana indigo and taking it to Persia in caravans.[40] Sarkhej indigo was taken to West Asia mainly by ship from Cambay, Broach, and Surat. Merchants' preference for the land or sea routes depended on how peaceful the political frontiers were and how safe the routes for caravans and ships were. Their decision also depended on the relative costs of carriage, including buying safe passage along the way, and on the careful weighing of the prospects of profits against possible risks involved in the journey. Coromandel indigo generally followed the maritime route to West Asia and was exported mainly by Indian and Asian merchants in the early seventeenth century.[41] In 1610, VOC officials reported about Persian merchants buying large quantities of indigo in Masulipatnam and exporting it to Hormuz, from where it was also taken to Aleppo and Eastern Europe via Basra and Babylon.[42]

Gujarati, Armenian, and Persian merchants dominated the indigo trade between Gujarat and West Asia.[43] Several letters and reports by English and Dutch company officials mention the presence of Armenian, Mughal, Persian, and Bania merchants in the indigo markets of Bayana and Sarkhej as potential competitors, and they often blame them for the scarcity of indigo, its high price, and their inability to procure indigo of the desired quality. The companies were often alarmed by the sheer volume of indigo exports by Asian merchants to West Asia. In 1628, for example, EIC officials attributed the high price

dyers used natural indigo imported from India to colour their yarn. A. Cecil Edwards, *The Persian Carpet: A Survey of the Carpet-Weaving Industry of Persia* (London: Duckworth, 1983), 33, 213.

39 Strange, *The Lands of the Eastern Caliphate*, 314, 317–18, 320; Edwards, *The Persian Carpet*, 32–3, 213; Jenny Balfour-Paul, *Indigo in the Arab World* (London: Curzon, 1997).

40 *EFI 1634–36*, Surat to London, 2 Jan. 1636, p. 138.

41 Raychaudhuri, *Jan Company in Coromandel*, 162–3.

42 VOC 1055, Resoluties, Masulipatnam, 15 June 1610, p. 121.

43 Gopal, *Commerce and Crafts in Gujarat*, 43–6.

of indigo in Agra to large-scale purchases of indigo (about 6,000 *man*) by Armenian and Muslim merchants.[44] In 1630, they expressed similar sentiments regarding Sarkhej indigo large quantities of which were reportedly bought by Armenian and Muslim merchants.[45] In 1636, VOC officials apprehended the presence of Asian merchants who had invested about Rs 350,000 in Bayana indigo, rendering the commodity scarce and expensive.[46] In 1639–40, exports of Bayana and Sarkhej indigo to West Asia by sea alone amounted to 3,120 *man* (about 156,000 Dutch pounds) and 2,580 *man* (82,560 Dutch pounds), respectively.[47] Thus, the European companies had to compete with Asian merchants in the indigo marts of Agra, Ahmadabad, and Surat as well as in the interior, where it was produced.

Those Asian merchants who followed the maritime route to West Asia freighted their indigo in both Indian and European ships. This was more so when the overland caravan routes were unsafe due to political disputes and warfare. The companies usually sold a part of their ships' tonnage to Asian merchants for this purpose. The companies also exported indigo to West Asia and usually earned a good profit, especially when the market was favourable. In the first half of the seventeenth century, the EIC and the VOC dispatched a part of their indigo to the Persian Gulf to be sold there. Both the companies were thus involved in intra-Asian trade, and they exchanged indigo and other commodities in West Asian markets for silk and precious metals, especially gold ducats and rials of eight, the specie they needed to purchase textiles and other commodities in Coromandel and other parts of India. In the 1640s, when indigo prices in Europe declined, West Asia became an alternative market for the companies.[48] Consequently, the EIC and VOC exports to West Asian markets, especially the Persian Gulf, grew substantially during this period. In 1640–41, the EIC exported 608 *man* (33,440 pounds) of Bayana and 448 *man* (14,336 pounds) of Sarkhej indigo and the VOC exported 1,368 *man*

44 In that year, they reportedly freighted to West Asia some 1,500 bales (6,000 *man*) of indigo on VOC and EIC ships. *EFI 1624–1629*, Surat to London, 21 Dec. 1628, p. 307.

45 *EFI 1630–1633*, Ahmadabad to Surat, 31 Dec. 1630, pp. 125–6.

46 VOC 1122, Directeur and Raad van Surat aan Bewindhebberen, 2 Dec. 1636, f. 518^{r}.

47 VOC 1134, Shipping List, Surat, 1639–40, p. 231. Shipping lists prepared by VOC officials in Surat do not provide complete cargo information for all ships departing from Surat in which indigo may have been exported to West Asia. Total exports may have been much larger than the figures in these shipping lists.

48 In 1641, the sale price of Bayana indigo in England fell from about 11^{s} per pounds to 7^{s} 6^{d} per pound. *EFI 1637–41*, London to Surat, 29 Nov. 1641, p. 311. A year later, EIC officials were even more apprehensive of the falling price in England on account of massive imports of indigo into Europe by the VOC. *EFI 1742–45*, Surat to London, 17 Jan. 1743, p. 84.

(43,776 Dutch pounds) of Sarkhej indigo to Gombroon.[49] With the decline of indigo production in India and the companies' loss of interest in indigo trade after 1650, indigo supplies to West Asia too seem to have considerably shrunk. However, Persia continued to be a substantial market for indigo and many Indian, Persian, and Armenian merchants continued their indigo trade with that region. In 1652, more than 7,096 *man* (about 331,760 Dutch pounds) of Bayana and Sarkhej indigo were exported by ship to West Asia.[50] In the second half of the seventeenth century, indigo continued to be an important article of trade between Gujarat and Persia. As John Fryer (an EIC surgeon from 1672 to 1681) tells us, in the last quarter of the seventeenth century, vast quantities of indigo, cotton, cotton-yarn and silks were exported from India by the Persian Gulf and Red Sea fleets that annually called at Surat.[51] An Armenian merchant, Hovhannes, was involved in large-scale indigo exports to West Asia. On one of the large consignments he sent to Basra he earned a 50 percent gross profit.[52] In the absence of alternative sources of indigo, Persia and other West Asian markets continued to depend on supplies from India in the eighteenth and nineteenth centuries.

Turkey was another major market for Indian indigo in this period. The potentiality of this market for indigo could be judged from the English adventure of re-exporting Indian indigo from London to the markets of Egypt and Turkey in the seventeenth century.[53] Such a reverse flow of indigo to Aleppo may have adversely affected Asian merchants trading with ports and places in the Ottoman Empire. At the end of the seventeenth century, Bayana indigo was the best and the most expensive variety in Smyrna. In 1698 and 1699, it was valued at a price twice as much as that of Guatemala indigo.[54] Sarkhej indigo, perhaps more than Bayana indigo, was imported into Smyrna in this period, possibly because it was cheaper and sold at a much lower price than Bayana or Guatemala indigo.[55] In Smyrna, as perhaps at other places in Turkey and elsewhere

49 *Dagh-Register, 1640–1641*, p. 317; VOC 1134, f. 489.

50 VOC 1188, Shipping List, Surat, 1652, ff. 371^r–377^v.

51 John Fryer, *A New Account of East India and Persia in Eight Letters being Nine Years Travel, 1672–1681* (London: R Chiswell, 1698), p. 112.

52 Niels Steensgaard, *Carracks, Caravans and Companies: The Structural Crisis in the European-Asian Trade in the Early 17th Century* (Copenhagen: Andelsbogtrykkeriet, 1973), 26.

53 Chaudhuri, *The English East India Company*, 185–6.

54 Chambre de Commerce Archives, Marseille, J/400–401, Tarif du pris des merchandises dentree et sortie de Smirne pour le droit du consulat de franco en lonnee, 1698, p. 9.

55 In 1698, a merchant firm Bourgois & Monnie imported to Smyrna 270 ocques (a measure of weight) of Sarkhej indigo on which it paid a duty of 1½ percent. Chambre de Commerce Archives, Marseille, J/400, Manifest des merchandises [Manifest of merchandise], Smyrna,

on the north-eastern Mediterranean littoral, Indian indigo competed with American indigo from Guatemala and, possibly, from Saint-Domingue. Being a part of the intra-European trade network, these ports were frequented by European merchants with products from colonies.[56]

European Demand for Indian Indigo

Indigo Trade of the Portuguese

Indian indigo reached the markets of Europe in the fifteenth and early sixteenth centuries primarily through the Levant. After the Portuguese sailed round the Cape of Good Hope and discovered an all-water route to India in 1498, an increasing proportion of indigo began to reach Europe through this transoceanic route. First the Portuguese and then the English, Dutch, and French exported large quantities of indigo in homebound ships. Initially, the Estado da India was mainly interested in pepper and spices. Not much is known about Portuguese interest in indigo early on. By the time the Portuguese arrived in India, indigo was already known to the Mediterranean world as a substitute for woad. The Portuguese occupied Hormuz in 1515 and established their foothold in the western Indian Ocean in the following decades, by which time indigo may have come to form a part of the cargo that they would take to Lisbon. By the middle of the sixteenth century, indigo had certainly made it to the list of commodities the Portuguese exported from India to West Asia and Lisbon. Nevertheless, the volume of exports to Europe remained modest because of the general resistance to indigo by woad manufacturers and dyers and some European states' prohibition against its use.[57]

Gradual acceptance of indigo by the European dyeing industry in the course of the century and improving prospects of trade and profits may have induced the Portuguese to export indigo from India—by far the only major source of commercial dyestuff to which they had access. But the Portuguese could not reach the interiors of Gujarat and Mughal north India where indigo was produced. Their use of violence to control and tax the maritime trade of

---

1698, p. 8. In 1699, another merchant firm, the Salvador & Ishac Cardeso, imported 135 ocques of Sarkhej indigo. J/401, Manifest des merchandises, Smyrna, 2 Nov. 1699, p. 1.

56 Imports of Guatemala indigo into Smyrna is reported in the customs charges as recorded by the French authorities there. Ibid.

57 Jamieson B. Hurry, *The Woad Plant and Its Dye* (New Jersey: Augustus M. Kelly, 1973), Chapter xvi.

the Indian Ocean put them in perpetual hostility with the Mughals and their officials in Gujarat. They could not, therefore, secure formal establishments in Agra and Ahmadabad for the procurement of indigo. The best they could do was to purchase in Cambay, where local merchants brought Bayana and Sarkhej indigo every year. Alternatively, they could purchase it in Goa, where ships from Gujarat brought large quantities of indigo and other commodities for sale.[58] In the last quarter of the century, as Van Linschoten notes, the demand for indigo in Portugal was fairly large and the Estado exported substantial quantities of indigo from India.[59] James Boyajian's study clearly shows the importance of indigo in the Portuguese Asian trade between 1580 and 1620. The Estado and private merchants imported into Lisbon large quantities of indigo that generally sold at prices amounting to four or five times that of the purchase prices.[60] Indigo was 'often among the most valuable of all the "spices", and progressively undermined the whole European woad industry'.[61] Anticipating this improvement prospects, the Habsburg king of Portugal, monopolised the indigo trade in 1587. Subsequently, all indigo exports from India to Lisbon were to be handled by the Estado on behalf of the monarch and no private exports of indigo to Lisbon were to be permitted. Apparently, the monopoly was strictly enforced. All chests and packs arriving in Lisbon were examined and were subject to clearance at the customhouse if they carried no monopoly goods like pepper, spices, or indigo. Indigo, however, continued to be exported from Goa to Lisbon every year on private accounts.

Boyajian's export figures for indigo on private account show that the crown monopoly of indigo trade was greatly weakened by the end of the century. Like the monopoly on the spice trade, the indigo monopoly too was possibly undermined by its large-scale imports into Lisbon by private merchants. In the seventeenth century, some indigo was exported to Lisbon by Portuguese merchants on private accounts. Tinoco de Carvalho was a merchant active in the Goa–Lisbon trade and his annual exports from Goa included indigo.[62] In

---

58 Gopal, *Commerce and Crafts in Gujarat*, 83–4.

59 Van Linschoten, *The Voyage of Jan Huyghen van Linschoten*, pp. 91, 229–30. Exports of indigo in some years of the 1580s and 1590s were rather substantial.

60 James C. Boyajian, *Portuguese Trade in Asia under the Habsburgs, 1580–1640* (Baltimore: Johns Hopkins, 1993), 45–6.

61 Jenny Balfour-Paul, 'India's Trade in Indigo: Its Ups and Downs', in Rosemary Crill (ed.), *Textiles from India: The Global Trade* (Calcutta: Seagull Books, 2005), 361. It, sometimes, formed three-quarters of the total private shipment of '*drogas*' (spices, including indigo). Balfour-Paul, *Indigo*, 44.

62 Ibid., 98.

1649, Portuguese merchants exported 100 *bahar* (or 48,000 pounds) of indigo to Lisbon and they dispatched a 'richly laden' carrack and galleon to Lisbon in 1656 whose cargo included indigo among other commodities.[63]

In the early seventeenth century, the Portuguese political and commercial preponderance in maritime Asia was increasingly challenged by their north European rivals. Portuguese ships in Asia were subjected to fierce naval and military assault and their trade monopolies in pepper, spices, and indigo were seriously undermined by the large-scale indigo trade of the EIC and the VOC.[64] While the Dutch monopolised the trade in fine spices and, to some extent, pepper, they and the English cornered for themselves much of the indigo trade forcing the Portuguese to be content with a small piece of the pie. The Portuguese purchases of indigo in Gujarat were still so substantial that the VOC and EIC apprehended them as potential buyers capable of unsettling the indigo market both in India and Europe. In 1613, the EIC factors in Ahmadabad reported, rather joyfully, that the indigo price had gone down from Rs 18 to Rs 14 per *man* because no Portuguese ships arrived in Surat in that season.[65] Portuguese hostilities with the Mughals in 1613–15 posed difficulties in obtaining supplies of indigo and textiles from Gujarat. This, together with the Anglo-Dutch naval assaults and consequent shipping disasters on the Cape route, precipitated the decline.[66] By 1620, thus, Portuguese exports of indigo (as also of textiles) from Gujarat and Goa had greatly declined.

It is hard to find data to quantify Portuguese exports of indigo from western India. It transpires from occasional estimates and some qualitative statements that their indigo purchases in the beginning of the seventeenth century were not insignificant. Thomas Best, testifying to the Portuguese voluminous trade at Cambay, writes that a fleet of more than 200 carracks and galleons used to procure the greatest part of the port's cargo, which they carried to Portugal. Indigo may have constituted a fair proportion of this trade. The Portuguese continued to be the major suppliers of indigo to Europe until, and even after, the EIC and VOC had established themselves firmly in Surat and had gained access to its vast hinterlands. In 1617–18, for example, VOC officials in Surat reported that the Portuguese procured about 5,000 packs

63 *Generale Missiven*, vol. II, 1639–1655, p. 379; *Generale Missiven*, vol. III, 1655–1674, p. 80.

64 M.N. Pearson, *Merchants and Rulers in Gujarat: The Response to the Portuguese in the Sixteenth Century* (Berkley: University of California Press, 1976).

65 BL, East India Company Correspondence with the East, 1, East India Company Original Correspondence, doc. no. 117, Ahmadabad, 9 Nov. 1613, ff. 198^{b}–199^{a}.

66 Boyajian, *Portuguese Trade in Asia*, 130.

(20,000 *man*) of Sarkhej indigo for Lisbon.[67] This is obviously an exaggeration, but the estimate indicates the scale of Portuguese trade in indigo in the early seventeenth century.

During the first three decades of the seventeenth century, Portuguese trade from Goa to Portugal and to Gujarat rapidly declined. Pieter van den Broecke, a VOC official in Gujarat, reported that whereas there used to come every year from 200 to 300 Portuguese *fusts* (or *fustas*; small galleys) to Cambay and Surat, only from 50 to 60 came in 1621, and the goods they carried were also of small value.[68] Pelsaert, too, lamented the declining trade of Cambay by saying that in 1626 only forty merchant *fusts* arrived with goods of little value and that this was the cause of the decline of Cambay and indeed of all Gujarat.[69] Michael Pearson's study of the Portuguese trade from Goa—the Estado's headquarters in Asia—clearly shows a sharp decline in the early seventeenth century. The value of trade between Goa and Gujarat declined from 2 million *cruzados* (or 2.6 million *xeraphins*) in 1600 to about 150,000 *xeraphins* in 1635.[70] Naturally, their exports of indigo would have been adversely affected. After 1620, the EIC and VOC no longer considered the Portuguese potential rivals in the indigo markets of Gujarat. Available figures from the subsequent period indicate intermittent and substantially reduced supplies of this commodity being shipped to Lisbon. In 1630, the Portuguese exported 325 quintals (about 36,400 pounds) of indigo, which amounted to 11.5 percent of the total value of their exports in that year.[71]

This decline was also a reflection on the changing dynamics of the European indigo market. Large-scale shipments of good-quality Bayana, Sarkhej, and

---

67 *The Dutch Factories in India* [hereafter DFI], *1617–1623: A Collection of Dutch East India Company Documents Pertaining to India* (ed.), Om Prakash (New Delhi: Munshiram Manoharlal, 1984), 62. During 1616–18, the Portuguese exported 37,002 kilograms (about 74,000 pounds) of indigo to Lisbon. Afzal Ahmad, *Portuguese Trade and Socio-Economic Change on the Western Coast of India*, 1600–1663 (New Delhi: D.K. Publishers, 2000), 151.

68 *DFI 1617–23*, pp. 151, 155, 235; M.N. Pearson, 'Goa-Based Seaborne Trade: 17th–18th Centuries', in idem, *The World of Indian Ocean, 1500–1800* (Aldershot: Ashgate Variorum, 2005), chapter III, 167.

69 Francisco Pelsaert, *De Geschriften van Francisco Pelsaert over Mughal Indië, 1627: Kroniek en Remonstrantie* [the writings of Francisco Pelsaert about Mughal India: chronicle and remonstrance], (eds.), D.H.A. Kolff and H.W. van Santen, ('s-Gravenhage: Martinus Nijhoff, 1979), p. 265.

70 Pearson, 'Goa-Based Seaborne Trade', 164–5. One *cruzado* was equal to 1.3 *xeraphins*.

71 A.R. Disney, *Twilight of the Pepper Empire: Portuguese Trade in Southwest India in the Early Seventeenth Century* (Cambridge, Mass.: Harvard University Press, 1978), 113–14. In Lisbon in 1630, the profits earned on the sale of indigo varied from 116 to 126 percent.

Coromandel indigo to Europe by the English and the Dutch affected the Portuguese prospects of sale and profits at home. After all, north-western Europe was a major market to which Lisbon re-exported a large part of its indigo imports from India.[72] Once the EIC and VOC began to import indigo on a large scale via the Cape, the Portuguese lost the continental European market for their indigo. Portuguese imports of Indian indigo into Lisbon were also adversely affected by substantial imports of American indigo in the seventeenth century, particularly in its second half.

Indigo Trade of the EIC and the VOC

By the time the EIC and the VOC began their commercial contacts with India in the early years of the seventeenth century, indigo had come into wider use in Europe and dyers had come to recognize its superior quality and its resistance to fading. The European demand was on the rise mainly because it was rapidly replacing woad. The changing relative value of commodities in Europe also contributed to this demand. As K.N. Chaudhuri has pointed out, by 1600, pepper, the most important of all Asian imports, had lost its relative value in Europe whereas indigo and Indian textiles (mainly calicoes) had become more profitable.[73] It is no surprise then that the profit-seeking European companies would turn to indigo, for which there was an extensive demand. Large exports of Indian indigo to Britain and the Dutch Republic was also occasioned by the growing demand for it in the period when Europe was in the grips of the Thirty Years' War (1618–1648). During the war, supplies of indigo from Europe's transatlantic colonies were interrupted and the shortages were made up by indigo from Asia. Between 1620 and 1650, therefore, indigo exports from India to Europe registered the highest growth (Table 3.1).

The EIC and the VOC were able to export large quantities of indigo from India and seriously challenge the Portuguese and the Levant Company in this trade mainly because of their access to the inland areas where the commodity was produced. Since its arrival in Gujarat in 1608, the EIC had exported large quantities of Bayana and Sarkhej indigo to England from Surat, the company's headquarters in western India. The VOC procured indigo on the Coromandel Coast and its exports from Surat after 1618 consisted mainly of the Bayana and Sarkhej varieties. By 1620, the English and the Dutch companies had emerged as the two most prominent indigo buyers in India. Each had certain advantages over the other but they came to face similar problems in the trade. Both entities were equally susceptible to the limitations of consumer demand in Europe and uncertainties of supplies in India, and their responses to such challenges, too, had

72 Chaudhuri, *The English East India Company*, 174.

73 Ibid., 21.

some common characteristics. The companies and other merchants engaged in this trade knew very well that success depended on their ability to buy the best-quality indigo at the lowest price. Competition among buyers often raised the price in India, and any large supplies of indigo from other sources could potentially depreciate its value in European markets. The companies had to guard against such potential or real threats and devise measures to avoid either of the situations. Over the next three decades, each competed with the other in the indigo markets of Bayana and Sarkhej, but at times they also collaborated with each other if circumstances so required. Their activities in the indigo market and their conduct in relation to one another depended to a large extent on the nature of their commercial pursuits in Asia, Anglo-Dutch political relations in Europe, and politico-economic developments in India and Europe.

Right from the beginning, the *Heeren XVII* were interested in obtaining spices, textiles, indigo, and many other commodities from Asia for European markets.[74] Every year, they provided their VOC officials in Asia with large capital to enable them to procure these commodities. Soon after their arrival in Asia, VOC authorities sensed the potential for profit in trading Asian goods within Asia. They thought that this was the most productive way of using the initial capital available to the company. The intra-Asian trade, they anticipated, would help the company subsidize its purchase of Asian goods or meet the costs of its extensive administration. In the company's scheme of this trade, Indian cotton textiles held a key position as a commodity that could be profitably exchanged for other merchandise, including pepper and fine spices in the East Indies. All that the VOC authorities needed was 'a little water to prime the pump'.[75] They expended the funds, therefore, primarily in buying textiles in Coromandel and Gujarat. The High Government in Batavia often instructed its officials in India to invest the available capital first in textiles for the East Indies and to buy other goods like indigo only when the investments for Batavia were complete and funds were still available.

The VOC officials on India's Coromandel Coast followed Batavia's instructions and invested capital primarily in textiles. They also usually bought some indigo for the home market. Coromandel indigo was neither of the best quality nor as abundant as in some parts of north and western India. Complying with Batavia's orders was not so easy for the VOC officials stationed in Surat and its dependent factories in Ahmadabad and Agra. Batavia insisted that the funds be primarily invested in textiles for the East Indies whereas the officials

74 *Heeren xvii* or Gentlemen Seventeen, the company's highest governing body in the Dutch Republic consisting of the representatives of the Amsterdam, Delft, Rotterdam, Middelburg, Hoorn, and Enkhuizen chambers.

75 Prakash, *European Commercial Enterprise in Pre-Colonial India*, 92.

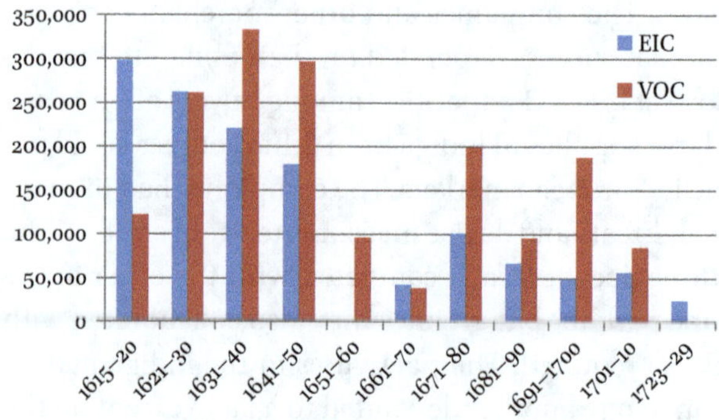

FIGURE 3.1 *Ten-yearly average annual exports of indigo by the* EIC *(in lb.) and the* VOC *(in Dutch pounds) from Surat, 1615–1729*
SOURCE: BASED ON THE FOLLOWING TABLE 3.1.

TABLE 3.1 *Ten-yearly average annual exports of indigo by the* EIC *(in lb.) and the* VOC *(in Dutch pounds) from Surat, 1615–1729*

	EIC (pounds)	VOC (Dutch pounds)
1615–20	297,572	121,757
1621–30	261,649	260,776
1631–40	220,075	332,316
1641–50	179,169	296,370
1651–60	—	95,818
1661–70	42,015	38,101
1671–80	100,529	198,683
1681–90	66,230	95,387
1691–1700	49,094	187,181
1701–10	55,808	84,490
1723–29	23,733	—

SOURCE: BASED ON FIGURES IN APPENDIX 1 AND APPENDIX 4

in Surat found indigo equally attractive and profitable and often bought large quantities of it. Their purchases of indigo were in response to the orders from *Heeren XVII* who found the best indigo from Bayana and Sarkhej among the most profitable Asian merchandise.[76]

76 In 1617, indigo afforded the highest profit in Amsterdam. *DFI 1617–1623*, Amsterdam to Pulicat, 19 Oct. 1617, p. 45.

Soon, therefore, the VOC's indigo trade took off. In the first five years (1615–20), the company annually bought an average of 121,757 Dutch pounds of indigo. In the next ten years, the annual average exceeded 260,000 Dutch pounds. These figures also include some indigo bought on the Coromandel Coast. The exports in the next two decades were higher than the average of the 1620s—about 332,000 and 296,000 Dutch pounds during 1631–40 and 1641–50, respectively. Due to a lack of data, it is not possible to figure out the percentage share of indigo in the total value of VOC exports from Surat over a long period. The available figures for some years might help us to understand the significance of indigo in the company's trade in Gujarat. In 1624–25 and 1625–26, for instance, indigo accounted for between 74 and 77 percent of the total value of exports from Surat to the Dutch Republic.[77] The percentage is less if we also include the values of exports from Surat to Batavia. The figures that Van Santen has collected for some years between 1622 and 1641 show that indigo accounted for more than 45 percent of the average annual value of all exports from Surat, including exports to the East Indies.[78] After the mid-1640s, however, the VOC's indigo trade rapidly declined. Indigo's share in the total average annual value of exports from Surat fell below 20 percent between 1644 and 1656.[79]

The EIC was primarily engaged in exporting Indian goods to Europe and less engaged in intra-Asian trade than the VOC. The production and supply conditions in India and the nature of consumer demand in Europe induced the EIC to diversify its imports. With no or limited access to Asian spices, the EIC's trading enterprise in India came to depend on the export of indigo and textiles from India to Europe. Thus, right from the establishment of its factory in Surat in 1608, the EIC invested in indigo and exported large quantities of it to England every year. In the following ten years, indigo was the most valuable merchandise the EIC exported from India.[80] Between 1615 and 1620, the company benefited from the availability of indigo at low prices due to lack of competition from the Portuguese. The EIC's average annual export during this period was approximately 298,000 pounds. Over the next three decades, its exports steadily declined. From an already reduced figure of 262,000 pounds

77 *DFI 1624–27*, An extract from the invoice of the *Schoonhoven*, 12 Oct. 1624, pp. 119; ibid., An extract from the invoice of the *Dordrecht*, April 1625, pp. 151–2; ibid., An extract from the invoice of the *Weesp*, April 1625, pp. 155–6; ibid., An extract from the invoice of the *Hollandia*, April 1626, p. 266; ibid., An extract from the invoice of the *Oranje*, April 1626, p. 267; ibid., An extract from the invoice of the *Gouden Leeuw*, April 1626, p. 268; ibid., An extract from the invoice of the *Mauritius*, April 1626, pp. 269–70.

78 Van Santen, 'De Verenigde Oost-Indische Compagnie in Gujarat en Hindustan', 32–3 (Table 1).

79 Ibid.

80 Chaudhuri, *The English East India Company*, 176.

per year during 1621–30, average exports fell to about 220,000 pounds during 1631–40. It declined further to 180,000 pounds a year during 1641–50. Thus, in thirty years, the EIC's indigo exports from India declined by about 40 percent.

Bayana and Sarkhej indigo were the two most sought-after varieties in Europe.[81] The former was preferred because of its generally superior quality. EIC and VOC officials were often instructed to buy Bayana indigo first. The Sarkhej variety was a second choice resorted to only if supplies of Bayana indigo were inadequate. Often, the VOC's annual orders for indigo in the early seventeenth century were in the proportion of two-thirds Bayana and one-third Sarkhej.[82] Sometimes, however, Sarkhej indigo was preferred for its low purchase price and the lower costs of transportation from Ahmadabad to Surat. The caravan route from Agra was longer and more exposed to insecurity and local chiefs' impunities. Further, Sarkhej indigo fetched prices in Europe that were sometimes only marginally less than those of Bayana indigo.[83] Under such circumstances, the companies exported more of the Sarkhej variety. Between 1624 and 1626, and again between 1638 and 1640, a large proportion of the VOC's indigo exports from Surat to the Dutch Republic comprised of Sarkhej indigo [see Appendix 1].[84] In general, however, the proportions of Bayana indigo in the VOC's total indigo exports from Surat were greater.

Until 1630, the EIC's indigo procurements too were overwhelmingly of the Sarkhej variety and for many years in the 1620s, the company did not buy any

81 The companies' annual indigo exports from Gujarat also included some Khurja, Hindaon, Dholka and Jambusar indigo. They intermittently bought these inferior sorts especially when the supplies from Bayana and Sarkhej were insufficient to meet their requirements.

82 Gentlemen Seventeen thus allocated the funds to be invested in indigo to the amount of *f.* 200,000 for Bayana and *f.* 100,000 for Sarkhej indigo. *DFI 1624–27*, General letter from Governor-General Peter de Carpentier at Batavia to the Directors at Amsterdam, 3 Jan. 1624, pp. 52–3.

83 In 1623–24 and in 1638–39, for instance, the VOC authorities desired that larger quantities of Sarkhej indigo than Bayana be exported to Europe because it could be bought cheaper in India and sold at high prices in Amsterdam. *DFI 1617–23*, Surat to Batavia, 25 Dec. 1623, p. 286.

84 The percentage share of Sarkhej indigo in the VOC's total annual indigo exports from Gujarat averaged about 70 during 1624–25 and 1625–26 and about 77 during 1637–40. Between 1621 and 1644, on an average, the proportion of Sarkhej indigo to that of Bayana was almost equal (49 and 51 percent respectively). This shows that the view that Sarkhej indigo was so poor in quality that it was consumed locally and that Europeans were mainly interested in Bayana indigo is untenable. George Winius and Markus Vink, *The Merchant-Warrior Pacified: The VOC and its changing political economy in India* (Delhi: OUP, 1991), 62.

Bayana indigo.[85] Available figures for some years between 1615 and 1630 show that on average Sarkhej indigo accounted for about two-thirds of the EIC's total annual indigo exports from India. Between 1633 and 1651, it still comprised some 40 percent of indigo exports from Gujarat.

The sudden growth of European trade in indigo did not last long. After 1650, exports from India rapidly declined (see Figure 3.1). Several circumstances contributed to this decline. First, the European demand for indigo was limited to the extent that it substituted woad. Without any considerable expansion in European textiles production, the demand stagnated and large imports from other sources adversely affected the commercial prospects of Indian indigo. K.N. Chaudhuri has pointed out that indigo as a substitute for woad had a limited demand in England and once this process of displacement was complete, consumption would stagnate unless there was a growth in textile production itself.[86] Secondly, after the Thirty Years' War, indigo supplies from Guatemala, and subsequently from other colonies, into Europe resumed and expanded. In the late seventeenth and eighteenth centuries, British Jamaica and South Carolina, French Saint-Domingue, and Dutch Java kept Europe supplied with indigo. Finally, at the interface of competition from transatlantic indigo supply chains and the demand being somewhat inelastic, Indian indigo lost its relative advantage in terms of value and profitability in Europe. Consequently, the EIC and the VOC turned their attention to textiles and other more profitable commodities. The companies, however, continued to export some indigo from India well up to the early eighteenth century, when indigo production in Jamaica, Saint-Domingue, and Java stabilized and Britain, France, and the Dutch Republic began receiving large quantities of it from their respective colonies. Thereafter, the VOC only intermittently purchased Bayana, Sarkhej, or other varieties and the EIC ceased to export any indigo from India.

The VOC, for example, purchased a mix of Bayana, Khurja, Sarkhej, Jambusar, Coromandel, Malabar, and Ceylon indigo. By 1710, Java had emerged as a stable source of good-quality indigo and, thereafter, the company's exports of Java indigo were the most consistent. It is interesting to note that after 1709–10, Bayana indigo is not mentioned at all in the statements of sales (Appendix 2). It is true that purchasing Bayana indigo had become difficult after the company gave up

---

85 In 1624, VOC officials reported that the English did not buy any Bayana indigo in the last three years. *DFI 1624–27*, Pieter van den Broecke at Surat to the Directors at Amsterdam, 11 Jan. 1624, p. 64.

86 Chaudhuri, *The English East India Company*, 176–7. The process was actually never complete. Woad continued to be in use in the seventeenth and eighteenth centuries, often in combination with indigo. Balfour-Paul, *Indigo*, 38–9.

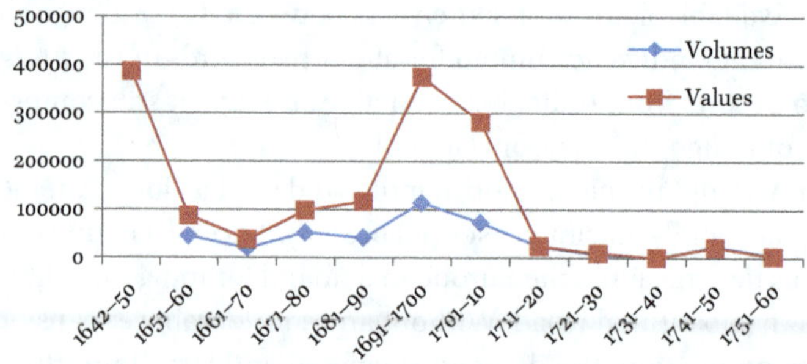

FIGURE 3.2 *Ten-yearly average annual quantities (in Dutch pounds) and values (in guilders) of indigo from India sold by the VOC in the Dutch Republic, 1642–1760*
SOURCE: BASED ON FIGURES IN THE FOLLOWING TABLE 3.2.

TABLE 3.2 *Ten-yearly average annual quantities (in Dutch pounds) and values (in guilders) of indigo from India sold by the VOC in the Dutch Republic, 1642–1760*

Years	Quantities	Values
1642–50	n.a.	385,021
1651–60	44,079	86,043
1661–70	18,924	36,723
1671–80	51,157	97,233
1681–90	41,278	115,889
1691–1700	112,705	374,865
1701–10	71,756	280,815
1711–20	22,749	24,311
1721–30	6,658	9,301
1731–40	136	177
1741–50	22,883	21,150
1751–60	3,183	2,757

SOURCE: VOC 4583, GENERALE STAETEN VAN D' OOST-INDISCHE COMPAGNIE VAN DEN JARE 1642 TOT DEN JAERE 1676 [GENERAL STATE OF THE EAST INDIA COMPANY FROM 1642 TO 1676]; VOC 4585, STAET GENERAEL VERHANDELDE GOEDEREN EN UIJTSTAEN SCHULDEN EN ONVERCOGHTE GOEDEREN VAN DE RESPECTIVE CAMEREN ONDER MEDIO APRIL 1677 GESLOTEN TOT MEDIO MEIJ 1683 [GENERAL STATE OF THE SOLD GOODS AND OUTSTANDING DEBTS AND UNSOLD GOODS OF THE RESPECTIVE CHAMBERS FROM MID-APRIL 1677 TO MID-MAY 1683]; VOC 4586, GENERALE STAETEN VAN VERHANDELDE GOEDEREN ALS ONVERCOGHTE GOEDEREN EN UIJTSTAEN SCHULDEN ETC VAN DE RESPECTIVE CAMEREN GESLOOTEN ONDER MEDIO APRIL 1684 EIJNDIGT MEDIO MEIJ 1688 [GENERAL STATE OF THE SOLD AND UNSOLD GOODS AND OUTSTANDING DEBTS OF THE RESPECTIVE CHAMBERS FROM MID-APRIL 1684 TO MID-MAY 1688]; VOC 4587, GENERALE STAETEN VAN VERHANDELDE GOEDEREN ALS ONVERCOGHTE GOEDEREN EN UIJTSTAEN SCHULDEN ETC VAN DE RESPECTIVE CAMEREN GESLOOTEN ONDER MEDIO APRIL 1690 TOT MEDIO MEIJ 1696; VOC 6989, BIJEENBRENGING VAN VERKOPINGEN IN DE RESPECTIVE KAMERS, 1693–1760 [STATEMENT OF SALES IN THE RESPECTIVE CHAMBERS, 1693–1760].

its Agra factory in 1713. On many occasions, therefore, the VOC officials in Surat were unable to comply with the orders for Bayana indigo from home.[87] At times, however, the VOC purchased large quantities of it, as in the early 1740s, yet the annual statements of sales in the Dutch Republic do not record it. The large demand for and the VOC's occasional large-scale purchases of Bayana and Sarkhej indigo, as well as that of Jambusar or Khurja, or Coromandel, indicates that the indigo industry in those regions was vibrant and responsive to sudden fluctuations in external demand. The figures in Table 3.1, above, and Appendix 1 show that after the sudden decline in the mid-seventeenth century, the volumes and values of the VOC's indigo exports from India were still quite significant. This was particularly so in the 1690s and 1700s, when the volume of exports was large and profits were high (Figure 3.2 and Table 3.2). In the VOC's total annual sale values, indigo from India accounted for 6.2 percent in 1692, over 9 percent in 1703, 8.7 percent in 1706, and 7 percent in 1709. From the 1710s onward, the VOC only occasionally purchased indigo in India, and that, too, on a very small scale. This was mainly because of low sale prices, which resulted from large imports into Europe through several competing indigo supply chains.

The EIC's indigo trade, too, underwent a similar metamorphosis. Its exports from India rapidly declined in the mid-seventeenth century owing largely to the factors enumerated above. Britain's colonial conquests in the Americas, specially its occupation of Jamaica in 1655, and the plantation economy that developed there gave rise to a commodity chain that sought to replace other indigo in British markets coming from outside its colonial territories. Britain's colonial and mercantilist policies, as embodied in the Navigation Acts passed between 1650 and 1673, too contributed to the rise of plantation-based and indigo planters-led commodity chain in its newly acquired territories in Central America.[88] Consequently, the EIC exported Indian indigo in the late seventeenth and early eighteenth centuries on a small scale.[89] The average annual imports of Indian indigo into Britain by the EIC during 1665–1729 was

87 In 1725, for example, Amsterdam placed an order for 150,000 Dutch pounds of Bayana indigo but Surat could not comply with it on account of its withdrawal of the factory from Agra and insecurity of the caravan route from there to Surat. VOC 9059, pp. 72, 76.

88 For details, see J.H. Parry, *The Age of Reconnaissance: Discovery, Exploration, and Settlement, 1450–1650* (Berkley: University of California Press, 1981), 263–4; Alan K. Smith, *Creating a World Economy: Merchant Capital, Colonialism, and World Trade, 1400–1825* (Oxford/Boulder: Westview Press, 1991), chapters 7–8.

89 In 1663, some 200 bales of Sarkhej indigo were ordered. High prices of indigo, however, continued to obstruct its exports. In 1664, only fifty bales were ordered with the provision to double this amount if it was procurable at 0.75 *mahmudi* per pound. In the subsequent years, orders for Sarkhej indigo varied between 100 and 200 bales, with some occasional jumps to 300 to 400 bales as in 1670 and 1671 and again in 1683 and 1693.

approximately 56,400 pounds. Imports were somewhat regular until 1712, after which it became intermittent, and by 1729 the company almost completely stopped buying indigo in India.[90]

Trading in Indian Indigo: Challenges and Responses

In their indigo trade, the VOC and EIC had to face challenges from many corners. Competition among buyers, especially between the Dutch and the English, often rendered the commodity scarce and expensive.[91] Sometimes, the competition was so intense that it frustrated the companies' officials in their indigo purchases. A Dutch factor in Agra reported in 1627 that competition for indigo was so intense that it not only drove up indigo prices, but it also caused a shortage of carts and camels, which raised the cost of transportation from Agra to Surat from Rs 1½–1¾ to Rs 2½ per *man*.[92] As discussed in Chapter 2, the VOC and EIC had recourse to advance-buying directly from producers in the villages in order to ensure that they obtained indigo of the desired quality and quantity. At times, even this could not guarantee that the producers would not sell indigo to competitors offering still higher prices. Companies' officials knew very well that their bulk indigo purchases often induced indigo manufacturers and merchants to raise the price and encouraged local governors to monopolise the sale of indigo. To keep the prices down, the companies often tried not to disclose the quantities they intended to buy in the season. Sometimes, they even colluded to purchase it jointly and then divide it. On several occasions in the 1620s, the VOC in Gujarat purchased it jointly with the EIC.[93] This last method proved quite effective in keeping the demand-induced price increases within limits. However, such measures were not always easy to carry out, especially when competition was intense and the commercial

90 Chaudhuri, *The Trading World of Asia*, 523 (Appendix 5, Table C.10).

91 The EIC and VOC records contain innumerable references to competition among buyers, especially between the Dutch and English, and its impact on prices. *DFI 1624–27*, Memorandum from Vapour at Agra to Batavia, 26 Oct. 1627, pp. 342, 352; VOC 1127, Directeur and Raad van Surat aan Bewindhebberen, 15 Feb. 1638, ff. 84v–85r; *Dagh Register, 1637*, pp. 270–1; *Dagh-Register, 1644–45*, p. 232.

92 *DFI 1624–27*, Memorandum from Vapour at Agra to Batavia, 26 Oct. 1627, p. 342.

93 *DFI 1624–27*, Pieter van den Broecke at Surat to the Directors at Amsterdam, 11 Jan. 1624, p. 64; ibid., Surat to Batavia, 4 Dec. 1625, p. 184. In 1625, VOC officials in Surat were instructed to cultivate cordial relationship with the English for the procurement of indigo and for defeating the trade monopoly of the Mughal governors and officials in Gujarat. *DFI 1624–27*, Governor-General De Carpentier at Batavia to Van den Broecke at Surat, 14 Aug. 1625, p. 169.

logic required the parties to proceed otherwise and act in ways that might be contrary to their mutual interests. On several occasions, the companies contemplated joint investments in indigo, but the parties were not able to keep the terms of agreement. The companies also imposed price-ceilings that to some extent kept prices at a reasonable level. Although the officials often found the companies' prices much below the current prices and were, sometimes, unable to purchase any indigo, establishing a price ceiling certainly helped in narrowing the difference between what the companies were willing to pay and what the sellers demanded for their indigo.

Private trade by company officials and free European merchants was another source of trouble, though perhaps more so for the EIC than for the Dutch.[94] The EIC claimed exclusive rights to import certain commodities from India to Britain and guarded its monopoly with much success. Indigo was one commodity that private merchants were not allowed to import.[95] Notwithstanding the prohibition, some company officials succumbed to the temptations of a lucrative private indigo trade, thereby undermining the commercial interests of their employer. In the early 1630s, company officials in London discovered that indigo was being imported into England and sold on private accounts.[96] The company grew increasingly concerned about such imports, which adversely affected the company's sales in London. The Court of Directors reproached the officials in Surat for their inability to stop this 'unlawful' practice and suspected

94 The VOC had a monopoly of all trade in Asia and between Asia and Europe and the company jealously guarded it. The intermittent voices from some VOC men calling for allowing private trade in certain sectors and in certain commodities fell on deaf ears. S. Arasaratnam, 'Monopoly and Free Trade in Dutch-Asian Commercial Policy: Debate and Controversy with the VOC', in idem, *Maritime Trade, Society and European Influence in Southern Asia, 1600–1800* (Aldershot: Ashgate Variorum, 1995), chapter VII. Despite this monopoly, as recent studies show, private trade had become rather common among VOC servants in Asia in the eighteenth century. Chris Nierstrasz, *In the Shadow of the Company: The Dutch East India Company and Its Servants in the Period of Its Decline, 1740–1796* (Brill, Leiden, 2012), chapters 8–10. It may be presumed that some indigo may have been exported from India on private accounts in the seventeenth century as well.

95 George Birdwood and William Foster, *The First Letter Book of the East India Company, 1600–1619* (London: Bernard Quaritch, 1893), 57–8. Indigo is not listed among commodities that EIC officials and seamen were allowed to import into Britain by the royal proclamation issued in 1631. BL, *By the King: A Porclamation for the better encouragement, and advancement of the trade of the East India Companie, and for prevention of excesse of private trade,* (London: R. Barker, 1631).

96 In 1633, they discovered that about 300 hundredweight (33,600 pounds) of indigo was reportedly sold in Dover to private merchants. BL, Court Minutes, Court of Committees held on 6 Sept. 1633, p. 65.

them of colluding with those on board ships in perpetrating private trade.[97] At the time when the EIC's indigo enterprise was under severe competitive pressure from American indigo, private imports from India and their adverse impact on prices and the market aggravated the company's difficulties. Despite repeated instructions from London, officials in Surat were unable to prevent indigo from being taken or smuggled on board the homebound ships. They expressed their shock and anger at the impudence of those who smuggled indigo aboard ships and went undetected, an activity that earned them disrepute and the criticism of their superiors in London.[98] This problem seems to have continued in subsequent years.

The EIC officials in Surat were still contemplating measures to stop this practice that included 'fixing a public inhibition upon the ships mainmasts, private admonitions to the masters, and keeping a strict watch to prevent the goods being carried aboard'.[99] Some EIC servants also exported indigo on private account to West Asia in the 1650s. This, too, was in contravention of the company's monopoly and adversely affected its commercial interests in the region. In 1651, Thomas Andrew bought for himself 50 bales of Khurja indigo and exported it to Gombroon. The transaction turned out to be unfavourable and he lost about Rs 10,000.[100] In 1652, the *Assada Merchant* carried to Gombroon 70 bales of indigo, 20 were for the company and 50 belonging to William Jesson, an EIC employee in Agra. The instructions accompanying the cargo stipulated that the best 20 bales were to be sold on the company's account and the rest on Jesson's. Surat officials justified this transaction by arguing that priority was given to the company's interests, and business was conducted in such a way that it gave no encouragement to private trade.[101] It seems that such activities were carried out with the tacit approval and cooperation of fellow officials and colleagues and they even misused the company's funds. Andrew and Jesson worked together in Agra and were in collusion with each other as both carried out their private indigo trade. Jesson favoured Andrew by letting him borrow Rs 21,000 from the company (at a monthly interest of ¾ percent) to discharge

97 In 1643, about 40,000 pounds of indigo was imported into London on the *Crispiana* and *Aleppo Merchant* on private accounts. *EFI 1642–45*, London to Surat, 27 Nov. 1643, p. 123. Another homebound ship, the *London*, had on board some indigo on private account. Ibid., p. 141.

98 *EFI 1642–45*, Surat to London, 28 Nov. 1644, p. 202.

99 *EFI 1646–50*, Surat to London, 25 Jan. 1647, p. 78.

100 *EFI 1651–54*, Thomas Andrew at Agra to the company, 25 Dec. 1654, pp. 301–2. He also traded on private account in other commodities. He had reportedly consigned musk worth £500 to England on his private account.

101 *EFI 1651–54*, Surat to Persia, 4 Oct. 1652, p. 134.

his liabilities and entered the transaction in the other person's name. Things turned out to be unfavourable for Andrew and he incurred substantial losses. In 1655 he was greatly indebted not only to the company but also to many private persons in Agra.[102]

In the second half of the century, even though the EIC's indigo imports from India had substantially declined, private trade in indigo continued to bother the authorities in India and London. In the 1670s, they imposed a penalty on private imports of indigo into London. A fine of 18 pence per pound and 12 pence per pound was imposed respectively on all Bayana and Sarkhej indigo imported in the company's ships and brought into its warehouses.[103] By the last quarter of the century, the EIC's trade monopoly had come to be challenged by British entrepreneurs aspiring to share commercial privileges and profits in Anglo-Indian trade. The company tried hard to preserve its trade monopoly. In 1681, it even secured a royal proclamation that prohibited all private trade in commodities whose import into England was an exclusive monopoly of the EIC and subjected all private traders to punitive action.[104] The so-called interlopers carried out frequent commercial ventures in the East and even established the New Company in 1698, which traded in Asia as the EIC's rival until the two merged in 1708.[105]

The indigo trade of the European companies and all other merchants also suffered intermittently from official interference. Some Mughal governors and high officials in Gujarat were involved in maritime trade of which indigo exports to West Asian markets was a major component.[106] They, sometimes, took advantage of the large European demand for indigo and monopolised the commodity, thereby forcing all merchants to buy indigo from them and their agents. EIC and VOC sources allude to local governors forcing their indigo upon the companies. In 1618, EIC officials were unable to purchase any indigo in Ahmadabad because the Mughal governor, Muqarrab Khan, had monopolised

102 Later, Andrew confessed that he used the company's funds for private trade and owed Rs 24,000 to the company and Rs 11,000 to private persons in Agra. *EFI 1655–60*, Surat Presidency, 1655, p. 9.

103 BL, *Court Minutes, 1671–73*, pp. 65, 91, 170–1.

104 BL, 'By the King: A Proclamation for the restraining of all his Majesties subjects but the East India Company, to trade to the East Indies' (London, 1681), no. 192.

105 Ian Bruce Watson, *Foundation of Empire: English Private Trade in India, 1659–1760* (New Delhi: Vikas Publishing House, 1980), 61–3.

106 In 1610, agents of the Queen Mother (mother of Jahangir) were reportedly purchasing indigo in Bayana for her ship sailing to Mocha. Finch, *Early Travels*, 123; Jourdain, *The Journal of John Jourdain*, 155–6.

the sale of this commodity.[107] In 1633, the Mughal Emperor Shahjahan declared the indigo trade in the whole of the empire a state monopoly. The sale of indigo was farmed out to a merchant-monopolist, Manohardas, for three years and all merchants and the companies were required to buy indigo from him and his agents. The EIC and VOC joined hands to resist and defeat the monopoly. On 29 November 1633, the EIC chief and the VOC director in Surat signed an agreement and pledged to abide by it.[108] They agreed not to buy any indigo without mutual knowledge and consent, and that none of them would buy any quantity at prices higher than those specified in the agreement. In view of the companies' resistance and protests by merchants and producers, Emperor Shahjahan withdrew the monopoly in 1634.[109]

While these measures blunted the adverse effects of competition and official interference in the European indigo trade in the short run, the EIC and VOC also took measures that would have some long-term implications for the indigo industry in India. The unpredictability of indigo supplies and prices in Agra, Ahmadabad, and Surat, and intermittent monopolies prompted the companies to look for alternative and more stable sources of indigo elsewhere in Asia and the Americas. From the mid-1630s, the VOC implemented measures to promote indigo production in its colonies in East and South-east Asia. The British also looked towards their transatlantic colonies to obtain indigo. Although it took a few decades for colonial Jamaica, and many more for South Carolina, to become stable sources of indigo supplies, Britain certainly began to obtain indigo from Spanish and, later, French colonies.[110] The Dutch colonial possessions in the New World were less suitable for indigo plantation than were the French and Spanish colonies. Some indigo from India, therefore, continued to enter European markets until the early eighteenth century, when large-scale supplies of indigo from America rendered Indian indigo undesirable in Europe.[111]

---

107 *EFI 1618–21*, Surat to London, 16 March 1618, p. 28.

108 VOC 1113, Contract ende capitulatie op den handel van den indigo [Contract and capitulation concerning the indigo trade], Surat, 29 Nov. 1633, ff. 230r–236r.

109 Bibliothèque Nationale, Paris, France, Blochet Supplementary Persan 482, Copy of Shahjahan's *farman* declaring the withdrawal of the indigo monopoly, 1634, f. 98a. Indigo producers too felt the brunt of the imperial monopoly and joined the forces rallying against it. In protest, peasants also reportedly uprooted their indigo plants. Irfan Habib, *The Agrarian System of Mughal India, 1556–1707* (New Delhi: OUP, 1999), 87–8.

110 These colonies participated openly or clandestinely in the intra-Caribbean trade and secured indigo supplies from Guatemala and Saint-Domingue. See, Chapter 4 notes 21 and 32.

111 Between 1650 and 1750, the Spanish and French had monopolised the world market and the indigo from their transatlantic colonies catered to the British and European demand for the blue dye. R.C. Nash, 'South Carolina Indigo, European Textiles, and the British Atlantic Economy in the Eighteenth Century', *Economic History Review*, vol. 63, no. 2 (2010), 363.

Indian Indigo in the Nineteenth Century: Global Demand and Distribution

Indian Indigo in Europe

At the end of the eighteenth century, the EIC and many European private merchants once again began exporting large quantities of indigo from India to Europe. Britain's colonial conquests in Bengal, the loss of indigo-producing transatlantic colonies (mainly South Carolina) in the 1770s, and the rapid growth in the demand for indigo due to expanding textile production in Europe set the stage for the emergence of Bengal indigo as a global commodity. The EIC's colonial government promoted indigo production in the Bengal Presidency. Exponential growth in its production occurred in the 1790s and soon India once again became the largest supplier of this raw material, initially to Britain and eventually to Europe and the wider world. Average annual exports from India to Great Britain, thus, rose from about 150,000 pounds during 1782–86 to about two million pounds during 1792–96 (three times more than the average in the preceding five years), and it exceeded three million pounds in the decade from 1801 to 1810 (Figures 3.3 and 3.4). Exports to Britain doubled to six million pounds in the next two decades and annual averages during the 1840s reached eight million pounds. Indigo exports from India to Britain and other parts of Europe and America grew consistently well up to the end of the nineteenth century (Table 3.3). After the 1830s, the volume of indigo exports to France and the United States increased substantially. The average annual value of indigo exported from Calcutta grew from about Rs 4 million during 1796–1805 to more than Rs 21 million during 1836–45. After a temporary fall during 1846–1855, exports increased rapidly and the average annual values exceeded Rs 38 million during 1886–1895 (Table 3.4 and Figure 3.5).[112]

At the end of the century, the introduction of synthetic indigo and its popularity gave a severe blow to natural indigo. Dyers in Europe and elsewhere began to use synthetic dye, hence the demand for indigo from India fell drastically. Joint endeavours by the colonial state in India, indigo planters, and chemists/botanists to make natural indigo competitive by introducing new plants (Java indigo) in India and new methods of cultivation, manuring, and

112 In 1873–74 and 1874–75, the values of indigo exports to London amounted to Rs 16.8 and 12 million respectively. In these years, the values of total indigo exports to all places including Britain exceeded Rs 26.3 and 19.8 million respectively. BL, P/188, Statement showing the total annual trade of dye-stuffs exported from Bengal during 1873/4 and 1874/5, p. 56. Large-scale indigo production continued in the 1880s and early 1890s. During 1881–82 and 1894–95, the average annual production of indigo in Bengal and Bihar alone exceeded 84,673 factory *man* (6.3 million pounds). WBSA, Agriculture, 10C/1, Statement of indigo, p. 94.

manufacturing, could not save the natural indigo industry.[113] There was a brief revival in the indigo trade during the late 1910s and early 1920s, when indigo exports to Britain, the United States, and Egypt were rather substantial. During 1914–15 and 1918–19, the average annual value of indigo exports to Britain amounted to Rs 7.8 million, whereas average exports to the United States and Egypt together exceeded Rs 6.3 million.[114] Soon thereafter, however, indigo production and exports declined. By the late 1920s, the production of commercial indigo in India had almost completely stopped. By then, synthetic indigo had inundated the markets of Europe, West Asia, Russia, and America as a better and less expensive substitute for natural indigo.

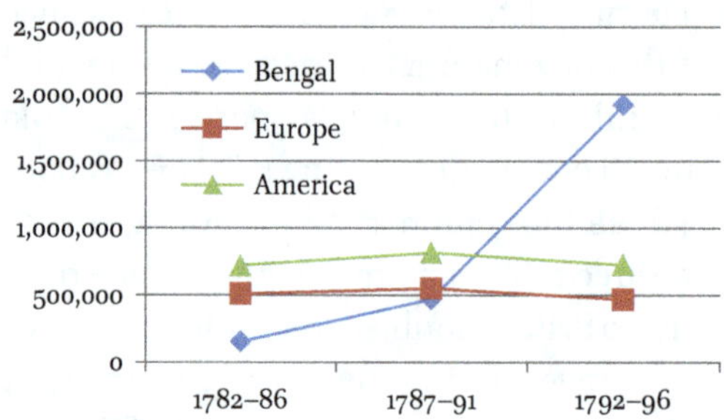

FIGURE 3.3 *Five-yearly average annual imports (in lb.) of indigo into Great Britain, 1782–96*
SOURCE: BASED ON FIGURES IN TABLE 4.3 IN CHAPTER 4.

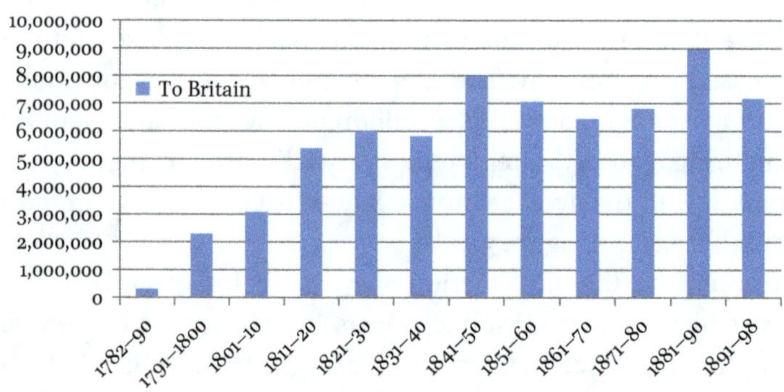

FIGURE 3.4 *Ten-yearly average annual exports (in lb.) of indigo from India to Great Britain, 1782–1898*
SOURCE: BASED ON FIGURES IN THE FOLLOWING TABLE 3.3.

113 For a recent analysis of these initiatives, see Prakash Kumar, *Indigo Plantations and Science in Colonial India* (Cambridge: CUP, 2012), chapters 3 (171–6) and 6.

114 *Statistical Abstract for British India, 1911–12 to 1920–21* (Calcutta: Superintendent of Government Printing, 1922), pp. 474–77, 542–43. In four years between 1915–16 and 1918–19, the total value of indigo exports to the United States amounted to Rs 16.3 million and to Egypt it amounted to Rs 11.27 million during 1816–1820. Ibid.; *Statistical Abstract for British India, 1920–21 to 1929–30* (Calcutta: Superintendent of Government Printing, 1931), p. 623

TABLE 3.3 *Ten-yearly average annual indigo exports (in lb.) from India to Great Britain, 1782–1898*

Year	To Britain	Total indigo
1782–90	294,697	1,604,471
1791–1800	2,277,312	3,138,995
1801–10	3,077,285	3,708,944
1811–20	5,371,897	5,517,009
1821–30	6,010,426	6,516,881
1831–40	5,804,447	6,288,556
1841–50	7,985,731	8,426,338
1851–60	7,051,632	7,913,248
1861–70	6,433,504	8,611,792
1871–80	6,808,144	8,730,064
1881–90	8,959,216	9,944,032
1891–98	7,168,112	7,819,056

SOURCE: REPORTS AND DOCUMENTS CONNECTED WITH THE PROCEEDINGS OF THE EAST INDIA COMPANY, PP. 26–7; NA, KEW, CUST 5/1A, 1B, 1C, 1D, 1E, 2–36, 38, 42, 44, 48, 50, 52, 54, 56, 58, 62, 64, 66, 68, 72, 75, 81,87, 92, 97, 102, 104–5, 107, 109, 111, 115, 119, 123, 125, 127, 131, 133, 135, 137, 141, 143, 147, 153, 155, 161, 159, 157.

Substantial quantities of Madras indigo were also exported to Europe, especially to Britain and France. By 1830, Madras alone was exporting over a million pounds to Britain, even though its quality was lower than that of Bengal indigo.[115] Exports more than doubled in the second half of the century as production expanded after the indigo peasants' rebellion against planters and manufacturers in Bengal in 1860.[116] Between 1861 and 1898, annual exports of Madras indigo to Britain averaged more than two million pounds. During this period, Madras indigo comprised 31 percent of total indigo imports from India into Britain, and in terms of value it amounted to 21 percent (Figure 3.6 and Table 3.5).

115 In 1828 and 1829, the imports into Britain were 742,500 pounds and 1,083,250 pounds respectively. John A. Phipps, *A Series of Treatise on the Principal Products of Bengal: 1 Indigo* (Calcutta: Baptist Mission, 1832), 19. According to John Phipps, it was an inferior indigo and was generally sold in Europe at very low prices, about half of the price of Bengal indigo. In terms of value, therefore, Madras indigo accounted for a low proportion although in volume the imports were rather substantial.

116 For details about this rebellion, see Blair B. Kling, *The Blue Mutiny: The Indigo Disturbances in Bengal, 1859–1862* (Philadelphia: University of Pennsylvania Press, 1966).

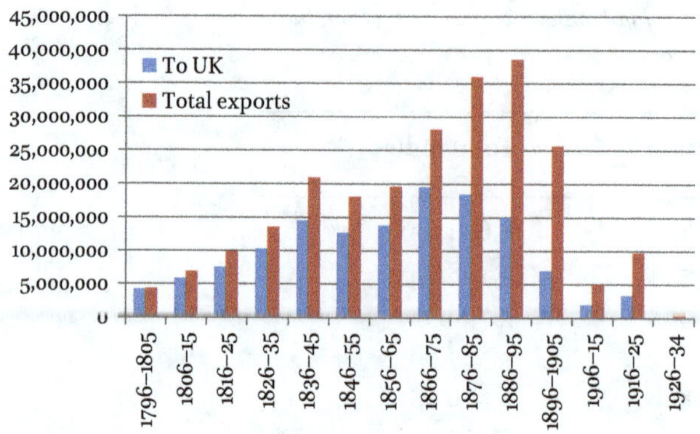

FIGURE 3.5 *Ten-yearly average annual values (in rupees) of indigo exports from India, 1796/97–1933/34*
SOURCE: BASED ON FIGURES IN THE FOLLOWING TABLE 3.4.

TABLE 3.4 *Ten-yearly average annual values (in rupees) of indigo exports from India, 1796/97–1933/34*

Years	To UK	Total exports
1796–1805	4,126,869	4,263,580
1806–15	5,811,951	6,858,442
1816–25	7,469,321	9,835,599
1826–35	10,208,840	13,476,366
1836–45	14,458,952	20,859,195
1846–55	12,631,545	17,985,211
1856–65	13,685,336	19,513,079
1866–75	19,484,167	28,028,981
1876–85	18,411,290	35,943,747
1886–95	15,011,404	38,533,702
1896–1905	7,020,399	25,550,662
1906–15	1,874,137	4,971,914
1916–25	3,312,274	9,700,200
1926–34	57,778	287,222

SOURCE: BASED ON FIGURES IN APPENDIX 5.

On a small scale, indigo was also exported from Bombay to Europe and West Asia. It was not a major centre of production and what was exported from there was a mix of Sind, Gujarat, Bengal, and even Manila indigo. Some indigo was sent to London and occasionally to France and the United States as well.

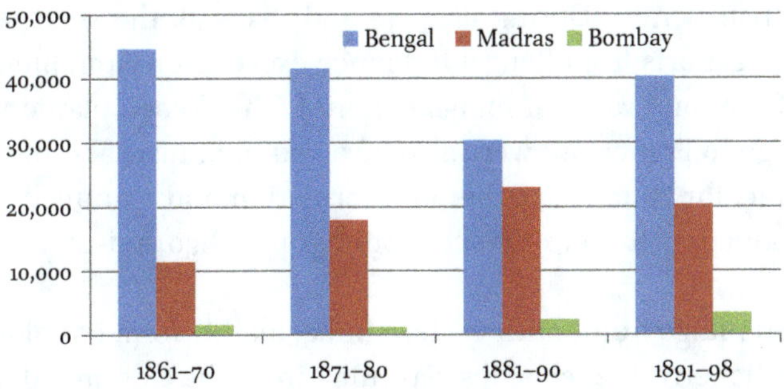

FIGURE 3.6 *Ten-yearly average annual imports (in cwt of 112 lb.) of indigo from Bengal, Madras, and Bombay into Great Britain, 1861–98*
SOURCE: BASED ON FIGURES IN THE FOLLOWING TABLE 3.5.

TABLE 3.5 *Ten-yearly average annual quantities (in cwt of 112 lb.) and values (in pound sterling) of indigo imports from Bengal, Madras, and Bombay into Great Britain, 1861–1898*

	1861–70		**1871–80**		**1881–90**		**1891–98**	
	Quantities	**Values**	**Quantities**	**Values**	**Quantities**	**Values**	**Quantities**	**Values**
Bengal	44,576	1,668,268	41,487	1,222,270	30,202	1,361,043	40,256	805,604
Madras	11,380	287,012	17,868	414,874	22,869	410,544	20,299	303,930
Bombay	1,486	17,156	1,079	20,204	2,260	33,550	3,347	46,130

SOURCE: CALCULATED FROM THE ANNUAL STATEMENTS OF IMPORTS INTO LONDON. NA, KEW, CUST 5/64, 66, 68,72, 75, 81, 81, 87, 92, 97, 102, 105, 107, 109, 111, 113, 115, 117, 119, 121, 123, 125, 127, 129, 131, 133, 135, 137, 139, 141, 143, 145, 147, 149, 151, 153, 155, 157, AND 159.

Exports to Britain increased somewhat in the last quarter of the century (Figure 3.6 and Table 3.5). Britain also occasionally received indigo from Ceylon albeit in trifling quantities, the maximum imports being 43,008 pounds in 1896.[117]

Next to Great Britain, France was the most important market for Indian indigo in the nineteenth century. After losing Saint-Domingue, France's main indigo-producing colony in the Caribbean, the expanding French textiles industry had come to depend almost entirely on indigo imported from India.[118] Many indigo planters of Saint-Domingue relocated to India and established

117 NA, Kew, CUST 5/155, Customs Records, 1896.

118 Cotton textiles industry flourished in France in the nineteenth century and a significant growth occurred in the second half of the century. Roger Price, *An Economic History of Modern France, 1730–1914* (New York: St. Martin's Press, 1981), 101–06.

indigo factories in British Bengal. During 1843–44 and 1857–58, the average annual values of indigo exports from Bengal to France exceeded Rs 4 million (about 22.3 percent of the total value of indigo exports). The French planters not only exported indigo to France but were also involved in industrial espionage. Pierre-Paul Darrac, for instance, gathered information and compiled a treatise on indigo production to help France to develop indigo industry in West Africa.[119]

France also imported indigo from south-eastern India, mainly from its colonial possession in Pondicherry. French ships returning from the Coromandel Coast invariably brought indigo along with other merchandise.[120] A brisk indigo trade went on from Pondicherry, and some Madras indigo too was taken there for export to Europe.[121] It is interesting to note that in the quotations of comparative prices by the Marseille Chamber of Commerce in the late 1890s only Madras, Pondicherry, and Java indigo are mentioned; Bengal indigo is conspicuously absent. Some Madras indigo was also sent to West Asia by Asian and European merchants.

Indian Indigo in Asian Markets

In the eighteenth century, Bengal emerged as a major textile production centre for the world market and by the early 1790s, it had also begun to produce indigo on a large scale. Although, the indigo industry grew mainly in response to the growing European demand, it also catered to the needs of India's flourishing textile industry, and some was also exported to Persia and parts of West and Central Asia. Keeping in mind the massive volume of textiles exported from Bengal, whose average annual value was about Rs 12 million during the first quarter of the nineteenth century, it is likely that local indigo consumption increased in parallel with the expanding production of textiles. According to one estimate, in the early 1820s Bengal consumed on average about

119 Pierre-Paul Darrac and Willem van Schendel, *Global Blue: Indigo and Espionage in Colonial Bengal* (Dhaka: the University Press, 2006), 33–6.

120 Indigo is listed in the declarations of the cargo on ships arriving in Marseille. It is mentioned in the cargo list of many French ships returning in 1851 from Bimlipatam and Pondicherry on the Coromandel Coast and from Calcutta in Bengal. Chambre de Commerce Archives, Marseille, 200 E 604, diverse dates, 1851. In the 1890s, the comparative price lists mention Pondicherry and Madras indigo along with Java indigo. Chambre de Commerce Archives, Marseille, Production et Commerce en France, Matieres Colorantes: grance and indigo, 1810–1900.

121 The British in Madras, sometimes, complained that much indigo produced in their territories ended up into French hands as it was smuggled into Pondicherry. BL, Madras Revenue Proceedings (P/440), 24, Proceedings of the Madras Government, Revenue Department, 12 Aug. 1869, p. 3212; ibid., 63, Proceedings of the Revenue Board, Madras, 1870, pp. 5885–8.

4 percent of the region's total indigo production. Soon thereafter, however, local demand for indigo suffered a setback as the production and export of Bengal piece goods rapidly declined. The annual value of textile exports fell by about two-thirds, from an average of Rs 12 million between 1800 and 1825 to about Rs 4.5 million in the next three decades. Furthermore, as consumers in Europe became increasingly conscious of quality and colour, the EIC began to export cotton and silk fabrics from Bengal and elsewhere in India to be dyed, painted, and printed in Britain. These developments must have adversely affected the consumption of indigo in India.

In the second half of the nineteenth century, indigo consumption in India seems to have improved. The cotton textile mills in western India (Ahmadabad, Surat, and Bombay) and the jute mills of Bengal may have generated enormous demand for indigo and other dyeing materials. Indigo supplies to these mills came mainly from Bengal, north India, and Madras. While indigo producers may have found a flourishing market for their indigo, the dye-houses attached to the mills seems to have taken away whatever opportunities were previously available to local small-scale dyers. In the late nineteenth century, large imports of cheap coloured cotton textiles and dyed cotton yarn from Europe also adversely affected the indigo dyeing industry in India.[122] The final blow to the natural indigo industry and to indigo dyers came from the introduction and popularity of synthetic indigo in the early twentieth century.

West Asia (mainly Persia) was the major market for indigo exported from Bombay. Large proportions of Bengal and Sind indigo exported from Bombay in the early nineteenth century were destined for the Persian Gulf. Between 1804–05 and 1826–27, more than half of the total average annual value of indigo exports from Bombay was to the Persian Gulf.[123] It was, however, Bengal that supplied large quantities of indigo to the Persian Gulf. Between 1807–08 and 1857–58, the average annual value of indigo exports from Calcutta to this region exceeded Rs 700,000.[124] Indigo was also produced in some parts of Persia,

122 During 1891–1895, the average annual imports of coloured or dyed cotton textiles into Bombay alone amounted to more than 166 million yards. C.G.H. Fawcett, *A Monograph on Dyes and Dyeing in the Bombay Presidency* (Bombay, 1896), 5–6.

123 During this period, annual average value of indigo exports to the Persian Gulf was Rs 36,899 and the average annual value of indigo exports to all places amounted to Rs 63,629. MSA, Returns and Statements: External and Internal Commerce, nos. 3, 4/5, 5/6, 8–16, 20–26, General statement of the value of merchandise exported from Bombay.

124 BL, Bengal Commercial Reports (P/174), 22, 25, 38, 44, 48, 49, 56, 59, 61–65, 63, 64, 66, 67, 68–69.

but the quality was poor and output insufficient to meet the local demand.[125] Good-quality indigo, whose consumption in Persia was rather high, had to be imported from India. In the nineteenth century, according to Willem Floor, the dye-works in Isfahan consumed about 150 kilogram (330 pounds) of indigo per day and those of Yezd consumed about 60,000 kilogram (132,000 pounds) per year.[126] Most indigo that Persian dyers used was imported from Sind, Bengal, and Madras by Asian and European merchants. The demand for indigo was on the decline, however, because of large imports of dyed piece goods from Bombay, which adversely affected the dyeing industry of Persia.[127] By the 1880s, average annual indigo imports from India had shrunk to 14,000 to 23,000 kilogram (30,800–50,600 pounds), nearly half of the average imports in former years.[128] Persian dyers and weavers persisted in their use of Indian indigo for dyeing yarn and textiles well into the early twentieth century, until they discovered synthetic dyes to be a convenient and user-friendly substitute.[129]

In the nineteenth century, indigo constituted a valuable export in the extensive trade that Indian merchants carried out with Central Asia and Russia.[130] It was exported in considerable quantities to Bukhara, Turkistan, and Khiva. Estimates show that indigo exports to Bukhara in the 1830s and 1840s varied from 500 to 3,500 camel loads a year.[131] Even in the early twentieth century, indigo continued to be a significant article of Indo-Russian trade. Although the Germans supplied huge quantities of synthetic dye, Russian dyers persisted in their use of the natural indigo, which kept the trade going. This trade gradually declined after 1904, when import duties on natural indigo and synthetic dyes were made equal, which worked in favour of the latter.[132] In the 1910s, the total

125 William Floor, *The Persian Gulf: Bandar Abbas, The Natural Trade Gateway of Southeast Iran* (Washington: Mage Publishers, 2011), 266–7.

126 Ibid., 513.

127 Willem Floor, 'The importation of indigo into Qajar Iran', *Studia Iranica*, vol. 35, no. 2 (2006), 242–3.

128 Floor, *The Persian Gulf*, 513.

129 Floor, 'The importation of indigo into Qajar Iran'.

130 Surendra Gopal, 'Indian Traders in Uzbekistan in the Eighteenth Century', in Surendra Gopal (ed.), *India and Central Asia: Cultural, Economic and Political Links* (Delhi: Shipra Publications, 2001), 25, 30–1; G.L. Dmitriyev, 'From the History of Indian Colony in Central Asia (2nd half of the XIX Century-Beginning of the XX Century)', in Gopal (ed.), *India and Central Asia*, 81–2.

131 Devendra Kaushik, 'Economic Relations between India and Central Asia in the 19th Century', in Gopal (ed.), *India and Central Asia*, 60–1.

132 Ibid.

annual import of indigo into Russia was estimated at from 12,500 to 15,000 cwt (1,400,000 to 1,680,000 pounds) worth more than 200,000 pounds sterling.[133]

For a short period after the First World War, Japan was a major recipient of Indian indigo. During 1918–19 and 1921–22, the average annual values of indigo exports to Japan approximated Rs 4.5 million. By the mid-1920s, synthetic indigo had come to dominate the world market and the natural indigo as a commercial dye came to the end of its *long-durée* moment. By 1934–35, Indian production of indigo completely stopped. One will have to wait and see to what extent recent and ongoing efforts in some parts of the world to revive the natural indigo dye industry succeeds in carving out a niche in a global market so inundated by artificial blues.

Trade in Indian Indigo: a Long-durée Perspective

If we compare the pattern of global trade in Indian indigo in the nineteenth century with that of the preceding period, three major changes are noticeable. The first was the major reconfiguration of the world indigo market and India's position in it. In terms of production, India became the primary manufactory of the world, and other production and supply chains that had formerly competed with Indian indigo and dominated the world market became relatively less significant. Imports of Guatemala and El Salvador indigo into Britain and continental Europe, for example, continued, but comprised a very small proportion of total indigo imports from all places.[134] Similarly, imports from Java continued and expanded after the introduction of the 'culture system' in the 1830s, but were hardly significant in comparison with imports from India. Europe also received some trifling quantities of indigo from Manila, where the industry seems to have flourished in the nineteenth century.[135] Another dimension of this reconfigured market was the expansion of consumer demand to places not previously known for importing indigo from India on a large scale. A wide range of new markets emerged where Indian indigo was in

133 D.T. Chadwick, *Report on Indo-Russian Trade* (Simla: Government Central Press, 1917), 62–3.

134 According to John Phipps, the average annual imports of Spanish [Guatemala] indigo during 1826–27 and 1830–31 amounted to about 400,000 pounds. Phipps, *A Series of Treatises on the Principal Products of Bengal*, 19.

135 China was the main market for Manila indigo, where it was taken in liquid as well as manufactured forms. Phipps, *A Series of Treatises on the Principal Products of Bengal*, 19. Bombay, too, sometimes, received some Manila indigo for re-export to West Asian markets.

much demand, including the United States, France, Russia, Penang (Malaysia), and later Egypt and Japan.

The second major change may be seen in the disjuncture that took place between demand and production or supply. It is true that the European appetite for indigo grew rapidly in the nineteenth century, and that certainly stimulated growth in production; but the exponential growth in the indigo industry in colonial India was also an outcome of speculative investments made by European capitalist entrepreneurs whose primary purpose was the remittance of income and trade surpluses from India to Europe. As early as 1819–20, a report on the commerce of Bengal stated, '[T]he quantity exported is entirely governed by the productiveness of the crop and not dependent upon or in any way influenced by the state of the markets in Europe'.[136] As David McCreery has recently summed it up, 'the amount of indigo delivered to London markets depended not entirely on actual or anticipated demand or even on price but on the need of the company and of private businesses in Bengal to remit payments and profits to Europe'.[137] This disjuncture between demand and supply many a time caused an overabundance of indigo and led to price collapse in European markets that in turn resulted in business failures and crises in the industry in India on a scale and intensity not known before.

Finally, the EIC's share in total indigo exports from Bengal was insignificant right from the late 1780s and exports fell primarily into the hands of private European merchants and their corporations. What is also important to note is that as the century progressed, Britain gradually lost its position as the sole importer and distributor of India's indigo. Large quantities of it began to be exported to continental Europe (mainly France) and the United States directly from India. Between 1837 and 1858, about a third of Calcutta's total annual indigo exports was destined for places other than Britain. In the last quarter of the nineteenth century, about two-thirds of total indigo exports went directly to places other than Britain.

The *long-durée* view of the global trade in indigo shows that Indian production and exports had an erratic trajectory, with periods of boom and slump. Several major and minor changes occurred in the structure of the world market, in the flow of global trade, and in the fortunes of competing indigo commodity

---

136 BL, Bengal Commercial Reports, 31, Report on the internal and external commerce of Bengal in 1819–20.

137 David J. McCreery, 'Indigo Commodity Chains in the Spanish and British Empires, 1560–1860', in Steven Topik, Zephyr Frank and Carlos Marichal (eds.), *From Silver to Cocaine: Latin American Commodity Chains and the Building of the World Economy, 1500–2000* (Durham: Duke University Press, 2006), 66.

chains. What did not change, however, was the quest for alternative sources of indigo. The search for stable and better alternatives was prompted mainly by European nations' desire for an alternative to imports from and dependence on territories over which they did not exercise political control. It was this persistent search for different sources of indigo that made it a global commodity, gave rise to competing production and supply chains, and eventually led to the discovery of synthetic indigo which caused the rapid and sure disappearance of the natural indigo industry. It is to this long historical continuity that we now turn our attention.

CHAPTER 4

The Making of the World Market: Indigo Commodity Chains

> ….tropical commodity chains are almost always truly "global"—not only do these chains cross national borders, they also connect producers to consumers across the boundaries of the world-system zones.
>
> —JENNIFER BAIR, *Frontiers of Commodity Chain Research, 16.*

Right from the sixteenth century, Europe's appreciation of indigo as a valuable merchandise and its desire to secure stable sources of supplies from its colonies contributed to the wider dispersal of indigo production and, consequently, the emergence of the world indigo market. Indigo was among the first agricultural exports to Europe from the colonies that the Spaniards established in the New World. With this began a new era in which indigo from India and America entered European markets, each initially supplementing the other but soon becoming rivals. Thereafter, indigo began to be produced in many parts of the world and the commodity assumed a global character (Map 4.1). Competing indigo commodity chains emerged and the fortunes of all those involved in production and trade in one came to be closely linked with those in another. This is well exemplified by the expansion and contraction in the volumes and values of exports and imports, and the waxing and waning of indigo chains in relation to one another.

In the seventeenth century, the search for alternative sources of supplies intensified as European nations began to harbour ambitions to dominate the continental market by supplying good quality indigo at competitive prices. The Dutch and the British, and later the French, aspired to obtain indigo supplies from India and their Asian and American colonies primarily as a measure to substitute imports of Spanish colonial indigo. The uncertainties of supplies from India and the challenges that the EIC and the VOC came to face in procuring it prompted their quest for alternative and more reliable sources. In the 1630s, the VOC began to explore the possibility of growing indigo in its various Asian colonies and at places where the company had some political influence. Since the EIC had no colonies in Asia, the English turned towards the Americas. Colonial conquests and the desire to make the colonies economically profitable for the mother countries enabled the Dutch Republic and England to replace Indian indigo, at least partially, with the dye obtained from their colonies.

 | DOI 10.1163/9789004311558_006

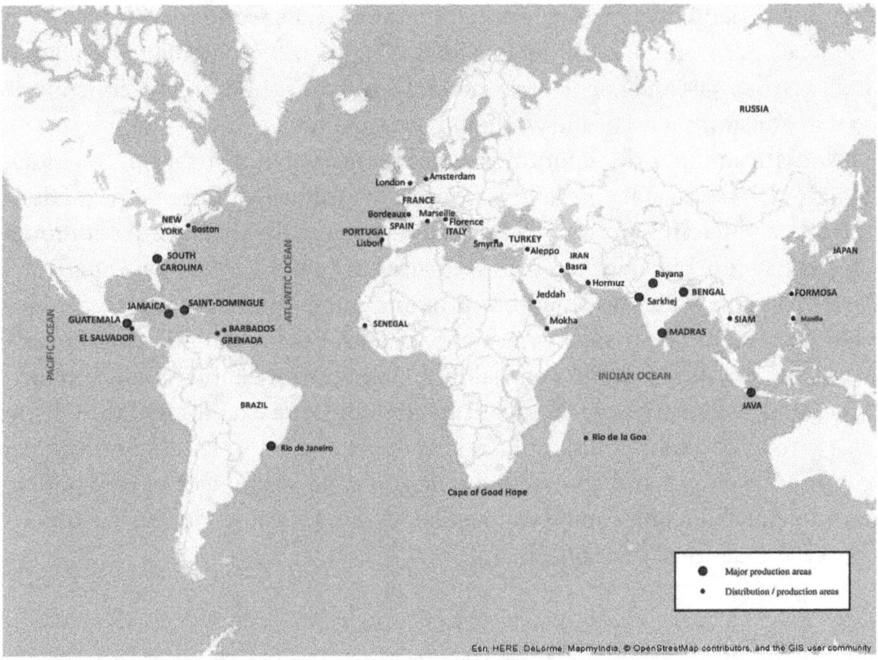

MAP 4.1 *World Map: major production and distribution areas*

In early seventeenth-century Europe, Guatemala indigo was well known for its superior quality. It had such a high reputation that merchants and dyers compared indigo from all other places with it.[1] Imports of Guatemala indigo were, however, modest during this period for three main reasons. Indigo production in the colonies did not increase to the extent that it could meet Europe's total demand. The Thirty Years' War (1618–48) adversely affected indigo production and interrupted imports into Europe. Finally, from the early years of the seventeenth century, the EIC and the VOC imported into Europe large quantities of indigo from India that almost entirely met the demand in terms of both quality and quantity. By the mid-seventeenth century, however, the situation had changed, and the world indigo market began to experience some major transformations that would have long-term implications for the industry in India. Large quantities of indigo from Europe's transatlantic colonies entered the continental market rendering its imports from India less desirable. At the end of the eighteenth century, India began to produce indigo on

1 In a letter to Batavia written in 1622, the directors of the VOC in Amsterdam referred to Guatemala indigo as a standard of quality. Collectie Geleynssen de Jongh [Geleynssen de Jongh Collection], 114, Bewindhebberen aan GG&R, Amsterdam, 20 Jan. 1622, f. 54^{r}.

an unprecedentedly large scale and it dominated the world market well up to the 1920s. A combination of factors, including the EIC's colonial conquests in India in the 1750s and decolonization in the Americas in the 1770s, contributed to this transformation of the world indigo market.

Notwithstanding the enormous exports and global distribution of Indian indigo, the search for alternative sources continued. Efforts were made in the late eighteenth and nineteenth centuries to make the existing commodity chains more effective and competitive as in Spanish Guatemala and Dutch Java. Attempts were also made to promote indigo production in some new colonies and to create new commodity chains. French ambitions to create a West African alternative in Senegal in the nineteenth century and Germany's success in finding a chemical substitute for indigo are examples of this. Below, we examine the causes and implications of the success or failure of the indigo commodity chains and analyse how their relative advantages in land, labour, technology, skills, and capital were embedded in local and global structures of power and political control.

South–East Asian Alternative: Indigo from the Dutch East Indies

In the early 1630s, the VOC's and the EIC's indigo purchases in India were interrupted first by a severe famine in Gujarat (1630–32) and then by the Mughal's short-lived imperial indigo monopoly (1633–34). This prompted the companies to try finding indigo elsewhere. The VOC first tried to promote indigo cultivation and manufacture in Siam (Thailand) where the company was more firmly placed than in northern India. It also had some political influence at the Siamese court. In 1636, VOC authorities in Batavia reported to Amsterdam that they were expecting samples of indigo from Siam and observed that plenty of labour would enable the VOC to export large quantities of indigo to Europe and break the monopoly of Indian indigo.[2] In that year, the VOC exported some 450 pots of indigo to Batavia for trial at home.[3] In 1637, some Bayana indigo seeds

2 *Generale Missiven*, vol. I, 1610–38, pp. 515–16.

3 *Dagh-Register, 1636*, p. 295. It seems that the company exported from Siam and Taiwan some liquefied or wet indigo (*natte werve* or *blauwe cangan*) to Amsterdam where it was either sold as such or after converting it into dry indigo cakes. In 1637, seeing that the quality was not good, indigo experts advised the company officials to not to show it to merchants without first mixing and diluting the liquid well so that the impure particles precipitated at the bottom and the liquid on top appeared as a shining blue substance. *Generale Missiven*, vol. I, 1610–38, Batavia, 9 Dec. 1637, p. 610.

were sent from Agra to Siam to promote its production.[4] In the 1640s, the VOC obtained some indigo from Siam for the home market and also some indigo seeds for Formosa (Taiwan) where the company tried to promote indigo cultivation as well.[5] In 1644–45, the company tried hard to grow indigo in Taiwan but could not succeed because the island's climate and land were not suitable for producing commercial indigo on any large scale.[6] Our sources do not tell us why the VOC did not succeed in Siam, a place that would go on to produce plenty of indigo in the nineteenth century for Chinese markets. Possibly, rice was a more profitable crop for peasants than indigo, of which the VOC was the only buyer.

Not buying indigo in India meant that the commodity would be available at low prices to its rival, the EIC, to export much of it to Europe. To deprive the EIC of the benefits of this advantageous trade, the VOC thought it necessary to buy indigo and keep the purchase prices high.[7] Considerations of better prospects for sales and profits in Europe and aspirations to dominate the European market underpinned Europe's search for alternative sources of indigo supplies. Thus, it would seem that while the VOC obtained indigo from its colonies in the East Indies, it did not entirely give up its indigo purchases in India. The VOC also promoted indigo culture in Batavia and, as early as 1636–37, company authorities even anticipated that the indigo from Siam and Batavia would almost entirely replace Indian indigo in European markets.[8] The experiments, however, did not meet the company's expectations, and the search for alternative indigo continued. In the 1660s, indigo was being planted in Timor on a trial basis, and its production was reported in the Cape as well in 1687.[9]

Indigo seeds, plants, and instructions regarding cultivation and manufacture were sent from Batavia to the Cape and to the Residency of Rio de la Goa (Mauritius). But, because of unsuitable climatic conditions and calamities, these trials were not successful.[10] Efforts to produce indigo in Mauritius

---

4 *Generale Missiven,* vol. I, 1610–38, Batavia, 9 Dec. 1637, p. 610.

5 In 1642, Batavia reportedly received a quantity of indigo from Siam. *Generale Missiven,* vol. II, 1639–1655, 23 Dec. 1642, 286.

6 VOC 1149, Vertoog aen de Edele Heer Francois Caron raad van Indien en Gouverneur van Formosa [Exposition of Mr. Francois Caron, councilor of the Indies and Governor of Formosa], Casteel Zeelandia, 13 Oct. 1645, ff. 736ʳ–737ʳ. In 1644, Siam sent 300 *catties* of indigo seeds to Taiwan. VOC 1157, Invoice of goods sent to Taiwan, Siam, 25 July 1644, f. 676ʳ.

7 Ibid.

8 *Generale Missiven,* vol. I, 1610–38, p. 610.

9 *Generale Missiven,* Vol. III: 1655–74, p. 681.

10 Western Cape Archives, Cape Town, South Africa (hereafter WCA), Inkomende Brieven [Incoming letters], C 362, Batavia to Cape of Good Hope, 30 Nov. 1697, pp. 108–9. In 1698, for example, rats destroyed the seeds soon after the sowing had taken place. C 363,

continued and intensified in the early eighteenth century. In the 1720s, instructions regarding sowing, harvesting, and manufacturing indigo were sent to Mauritius and VOC officials were encouraged to make every possible effort to promote the industry.[11] Indigo vats were constructed in 1726, and Arent Sonnemans and David van Mitsky were sent from Batavia as indigo experts to oversee production. To facilitate this, twelve copper pots were sent together with a copy of a manual prepared by Gijsbert Penning and Arij Tob, indigo-makers in Cheribon and Priangan.[12] Nothing, however, could lead the VOC to the desired outcome. Experiments with indigo cultivation continued at the company's gardens at Rondebosje and Nieuwland in the Cape. Trials with different seeds were carried out in different seasons to find out in which part of the year indigo plant grew best.[13] By the 1750s, however, the impossibility of indigo production in the Cape had become obvious. Plants could not grow properly because cold winter and hot summer wind devastated indigo plants in the fields. The project was subsequently given up.

Efforts to produce indigo in Java seemingly intensified in the 1690s and 1700s. The company recruited some indigo experts in India to promote indigo culture in Java. In 1693, four such persons were sent to Batavia from the Coromandel Coast and an indigo grower from Agra was sent to Batavia in 1702.[14] The VOC officials also proposed that two or three poor Dutch young men be brought to India to learn the art of indigo making, the intent being that they would later serve in the East Indies to improve indigo production there.[15] A report on indigo production written in 1696 shows that some parts of Java, including Banten, Tanjungpura, and Semarang, produced some good-quality indigo.[16] The VOC also promoted indigo culture in Ambon and Cheribon. In 1697, indigo was

Mauritius to Cape of Good Hope, 10 Feb. 1698, pp. 19–20. In 1726, plants shrivelled on the ground because of drought. C 422, Rio de la Goa to Cape of Good Hope, 26 Dec. 1726, p. 12. WCA, Verklaring [Statement], C 2527, Report to the governor of the Cape of Good Hope, 13 Jan. 1755, pp. 19–23.

11 WCA, Uitgaande Brieven [Outgoing letters], C 1466, Cape of Good Hope to Rio de la Goa, 23 Nov. 1723, pp. 298–9; C 1467, Cape of Good Hope to Rio de la Goa, 10 May 1724, p. 158; C 1467, Cape of Good Hope to Rio de la Goa, 6 Nov. 1724, pp. 790–1.

12 WCA, C 422, Batavia to Cape of Good Hope, 5 Dec. 1726, pp. 116–17; C 422, Rio de la Goa to Cape of Good Hope, 26 Dec. 1726, p. 14; C 425, Batavia to Cape of Good Hope, 27 Oct. 1727, pp. 45–6.

13 WCA, C 2527, Report to the governor of the Cape of Good Hope, 13 Jan. 1755, pp. 19–23.

14 *Generale Missiven,* vol V: 1686–97, p. 639; VOC 1666, Directeur en Raad van Surat aan GG&R [Director and the Council of Surat to Governor-General and Council], Surat, 23 Feb. 1702, p. 99.

15 VOC 1666, Directeur en Raad van Surat aan GG&R, Surat, 23 Feb. 1702, p. 99.

16 VOC 7779, A report on indigo, Java's Oost-hoeck, 20 July 1696, pp. 243–46.

reportedly grown and processed in several villages in Cheribon, although the amount the company could procure was small and of poor quality.[17] This was mainly because of unsuitable climate and water, a shortage of labour, and a lack of experienced men to cultivate and process indigo. Production picked up in the eighteenth century, but even then the VOC's total procurements of Java indigo rarely exceeded 40,000 pounds. On average, the company's annual procurement of Java indigo between 1704 and 1781 was about 27,700 pounds (Appendix 3). The region, however, lacked no potential to produce indigo on a large scale.[18]

Indigo production expanded rapidly in the nineteenth century, particularly after 1830, when the Dutch colonial state in Indonesia carried out agrarian reforms and introduced the culture system and consignment system. Figures for government and private exports show that the production of indigo increased substantially. Indigo exports on private account increased from 45,000 Dutch pounds in 1831 to 2.12 million Dutch pounds in 1840.[19] While indigo production declined in the second half of the nineteenth century (even as that of coffee and sugar increased rapidly), indigo remained a major export commodity up to the early twentieth century (Table 4.1 and Figure 4.1).

It may be observed that in restructuring Java's colonial agrarian economy in the eighteenth century, the VOC's primary interest was to secure pepper, and indigo occupied second place. Later, in the nineteenth century, coffee and sugar became important commodities that the VOC successfully promoted on the island. Java and other parts of South-east Asia also produced some cotton textiles and they may have consumed a part of the locally produced indigo.

Indigo from the Dutch West Indies

Attempts were also made to obtain indigo from the Dutch West Indies. Its major colonies there, such as Curaçao and Surinam, were not suitable for indigo cultivation. Attempts to grow indigo in Essequibo in the mid-eighteenth century too were unsuccessful.[20] The West India Company and private Dutch traders obtained indigo supplies from other European colonies by participating in the

17 VOC 1599, Daily report of the visit to Periangan, Cheribon, 6 Nov. 1697, pp. 16–43.

18 In some years, total production was large. In 1759–60 and 1763–64, the VOC procured more than 131,000 and 178,000 pounds respectively. NA, Boekhouder-Generaal te Batavia, 11830, p. 107 and 11831, p. 107.

19 J.S. Furnivall, *The Netherlands India: A Study of Plural Economy* (New York: The McMillan Company, 1944), 129.

20 Eric Willem van der Oest, 'The Forgotten Colonies of Essequibo and Demerara, 1700–1814', in Johannes Postma and Victor Enthoven (eds.), *Riches from Atlantic Commerce: Dutch Transatlantic Trade and Shipping, 1585–1817* (Leiden: Brill, 2003), 349.

TABLE 4.1 *Five-yearly average annual imports (in Dutch pounds) of Java indigo into the Dutch Republic, 1831–1913*

Year	Dutch pounds	Values in *f.*
1831–35	242,800	1,044,000
1836–40	2,123,000	6,371,000
1841–45	1,653,000	4,961,000
1846–50	1,256,000	4,193,000
1851–55	—	3,250,000
1856–60	—	3,452,000
1861–65	—	4,229,000
1866–70	—	3,227,000
1871–75	—	1,900,000
1876–80	—	3,000,000
1881–85	—	3,700,000
1886–95	NA	NA
1896–1900	1,174,000	3,522,000
1901–05	1,018,000	3,054,000
1906–13	152,000	456,000

SOURCE: FURNIVALL, *THE NETHERLANDS INDIA*, 129, 171, 207, 318. ORIGINAL FIGURES IN KILOGRAMS HAVE BEEN CONVERTED INTO DUTCH POUNDS (1 KILOGRAM = 2 DUTCH POUNDS).

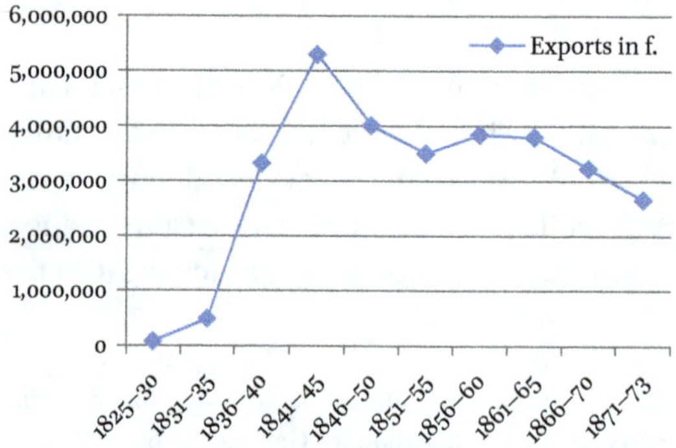

FIGURE 4.1 *Five-yearly average annual values (in guilders) of indigo exports from Java, 1825–73*
SOURCE: BASED ON FIGURES IN APPENDIX 7: VOLUMES AND VALUES OF INDIGO EXPORTS FROM JAVA, 1822–73.

intra-Caribbean transit trade.[21] In the eighteenth century, indigo from the French and Spanish colonies was imported into the Dutch Republic mainly through Curaçao and Surinam and, in some years as during the War of Jenkins' Ear (1744–1749), the imports were rather large.[22] Between 1745 and 1749, Dutch ships brought to Amsterdam about one million pounds of indigo, mostly from the French colony, Saint-Domingue.[23] In 1759, for example, Amsterdam received 575,170 pounds of indigo in 42 West India ships the sale value of which amounted to 3.35 million guilders (more than 46 percent of the total sale value of all goods brought in those ships).[24]

Some private merchants who traded in the Caribbean and across the Atlantic also brought some indigo to Amsterdam. In 1750, a private Amsterdam-bound ship from the Caribbean had on board 59 barrels (9,590 pounds) of indigo.[25] Of the total indigo imports into the Dutch Republic, some was re-exported to Britain. During 1782–96, the Dutch annual exports to Great Britain averaged about 25,000 pounds.[26] Thus, for about one and a half centuries before India would once again take the centre-stage in the world indigo market, an overwhelming part of European imports of indigo was from its transatlantic colonies.

Indigo from Britain's American Colonies: Jamaica and South Carolina

The efforts made by the English to explore sources of indigo supplies from their West Indian and American colonies were more successful than those of

21 Dutch ships either sailed directly to French, Spanish, and English colonies in the West Indies or were engaged in intra-Caribbean trade centred in Curaçao. Wim Klooster, 'Curaçao and the Caribbean Transit Trade', in Postma and Enthoven (eds), *Riches from Atlantic Commerce*, 203–4.

22 Indigo accounted for 1.7 percent of the total imports into the Republic by the *Middelburg Commercie Compagnie* between 1723 and 1744 and about a million pounds of indigo were imported into Amsterdam during the war (1744–49). Klooster, 'Curaçao and the Caribbean Transit Trade', 203n, 215–6. John Garrigus, 'Blue and Brown: Contraband Indigo and the Rise of a Free Colored Planter Class in French Saint-Domingue', *The Americas*, vol. 50, no. 2 (1993), 244–6.

23 Klooster, 'Curaçao and the Caribbean Transit Trade', 215–6.

24 Victor Enthoven, 'An Assessment of Dutch Transatlantic Commerce, 1585–1817', in Postma and Enthoven, (eds), *Riches from Atlantic Commerce*, 441.

25 Cornelis Ch. Goslinga, *The Dutch in the Caribbean and in the Guianas, 1680–1791* (Assen: Van Gorcum, 1985), 208.

26 BL, Home Miscellaneous, 449, Selection of Papers exhibiting a View of the East India Company's Commercial Concerns, pp. 57–59.

the Dutch. After the English acquisition of Jamaica in 1655, indigo production in the colony began on a large scale. Indigo production seemingly continued and even expanded despite the British parliament's imposition of a duty of 3s. 6d. on indigo in 1670.[27] By 1672, there were about sixty indigo manufactories in Middlesex County alone producing some 50,000 pounds a year.[28] In 1687–88 and 1688–89, Jamaica exported to England 110,116 pounds and 132,704 pounds of indigo, respectively.[29] Exports increased in the following decade. During 1698–99 and 1699–1700, average annual exports exceeded 202,600 pounds. Over the next three decades, Jamaica's average annual exports of indigo to Britain exceeded 166,600 pounds (Table 4.2).[30] In addition to its own production, Jamaica also exported large quantities of indigo that it obtained from Spanish and French colonies in exchange for slaves and clothes. Exports of Spanish indigo to England were fairly large between 1721 and 1725, when average annual exports exceeded 250,000 pounds. In the 1730s, exports from Jamaica of both its locally

TABLE 4.2 *Ten-yearly average annual imports (in lb.) of American indigo into Great Britain, 1701–1780*

Year	Jamaica	Carolina	Total
1701–10	194,563	—	242,274
1711–20	136,656	—	307,721
1721–30	168,614	—	551,203
1731–40	39,047	6,908	331,692
1741–50	94,395	63,157	691,145
1751–60	63,443	307,179	912,913
1761–70	46,084	453,153	1,392,985
1771–80	113,164	882,279	1,132,156

SOURCE: NA, KEW, CUST/3/5-80, CUSTOMS RECORDS FOR 1701–1780.

27 G. Terry Sharrer, 'The Indigo Bonanza in South Carolina, 1740–90', *Technology and Culture*, vol. 12, no. 3 (1971), 447.

28 Daurel Alden, 'The Growth and Decline of Indigo Production in Colonial Brazil', *Journal of Economic History*, vol. 35 (1965), 41.

29 Ibid., 42. It was reported in 1692 that about seventy percent of Britain's total imports of American indigo in the preceding four years came from Jamaica. NA, Kew, CO 138/7, 11 Oct. 1692.

30 In some years, exports were fairly large. In 1704, it exported some 250,000 pounds to England whose sale value was £93,750. NA, Kew, CO 137/6, No., 34 and CO 138/11, pp. 107–8. The average for the years 1726–1730 was 283,779 pounds.

produced and Spanish/French indigo rapidly declined. The average annual exports of Jamaica indigo and Spanish/French indigo to Britain during 1731–1740 were about 39,000 pounds and 87,392 pounds, respectively. Indigo exports from Jamaica increased starting in the 1740s, but then Britain's mainland American colony of South Carolina emerged as a major producer for the home market.

In the second half of the eighteenth century, Jamaica remained a minor supplier and in some years—1771–72, 1774–75, and 1778–79, for example—indigo exports were substantial.[31] In the 1780s, average annual British imports of indigo from Jamaica and the West Indies exceeded 142,000 pounds (Table 4.3). Thereafter, however, imports rapidly declined. Jamaica's exports of indigo to England in the eighteenth century consisted mainly of Spanish and French indigo. It was reported in 1758 that almost all indigo that left Jamaica was grown in French or Spanish colonies.[32] This was despite several attempts by the government to restrict Jamaica's intra-Caribbean trade by prohibiting trade

TABLE 4.3 *Five-yearly average annual imports (in lb.) of indigo into Great Britain, 1782–96*

Place	1782–86	1787–91	1792–96
Holland (Java)	35,422	15,929	25,218
France (WI colony)	—	72,504	17,310
Portugal (Brazil)	56,984	98,387	67,146
British America	576,246	749,026	691,170
British West Indies	142,429	66,929	34,866
India (Bengal)	152,690	470,805	1,917,561
Spain (Guatemala)	314,473	293,484	305,523
Others	97,949	112,949	24,699
Total	1,376,193	1,880,013	3,083,493

SOURCE: BL, HOME MISCELLANEOUS, 499, SELECTION OF PAPERS REGARDING THE EAST INDIA COMPANY'S COMMERCIAL CONCERNS, PP. 57–9.

31 Total exports to Britain in these years were 221,602 pounds, 209,915 pounds, and 169,820 pounds respectively.

32 In the second half of the eighteenth century, Jamaica exported large quantities of French indigo from Saint-Domingue's southern provinces to Great Britain. Garrigus, 'Blue and Brown', 245–6. In 1774, it exported 131,400 pounds of indigo to Great Britain and Ireland. *An Abridgment of Mr. Edward's Civil and Commercial History of the British West Indies*, vol. 1, (London: J. Parsons, Paternoster-Row, and J. Bell, 1794), 119–20.

with Spanish and French colonies and imposing higher duties on goods from non-British American colonies.[33]

Britain also obtained some indigo supplies from its other colonies. Antigua, Barbados, and Montserrat were important suppliers of indigo in the early eighteenth century. In 1671, the governor of the Leeward Islands wrote to the Council of Plantations that Antigua had the potential to replace East Indian indigo.[34] In the 1720s, New England and New York produced large quantities for the home market. In 1776, Britain imported some 27,638 pounds from Grenada and its dependencies. Subsequently, however, production rapidly declined as the imports from this colony into Great Britain and Ireland in 1787 amounted to less than 3,000 pounds.[35] Planters in Jamaica and other British colonies in the West Indies gradually gave up indigo production in favour of other, possibly more profitable, agricultural crops such as sugar and coffee.[36]

In the 1740s, South Carolina became the most prominent British colony to produce indigo on a large scale.[37] Although, experiments with indigo production there had begun in the 1670s, it remained primarily a rice-producing colony. The War of Jenkins' Ear and King George's War (1744–48) disrupted South Carolina's rice trade and induced planters to turn to indigo as an alternative crop. The Seven Years' War (1756–63), which interrupted supplies of Spanish

---

33 As early as 1716, an act was passed in Jamaica that sought to prevent trade with foreign (mainly Spanish and French) territories. NA, Kew, CO 138/16, pp. 301–2. Merchants continued to trade with foreign territories in the Caribbean clandestinely. To stop this, the governor of Jamaica proposed the British government to subject all Spanish and French indigo imported into Jamaica to a high duty. NA, Kew, CO 5/1265, Lt. Governor Keith to the Council of Trade and Plantations, 25 Nov. 1717, pp. 89–90. In 1724–1725, British merchants trading with Jamaica complained that indigo planters turned to producing sugar because they were discouraged by large-scale indigo production by the French in Hispaniola. NA, Kew, CO 388/24, no. 145, Merchants Trading to Jamaica to the Council of Trade and Plantations, 31 May, 1724. In England, indigo from foreign countries was subjected to higher duties than indigo from British plantations. NA, Kew, CO 137/14, ff. 1^{b}, 2^{b}. NA, Kew, CO 5/1265, nos. 89 and 89/i; CO 5/1293, pp. 134–5.

34 NA, Kew, CO 1/27, no. 52, Governor of Leeward Islands to the Council of Plantations, 9 Dec. 1671.

35 *An Abridgment of Mr. Edward's Civil and Commercial History*, 261, 267.

36 *Reports and Documents connected with the Proceedings of the East India Company in regard to the Culture and Manufacture of Cotton-Wool, Raw Silk, and Indigo in India* (London: J.L. Cox and Sons, 1836), iii. Bryan Edward attributes the decline in Jamaica's indigo culture to the high duties imposed on indigo exports. This was deliberately done in order to encourage sugar production on the island. Bryan Edward, *The History Civil and Commercial of the British Colonies in the West Indies* (London: John Stockdale, 1801), 335.

37 For a detailed description of the indigo production processes in South Carolina see, Sharrer, 'The Indigo Bonanza in South Carolina', 448–53.

and French indigo into Europe, provided further incentives to Carolina planters to exploit market opportunities in Britain and Europe, where the demand for indigo in the expanding textile industry was on the rise. Like the colonies in the Caribbean, agriculture in South Carolina was based on slave labour and, therefore, European plantation owners could quickly turn to indigo, which had become more profitable than rice.[38] Plenty of cultivable land made it possible for South Carolina planters to combine indigo production with the cultivation of rice or other subsistence crops within the same plantation. Indigo complemented the rice economy as planters could grow rice on low-lying, swampy land and indigo on higher sandy land.[39] Such circumstances favoured South Carolina and indigo from there became the colony's principal export to Britain, and it soon emerged as British America's largest indigo supplier to Europe.[40] In the 1740s, several essays and pamphlets on indigo production were published and were accessible to Carolinian planters. The literature not only convinced them of the commercial benefits of indigo, but also served as a useful guide to indigo production and manufacture.[41] The indigo industry in Carolina also benefitted from the bounty of 6d. per pound that Britain allowed on all indigo directly imported from its American colonies through an act of parliament passed

38 For a recent study of the role of slavery and race in the making of the South Carolina indigo, see Andreas Feeser, *Red, White, and Black Make Blue: Indigo in the Fabric of Colonial South Carolina Life* (Athens: University of Georgia Press, 2013).

39 David J. McCreery, 'Indigo Commodity Chains in the Spanish and British Empires, 1560–1860', in Steven Topik, Zephyr Frank and Carlos Marichal (eds), *From Silver to Cocaine: Latin American Commodity Chains and the Building of the World Economy, 1500–2000* (Durham: Duke University Press, 2006), 56; Scott David Edelson, 'Colour and Enterprise: South Carolina Indigo and the Atlantic Economy, 1745–1795' (PhD thesis, Lincoln College, University of Oxford, 1994).

40 In 1747, exports from the colony exceeded 150,000 pounds. David L. Coon, 'Eliza Lucas Pinckney and the Reintroduction of Indigo in South Carolina', *The Journal of Southern History*, vol. 42, no. 1 (1976), 70–1. In the 1760s, Carolina indigo amounted to about one-fourth of the total indigo imports into Europe. R.C. Nash, 'South Carolina Indigo, European Textiles, and the British Atlantic Economy in the Eighteenth Century', *Economic History Review*, vol. 63, no. 2 (2010), 363–6. On the eve of the American Revolution, annual indigo exports from South Carolina exceeded 1.1 million pounds. Alden, 'The Growth and Decline of Indigo Production in Colonial Brazil', 45.

41 Coon, 'Eliza Lucas Pinckney and the Reintroduction of Indigo', 71–5. Carolina's French immigrants, some of whom were indigo experts, contributed to the colony's successful indigo enterprise. Arthur H. Hirsch, 'French Influence on American Agriculture in the Colonial Period with Special Reference to Southern Provinces', *Agricultural History*, vol. 4, no. 1 (1930), 8–9. See also, 'Letter from Mrs. Charles Pinckney to Harriott Horry', annotated by Joseph W. Barnwell, *The South Carolina Historical and Genealogical Magazine*, vol. 17, no. 3 (1916), 101–2.

in 1748.[42] Exports from South Carolina to Britain consequently increased. In 1775, London Customs House officials reported that indigo imports from South Carolina and Georgia expanded so much that it satisfied English demand and large quantities were available for re-export to the Dutch Republic, Germany, Russia, and other countries.[43] Britain, nevertheless, continued to import indigo from other sources, especially Guatemala indigo through Spain. Between 1782 and 1796, about one-fourth of the total average annual indigo imports into Britain came through Holland, France, Spain, and Portugal (Table 4.3). During the American Revolution, South Carolina lost its major market, which adversely affected the indigo industry there. Exports to Britain dropped from an annual average of 1.32 million pounds during 1773–1775 to about 34,000 pounds in 1776–1777. Consequently, Britain's total average annual indigo imports from the Americas decreased from 1.6 million pounds during 1771–75 to mere 640,000 pounds during 1776–1780. During the revolution, some South Carolina indigo found its way to England through Spanish Florida, from where average annual exports rose to over 130,000 pounds during 1775–78 from an average of less than 16,000 pounds in the preceding five years.[44] The indigo industry in South Carolina, as also in Georgia, seemingly revived soon after the American Revolution, and Britain continued getting large quantities of it. Between 1783 and 1795, South Carolina's average annual exports exceeded 596,000 pounds.[45] In 1785, EIC authorities in London instructed company officials in Bengal not to send any poor-quality indigo because, they wrote, 'there is annually a great supply of Carolina indigo at low prices which will answer the same purposes and which from the low freight and small expense attending the importation will always have an advantage over any of the like qualities imported by us'.[46] In the 1790s as well, the EIC apprehended the adverse consequences of large imports of Carolina, Georgia, and Mississippi indigo into Britain on its trade from Bengal.[47] But once the EIC gave up its monopoly of the indigo trade in 1788, large volumes of

42 Alexander Hewatt, *An Historical Account of the Rise and Progress of the Colonies of South Carolina and Georgia*, vol. 2 (London: Alexander Donaldson, 1779), 139. Edelson, 'Colour and Enterprise', 30–33, 40.

43 NA, Kew, T 1/516, Report on papers related to the mode of allowing the bounty on indigo, London, 22 Nov. 1775, ff. 238a–239a.

44 NA, Kew, CUST 3/70-78, Imports into Britain, 1697–1785.

45 Average annual exports prior to the American Revolution amounted to about 416,500 pounds. Edelson, 'Colour and Enterprise', table 11, South Carolina indigo exports, 1747–1800.

46 BL, East India Company Correspondence with India, 628, Dispatches to Bengal, 11 April 1785, p. 608.

47 BL, Board's Collections: collections of papers in support of East India Company Draft Dispatches, 1796–1858 (hereafter Board's Collections), 60, doc. no. 1369, Extract proceedings of the Board of Trade in Bengal, 28 Oct. 1796, pp. 123–4.

indigo began to be exported by private European merchants whose main interest was the remittance of funds from the colony and who were not much concerned with the equations of demand and supplies in the home market. By the end of the century, therefore, large imports from Bengal almost completely replaced Carolina indigo in Britain and the European market. Consequently, most Carolina and Georgia planters switched to cotton, which had become more lucrative and the European market for which was rapidly expanding.[48]

Even though, Britain obtained large supplies of indigo from its transatlantic colonies, the poor quality of the dye was a continuous concern. Adulteration was another source of irritation, and voices were raised against it. In the early 1690s, an act was passed in Montserrat, and endorsed by the queen that sought to prevent the making and receiving of adulterated indigo.[49] Indigo from Jamaica and South Carolina, being inferior in quality to that from the Spanish and French American colonies, was used mainly by the dyers of coarse cotton and linen textiles. Dyers and finishers of high-quality woollen and silk clothes grew disenchanted with the poor quality and became increasingly dependent on the supplies of French and Spanish colonial indigo.[50] In Britain, in the eighteenth century, several experiments were carried out with different plant species to find out if the type of plant determined the yield and quality. These showed that the quality and purity of indigo depended on, apart from the type of plant, the precision with which manufacturing procedures were carried out. Measures were accordingly recommended to indigo producers for improving the quality.[51] The problem, however, never seems to have been resolved. Even in the 1830s, the quality of indigo manufactured in the United States was reportedly much inferior to the dyestuffs from Bengal or elsewhere.[52]

---

48 Sharrer, 'The Indigo Bonanza in South Carolina', 455.

49 NA, Kew, CO 153/4, Order of the Queen in Council, 28 May 1691, pp. 335–6. In pursuance of this act, the Council of Assembly of Montserrat ordered seizure and destruction of adulterated indigo. NA, Kew, CO 155/1, Minutes of Council of Assembly of Montserrat, 1 Feb. 1694; ibid., 7 April 1694, pp. 326–7.

50 English dyers and textile manufacturers were so much used to Spanish indigo that they were alarmed at the slightest threat of war and even advocated continuation of trade in times of war. Jean O. McLachlan, *Trade and Peace with Old Spain, 1667–1750* (Cambridge: CUP, 1940), 10.

51 James Crokatt and Edward Leigh, *Observations concerning indigo and cochineal* (London, 1746); James Crokatt, *Further observations intended for improving the culture and curing of indigo and c. in South Carolina* (London, 1747), 1–25; John Ledyard, *Methods for improving the manufacture of indigo: originally submitted to the consideration of the Carolina planters and now published for the benefit of all the British colonies whose situation is favorable to the culture of indigo* (London, 1776).

52 William Partridge, 'On the Manufacturing of Indigo in the United States', *Silliman's Journal*, vol. 6, no. 3 (1830), 193–8.

British concern about the loss of money in buying foreign—whether French, Spanish, or Indian—indigo kept up their quest to obtain indigo supplies from the colonies. In 1671, the governor of the Leeward Islands observed that Antigua's indigo would induce the British government to prohibit imports of East India indigo, which 'rob England of money'.[53] Pamphlets and publications urged the colonies' indigo manufacturers to pay attention to quality and to produce the best indigo they could in order to replace all other varieties in the home market. The author of a pamphlet calculated the average annual indigo consumption in England in 1745 at about 680,000 pounds and wished that South Carolina could supply a good proportion of that. This was possible, the author believed, if planters were careful to produce indigo comparable in quality with those of the French colonies.[54] Another account holds that, around the middle of the eighteenth century, Britain annually consumed about 600,000 pounds of French indigo, at a cost to the nation of some £150,000 per year.[55] Merchants and dyers bewailed the planters' failure to meet their requirements. The mercantilist ambitions of the Britons to obtain indigo from their colonies and thereby stop the loss of money in buying the commodity from others prompted the EIC to promote indigo production on a large scale in its colonial possessions in India in the last quarter of the eighteenth century.

Indigo from Spanish, French, and Portuguese Colonies in America

The Spaniards pioneered the production of commercial indigo in the Americas. Right after the establishment of their colonies in the New World, the Spanish settlers of Guatemala and El Salvador began to produce indigo on a large scale.[56] The primary motivation for this was, as some recent

53 NA, Kew, CO 1/27, no. 52, Governor of the Leeward Islands to the Council of Plantations, 9 Dec. 1671.

54 Between 1734 and 1745, average annual imports of indigo into England amounted to 681,806 lb., but discounting the inflated reporting at the customs house, the author puts the average consumption at 500,000 lb. a year. Crokatt, *Further observations*, pp. ii, 2.

55 Hewatt, *An Historical Account of the Rise and Progress of the Colonies*, 139. Even in the late eighteenth century, Britain imported large quantities of Spanish-American indigo. Average annual imports between 1782 and 1796 exceeded 304,000 pounds. BL, Home Miscellaneous, 449, Selection of papers exhibiting a view of the East India Company's commercial concerns, pp. 57–9.

56 Spain received substantial quantities of indigo during 1580–1595 from Honduras and New Spain, which indicates that the industry was rather well-establish in the sixteenth century. Between 1606 and 1620, annual imports from the colony averaged 250,000 pounds. Robert

studies have shown, to substitute import of woad from other woad-growing European countries like France and Germany. By the mid-sixteenth century, indigo was gaining popularity among dyers as a cheaper and better substitute for woad even though its use was subject to prohibition and criminal prosecution in several European countries. As was perhaps anticipated, indigo from Guatemala became a better substitute for woad to Spanish dyers and its large-scale imports contributed to the decline of the woad industry elsewhere in Europe.

The native Maya knew the plant and were familiar with the art of extracting indigo, and by the mid-sixteenth century, European settlers were involved in its production. Plenty of suitable land was available, but the shortage of labour and capital was a serious obstacle to the growth of the industry.[57] In view of health hazards involved in indigo production, planters were not allowed to employ native Indians on their farms and the available slaves and mulatto and mestizo labourers were not as suitable or efficient as the native Indians for the kind of work indigo production required.[58] Despite prohibitions and punitive measures adopted by the crown, some planters employed Maya anyway. Data on production and exports of Guatemalan indigo for the sixteenth and seventeenth centuries is not available, but given that it replaced the substantial imports of Bayana and Sarkhej indigo in European markets in the 1650s, and that the colonial economy of Guatemala was based on indigo, and paid for all its imports, it is clear that production was rather substantial in the seventeenth and early eighteenth centuries. From the mid-eighteenth century, indigo production increased rapidly as a result of the lifting of the ban on the employment of Maya labour in 1738 and the reforms introduced by the Spanish monarchy, as well as other initiatives of indigo merchants, who had recently begun relocating from Spain to the colonies.[59] By the late 1770s, indigo culture in Guatemala had attained full growth and the commodity had come to dominate the agrarian economy. Average annual indigo exports into Spain in the last quarter of century varied from about 600,000 pounds to 1,200,000

S. Smith, 'Indigo Production and Trade in Colonial Guatemala', *The Hispanic American Historical Review*, vol. 39, no. 2 (1959), 197.

57 Idem, 'Statutes of the Guatemalan Indigo Growers' Society', *The Hispanic American Historical Review*, vol. 30, no. 3 (1950), 336; idem, 'Forced Labour in Guatemalan Indigo Works', *The Hispanic American Historical Review*, vol. 36, no. 3 (1956), 319.

58 The prohibition came from the colonial government and it had the approval of the crown as early as 1563. Idem, 'Indigo Production and Trade in Colonial Guatemala'; idem, 'Forced Labour in Guatemalan Indigo Works', 319.

59 Troy S. Floyd, 'The Indigo Merchant: Promoter of Central American Economic Development, 1750–1808', *Business History Review*, vol. 39, no. 4 (1965), 466–88.

pounds (Figure 4.2). In the early nineteenth century, indigo production in Guatemala was still substantial, although it was gradually declining. A number of circumstances precipitated the decline, the most important of which was the competition that Guatemala indigo had come to face in Europe with imports from Spain's other possessions and from the Dutch East Indies and British India.[60] High taxation on indigo sales in Guatemala, which amounted to some 25 percent of the price, and the cost of exporting it to England and Holland, the two major markets, amounting to about 20 percent, made it impossible for merchants to sell it at competitive prices in Europe.[61] By the time the government was persuaded to reduce production and trade taxes as measures to make Guatemala indigo competitive and thereby save the declining industry, the colony was in the grips of a national revolution. With independence from Spain in 1821, Guatemala indigo lost its European market forever. The government abolished the Indigo Growers' Society in 1826, and by the end of the decade the indigo industry came to an end. By then, the centre of indigo production had shifted from Guatemala to what became El Salvador, where it continued to be produced on a substantial scale in the 1820s and 1830s. In 1826, it exported about 1,200,000 pounds but dropped to 873,750 pounds in 1834 due to labour problems and uprisings.[62]

Since the beginning, indigo from Guatemala was universally recognized as the best in European market and was always a point of reference when merchants and dyers compared the quality of indigo from elsewhere. It was because of this superior quality that Guatemala indigo could successfully compete with all other indigo in Europe despite its high prices due to relative disadvantages in transportation costs and the availability of labour and capital.[63] What made it so good in quality? This remains unexplained in the sources and the literature. Guatemala indigo came in as many types and grades as

60 Spain received about 3 million pounds of indigo from its colony of Caracas during 1793–96 and during 1797–1800, exports from this colony amounted to 792,210 pounds. Smith, 'Indigo Production and Trade in Colonial Guatemala', 208–9. Britain's large-scale imports of Bengal indigo 'heralded the end of the uncompetitive market in Europe' and the locust plagues in 1801, and intermittently throughout the decade, devastated the crop and caused a 50 percent reduction in production. Floyd, 'The Indigo Merchant', 484.

61 About 80 percent of indigo that Spain received from Guatemala was re-exported to textile production centres of England and Holland. Smith, 'Indigo Production and Trade in Colonial Guatemala', 200.

62 Christopher M. White, *The History of El Salvador* (Westport: Greenwood Press, 2009), 52–6.

63 Robert S. Smith has examined in detail the issues of labour and capital in the Guatemala indigo industry. Smith, 'Indigo Production and Trade in Colonial Guatemala'.

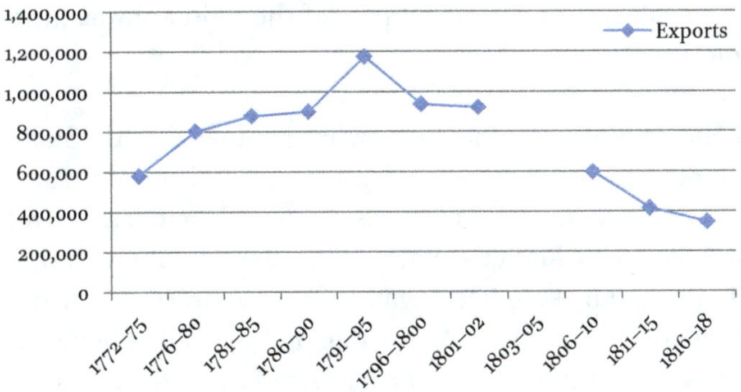

FIGURE 4.2 *Five-yearly average annual exports (in lb.) of Guatemala indigo to Europe, 1772–1818*
SOURCE: BASED ON FIGURES FROM SMITH, 'INDIGO PRODUCTION AND TRADE IN COLONIAL GUATEMALA', 197–8.

indigo from any other place. There were three main grades: the best (*flor*), middling (*sobrestiente*), and ordinary (*corte*), each of which was further classified into various subgrades depending on purity and colour. More than 90 percent of total exports in the 1790s consisted of the ordinary sort and the share of the best-quality indigo varied between 2.5 and 6.2 percent.[64] In general, the quality was much better than indigo from other sources. Climate, quality of water, type of plant, and precision with which manufacturing processes were carried out, it seems, contributed to the superior quality of Guatemala indigo. In 1796, EIC authorities in London laid out the structure of the British demand for indigo and the share of Guatemala indigo in it. They wrote,

> [A] proper assortment of indigo for the general demand should consist of about equal proportion of fine, middling and ordinary. The fine has hitherto been almost exclusively furnished by Spain, who have always been remarkably attentive as to quality and it is with regret we perceive, they are still extending their concerns, the imports from thence in the last year having exceeded considerably those of former periods. The middling was mostly supplied by the French which was completely supplanted by the

64 Ibid., 185. Miles Wortman attributes the decline of Guatemala indigo in European markets since the late 1780s to producers' greed and large-scale production of lesser-quality indigo. Miles Wortman, 'Government Revenue and Economic Trends in Central America, 1787–1819', *The Hispanic American Historical Review*, vol. 55, no. 2 (1975), 557–9.

> production of Bengal; and the principal part of the ordinary was introduced from America.[65]

The next best, and the only variety that somewhat competed with Guatemala in European markets in the eighteenth century, was indigo from Saint-Domingue (Haiti). In the second half of the seventeenth and eighteenth centuries, Saint-Domingue was France's major transatlantic colony and its slave-based plantation economy supplied sugar, coffee, cotton, and indigo in large quantities to France and Europe.[66] As the demand for indigo increased in France in the eighteenth century, production accelerated and the island became France's most important source of indigo. A part of what France received from there was re-exported to Britain and other parts of Europe. In the mid-eighteenth century, Britain alone consumed some 600,000 pounds annually and considerable exports of French colonial products, such as indigo, sugar, and coffee, to Germany, Holland, and Italy were reported in the 1760s.[67] In 1770, Saint-Domingue reportedly produced about 2 million pounds of indigo, and between 1783 and 1789 annual production varied from 1.86 to 0.93 million pounds.[68] As these figures indicate, production began to decline in the early 1780s and within a few years it fell by fifty percent.

Unlike the indigo monoculture in Guatemala, the dynamic agrarian economy of Saint-Domingue produced a variety of commercial crops. In the eighteenth century, a large proportion of sugar, coffee, cotton, and indigo supplied to Europe came from this colony. The production of coffee and sugar was already rapidly increasing in the last quarter of the century. When indigo production began to decline in the 1780s, the newly available land and slave labour were quickly employed in producing other commercial crops, which were equally or more profitable. In a letter to Bengal in 1792, the EIC's Court of Directors noted that Saint-Domingue produced about 5 million pounds of coffee and 2 million pounds of indigo in 1770 and it produced 76 million pounds of coffee and less than one million pounds of indigo in 1789.[69] The decline in

65 BL, Board's Collections, 60, doc. no. 1369, State of the Indigo Manufacture etc., Extract of Commercial letter to Bengal, 27 July 1796, p. 43.

66 France's another colony in America, Louisiana produced indigo on a fairly large scale in the eighteenth century. Jack D.L. Holmes, 'Indigo in Colonial Louisiana and the Floridas', *Louisiana History: The Journal of the Louisiana Historical Association*, vol. 8, no. 4 (1967), 329–49.

67 NA, Kew, SP 78/271, Rochford's report from Paris, 1766, ff. 201[a]–[b].

68 BL, Board's Collections, 60, doc. no. 1369, Extract Court's Commercial Letter to Bengal, 30 May 1792, pp. 9–10.

69 Ibid., pp. 9–10.

indigo production happened at the time when Europe had begun to receive large quantities of indigo from colonial India and Java, and these Asian varieties were fast replacing American indigo in Europe. A report compiled in 1792 noted that, 'in proportion as the imports from Bengal have increased, there has been a diminution from other parts. The consumption of the French indigo in this country [England] is in a manner entirely supplanted by that from Bengal'.[70] About the same time, slave rebellions and political crisis caused major restructuring of Saint-Domingue's agrarian economy. War and revolution disrupted indigo production and exports and the new political economy of Haiti (formerly Saint-Domingue) in the early nineteenth century induced planters to produce more lucrative crops like coffee and cocoa.[71]

In the second half of the eighteenth century, Portugal also sought to find an alternative source of indigo in South America.[72] Attempts were made in the 1750s and 1760s to produce indigo in Brazil for home and European markets, primarily to substitute imports from other countries, particularly Spain, with which Portugal had territorial disputes, and to generate revenues for the state by exporting surpluses to other countries.[73] It was a slave-based plantation, but unlike all other indigo producing colonies, indigo production in Brazil was in private hands while trade was a state monopoly, a model that the EIC would follow in Bengal in the 1780s. It was a crown-sponsored enterprise and all manufacturers were to deliver indigo to the government at a fixed price for export to Portugal on royal account. Because of this monopoly, no private merchants invested in indigo and the industry depended entirely on the government's financial support. The model seems to have worked quite well in the 1780s and 1790s when large quantities of Brazil indigo were exported to Lisbon. According to Charles Boxer, 'there were 206 establishments processing the indigo produced on plantations in the region of Cape Frio, and the captaincy's

70 Ibid.

71 Willem van Schendel, 'Asianization of Indigo: Rapid Change in Global Trade around 1800', Peter Boomgaard, Dick Kooiman and Henk Schulte-Nordholt, *Linking Destinies: Trade, Towns and Kin in Asian History* (Leiden: KITLV Press, 2008). Diversification of crops in Saint-Domingue was a part of the recent trend in America i.e., 'the economy of abundance' that advocated diversity of agricultural production. The Spanish American colonies too experienced this transformation contributing to the circumstances that led to the end of the 'indigo-age'. Floyd, 'The Indigo Merchant', 485.

72 Not much has been written on the Portuguese indigo enterprise in Brazil or its other colonies. Lack of literature in English restricts any analysis at length of the significance of indigo from Portuguese colonies and its impact on the world indigo market in the eighteenth and early nineteenth centuries.

73 Alden, 'The Growth and Decline of Indigo Production in Colonial Brazil', 48.

total output had reached 5,000 *arrobas* in 1796'.[74] Since Portugal's dyeing industry was not as big as those of Britain, the Dutch Republic, France, and German and Italian city states, a large quantity of indigo was re-exported to these countries.[75] Average annual exports to Britain alone approximated 75,000 pounds between 1782 and 1796.[76] In the early years of the nineteenth century, however, production declined, partly for lack of incentives and financial support from the government to indigo manufacturers, and partly because of the disruption of trade during the Napoleonic Wars and the French occupation of Portugal, as well as the general interruption of trade in Europe in this period.[77] By the end of the 1820s, the indigo industry ceased to exit.

The Nineteenth-century Indigo Commodity Chains

In the nineteenth century, it is true that the Indian indigo industry dwarfed all other commodity chains and caused the rapid decline and even disappearance of many. Many indigo chains, however, held on and complemented and competed with Indian or other indigo in the world market. The Dutch had finally succeeded in finding a South-east Asian alternative in Java from where they secured large quantities from 1830 onward (Table 4.1 above). Although, the United States imported substantial quantities of Bengal indigo, they also produced some of their own for domestic consumption. In Guatemala, government and indigo manufacturers and merchants took measures to revive the indigo industry, which delayed the disappearance of Guatemala indigo industry by at least a quarter of a century. However, it was another Spanish colony, the Philippines, where the industry actually flourished in the nineteenth century and from where indigo came to be exported in large quantities to Spain, China, India and West Asia, and also to the United States.[78] Siam too emerged as a

---

74 C.R. Boxer, *The Portuguese Seaborne Empire, 1415–1825* (London: Hutchinson & Co., 1969), 196–7. *Arroba* was a unit of weight equal to about 32 pounds.

75 In 1786–87, imports were large and Portugal re-exported 118,328 pounds of this indigo to other European countries. In 1796 indigo imports from Brazil into Portugal amounted to 264,768 pounds. Boxer, *The Portuguese Seaborne Empire*, 55–6.

76 BL, Home Miscellaneous, 499, Selection of papers regarding the East India Company's commercial concerns, pp. 57–9.

77 Alden, 'The Growth and Decline of Indigo Production in Colonial Brazil'. Charles Boxer attributes the decline to its poor quality and, therefore, inability to compete with indigo imports from colonial India. Boxer, *The Portuguese Seaborne Empire*, 196–7.

78 John Phipps, *A Series of Treatise on the Principal Products of Bengal: 1 Indigo* (Calcutta: Baptist Mission, 1832), 48, 180. According to an estimate, Manila exported 400–500 ton

major producer and supplier of indigo primarily for China in the nineteenth century.

After losing Saint-Domingue in 1804, France came to depend heavily on supplies of indigo from British India and Java colonies. It tried to develop new sources of indigo in its colonies in India and Africa. In the 1820s, they sought to replicate the Indian system of indigo production in Senegal. They collected information on indigo plants and methods of cultivation and processing for guidance to the planters in Senegal.[79] They sent indigo seeds from India to be sown there. Even though the dyeing industry was well advanced in western Africa, the French in Senegal were unsuccessful in producing good-quality indigo on a large scale. As late as 1855, the French were complaining about the poor quality of indigo from Senegal but were quite optimistic that the industry could be developed in the colony if production processes were carried out with much care and diligence.[80] In the nineteenth century, France bought most of its indigo from British Bengal, but it also received some from its colony, Pondicherry.[81] In this instance, as in the cases mentioned above, the purpose was to secure a product from the colony that would make France self-sufficient in indigo and also enable it to export to other markets in Europe and Asia. Imports from India almost entirely met the domestic demand and also enabled it to export some indigo to the Eastern Mediterranean regions.[82]

In their search for alternative sources of indigo in the nineteenth century, the Germans took a different path. Instead of exploring natural resources in the colonies, they had recourse to chemical and botanical sciences and

of indigo in 1797. Some US merchants were reportedly buying indigo in Manila for home market in 1796–97. Peabody Essex Museum Archives, Salem, Log 1302, 1796–1797, p. 235. I am thankful to David Doran for this reference.

79 The primary purpose of Paul Darrac's treatise on Bengal indigo was to pass on the indigo knowledge to the planters and manufacturers of Senegal. Pierre-Paul Darrac and Willem van Schendel, *Global Blue: Indigo and Espionage in Colonial Bengal* (Dhaka: The University Press Limited, 2006).

80 Chambre de Commerce Archives, Marseille, MP 327, Production and commerce in France, Note on indigo of Senegal, 24 June, 1857, pp. 1–4.

81 French Pondicherry and British Madras were rival exporters of indigo to Europe. Indigo is listed among other goods imported into Marseille in ships returning from Pondicherry and other ports on the Coromandel Coast. Archives Départementales des Bouches-du-Rhône [Departmental archives at Bouches-du-Rhône], Marseille, 200 E 604, Declaration of ships' cargoes, Marseille, 1851.

82 In the 1850s, the French were exporting indigo to Damascus (Syria). They were even contemplating sending it directly from Calcutta to Damascus via the Suez. Chambre de Commerce Archives, Marseille, MP 327, Letter of the Ministry of Agriculture and Commerce to the Consul at the Republic of Damascus, Paris, 20 Feb. 1852.

laboratories and carried out experiments with new chemical sources of blue colour. After extensive trials and the expenditure of enormous amounts of money, they developed a synthetic substitute for indigo and launched the product in 1897 on the world market.[83] This was a major breakthrough in the history of the blue dye and had the most debilitating impact on the global natural indigo industry.

Quality and Profitability as Factors in Global Indigo Trade

From the sixteenth to nineteenth centuries, a vibrant world market existed in which indigo from various regions complemented and competed with each other. Each of the commodity chains discussed above was an outcome of a search for an alternative source of indigo to substitute for imports from other countries and to make colonies economically beneficial for the metropolis. Each was a product of a specific set of circumstances created through the dialectics of local and global political and economic forces. While some commodity chains like in Guatemala, India and Java, had longer lifespans during which they dominated the world market, the fortunes of many others did not last for more than a few decades. To what extent did the purely market economic forces of supply and demand cause the fluctuations in world indigo production and trade? Did the decline in production at one place lead to growth of the industry at another, or did less expensive, good-quality indigo from one place replace the expensive and poor varieties from another? In the literature, the quality and price competitiveness of indigo have generally been invoked to explain the rise and demise of the indigo industry. The loss of European demand for Indian indigo after the 1640s, for example, is generally attributed to the poor quality of indigo and its inability to compete with better, low-priced American indigo.[84] The success of Carolina indigo in the second half of the eighteenth century and the late-eighteenth century decline of Guatemala indigo are attributed to the former's price competitiveness and the latter's lack of it

83 In a recent study, Prakash Kumar has examined the processes that went into the making of synthetic indigo. Prakash Kumar, *Indigo Plantations and Science in Colonial India* (Cambridge: CUP, 2012), Chapters 4–5.

84 W.H. Moreland, *From Akbar to Aurangzeb: A Study in Indian Economic History* (London: Macmillan Press, 1923), 113–4; K.N. Chaudhuri, *The Trading World of Asia and the English East India Company, 1660–1760* (Cambridge: CUP, 1978); Holden Furber, *Rival Empires of Trade in the Orient, 1600–1800* (Minneapolis: University of Minnesota Press, 1976).

combined with its declining quality.[85] Similarly, the rapid growth in the indigo industry in Bengal in the late eighteenth and early nineteenth centuries is attributed to its high quality and the low prices at which it was sold in European and North American markets. It is also explained as the British response to the loss of American colonies and to the collapse of indigo production in Europe's former transatlantic colonies.[86] It is worth examining the role that quality and profitability played in the world indigo market.

Separated by thousands of miles from each other, the centres of indigo production around the world by and large followed the same manufacturing procedures. Yet, they produced indigo of varying qualities and catered to local and external demand that varied in terms of the quality sought by dyers and manufacturers and the prices they were willing to pay. To a large extent, the success of indigo enterprise depended on its quality, which determined its marketability. The quality of indigo from any given place was always judged by its purity of content, richness of colour, and dyeing capacity in comparison with indigo from another place. Quality was also directly proportional to yield. Producing the best-quality indigo was always expensive and, in view of the demand, most producers preferred greater output to better quality. Ordinary or low-quality indigo, therefore, comprised the largest proportion of the total indigo put on the market throughout the period under study.

As mentioned above, climate and manufacturers' care and meticulousness in carrying out production processes determined the quality, but the price at which the product would be sold depended on the costs of production, transportation, access to markets, and fees such as import and export duties. Wages paid to labourers constituted a major component of the production costs, hence, the availability of abundant and cheap labour and producers' control over it gave some regions advantages over others and enabled them to market their produce at competitive prices.[87] Distance from markets and the expense

85 Floyd, 'The Indigo Merchant', 484; Wortman, 'Government Revenue and Economic Trends', 259.

86 Boxer, *The Portuguese Seaborne Empire*, 197; Van Schendel, 'Asianisation of indigo'.

87 Abundance of cheap labour was always a major consideration in exploring the possibilities of indigo production. Availability of cheap labour, thus, inspired the VOC to promote indigo production in Siam and Java and contributed to the success of British-led Bengal indigo production from the seventeenth to the nineteenth century. Planters in the American colonies, on the contrary, had to confront situations when labour shortages impeded the enterprise. Their control over slave labour gave them some advantages over their Indian counterparts who could not exercise similar control over labour. But, once slaves rebelled in the early nineteenth century and slave trade became illegal, the entire indigo production system collapsed.

of transportation added to the costs and had to be accommodated in the price. Finally, and perhaps more important, the costs of accessing the market—whether buying protection from the local and imperial administration, or paying export and import duties—raised costs and thus prices.

In the period under review, indigo travelled varying distances and producers worked with different forms of labour—family/household labour, wage workers, bonded and slave labour. Each region that produced commercial indigo was successful at one time or another and failed only when a better-quality indigo from another region was put on market at a competitive price. This was particularly so when demand did not keep pace with augmented supplies from various quarters. The European market for indigo was saturated by the 1640s, and any further supplies were bound to create competition.[88] Large supplies of Guatemala indigo in the late 1640s and 1650s, thus, adversely affected the sale of Indian indigo in Britain, as the falling sale prices of Bayana and Sarkhej indigo indicate (Figure 4.3). Purchase prices in India began rising in the 1630s, and this rendered imports of Indian indigo less profitable in Europe (Figure 4.4).[89]

Indigo prices in India rose sharply in the 1630s. The average purchase price of Bayana indigo went up from 16 stivers per Dutch pound during 1621–30 to 28 stivers per Dutch pound during 1631–40, and that of Sarkhej indigo more than doubled, from 10 stivers to 21 stivers per Dutch pound, in the same periods. W.H. Moreland's price data on Sarkhej indigo between 1609 and 1663 show that the prices were high for much of the 1630s and 1640s.[90] Droughts and famines disrupted indigo production in Gujarat between 1630 and 1632 and the Mughal imperial indigo monopoly of 1633–34 raised the prices and temporarily interrupted trade. These developments prompted the Europeans to look elsewhere for indigo supplies. Their imports of Guatemala indigo, consequently, increased after the end of the Thirty Years' War in 1648. In terms of price, this was the most expensive variety of indigo, but because of its superior quality, European dyers did not mind paying a high price. Later, European countries took measures to promote indigo production in the colonies and secure imports from there. Even though, indigo from those colonies could not match the quality of Guatemala indigo, lower costs of production and

88 According to K.N. Chaudhuri, the demand for indigo in Europe was limited and saturated as soon as indigo had replaced woad. Chaudhuri, *The Trading World of Asia*.

89 EIC officials in Surat noted that with the rise in costs of indigo in India, indigo prices at home declined to 4 shillings per pound of Bayana and 3 shilling and 4 pence per pound of Sarkhej indigo. *EFI 1646–50*, Ahmadabad to Surat, 19 March 1646, p. 32.

90 Moreland, *From Akbar to Aurangzeb*, 162–4.

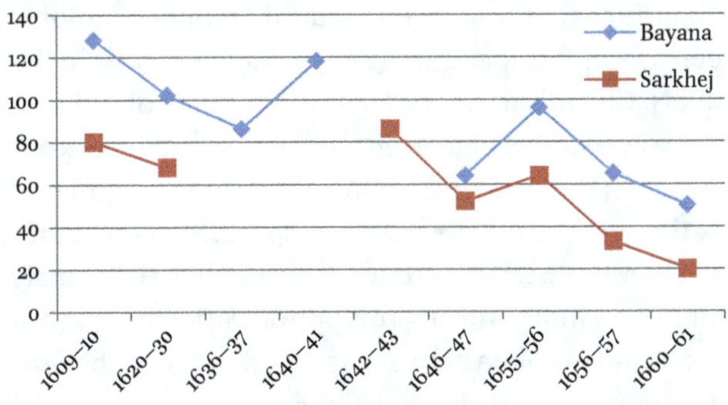

FIGURE 4.3 *Sale prices of Bayana and Sarkhej indigo in London (pence/lb.)*
SOURCE: BASED ON PRICES IN THE FOLLOWING TABLE 4.4.

TABLE 4.4 *Sale prices (per lb.) of Bayana and Sarkhej indigo in London*

1609–10	8s	5s
1620–30	6s-6s 6d	4s–4s 6d
1636–37	5s 6d	—
1640–41	7s 6d	—
1642–43	—	5s 6d
1646–47	4s	3s 4d
1655–56	6s	4s
1656–57	3s 10d–4s 1d	2s–2s 1d
1660–61	3s 2d	1s 4d

SOURCE: E/3/1, MORELAND, *FROM AKBAR TO AURANGZEB*, 111; BL, COURT MINUTES, 18, P. 280; BL, COURT MINUTES, 20, P. 216; BL, L/MAR/C/4, F. 170[b].

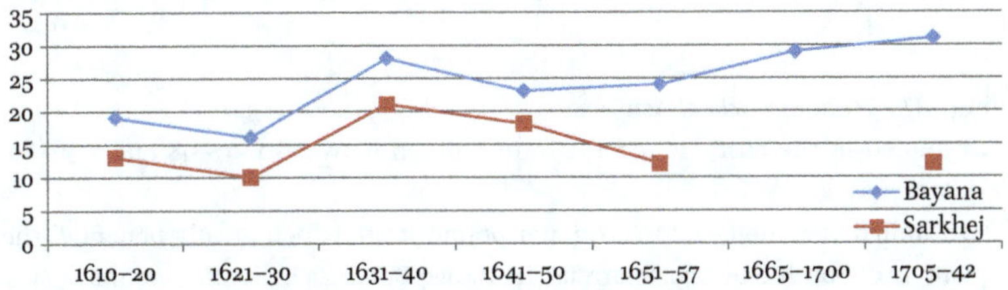

FIGURE 4.4 *Average annual prices (stivers/Dutch pound) of indigo in India, 1610–1742*
SOURCE: BASED ON PRICES IN APPENDIX 8.

transportation as well as bounties that it enjoyed certainly rendered colonial American indigo less expensive in Europe. Purchase prices were even higher in the eighteenth century. K.N. Chaudhuri has noted that the value of indigo in the mid-eighteenth century was twice as high as in the seventeenth century.[91]

Purchase prices of Indian and Jamaican or Carolina indigo in the eighteenth century were more or less the same, but if we take transportation, insurance, and handling costs into consideration, the differences may not have been insignificant. Purchase prices of Indian indigo during this period varied from 12d. to 16d. per pound that of Jamaica and Carolina between 12d. and 18d., and the price of Guatemala indigo ranged between 30d. and 36d. (2s. 6d. to 3s.) per pound.[92] A bounty of 6d. per pound (10–15 percent upon sale) that Carolina indigo enjoyed in London gave it a huge advantage over other varieties, especially those coming from long distances.[93] Despite sudden fluctuations in the sale prices of Indian indigo in European markets caused by expansion or contraction in production or supplies from elsewhere, the available sale prices for the first half of the eighteenth century indicate a downward trend. In the Dutch Republic, for example, the prices of Bayana indigo during the period 1696–1709 averaged 78.8 stivers (a little less than 4 guilders) per Dutch pound and those of Sarkhej averaged 44 stivers (2 guilders and 4 stivers) per Dutch pound, much lower than the average annual sale prices during the first half of the seventeenth century (Appendix 3). The average price of Sarkhej indigo from 1711 to 1747 was about 22 stivers (1 guilder 2 stivers) per Dutch pound. Indigo prices in London also declined in the course of the seventeenth century, from 5s. (60 pence) or more per pound for Bayana and 4s.–5s. per pound for Sarkhej indigo in the early seventeenth century to about 2s. per pound at the end of the century.[94]

The prices of Bengal indigo show an upward trend in the nineteenth century. Its average prices in Bombay, for example, rose from Rs 57 per *man* (of 41 *seer*) during 1812–17 to Rs 120 per *man* during 1820–27. Indigo prices in Calcutta too increased from Rs 121 per factory *man* (74.67 pounds) during 1843–1850 to Rs 277 during 1871–80 and Rs 256 per *man* in the following decade (Figure 4.5). Thereafter, prices went down, but even then they were much higher than the early nineteenth century prices. Indigo disturbances in Bengal in the late 1850s

91 Chaudhuri, *The Trading World of Asia*, 332–4.

92 Prices as quoted in the customs records from London between 1697–98 and 1779–80. NA, Kew, CUST/5.

93 All foreign indigo was subjected to a 6d. per pound tariff, which greatly benefited the indigo planters of South Carolina. Sharrer, 'The Indigo Bonanza in South Carolina', 454.

94 Chaudhuri, *The Trading World of Asia*, 332–3.

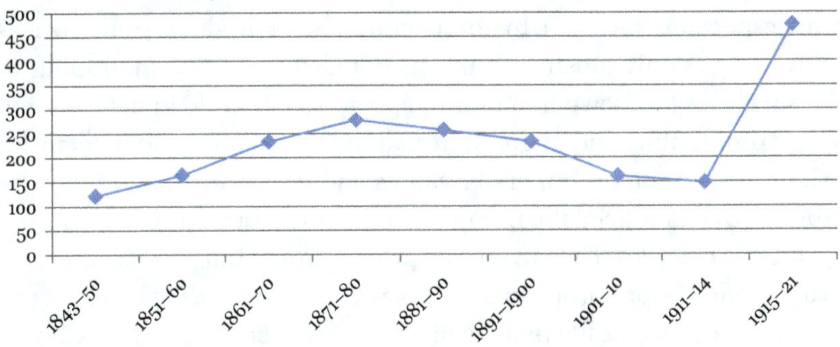

FIGURE 4.5 *Ten-yearly average annual indigo prices (Rs/factory* man) *in Calcutta, 1843–1921*

SOURCE: BASED ON CALCUTTA PURCHASE PRICES IN APPENDIX 9.

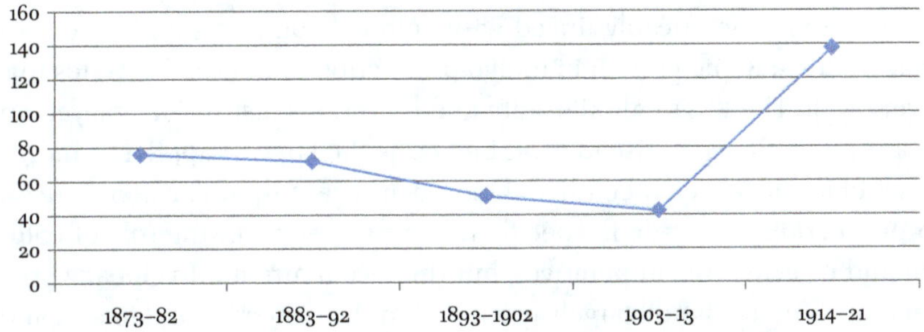

FIGURE 4.6 *Ten-yearly average annual prices (pence/lb.) of Bengal indigo in London, 1873–1921*

SOURCE: BASED ON LONDON SALE PRICES IN APPENDIX 9.

and early 1860s and comparatively higher costs of production in Bihar may have contributed to this price rise. The sale prices in London, on the other hand, declined from 6s. 3d. per pound during 1873–82 to 3s. 6d. per pound during 1903–13 (Figure 4.6). This was possibly caused by a substantial increase in imports of Indian indigo into Europe between the late 1860s and 1897. The average prices were low also because a good proportion of imports consisted of indigo of a comparatively poor quality from the Madras Presidency (see Table 3.6). Purchase prices in Calcutta and sale prices in London were unusually high due to a sudden increase in the global demand for indigo during the First World War (1914–18).

Quality, price competitiveness, and profitability were important factors in the global indigo trade and certainly played an important role in its success or failure as a trading commodity. But, the politico-economic imperatives of colonialism, especially the desire to obtain commercial products from the colonies that would not only substitute imports but also enable the metropolis to export the surpluses to elsewhere in Europe, played a key role in determining the price and profitability and, thereby, in shaping the commercial trajectories of indigo commodity chains. Imperial rivalries and the desire to dominate the intra-European trade induced the European powers to restructure the agrarian economy of their colonies. The large-scale production of indigo—as of tobacco, sugar, and coffee—for European markets, was an outcome of the strategies to make colonies economically beneficial for the mother country and stop or, at least minimize, the loss of money in buying these commodities from their European rivals.[95] Colonial imports were accorded with government favours, like bounties, lower customs, freight, and warehouse charges, to allow them to compete in the European market. The success or failure of the indigo trade in Europe was, thus, inextricably linked with colonial conquests and European imperial rivalries. Rapid growth in indigo production in Bengal illustrates this point very well. The EIC's colonial state and its various institutions played an important role in Bengal's rise to prominence as the largest supplier of indigo to the world in the late eighteenth and nineteenth centuries. The literature on indigo production and trade in specific regions underscores the role of colonialism and its economic imperatives, but the recent attempt to globalize the perspective on indigo is still largely grounded in the dialectics of demand and supplies.[96]

---

95 W. Roxburgh and Alexander Anderson, 'Papers in Colonies and Trade', *Transactions of the Society, Instituted at London, for the Encouragement of Arts, Manufactures, and Commerce*, vol. 28 (1810), p. 249. A century later, Arthur Hirsch wrote, 'England's colonial possessions would furnish her with staples needed for food and raiment. Furthermore, why should England make hazardous journeys to the Baltic lands to procure what she could raise herself; why remain in virtual economic bondage to countries that were her traditional rivals and enemies, when the road to economic independence lay invitingly before her. Had not writers and mariners for more than a century pointed out that goods for which England was paying handsome tribute to rival countries could be produced at slight cost within her own possessions? Then too, England's political safety required a larger measure of economic independence. Accordingly, England's economic freedom became a slogan, and colonization in America a crusade'. Hirsch, 'French Influence on American Agriculture', 2.

96 Furnivall, *The Netherlands India*; Smith, 'Indigo Production and Trade in Colonial Guatemala'; Floyd, 'The Indigo Merchant'; Alden, 'The Growth and Decline of Indigo Production in Colonial Brazil'; Wortman, 'Government Revenue and Economic Trends'; R.J. Barendse, *The Arabian Seas: The Indian Ocean World of the Seventeenth Century* (New York: M.E. Sharpe, 2002), 231–2; Darrac and Van Schendel, *Global Blue*.

Two important points must be emphasized. Apart from Europe's intervention in colonial economies, the agrarian ecology of the indigo-producing regions and indigo's value and profitability in relation to other commodities such as rice, coffee, and cotton, among others, also played a significant role in the development and longevity of the world indigo market. Also, colonial intervention in and engagement with indigo in each of the commodity chains varied widely in form and substance, as did the outcomes. How these interventions were carried out in the colonies and what the challenges and limitations were are questions that have not been fully explored. These questions are particularly relevant for any study that engages with global economic divergence and the notion of a top-down trajectory of economic growth in India and other parts of Asia.[97] The following chapter is an analysis of the role of the Mughals and the EIC's colonial state in indigo production and trade. On several occasions in the early seventeenth century, Mughal emperor Shahjahan and some governors of Gujarat contemplated measures to benefit from the indigo trade by monopsonizing and monopolising it. In the beginning, the EIC's colonial state also asserted its control over the indigo trade. Such attempts, however, did not go uncontested. Merchants and agency houses, brokers and intermediaries, and producers were mindful of their commercial interests and took every opportunity to resist, circumvent, or simply flout state intervention in the indigo market. A commodity-focused perspective leads us to a nuanced understanding of these processes and enables us to examine the challenges to and limitations of state control of the indigo economy.

97 Jan Luiten van Zanden, *The Long Road to Industrial Revolution: The European Economy in a Global Perspective, 1000–1800* (Brill: Leiden, 2009).

CHAPTER 5

The Political Economy of Indigo: States, Merchants, and Producers

> [T]he characters of a merchant and a sovereign are inconsistent with each other, and cannot unite but with danger to both. The spirit of trade makes them bad sovereigns, and the spirit of sovereignty makes them bad traders.
>
> —JOHN COCHRANE, C. 1800

The Mughal state played a limited role in the indigo industry in the seventeenth century. The patterns of indigo production and exchange then were determined more by market economic forces than by state policies. Producers and merchants got no particular incentive from the state in the form of reduced production or trade taxes.[1] Due to the absence of a consistent Mughal policy regarding commodity production and trade or, as Michael Pearson has described it, the Mughal state's hands-off attitude towards trade, especially maritime trade, individual Mughal nobles and high officials sometimes contemplated measures to benefit from the indigo trade. By exerting political influence, they attempted to obtain indigo from producers at low prices and sell it to the European companies at higher rates. Such interference, of which there are several instances in the early seventeenth century, was not unique to indigo.[2] It was a characteristic of an economy in which merchants, political elites, and producers interacted in a complex relationship of competition,

1 Indigo was a cash crop that was assessed at high rates for taxation purposes. Abul Fazl, *Ain-i Akbari*, (tr.), H.S. Jarrett, vol. 3 (Calcutta: Baptist Mission Press, 1894), Nineteen-Year and Ten-Year assessment rates, pp. 72–95. Shireen Moosvi, *The Economy of Mughal Empire c. 1595: a Statistical Study* (New Delhi: OUP, 1987), 104–25. There are two recorded exceptions, however, when Firuz Shah Tughlaq of the Delhi Sultanate and Mughal Emperor Akbar reduced tax on some commodities and professions including indigo and its manufacture. Edward Thomas, *The Revenue Resources of the Mughal Empire in India, from A.D. 1593 to A.D. 1707: A Supplement to The Chronicles of the Pathan Kings of Dehli* (London: Trübner & Co., 1871), 5–6, 17–9.

2 Instances of engrossing and monopolising staple commodities like indigo, cotton goods, lead, spices, and even food-grains by Mughal officials and provincial governors in the seventeenth century are numerous. W.H. Moreland, *From Akbar to Aurangzeb: A Study in Indian Economic History* (Delhi: D.K. Publishers, 1994 reprint), 146–7. On the basis of such occurrences, Moreland concluded that 'industrial or distributive enterprise must have been

 | DOI 10.1163/9789004311558_007

contestation, and cooperation. Interventions that temporarily interrupted production and trade and adversely affected the fortunes of those involved in the industry also impacted and reconfigured relationships between merchants and producers and among their numerous constituents. The nature of the economy would not change much in the colonial period in so far as the complexity of this relationship is concerned. At this juncture it is worth examining the circumstances that led to intervention in the indigo market by Mughal rulers, nobles, and governors, and the British colonial state's take on indigo and the outcome. It is also necessary to analyse the responses and reactions that such interventions bred among merchants and manufacturers in order to explicate their position vis-à-vis the state in the market place.

State, Merchants, and Indigo Producers in the Seventeenth Century

Some members of the Mughal imperial household and provincial governors and high officials invested their resources in trade of which indigo exports to West Asia was a significant component.[3] They were, at times, encouraged to benefit from the large-scale European purchases and extraordinary competition among merchants for Bayana and Sarkhej indigo. They exerted their political influence, monopolised the purchase and sale of the commodity, and forced the Europeans to buy from them and their agents. Imposing a monopoly enabled them to secure indigo supplies that they intended to export to West Asia on the one hand and sell it, or the remainder, to merchants and the European companies at high prices on the other. The monopoly also implied that producers and intermediary merchants were coerced to sell their indigo to none other than the monopolist or his agents. In this way, they also effectively contained competition in West Asian markets.

seriously discouraged by the risk that novel demands might be imposed in the event of any profitable development of business'. Ibid., 291–2.

3 Several Mughal princes, princesses, and royal ladies owned ships and participated in Indian Ocean maritime trade. Shireen Moosvi, *People, Taxation, and Trade in Mughal India* (New Delhi: OUP, 2008), 244–74 (chapters 14–5). In 1610, the agents of the Queen Mother (mother of Mughal Emperor Jahangir) were reportedly purchasing indigo in Bayana for her ship sailing to Mocha. William Finch, *Early Travels in India, 1583–1619*, (ed.) William Foster (London: OUP, 1921), 123; John Jourdain, *The Journal of John Jourdain, 1608–1617* (ed.), William Foster (Cambridge: Hakluyt Society, 1905), 155–6. In 1637, a Mughal merchant, Shaikh Daud reportedly bought 300 *man* of Bayana indigo for Hakim Masih-uz Zaman. *Dagh-Register, 1637*, p. 270. Mirza Shaikh, the Mughal ambassador to the Ottoman court, similarly, is reported to have bought 310 packs of indigo to take to Turkey via Sind and Basra. Ibid.

In 1618, the Mughal governor of Ahmadabad, Muqarrab Khan, monopolised the sale of indigo.[4] In the early 1620s, the Mughal prince, Dawar Bakhsh, his *diwan*, Mohammad Taqi, Saif Khan, governor of Cambay, Hamid Khan, governor of Broach, and the governors of Surat and Dholka were involved in the indigo trade and tried to benefit from it by forcing their indigo upon the companies and Portuguese merchants. To accomplish this, they used their political connections and bureaucratic powers. On many occasions, they succeeded in persuading provincial governors to prohibit merchants to sell or weigh indigo to the Europeans until and unless their own indigo was disposed of.[5] Their intention was to sell indigo to the companies at high prices. On many occasions, the officials of the English and the Dutch East India Companies (EIC and VOC) succumbed to the pressure and accepted the offer.[6] Such interference in the indigo trade was possibly a response to the changes in the structure of the commodity market affected by the coming of the EIC and the VOC in Gujarat. Unlike the Portuguese who had no access to indigo-producing villages and bought indigo from Mughal entrepreneurs and local merchants, the EIC and VOC began to purchase it directly from primary producers in the villages of Sarkhej, Bayana, and Dholka, among others. This came as a challenge to all those who, until then, had been making fortunes by selling indigo and other commodities to the Europeans in Surat and other port cities. The response came in the form of political intervention in the economy and local governors' attempts to force their indigo upon the companies. Large European demand and the Anglo-Dutch competition to secure indigo supplies also prompted this kind of response. It seems that initially, at least, the EIC also had to procure indigo from monopolists because of disputes with the Mughals in the early 1620s

4 *EFI 1618–21*, Surat to London, 16 March 1618, p. 28; Moreland, *From Akbar to Aurangzeb*, 114.

5 In 1622, the governor of Dholka induced Mohammad Taqi, the *diwan* of Prince Dawar Bakhsh, to forbid all merchants of Sarkhej to sell or weigh their indigo to anyone. His intention was to sell his indigo to the English. *EFI 1622–23*, Ahmadabad to Surat, 26 Dec. 1622, pp. 172–3; ibid., Ahmadabad to Surat, 22 Jan. 1623, p. 185. Muhammad Taqi, similarly, forbade merchants to sell or weigh indigo until his own indigo was sold. *EFI 1622–23*, Ahmadabad to Surat, 3 April, 1623, p. 217; ibid., Ahmadabad to Surat, 2 May 1623, p. 230.

6 *EFI 1618–21*, Ahmadabad to Surat, 13 Nov. 1621, pp. 329–30. EIC officials reported that they 'have been forced by Himmat [Hamid] Khan's importunity to agree with him for the purchase of his indigo at Broach'. Ibid., Ahmadabad to Surat, 30 Nov. 1621, p. 339; ibid., Broach to Surat, 8 Dec. 1621, p. 341. EIC officials in Agra noted that Mohammad Taqi demanded Rs 10 per *man* and the prince's broker, Gurdas, asked for Rs 12 ½ per *man* whereas the market price was not more than Rs 8 or 8 ¾ per *man*. *EFI 1622–23*, Ahmadabad to Surat, 7 April 1623, p. 219 and Ahmadabad to Surat, 29 Nov. 1623, pp. 328–9.

and limited access to the hinterlands.[7] Once peace was established and the EIC regained access to the interior, the English and the Dutch began to compete for indigo. This, coupled with other circumstances, paved the way for yet another major political intervention in the indigo market.

Shahjahan's Indigo Monopoly

In 1633, Mughal Emperor Shahjahan declared the indigo trade in the whole of the empire a state monopoly. The initial idea behind the monopoly, as the EIC officials noted, was to force all merchants to buy indigo from the emperor at his price and to pay a year in advance. Upon some show of resistance by producers and merchants, the emperor gave up this plan and farmed out the sale of indigo to a merchant-monopolist, Manohardas, for a three-year term.[8] The latter obtained the sole right of buying all indigo grown in the empire, and all merchants and the European companies were required to buy from him and his agents. At the end of the term, he was to pay to the emperor a sum of Rs 1,100,000 (Rs 200,000 rupees every year out of his profits and Rs 500,000 in repayment of a loan made to him out of the royal treasury).[9] The contract stipulated that if the enterprise failed because the Europeans were not buying indigo from him, or for any other reason, the contractor would simply repay the loan. Some EIC officials regarded the monopoly as a state policy of expropriating the surplus profits of the indigo trade, a measure to control the industry, or as an outcome of the 'immeasurable' greed of the Mughals.[10] Modern scholarship holds that the monopoly was the Mughal response to the economic and political threat that the VOC's credit extension, in the form of cash advances to producers, and its penetration of the rural economy apparently posed to the empire.[11] Advance buying was undoubtedly an important aspect of the commodity trade in India and, as we have discussed earlier, its role in

7 In 1623, thus, the company bought 1,200 *fardles* of the prince's indigo and was negotiating with Gurdas, the prince's broker, for 2,500 *fardles* more. *EFI 1622–23*, Ahmadabad to Surat, 2 Dec. 1623, pp. 330–1.

8 *EFI 1634–36*, Surat to London, 31 Jan. 1634, p. 7.

9 *EFI 1630–33*, Agra to Surat, 12 Nov. 1633, pp. 324–6.

10 H.W. van Santen, 'De Verenigde Oost-Indische Compagnie in Gujarat en Hindustan, 1620–1660' (PhD dissertation, Leiden University, 1982), 133.

11 According to Van Santen, the monopoly was a response to the danger of the company servants acquiring land rights, which forced the Mughals to take over the supply of credit. Van Santen, 'De Verenigde Oost-Indische Compagnie in Gujarat en Hindustan', 133. Later, George Winius and Markus Vink noted that the Dutch penetration into indigo production areas and their credit extension making the farmers and producers dependent on the VOC formed 'not only an economic but a political threat' to the Mughals and the monopoly

the indigo market was rather important. It was a common practice and both the VOC and the EIC and other indigo merchants advanced large amounts of money as credit to peasants and manufacturers. This practice was not limited to indigo; large sums were also advanced to textile weavers and producers. Thus, the Dutch credit extension in the indigo market does not adequately explain the causal dynamics of the monopoly.[12] A combination of factors such as an unusual scarcity of indigo in Gujarat, fierce competition for the commodity, and several previous and current examples and models, I suggest, went into the making of the monopoly.

Indigo production in Gujarat was seriously disrupted by famine and the ensuing mortality during 1631–32.[13] EIC officials in Surat lamented the impact of the dreadful famine on indigo production in these words:

> Soe that the tymes here are soe miserable that never in the memory of man any the like famine and mortallity hapened. This that was in a manner the garden of the world is nowe turned into a wildernes, haveinge fewe or noe men left to manure theire grownd nor to labour in any profession; soe that places here that have yealded 15 bayles cloath made there in a day hardly yealds nowe three in a moneth. Amadavaz [Ahmadabad], that likewise yealded 3,000 bayles indico yearely or more, nowe hardly yealds 300; yett a plentifull yeare for yts grouth, but fewe men liveinge to gather it, but lies rottinge on the grownd.[14]

In January 1632, the EIC's President Hopkinson wrote to London,

> [T]he countrie in a miserable estate through famyne and mortalitie. Inundacion of waters admirable. A mortalitie unspeakeable. Swally and the places neere adjoining wholly dispeopled.... No workmen left, insomuch that one half for reaping and making the crop of Cirques [Sarkhej] indico

was a response to that. George Winius and Markus Vink, *The Merchant-Warrior Pacified: The VOC and its changing political economy in India* (Delhi: OUP, 1991), 62.

12 Hiromu Nagashima has, recently, argued that the monopoly may not be attributed to the Mughal apprehension of the Dutch involvement in agrarian economy and the latters' desire to obtain proprietary rights in land. Hiromu Nagashima, 'The Mughal Dynasty and Markets', in Harada Masami (ed.), *History of the Markets in Japan and Asia* (Osaka: Seibundo Shuppan, 2012), 239–72.

13 *EFI 1630–33*, Surat to Persia, 6 Oct. 1630, p. 59; Ali Mohammad Khan, *Mira't-i Ahmadi*, Part I (ed.), Syed Nawab Ali (Calcutta: Baptist Mission Press, 1928), pp. 205–6.

14 *EFI 1630–33*, Surat to London, 9 Dec. 1631, pp. 178–9.

> was offered for that labour. The only indigo they can hope to obtain is that of Agra.[15]

Famine and mortality caused great scarcity of indigo in Gujarat. Prices rose so high that they became equal to those of Bayana indigo. Under these circumstances, the European companies and all other merchants turned towards Agra for Bayana indigo. Indigo, after all, was the most important single commodity that the EIC and VOC exported from Surat to Europe. The failure of the Sarkhej indigo industry put enormous pressure on the Bayana indigo market. The companies and all other merchants fiercely competed with each other for the commodity. These developments induced the emperor to declare the indigo trade a state monopoly. The English officials in Surat were of the view that the monopoly was inspired by the Anglo-Dutch competition for indigo and held the VOC responsible for it. They noted that the emperor took the trade into his hands on the suggestion of the governor of Surat, with whom the Dutch had agreed to buy all indigo produced in the country.[16]

The monopoly need not be understood as the emperor's initiative to control the economy and trade. It was proposed by those nobles and governors who were involved in indigo trade and aspired to turn market conditions to their advantage. The governor of Surat, Mir Musa Muizzul Mulk, proposed the monopoly to the emperor. Another noble, Mir Jumla, was also involved in this project. In the words of the EIC officials, Mir Jumla 'did not only cherish but hatch it for his own advantage' as he carried out extensive indigo trade with West Asia.[17] It seems that these advocates of monopoly were also inspired by the precedents mentioned above. They also possibly drew some inspiration

15 Ibid., Surat to London, 23 Jan. 1632, pp. 192–3.

16 *EFI 1634–36*, Surat to London, 31 Jan. 1634, p. 7. The English very much apprehended 'the King's' miserableness, the Governor's baseness, and the cunning projects of the Dutch'. Ibid., p. 8. They wrote, '[T]he high price of indigo is entirely due to the competition between the English and the Dutch and to their allowing their ships to be used by native merchants for its transportation, for although it is not unusual to send Biana indigo overland to Persia via Lahore, no one would dream of dispatching any from Sarkhej by that route. Hence arose the scheme of the monopoly, which was greatly helped by the foolish bargain made by the Agra factors [of the VOC]'. Ibid., 2 Jan. 1636, p. 142.

17 *EFI 1634–36*, Surat to London, 29 Dec. 1634, p. 72. Mir Jumla sent overland to Persia 1,200 *fardles* of indigo in 1633. Ibid. For an analysis of portfolio capitalism and the role of Mir Jumla in politics and trade in the early seventeenth century, see Sanjay Subrahmanyam, *The Political Economy of Commerce: Southern India, 1500–1650* (Cambridge: CUP, 1990), 322–7; Jagdish Narayan Sarkar, *The Life of Mir Jumla: The General of Aurangzeb* (New Delhi: Rajesh Publications, 1979), 83–6. In 1641, the cargo that his vessel carried to Gombroon

from other examples of monopoly, such as the Safavid emperors' control over the silk trade of Persia. EIC officials noted that the governor of Surat imitated the silk contracts in Persia and tried to force the European companies to contract with him for indigo.[18]

The limited success with which the monopolies were implemented and the effectiveness with which such interventions were resisted by the affected parties reveal the inability of the state or its officials to control the economy. Merchants, peasants, and producers resisted the monopoly and often succeeded in forcing their way out of it. In 1623, indigo merchants protested Mohammad Taqi's prohibition, reported the matter to the governor of Gujarat, Hakim Masih-uz Zaman, and secured from him the freedom to buy and sell indigo as they wished.[19] At other times, they stopped buying indigo or financing its production. Without advances from merchants, peasants and producers were unable to undertake indigo cultivation and manufacture. The fear that their labour would not be rewarded de-incentivised them. Many, therefore, stopped producing indigo, uprooted the plant, or migrated to other places.[20] Recourse to such actions often rendered the monopoly unworkable.

For buyers, the monopoly meant paying higher prices and depending wholly on the monopolist for quantity and quality. Being the largest buyers and thereby the prime victims, the English and the Dutch took serious note of the monopoly and did their best to resist it. They knew quite well that their large-scale purchases of indigo and competition with each other raised the prices and induced those in positions of power to take advantage of their rivalry. To fight the monopoly, the companies agreed either not to buy at all for some time or to buy in common and divide it, as they did in 1625.[21] Such arrangements were, however, temporary and competition resumed soon thereafter. The indigo monopoly of 1633 was a major challenge for both the companies.

included 400 bales of Coromandel indigo. Subrahmanyam, *The Political Economy of Commerce*, 324.

18 *EFI 1634–36*, Surat to London, 29 Dec. 1634, p. 70.

19 *EFI 1622–23*, Ahmadabad to Surat, 3 April, 1623, p. 217; ibid., Ahmadabad to Surat, 2 May 1623, p. 230.

20 *EFI 1630–33*, Agra to Surat, 12 Nov. 1633, p. 326. In view of the flight of peasants from villages and their refusal to cultivate indigo, Shahjahan gave up the plan of taking indigo trade in his hands and farmed it out to Manohardas in 1633. *EFI 1634–36*, Surat to London, 31 Jan. 1634, p. 7.

21 The English and the Dutch factors in Agra agreed not to compete with each other in the market and to buy indigo in common and divide it. *EFI 1624–29*, Consultations, Surat, 28 Nov. 1625, p. 111.

They joined hands once again and adopted measures that would make the monopoly ineffective.

On 29 November 1633, the EIC chief and the VOC director in Surat signed an agreement and pledged to abide by it.[22] They agreed to abstain from buying indigo for a year and if, in that period, they had to buy it, they agreed to buy it with mutual consent and at prices not higher than specified in the contract. Article 12 of the contract also stipulated that under no circumstances would either of the companies allow its ships to freight any indigo belonging to local merchants to West Asia. They also enlisted the support of Asaf Khan and Afzal Khan, the two pre-eminent Mughal nobles at the court, in obtaining commercial freedom that the companies formerly enjoyed.[23] The EIC even called for giving up their entire establishments in Gujarat and northern India if the monopoly was not abandoned. All these measures proved rather effective. Europeans' refusal to buy indigo and the ensuing loss of revenues convinced the governor of Surat and other high officials in the Mughal bureaucracy of the ill-consequences of the monopoly. The governor, who had been the initiator of the monopoly, argued for its repeal.[24] The joint Anglo-Dutch resistance and widespread protest by merchants and producers resulted in the withdrawal of the monopoly in 1634.[25]

Interpreting Mughal State Intervention in the Indigo Economy

Attempts to monopolise indigo or to benefit from its trade, were intermittently made by some Mughal governors of Gujarat in the subsequent period.

22 VOC 1113, Contract ende capitulatie op den handel van den indigo [Contract and capitulation concerning the indigo trade], Surat, 29 Nov. 1633, ff. 230^r–236^r. The contract was for a year at the end of which the companies would decide if it needed to be continued. *EFI 1630–33*, Consultations, Surat, 15 Nov. 1633, pp. 327–8. M.S. Commissariat, *A History of Gujarat, 1573–1758*, vol. II (Bombay: Orient Longmans, 1957), 304–5.

23 *EFI 1634–36*, Surat to London, 29 Dec. 1634, p. 71.

24 Ibid., pp. 70–1.

25 Bibliothèque Nationale, Paris, Blochet Supplementary Persan 482, Copy of Shahjahan's farman declaring the withdrawal of the indigo monopoly, 1634, f. 98^a; *EFI 1634–36*, Surat to London, 29 Dec. 1634, p. 72. Irfan Habib, *The Agrarian System of Mughal India, 1557–1705* (New Delhi: OUP, 1999), 87–8. A copy of Shahjahan's farman (dated 29 Ramadan, 1044 A.H. or 19 March 1635) shows that the emperor withdrew the monopoly and allowed the VOC and other merchants to buy indigo anywhere and from any person and ordered his officials not to force anyone to buy indigo from the government. NA, Collectie Geleynssen de Jongh, 100, Briefboek van verscheyde soo becoomen als versonde brieven als formannen int Persiaens geschreven ende int Nederlants getranslateert begonnen anno 1639 in Agra [Letter-book of various letters received and sent as well as farmans written in Persian and translated into Dutch beginning in 1639 in Agra], not foliated (letter no. 3).

In 1638, the European companies were forced to buy indigo belonging to the wife of Azam Khan, governor of Ahmadabad, at a higher-than-market price. The governor forbade any sale or weighing of indigo by other merchants until his indigo was disposed of and delivered to the companies.[26] In 1646, the new governor of Ahmadabad levied duties that formerly had been remitted to indigo producers and, a year later, he forced the *banjaras* (itinerant traders) to sell their sugar to him and contemplated monopolising the indigo trade.[27] In 1656, the Mughal prince and governor of Gujarat, Murad Bakhsh, attempted through his *diwan* to force manufacturers to buy indigo leaves from him and would not allow the latter to either buy from others or manufacture any indigo.[28] As on earlier occasions, these monopolies were resisted by the companies and merchants.

Sometimes, the Mughal state intervened in a positive way. As adulteration became common and the quality of indigo deteriorated in the 1640s, merchants and the companies complained to the governor and solicited corrective measures from him. The authorities tried to assuage the complainants by forcing manufacturers not to adulterate indigo. In 1640, Gujarat's governor, Azam Khan, strictly forbade producers to adulterate indigo. In 1646, similarly, responding to merchants' complaints about the unscrupulousness of indigo-makers to mix oil and sand in indigo, the governor of Gujarat issued strict orders commanding producers to manufacture pure and good-quality indigo.[29] Although, our sources do not reveal the effectiveness of such measures, it seems

26 The VOC factor, S. Silvius, was forced by the governor to buy 400 *man* of poor-quality indigo at 2½ to 3 rupees per *man* higher than the market price. VOC 1127, Directeur en Raad van Surat aan GG&R, 3 May 1638, f. 116^{v}. The governor tried to monopolise the entire indigo trade and to accomplish this, he purchased 1,000 *man* indigo seeds to grow indigo. Ibid., The companies were left with no option but to petition against this monopoly to the emperor. We do not know if the matter was taken to that level and what the outcome was. The English were forced to buy 69 bales of 'very coarse indigo' by the governor. *EFI 1637–41*, Surat to London, 28 Jan. 1640, p. 232.

27 *EFI 1646–50*, Ahmadabad to Surat, 22 Dec. 1646, p. 64. This raised the price of indigo in Ahmadabad by two rupees per *man*. Ibid., *EFI 1646–50*, Ahmadabad to Surat, 17 May 1647, p. 130.

28 *EFI 1655–60*, Inland Factories, 1656, p. 76. It was not uncommon for the Mughals to collect land revenue partly in kind, especially from peasants who grew indigo. Some Mughal governors of Gujarat, such as Isa Tarkhan (1644) and Prince Aurangzeb (1646) collected large quantities of indigo plant and attempted to get indigo made out of it. Van Santen, 'De Verenigde Oost-Indische Compagnie in Gujarat en Hindustan', 157. The former had collected indigo plants worth Rs 7,000. Ibid.

29 *EFI 1637–41*, Surat to London, 29 Dec. 1640, p. 274; *Dagh-Register, 1640–41*, p. 313; *EFI 1646–50*, Ahmadabad to Surat, 30 March 1646, pp. 31–3.

that producers were reluctant to obey the governors' injunctions because they could not afford to make pure indigo because of poor returns.[30] Quality, therefore, remained a major concern for the companies and other merchants for much of the 1640s and 1650s.

As a form of Mughal official intervention, monopolies—and people's resistance to them—characterised the commodity markets in early modern India.[31] Not only the imperial household and the nobility but also mercantile elites exerted their influence whenever an opportunity arose and attempted to exercise monopolistic and monopsonistic control over the market.[32] Those affected by it often adopted non-confrontational modes of resistance, like suspending their business transactions, withdrawing from the market, and petitioning those in positions of power until their grievances were redressed.[33]

It transpires from the circumstances that went into the making and dismantling of the monopolies that Mughal state, at least in terms of its ability to control and dominate the economy, was weak. Mughal intervention in the indigo economy as discussed above was spontaneous and opportunistic and did not reflect a clear and consistent imperial policy. The emperor's 1633 endorsement of the monopoly proposed by the governor of Surat, and backed by Mir Jumla, and its revocation a year later on the recommendations of the same governor and of Asaf Khan and Afzal Khan typifies the fickle nature of state policy vis-à-vis the commercial economy of Mughal India. Merchants and the companies were aware of this and knew very well how to benefit from this. Thus, in their fight against Shahjahan's indigo monopoly, the English and

30 The Dutch officials noted in 1645 that producers began to adulterate indigo as soon as the said governor left Ahmadabad. *Dagh-Register, 1644–45*, p. 232.

31 Rulers and imperial officials also occasionally exerted their monopsonistic control in the textile markets. In 1641, the emperor and Asif Khan forbade weavers, dyers, and other artisans to make any cloth for any other merchants before their orders for cloth (worth Rs 160,000) were complete. *Dagh-Register, 1640–41*, p. 308.

32 On many occasions in the first half of the seventeenth century, Virji Vora acted as a monopsonist buyer forcing other merchants out of his way and purchasing commodities that the European companies imported into Gujarat. *EFI 1624–29*, Consultations, Surat, 10 July 1625, p. 90; *EFI 1624–29*, Consultations, Surat, 24 Sept. 1625, p. 94; *EFI 1634–36*, Consultations, Surat, 8 April 1634, p. 24; ibid., Surat to London, 28 April 1636, p. 218.

33 For an analysis of the everydayness of resistance in the merchant-state relationship in Surat, see Douglas Haynes, 'From Avoidance to Confrontation? A Contestatory History of Merchant-State Relations in Surat, 1600–1924', in Douglas Haynes and Gyan Prakash (eds), *Contesting Power: Resistance and Everyday Social Relations in South Asia* (New Delhi: 1991), 239–89; Ghulam A. Nadri, 'The Trading World of Indian Ocean Merchants in Pre-Colonial Gujarat 1600–1750', in Om Prakash (ed.), *The Trading World of the Indian Ocean, 1500–1800* (New Delhi: Pearson, 2012), 236–9.

the Dutch solicited support from Asaf Khan and Afzal Khan because these eminent nobles were political rivals of Mir Jumla, who not only supported the monopoly but also benefited from it.[34] The indigo monopolies illustrate that political power was an adjunct, and often subservient, to merchant capital and capitalist ambitions, which must be seen as the dominant forces in the political economy of Gujarat and Mughal India. Monopolies were the initiatives of capitalist-noblemen who used or abused their political power for economic gain. Paradoxically, merchant capital itself provided the antidote and that too through political channels.

Merchant capital succeeded in expropriating the labour of indigo producers far more than the Mughal emperor, provincial governors, or officials. Merchants were the main beneficiaries of the flourishing indigo industry, with profits trickling down to peasants and manufacturers as well. In the first half of the seventeenth century, indigo producers benefited from the large demand from and the competition among buyers. The European companies' endeavours to keep the purchase prices low by means of joint-buying and price ceilings did not always work. EIC and VOC officials were, at times, forced to ignore the price ceiling and purchase the commodity at the current market prices, which were higher than the ones fixed by the companies. This, however, was no longer the case after the 1640s, when European demand fell sharply and the companies cut their annual indigo purchases in India. The cessation of competition adversely affected indigo producers and intermediary merchants, who lost their bargaining position in the market. We do not know to what extent the expanding textile industry in India kept up the demand for indigo in the late seventeenth and eighteenth centuries. It may nevertheless be construed from the large European exports of dyed and printed cotton and silk textiles from Gujarat, Bengal, and Coromandel that local consumption of indigo had increased during this period.[35] In fact, the VOC and EIC's intermittent export of large quantities of indigo to Europe in the second half of the seventeenth century indicate that the industry was still quite vibrant. Indigo producers and local merchants continued to share the benefits accruing from the industry.

34 *EFI 1634–36*, Surat to London, 29 Dec. 1634, pp. 71–2.

35 Exports of cotton and silk textiles, especially from Bengal, increased considerably in the late seventeenth and Eighteenth centuries. Om Prakash, *The Dutch East India Company and the Economy of Bengal, 1630–1720* (New Jersey: Princeton University Press, 1985), chapter 3; Sushil Chaudhury, *From Prosperity to Decline: Eighteenth Century Bengal* (New Delhi: Manohar, 1995), chapter 7. Om Prakash, *European Commercial Enterprise in Pre-Colonial India* (Cambridge: CUP, 1998), chapters 5 and 6.

State, Indigo Planters, and Peasants in Colonial India

The EIC's takeover of Bengal and the expansion of its political control elsewhere in India in the late eighteenth and early nineteenth centuries changed the nature of India's political economy. The colonial state sought to exercise control over the economy. To achieve this, the company restructured the agrarian economy of the territories it possessed and created institutional and legal infrastructures to promote production and trade as well as to facilitate deeper penetration of British/European merchant capital in the economy.[36] The transformation of the EIC from a profit-seeking trading company to a colonial power, however, implied a marked shift in peoples' perception of the company and of its function. Maximisation of profit from trade that had until then benefitted the company's shareholders was no longer enough. In its new incarnation, the company began to be seen as Britain's political and administrative representative in India whose primary purpose was to make the colony economically beneficial for Britain. Consequently, voices began to be raised in England against the company's trade monopoly, and by 1813 trade with Asia was opened up for all Britons.

Indigo production and trade in the late eighteenth and nineteenth centuries were embedded in the politics of empire and colonial expansion. The changing characteristics of the relationship between the state and the economy under colonialism, which were mainly inspired by a series of political-economic developments in Europe, played an important role in shaping the indigo industry. The company regarded indigo as one of the most valuable exports from India and promoted this branch of trade. In the 1770s, the company began to make determined efforts to encourage indigo production in its territories in India. It adopted a series of measures that would intensify production and transform indigo from a monopoly commodity to a product freely exported by the British, European, and American merchants. Within the first decades of colonial rule, the EIC's take on indigo underwent a major transformation. The colonial state moved away from controlling its production and trade and limited itself to a supervisory role in promoting the indigo industry in the colony. Let us examine the role of the EIC and its colonial state in the growth and expansion of India's indigo industry in the late eighteenth and nineteenth centuries.

---

36 For an analysis of the linkages between colonial expansion and empire and the economic imperatives of colonialism, see H.V. Bowen, *Elites, Enterprise and the Making of the British Overseas Empire, 1688–1775* (London: Macmillan Press, 1996).

The Colonial State and the Indigo Industry

After the conquest of Bengal in 1757, and more so after the acquisition of the *diwani* (the right to collect land revenue) in 1765, the East India Company initiated measures that would facilitate appropriation of agrarian surpluses from its territorial possessions. With the newly found revenue resources, the company funded its investments in textiles (primarily cotton and silk piece goods) in Bengal and elsewhere in South Asia and in this way remitted a part of its revenue surpluses to Britain. As the revolution in the English textile industry and the spectacular expansion in cloth production rendered Bengal piece goods somewhat undesirable in European markets, the company began to invest its resources in agricultural raw materials, the most important of which was indigo. Cotton, silk, and sugar also attracted the company's attention and it promoted their production in Bengal for export purposes. To meet expectations, however, the company came to rely on indigo as this commodity offered the best prospects for production in Bengal and trade and profits in Europe.[37] The company therefore undertook to promote indigo production in the territories it possessed in eastern and south-eastern India.

Bengal was fit for indigo production because its extensive landmass was irrigated by several major and many minor rivers, and because of the fertility of the soil from the deposition of alluvium by annual inundation.[38] What was needed was a little stimulus. Some progress in this regard had already been made in the 1760s, when the company tried to obtain indigo seeds and knowledge of its cultivation from Gujarat to promote the industry in the territories it possessed in Bengal and Madras.[39] Efforts to produce indigo in Bengal,

37 Bengal did not produce cotton for export and experiments with sugar production were not successful as it could not compete with sugar imported into European markets from the West Indies. B.B. Chowdhury, *Growth of Commercial Agriculture in Bengal, 1757–1900* (Calcutta: R.K. Maitra, 1964), 75, 83. Sugar exported from British India was much inferior in quality than that from Mauritius and the West Indies and it paid higher duties in Britain than the West Indian sugar. John Crawfurd, 'A Sketch of the Commercial Resources and Monetary and Mercantile System of British India' (1837), in K.N. Chaudhuri, *The Economic Development of India under the East India Company, 1814–58: A Selection of Contemporary Writings* (Cambridge: CUP, 1971), 253.

38 As Blair Kling has noted 'Bengal had the natural endowments to produce the finest indigo in the world'. Blair B. Kling, *Partner in Empire: Dwarkanath Tagore and the Age of Enterprise in Eastern India* (Berkeley: University of California Press, 1976), 55; Sugata Bose, *Peasant Labour and Colonial Capital: Rural Bengal since 1770* (Cambridge: CUP, 1993), 9–12.

39 In 1763, the company's authorities in Surat instructed the resident at Cambay to procure a quantity of indigo seeds to promote its cultivation elsewhere. William Bowyear, the British Resident at Cambay, procured a quantity of 'the best Tarapore seed' and consigned

however, intensified in the following decades. By the 1780s, the nascent colonial state had survived its initial difficulties and an administrative structure was in place.[40] By then it was clear to the company's authorities in London and India that British sovereignty in Bengal and its extension elsewhere in India engendered commercial aspirations and that its political ascendancy would be meaningful only when net economic benefits were derived from it.[41] A restructuring of the colony's agricultural economy, consequently, followed the military conquest and the acquisition of the *diwani* rights in 1765. A coincidence of circumstances such as a growing demand for indigo at home, Britain's dependence on the supplies of French- and Spanish-American indigo in the aftermath of the loss of its indigo-producing American colonies in the 1770s, and the nationalist-mercantilist reactions against Britain's indigo purchases from rival European nations, induced the EIC to promote indigo in the colony as a profitable agro-industrial product. This promised fiscal and commercial advantages, for the company authorities believed, and rightly so, that the large-scale cultivation of indigo would enhance the income from agrarian taxation and would also enable the company to control indigo markets and procure, on

it to Surat together with a description of the methods of its cultivation and processing. MSA, Mumbai, Surat Factory Diary, 16/II (1761–1763), Cambay to Surat, 14 April 1763, pp. 485–6; ibid., Cambay to Surat, 4 May 1763, pp. 495–6. Interestingly, the resident was specifically instructed to procure 'Lahore indigo' seeds. Ibid. Lahore indigo actually refers to the variety from Bayana that was taken to West Asia through Lahore. Moreland, *From Akbar to Aurangzeb*, 109; K.N. Chaudhuri, *The English East India Company: The Study of an Early Joint-Stock Company, 1600–1640* (London: Frank Cass & Co., 1965), 175. In 1787, EIC officials at Cambay were directed to procure a small quantity of indigo produced there and send it to London with information regarding the costs and quantity of it, as well as to procure some of the 'choicest' seed to be packed in two parcels, one for Bengal and the other for Madras for trial cultivation there. BL, East India Company Draft Dispatches submitted to Board of Control, 55, Draft Paragraph proposed by the Court of Directors to be sent to their Presidency of Bombay, London, 2 Nov. 1787, pp. 554–5.

40 The Regulating Act of 1773 laid the foundation and the Ilbert Bill of 1784 seemingly concluded the discussion about the nature and form of the administrative structure that would come up to the expectations and aspirations of the people of Britain and their sympathies with the Indians.

41 There is a good deal of debate among scholars on the issues of interconnectedness of the empire and economy during the initial stages of colonial expansion. P.J. Marshall, 'British Expansion in India in the Eighteenth Century: A Historical Revision', in P.J. Marshall, *Trade and Conquest: Studies on the Rise of British Dominance in India* (Aldershot: Ashgate, 1993), chapter VII; idem, *East India Fortunes: The British in Bengal in the Eighteenth Century* (Oxford: Clarendon Press, 1976); Nicholas B. Dirks, *The Scandal of Empire: India and the Creation of Imperial Britain* (Cambridge, Mass.: Harvard University Press, 2006), 155–8.

a guaranteed basis, whatever quantity was required for Europe. Therefore, EIC-ruled Bengal became the focus of all attention.

The company's directors in London instructed their officials in India to extend all possible encouragement to indigo cultivation and manufacture. They regarded indigo as 'an article which, considered in a political point of view, has every claim to our attention, as having a tendency to render the company's possession in Bengal more valuable by creating from the soil and labour of the natives an export commerce, capable of being carried to a very great extent'.[42] In 1788, Governor-General Lord Cornwallis wrote to the company in London that 'indigo which is but recently exported from Bengal as an article of foreign commerce, absolutely creates a new source of wealth to it, capable perhaps of being in time rendered equal to the demands of the greatest part of Europe'. He went on to say 'it affords a happy means of employing the waste lands of the country, improving the revenue, and repairing the loss of other branches of trade, the great importance of encouraging it, is therefore, evident'.[43] Two years later, the promotion of indigo in Bengal was similarly noted to be the 'object of highest importance'. The Privy Council in London considered it 'as a national object likely in time to afford such supply of indigo to Great Britain as to render any importation of that article from foreign countries unnecessary'.[44]

With regard to the indigo project in India, the EIC had two main objectives. As a merchant, the company sought to keep its monopoly of indigo trade and benefit from the increasing British and European demand for it. As a ruler, the company sought to promote the industry within its colonial possessions to maximize revenues from agrarian taxation. To accomplish these, it initiated measures that would come to rapidly expand indigo production in Bengal for exports to Europe.

In the complex processes that went into making Bengal the world's largest producer of the best natural indigo in the nineteenth century, the colonial state, European and Indian merchant capital, and local labour all played a significant role. Their relationships were full of complementarities, competition, and contestations. With the unprecedentedly rapid expansion of the industry, competition and contestations intensified, and coercion—even violence—came to be associated with the industry. This was mainly because the new indigo

---

42 Court's letter of 28 March 1788, quoted in Chowdhury, *Growth of Commercial Agriculture in Bengal*, 75.

43 WBSA, Board of Trade, Indigo, 1810–1811, Proceedings, 6 Dec. 1811, p. 37.

44 BL, Home Miscellaneous, 434, Short Sketch of the measures adopted for the introduction of indigo and the promotion of agriculture in Bengal between the years 1779–1790, Bengal (Hugli), 30 Dec. 1790, p. 599.

enterprise was based on an odd combination of European model of capitalist production seeking to control labour and maximise profits, a mercantilist colonial state that wished to control the economy and trade, an indigenous production system that still largely depended on family labour and skills, and a system of control through monetary advances managed by a hierarchy of local intermediaries. The literature on colonial-period indigo industry recognizes the contested relationship between peasants and planters and generally emphasizes an almost total subordination of indigenous labour to European capital and capitalistic relationships.[45] The evidence often presented in support of this view is that the peasants were excessively exploited by the planters and manufacturers. The literature also underscores that the colonial state and its frameworks of law and administration privileged the interests of European indigo entrepreneurs in the colony, thereby facilitating their indigo enterprise.[46] The company's measures to promote indigo certainly benefitted the indigo planter-manufacturers and the company in the long run. But the notion of a European triumph in the indigo enterprise spearheaded by a company-planter syndicate does not really match its complex developmental trajectory.

Competition and contestations between the company and indigo planters and among planters themselves were as intense as between planter-manufacturers and peasants. To see this in the binary terms of European success and Indian failure is to miss the nuances and dynamics of production relations in the indigo industry and the relative autonomy and interdependence among these economic actors. Evidence of loss on European side is not lacking and one comes across references to Indian entrepreneurs who made fortunes from their indigo enterprise. With regard to peasants, it should be noted that their experiences and fortunes varied widely depending on their location and the type of contract they had with indigo planter-manufacturers and the production regime they had to work under. Thus, while the peasantry in some parts of Bengal

45 S.K. Mittal, *Peasant Uprisings and Mahatma Gandhi in North Bihar: A Politico-Economic Study of Indigo Industry, 1817–1917 with special reference to Champaran* (Meerut: Anu Prakashan, 1978); Abhijit Dutta, *Christian Missionaries on the Indigo-Question in Bengal (1855–1861)* (Calcutta: Minerva Publications, 1989); Raaj Sah, 'Features of British Indigo in India', *Social Scientist*, vol. 9, nos. 2–3 (Sep–Oct. 1980), 67–79; Amiya Roa and B.G. Rao, *The Blue Devil: Indigo and Colonial Bengal—with an English Translation of Neel Darpan by Dinbandhu Mitra* (Delhi: OUP, 1992); Prabhat Kumar Shukla, *Indigo and the Raj: Peasant Protests in Bihar, 1780–1917* (Delhi: Pragati Publications, 1993); Ananda Bhattacharya, *Indigo Rebellion: A Selection (1859–1862)* (Kolkata: Dey's Publishing, 2012).

46 Shukla, *Indigo and the Raj*, 34; Peter Robb, *Peasants, Political Economy, and Law* (Oxford: OUP, 2007), 33, 182; Indrajit Ray, 'The indigo dye industry in colonial Bengal: A re-examination, *Indian Economic and Social History Review*, vol. 41, no. 2 (2004), 199–224.

suffered heavily under the un-remunerative contract system in the mid-nineteenth century, those of Bihar, Banaras, Agra, and Awadh did not share the same fate. What follows below is an analysis of the dialectics between the EIC's policies regarding indigo, and planters' and peasants' responses to those policies.

The EIC's Indigo Enterprise in Colonial India: Opportunities and Challenges

The revival of indigo exports from India to Britain in the 1780s initiated a new phase in the history of the commodity.[47] The company's initiatives to promote production and exports and private merchants' readiness to undertake indigo manufacture contributed to the expansion of the industry in the Bengal Presidency to an extent that it soon dwarfed all other regions in the world in the supply of this natural blue dye. While the company aspired to keep to itself the benefits of indigo exports to Britain and Europe, the voluminous European demand aroused commercial aspirations of European planter-manufacturers, who were keen on becoming part of this lucrative commodity trade. What followed was a continuous contestation between the company and planter-manufacturers each trying to control the market and turning the terms of trade in its favour.

Initially, the company allocated production to private entrepreneurs and kept exports to itself.[48] Not content with this, the indigo planter-manufacturers desired to share the profits from trade. In 1785, they demanded and secured permission from the company to export indigo to Britain on company ships.[49]

47 The revival was partly because of Britain's loss of its indigo-producing American colonies but mainly as a result of Britain's desire to substitute Indian imports for transatlantic indigo, mostly French and Spanish.

48 The company purchased indigo through advance contracts with British/European indigo manufacturers, who owned indigo manufactories and, on receiving an advance, undertook to supply the stipulated amount of indigo to the company. Between 1779 and 1784, the company bought indigo from John Prinsep and, from then until 1788, from several indigo planters and mercantile houses. BL, Home Miscellaneous, 434, Short Sketch of the measures adopted for the introduction of indigo and the promotion of agriculture in Bengal between the years 1779–1790, Bengal (Hugli), 30 Dec. 1790, p. 601. Amlesh Tripathi, *Trade and Finance in the Bengal Presidency, 1793–1833* (Calcutta: OUP, 1979), 41. Mercantile houses such as Fairlie & Co., Colvins and Bazett, Campbell and Radcliff supplied indigo to the company. Chowdhury, *Growth of Commercial Agriculture in Bengal*, 76.

49 BL, East India Company Correspondence with India, 10, General Letter, 17 Jan. 1785, p. 80; ibid., General Letter, 31 Dec. 1785, p. 194. In 1786, the company contracted with a manufacturer, Mr. Boyce, to buy all his indigo at a certain price allowing him 400 Rupees per month as maintenance and half of the net profit on sale in London. BL, East India Company Correspondence with India, 10, General Letter, 7 March 1786, p. 237.

By 1788, it was clear to the company that what the private European indigo manufacturers aspired for was a share in the profit from trade and distribution. Consequently, the company gave up its monopoly of indigo trade and allowed private exports to Britain.[50] The company anticipated that opening up the indigo trade to private merchants and coupled with large cash advances would encourage them to establish manufactories and export indigo to Europe, which would intensify production in the colony. It was, however, belied in its expectations as many indigo contractors purchased 'foreign' indigo from Agra and Awadh and delivered it to the company for exports to Europe.[51] With its shipping monopoly between India and Britain, the company could still manipulate the transportation of indigo in London to keep transactions in its favour. The terms that regulated private indigo exports were unfavourable to manufacturers. The company valued indigo at one-fourth to one-third less its sale value in London, and subjected it to high charges for freight, warehousing, and, sometimes, demurrage. Besides, indigo paid a 5 percent import duty in Britain.[52] The company also kept the pound sterling–rupee exchange high (2s. and 4½ d. per rupee, which was about 14 percent higher than the usual 2s. per

50 This is in contrast to the EIC's policy with regard to opium. The company kept its monopoly of opium exports to China whereas it allowed private exports of indigo to Britain. This could be attributed to three main factors. First, the company's indigo trade was not profitable. It suffered losses on account of high purchase prices in India and low sale prices in London. Second, promoting indigo production through private investments served two important purposes namely, enhancing the revenue resources of the colony and remitting the revenue and income surpluses to the metropolis. Third, colonial conquests had engendered commercial aspirations among British entrepreneurs who then turned to indigo that had the potential to become one of the most important exports from India to Europe. The company temporarily stopped exporting it to Britain. But it did not want to lose the fiscal benefits that large-scale indigo production in Bengal promised. By allowing private trade in indigo, it sought to promote indigo production in Bengal and continue to drive fiscal benefits from it. BL, Home Miscellaneous, 434 Short sketch of the measures adopted for the introduction of indigo and the promotion of agriculture in Bengal between the years 1779–1790, Bengal (Hugli), 30 Dec. 1790, pp. 600–1.

51 Agra came under the company's control in 1803 and was therefore no longer foreign. Awadh was taken over by the company in 1856.

52 In his memorandum, John Cochrane, complained that the company kept one-fourth of the value of indigo to itself, charged exorbitant freight rates, kept the pound sterling-rupee exchange rates very high. The contract-based transactions were progressively disadvantageous to manufacturers. BL, Home Miscellaneous, 406, Memorandum by John Cochrane on India Trade and Shipping (not dated), p. 86.

rupee) and, therefore, in its favour. As this sort of transaction was unfavourable to manufacturers, many of them were forced to either leave the industry or use alternative means to send their indigo to Europe. Also, the company could not stop the contractors from importing foreign indigo into Bengal and delivering it to the company. Either way, the company failed to induce merchants to establish manufactories and process the plant cultivated within the company's provinces.

The company's pursuit of its commercial ambitions created conditions in which a clash of interests between the company and indigo planter-manufacturers was imminent. The company could not persuade or coerce indigo planter-manufacturers to comply with the rules that it framed for the industry. The planter-manufacturers followed their own path and did what was in their best interest. Thus, contrary to the company's wishes, they used the company's money to buy foreign indigo instead of establishing manufactories in Bengal.[53] At times, they declined to supply indigo at the price fixed by the company's appraiser.[54] To send their indigo to Europe, some even had recourse to other European merchants and the companies that provided remittance services at low costs.[55] In the beginning, thus, the company failed as a sovereign because, contrary to its expectations, indigo manufactories were not established within the territories it possessed in Bengal. It also failed as a merchant because despite all its manipulations, high purchase prices in India rendered its indigo transactions in Britain unprofitable.[56]

---

53 EIC officials alleged that the contractors bought 'foreign' indigo from 'other countries' (Awadh and Agra) and delivered to the company. Indigo from these regions was reportedly cheap because of the availability of labour at lower wages than in Bengal. BL, Home Miscellaneous, 434, Short sketch of the measures adopted for the introduction of indigo and the promotion of agriculture in Bengal between the years 1779–1790, Bengal (Hugli), 30 Dec. 1790, pp. 603–4.

54 BL, Home Miscellaneous, 393, Report of Commercial Occurrences, Bengal, 12 Sept. 1787, pp. 22–4.

55 BL, East India Company Correspondence with India, 11, Commercial Letter, 25 Jan. 1792, pp. 191–2. The Ostend Company, for instance, charged £16 per ton of 16 cwt. or 2d per lb. that was about one-third less than the freight the EIC charged from merchants. BL, Home Miscellaneous, 393, Report of Commercial Occurrences, Bengal, 16 Nov. 1790, pp. 501–2.

56 The company bought indigo at high prices (Rs 200–220/factory *man*) because its main concern then was to remit funds to Britain rather than to profit from indigo trade. The poor quality of indigo too may have contributed to lower or no profitability in Europe. As Tripathi has observed that the dye exported from Bengal was allegedly adulterated as the low-quality indigo from Awadh and Agra was mixed with the better one from Bengal. Tripathi, *Trade and Finance in Bengal Presidency*, 41.

By 1790, the company had forfeited its exclusive rights to export indigo to Britain. From then onward, the commodity was exported mainly by private European indigo planter-manufacturers and by commanders and officers of EIC ships.[57] However, the company knew that the benefits of extensive indigo cultivation in Bengal, in terms of revenue it would generate, were as significant as profits from trade. In framing its policies regarding indigo, therefore, the company's fiscal interests had definite precedence over commercial interests.[58] What the company aspired for as a sovereign, however, could not be accomplished by commercial measures alone. To make indigo a staple product of Bengal that would meet the entire European demand, the company had to resort to political legislation. Many indigo contractors established manufactories in Bengal and Bihar, and the number multiplied in 1792, when Governor-General Lord Cornwallis allowed private Europeans to hold land on lease in the Presidency. In 1792–93, consequently, a number of indigo works were established in the company's provinces.[59] But the nascent industry had to be protected against competition from foreign indigo. The company contemplated measures to restrict indigo imports into Bengal (Calcutta) from Agra and Awadh, but it could not successfully put them into effect. It imposed a 5 percent duty on imports from those regions and 'foreign' indigo was discriminated against Bengal indigo in other ways too.[60] As early as 1788, the company contemplated restricting the tonnage to the indigo that was produced within the company's provinces. To ensure that only the product from the colony was

57 In 1795, indigo procured through company's advances amounted to 542,841 pounds, indigo as individual consignment amounted to 1,508,187 pounds, and 904,834 pounds was on the accounts of commanders and ships' crews. BL, Board's Collections: collections of papers in support of East India Company Draft Despatches [hereafter Board's Collections], 60 (doc. no. 1369), State of the Indigo Manufacture etc., Extract of Commercial letter to Bengal, 27 July 1796, p. 44.

58 P.J. Marshall, *Problems of Empire: Britain and India, 1757–1813* (London: Routledge, 1998), 94.

59 BL, Home Miscellaneous, 406, Memorandum by John Cochrane on India Trade and Shipping, p. 88. John Cochrane wrote that an 'actual mania prevailed; and several merchants, not content with the slow returns of the farms, launched, through new channels, into the very gulph of speculation'. Ibid. The first indigo factory in Bihar was established in 1783 and indigo works multiplied very quickly. Tripathi, *Trade and Finance in Bengal Presidency*, 41.

60 In 1790, when the company had to cut down its indigo investments, it reduced its contracts for Awadh indigo by two-thirds while that of Bengal by one-third. WBSA, Board of Trade: Commercial, vol. 84, Proceedings, Fort William, 29 Jan. 1790, pp. 240–3.

carried aboard company ships, it insisted that each chest or cask be identified by the factory mark stamped on it.[61]

Notwithstanding these restrictions, European merchants and manufacturers could still import large quantities of foreign indigo into Calcutta by securing from the company remission of duties, by purchasing indigo at low prices to offset the Calcutta duties, or by smuggling.[62] The company's endeavours to protect and promote the industry within its territory certainly led to contestations among European indigo planter-manufacturers of Bengal and those located outside of it or who dealt with indigo produced in Agra and Awadh. In 1790, an English merchant and indigo planter in Bengal, Carl Blume, proposed a detailed scheme to the company that envisaged discrimination against foreign indigo and preference for indigo produced within the company's territories.[63] In 1796, a memorandum signed by some fifty-eight merchants and mercantile firms complained to the company about the injury that Bengal indigo suffered from 'foreign' indigo imports and desired that the company restrict these.[64] In another memorandum, some merchant firms trading in foreign indigo defended their trade and argued that the indigo they imported from outside the company's provinces actually contributed to Bengal's total indigo exports to Europe.[65]

After much deliberation, the Court of Directors in London and the Board of Trade in Bengal decided to restrict the import of 'foreign' indigo into

---

61 BL, East India Company Correspondence with India, 11, Commercial Letter, 25 Jan. 1792, p. 192.

62 In December 1789, some merchants and manufacturers petitioned and obtained from the company a temporary remission in the Calcutta duties on indigo they imported from the Banaras, Agra, and Awadh. BL, East India Company Correspondence with India, 11, Commercial Letter, 7 Dec. 1789, pp. 22–3. They also petitioned for remission in freight charges and duties in London, which was referred to the Court of Directors and the Board of Trade. Ibid., In 1792, the company declined to grant any remission in the *zemindari* and *manji* duties in Calcutta. BL, East India Company Correspondence with India, 11, Commercial Letter, 25 Jan. 1792, pp. 191–2. Many merchants and contractors cheated the company by buying cheap Agra and Awadh indigo and passing it on to Britain and Europe as Bengal indigo. BL, Home Miscellaneous, 406, Memorandum by John Cochrane on India Trade and Shipping, pp. 88–9.

63 He also proposed the abolition of the 5 percent duty in London, a reduction in warehouse room charge from 2½ to 1 percent, and 3 pence per pound as freight. BL, Home Miscellaneous, 434, Memorandum of measures and means to introduce, improve, and enlarge the manufacture of indigo in Bengal and Bahar, Hugli, 30 Dec. 1790, pp. 615–6.

64 BL, Board's Collections, 60 (doc. no. 1369), State of the Indigo Manufacture etc., Extract proceedings of the Board of Trade, Bengal, 28 Oct. 1796, pp. 51–60.

65 Ibid., 67–72.

Calcutta by imposing prohibitive duties and by accepting on board EIC ships only indigo that was produced within the colony.[66] The company considered subjecting all indigo imports from outside the company's territories to an additional 15 percent duty in Calcutta.[67] But it knew that shutting the doors of Calcutta to foreign indigo would not be without repercussions. Bengal indigo competed in Europe with that from Spanish- and Franco-American colonies, Java, the Philippines, Manila, and Mauritius. Restricting import of indigo from Awadh and Agra into Calcutta would adversely affect Bengal's indigo supplies to Europe, which, in turn, would encourage imports from elsewhere, particularly Central and South America and Java. Further, the company understood that the closure of the eastward traffic from Agra and Awadh to Calcutta would result in indigo flowing westward to Gujarat and from there to Europe through other channels.

The company knew very well that the competition was not just between Bengal and 'foreign' indigo but also between Indian indigo and the dye from the West Indies and America.[68] Any reduction in supplies from Bengal would encourage imports of American, Java, and other indigo into Europe, which would deprive Bengal and the company of all fiscal benefits (revenues) accruing from its large-scale production. The Bengal government was, therefore, less inclined to restrict imports of foreign indigo because it competed with the cheap North American indigo in European markets.[69] The Bengal Board of Trade rightly observed that 'if any impediments be thrown in the way of the Oude [Awadh] indigo we apprehend that, exclusive of the other bad effects, they would operate as an encouragement to the numerous rivals in this article, and that in particular they would act like a bounty to the indigo of the

66 The Board of Trade in Bengal did not oppose the import of indigo into Bengal from Upper India for export, but the Court of Directors in London proposed that such imports must be restricted and subjected to high import duties in order to protect the nascent indigo industry of the Presidency. Chowdhury, *Growth of Commercial Agriculture in Bengal*, 76–7.

67 BL, Board's Collections, 60 (doc. no. 1369), Extract of Commercial letter from Bengal, 15 August 1797, pp. 127–8.

68 The Board of Trade in Bengal noted, 'competition is not confined between Bengal and Awadh and countries west of it, but between all indigo exported from Calcutta and that carried to Europe from other parts of the world'. BL, Board's Collections, 60 (doc. no. 1369) State of the Indigo Manufacture etc., Extract proceedings of the Board of Trade, Bengal, 28 Oct. 1796, pp. 115–6.

69 BL, Board's Collections 60 (doc. no. 1369), Extract Bengal Separate Consultations, 5 March 1798, pp. 130–1. In 1788, the Bengal Board of Trade had noted the opposition of those dealing with West Indian and American indigo in London to Bengal indigo.

Carolinas, Georgia, and the Mississippi'.[70] One notices in the deliberations of the Court of Directors, the Board of Trade, and the Governor-General and Council that not only were the company's fiscal aspirations at times incompatible with its commercial interests but also that its overall economic interests in the colony were sometimes not in accord with the national interests at home. In consideration of the latter, the company had to act against the imperatives of the colonial state and disregard the voices that demanded restrictions on the import of foreign indigo into Bengal.[71]

By 1800, Bengal had become the largest producer of indigo in the world and it catered to large demand for it in Europe.[72] During 1796–1800, out of the total average annual imports of indigo into Britain, amounting to 3.87 million pounds, Bengal alone contributed 3.32 million pounds. Certainly, the company's administrative and judicial measures, its large-scale annual purchases, and monetary advances to indigo planters contributed to this. Although the company lost its exclusive right to export indigo from India to Britain, it continued to participate in trade by exporting indigo to Britain either on its own account or for manufacturers who had received advances from it. Soon, indigo manufacturers challenged even this right of the company. In the absence of a corresponding proportional rise in European demand, any expansion in indigo production was bound to have serious commercial implications. As early as 1795, indigo merchants had expressed concern about the impending danger of London markets being overstocked with Bengal indigo.[73] Prospects of high demand for indigo in Europe had induced private European merchants in Bengal and adjoining provinces to invest in indigo, whose exports then became a

---

70 Ibid., 123–4.

71 Thus, the proposal to impose an additional 15 percent duty on 'foreign' indigo brought into Calcutta was rescinded in 1798 by the Governor-General. BL, Board's Collections, 60 (doc. no. 1369), State of the Indigo Manufacture etc., Extract Bengal Separate Consultations, 5 March 1798, p. 135; ibid., Extract of Separate letter from Bengal, 16 March 1798, pp. 137–8. This was much to the disappointment of those manufacturers located in the company's provinces. John Cochrane, thus, characterised the import of 'foreign' indigo into Bengal as 'unmercantile traffic' and blamed the government for allowing and protecting it. BL, Home Miscellaneous, 406, Memorandum by John Cochrane on India Trade and Shipping, pp. 88–9.

72 Chowdhury, *Growth of Commercial Agriculture in Bengal*, 80–3. In 1795, out of the total indigo imports of about 4.4 million pounds into Britain, approximately 3 million pounds came from Bengal. Tripathi, *Trade and Finance in Bengal Presidency*, 42.

73 BL, Board's Collections, 60 (doc. no. 1369), State of the Indigo Manufacture etc., Extract of Commercial letter from Bengal, 15 May 1795, p. 31.

means of transmitting their wealth to Europe.[74] Government encouragement was still quite crucial, and it was readily solicited by manufacturers. In 1801, indigo planters like Fairlie, Colvins, and Bazett petitioned the Bengal government for its continued encouragement and also requested early advances from the company to be distributed among peasants.[75]

By the early nineteenth century, however, the industry had expanded so much that no further encouragement from the company was needed. Planter-manufacturers apprehended that if the company continued to advance money and purchase indigo for export, it would further enhance production, for which there was no corresponding increase in the demand.[76] In 1809, the Bengal government worried that indigo cultivation had increased so much and that so many new factories had been established that the produce during a favourable season would far exceed the ordinary demand.[77] In 1810–11, the Court of Directors also expressed concern over Bengal indigo overstocking the London markets and depressing prices.[78]

In 1811, Alexander Nowell, an indigo manufacturer in Bengal, expressed his concern to the Court of Directors about the company's purchases and cash advances to manufacturers causing a 'ruinous extension of manufacture' and requested that they restrict the company's participation in the trade.[79] By involving itself, he argued, the company had caused uncommon extension of

74 In the 1790s, a large number of them were engaged in its culture in Banaras where they got tracts of land on lease for indigo cultivation. In 1793, there were about 40 such planters and manufacturers in Banaras producing indigo for the home market. Kamala Prasad Mishra, *Banaras in Transition (1738–1795): A Socio-Economic Study* (New Delhi: Munshiram Manoharlal, 1975), 154. In the early nineteenth century, many districts of the Agra and Awadh produced large quantities of indigo. Asiya Siddiqi, *Agrarian Change in a Northern Indian State: Uttar Pradesh, 1819–1833* (Oxford: Clarendon Press, 1973), 141–53.

75 BL, Home Miscellaneous, 737, Mr. Fairlie to John Malcolm, Calcutta, 6 Nov. 1801, pp. 101–4.

76 The company's investments in Bengal indigo in the 1800s were rather large. In 1810, the company's allocation of funds for indigo amounted to 2 million rupees out of the total 8.43 million for all Bengal goods. BL, Home Miscellaneous, 374, Extract Letter to Bombay, 5 Jan. 1810, p. 195. For 1811–1812, the company allocated 4.5 million rupees to be invested in indigo. WBSA, Board of Trade, Indigo: 1811–1812, vol. 1. Proceedings, Fort William, 20 Sept. 1811, pp. 2–3.

77 BL, East India Company Correspondence with India, 14, Extract of commercial letter, Bengal, 3 March 1809 (not foliated).

78 WBSA, Board of Trade: Indigo 1811–1812, Proceedings, Fort William, Calcutta, 20 Sept. 1811, p. 5.

79 *Papers Relating to East India Affairs* (1811), no. 1, p. 1. Between 1807–08 and 1811–12, the company purchased 33,173 *man* or 2,487,975 pounds of indigo (worth more than 5 million rupees). WBSA, Board of Trade: Indigo, vol. 1, Proceedings, Fort William, 6 Dec. 1811, p. 58.

production which would lead to overstocked markets in Europe, falling prices and profits, the ruin of indigo planters, and the loss of benefits that the company derived from its production, and ultimately it would prompt other countries to manufacture indigo for Europe. Considering that the company's trade was no interference with the liberty extended to all merchants, the Court denied Nowell's petition. As one of the established indigo manufacturers of Bengal, Nowell was concerned about his long-term business interests and perceived the company's role as a facilitator and not as a competitor. Those who benefited from the company's indigo purchases may not have held the same opinion about the company's role as a sovereign. The company continued to invest in indigo, and many manufacturers, including some local ones, received advances and contracted to supply indigo to the company. The directors in London knew very well the precarious nature of the indigo market and were opposed to any measures undertaken by the company that would lead to an exponential growth of indigo production in the colony. They disapproved any suggestion of the company becoming a manufacturer. They also did not approve the promotion of the indigo industry in the Madras Presidency because they knew that any substantial increase in production would adversely affect the markets in India and Europe.

By the time the company's charter was up for renewal in 1833, British private traders and their capital dominated the colony's indigo industry. With the Charter Act of 1833, the company finally lost whatever control it had exercised until then as a sovereign to restrict Europeans from penetrating the agrarian economy of the colony.[80] Whether the European entrepreneurs should be

80 The company proceeded very cautiously in allowing Europeans to settle in indigo districts and lease or own land because it apprehended an unhappy outcome. It was not in favour of making India a settler colony and repeat what had happened to Britain's North American colonies in the 1770s. John Crawfurd, *A View of the Present State and Future Prospects of the Free Trade and Colonisation of India* (London: Ridgway, 1828), 47–9. When required, the company exerted its control over them. In 1794, the company withdrew the privilege it had earlier granted to indigo manufacturers in Bengal of holding land on lease and, in Banaras, it limited the size of individual holdings to a maximum of 50 *bighas*. This restriction was prompted by an affray between the servants of an opium contractor and an indigo planter. BL, East India Company Correspondence with India, 11, Revenue Letter, Bengal, 29 Dec. 1794, pp. 407–8. After the district was ceded to the company by the Nawab of Awadh, the colonial government passed a regulation in 1789–90 that allowed private European merchants to lease land or become proprietors to grow indigo or another crop. Taking advantage of this, a large number of European merchants obtained leases of large areas of land for indigo cultivation. There were more than 40 indigo planters settled in Banaras in the early 1790s. Mishra, *Banaras in Transition*, 154.

allowed to settle in the interior and engage in capitalist agricultural farming had been a major question in Britain in the 1820s.[81] The proponents of free trade won the debate and the new act in 1833 did away with the license system and allowed the unrestricted settlement of Britons and Europeans in the colony. It is interesting to note that in their demand for free trade, people often cited the example of how private British capital and enterprise had rendered Bengal indigo the best and the highly valued in the world market. The indigo industry, thus, served as a prime example of free capitalist enterprise and a model to be replicated in other spheres of commodity production in the colony. In this respect, indigo contributed to the EIC's eventual loss of its trade monopoly in Asia. The industry was itself a major beneficiary of the unrestrained settlement of Britons and other Europeans, and of the penetration of their capital in the colony's agrarian economy. This is evident from the rapid growth in indigo production in Bengal in the late 1830s and 1840s.[82]

Peasants, Indigo Manufacturers, and the State

Competition and contestations occurred among planter-manufacturers, too. In an industry that was both dynamic and highly precarious due to uncertainty of production and instability of demand, many merchants and manufacturers made fortunes, but many suffered failures.[83] To thrive one had not only to produce indigo successfully; one also had to be attentive to the factors that shaped the market. One major factor that adversely affected the indigo enterprise was competition. We have seen above how the manufacturers of Bengal competed with and challenged planter-manufacturers and merchants trading in

---

81 Crawfurd, *A View of the Present State and Future Prospects*; 'East India Monopoly—Export Trade to India', *The Oriental Herald*, vol. 19, no. 59 (Nov. 1828), 185–203; 'East India Monopoly—Import Trade', *The Oriental Herald*, vol. 19 no. 60 (Dec. 1828), 387–402. See also BL, IOR A/2/15, Minutes of Evidence on the East-India Company's Affairs, 29 April 1813, pp. 493–5.

82 Average annual value of indigo exports from Bengal increased from Rs 13.4 million during 1826–35 to Rs 20.8 million during 1836–45 (Table 3.4 in chapter 3).

83 When the indigo market in Britain collapsed in the decade following 1826, many indigo planters lost their fortunes and almost all major agency houses in Bengal went bankrupt. Chowdhury, *Growth of Commercial Agriculture in Bengal*, 84–111; Kling, *Partner in Empire*; Chaudhuri, *Economic Development of India*, 21. In a recent study of the commercial enterprises of perhaps the richest and the largest agency house in Calcutta, John Palmer and Co., Anthony Webster has underlined the role of indigo in bringing about the ruin of this agency house. Anthony Webster, *The Richest East India Merchant: The Life and Business of John Palmer of Calcutta, 1767–1836* (Woodbridge: Boydell Press, 2007), 34, 58–60, see especially chapter six; idem, *Twilight of the East India Company*, 87–91.

'foreign' indigo. Within Bengal, too, the planter-manufacturers competed with each other, and that intensified conflict between them and the peasants. The planter-manufacturers knew very well that they were competing in Europe with good-quality Spanish and French indigo and that unless they produced indigo of a superior quality or at very low costs, they could not undersell their rivals.[84] They therefore sought to minimise the costs of production by controlling the peasants who cultivated indigo for them.[85]

As the number of European planter-manufacturers increased in the colony, they began competing with each other to secure peasant labour to grow indigo. Initially, this worked to the advantage of the peasants, but exploitation and violence against them soon intensified. Affrays, sometimes violent, among peasants were often manifestations of competition among manufacturers. In 1794, for instance, a conflict occurred between servants of an opium contractor and an indigo planter in Banaras, apparently, over the control of peasants.[86] Fierce competition and violent clashes proliferated in the early nineteenth century. In the Saran district of Bihar in 1810, an altercation involving arson and physical assaults on natives and Europeans occurred between the assistant and employees of Mr Moran, who wanted to establish an indigo manufactory, and those of Mr Douglas, who owned a manufactory nearby and did not want the former to compete with him.[87] In 1830, a violent affray was reported among peasants belonging to two indigo planters, Pratt and Buckland. The Bengal government noted that 'mutual hostile proceedings of Messrs Pratt and Buckland have engendered discord and ill will between their *ryots* [peasants] and dependents'. A letter from Mr Hawkins, Magistrate of the Purnea District, to Mr Warner, Commissioner of the Division, illuminates this point. He wrote,

> Mr. Pratt either bought or rented a piece of land near Mr. Buckland's cultivation in which he built a pair of vats with the alleged intention of working off his own plant. Mr. Buckland apprehensive that his ryots would carry their plant to a factory immediately at hand rather than take it a longer way, built [vats] close to Mr. Pratt, and from that moment

84 The Court of Directors repeatedly told the company in India that unless a material alteration in price or quality is achieved it cannot compete with American indigo in European markets.

85 They also did their best to improve the quality of indigo and this was testified to by the Court of Directors already in 1795.

86 BL, East India Company Correspondence with India, 11, Revenue Letter, Bengal, 29 Dec. 1794, pp. 407–8.

87 *Papers relating to East India Affairs* (1813), no. 5, Extract of the Bengal Judicial Consultations in the Criminal Department, 20 July 1810, p. 12.

> commenced a course of hostile measures. They have mutually been endeavouring to harass and annoy by bringing complaints through their dependents against the servants and ryots of each other.[88]

Competition did, in many cases, lead to clashes and coercion of the peasants, but the relationship between planter-manufacturers and peasants was neither always nor in all cases acrimonious and violent. Circumstances including the systems of land tenure and production contracts determined the degree of control the planter-manufacturers could exercise over peasants. In Lower Bengal, where the former did not have the right to own land or hold it on lease to grow indigo, a control over peasants was crucial to ensure regular supplies of indigo plant to manufactories they owned. The planter-manufacturers had recourse to the notorious advance contract system that kept the peasants in seemingly perpetual control and forced them to cultivate indigo for the manufacturers. In Bihar, Banaras, Agra, and Awadh, where Europeans were allowed to lease or own large tracts of land, many planter-manufacturers cultivated indigo themselves with the help of hired labourers (*nij* cultivation). This was, however, not as cost-effective as making peasants produce under the advance contract system.[89] Most manufacturers, therefore, gradually moved to the latter system. The contract system in force in these provinces was somewhat different and less exploitative than that commonly found in Bengal.

In Bihar in the nineteenth century, the practice of taking villages in farm (*theeka*) was a common and preferred system by which the manufacturers ensured the supplies of indigo plant/leaves to their manufactories.[90] They became landowners and held the land either in perpetual or temporary lease on payment of rent to the *zamindar* or government. They then divided the land among peasants in small lots of three to seven acres and assessed the holdings according to their comparative values. The peasants were required to set aside a portion of land (the best and most productive part of the holding) to grow indigo. The manufacturers provided the seed and the peasants supplied the

---

88 BL, Board's Collections, 1373 (doc. no. 54577), Affray in Purneah, 1830, Extract Fort William Judicial Consultations, 13 July 1830, p. 3; ibid., Extract Fort William Judicial Consultations, 7 Sept. 1830, pp. 9–10.

89 A *bigha* of land yielded about 15–20 bundles (each weighing 3½–4 *man*) of leaves. The cost of cultivating a *bigha* of land under the *nij* system amounted to about Rs 4. Thus, the European manufacturers preferred the *raiyyati* system because they could obtain the crop at less than half of the costs of *nij* cultivation.

90 Hugh Martin-Leak, 'An Historical Memoir of the Indigo Industry of Bihar', *Economic Botany*, vol. 29 (1975), 361–71; Badshaah Chaube, *Betia Raj aur Champaran ke Kisan* [Betia Estate and the Peasants of Champaran] (Patna: Impression Publication, 2011), chapter 4.

crop to the factory.[91] In either case, control over peasants and labourers was necessary to keep production costs low and so thrive in a highly competitive indigo market.

Initially, the planter-manufacturers lured the peasants with cash advances with which the latter could meet their household expenses, pay taxes, or invest in the next cycle of production. As long as indigo was sown on alluvial soil not under rice cultivation, peasants were for it because it supplemented their income. But as production expanded and spread to land formerly used for growing food grains, peasants grew discontented. They became reluctant to grow indigo because it was not as remunerative as rice, especially when the latter's price was high, as it was in the 1850s.[92] Contemporary descriptions of indigo production show that indigo cultivation was less profitable for peasants. It could even be ruinous because they had to bear the risks of crop failure caused by early inundations (quite common in Lower Bengal), drought, untimely and heavy rainfall, or any other natural and man-made calamities.[93] There was among peasants, we are told, an almost universal dislike for indigo, and they were indisposed to accept advances and cultivate indigo. Under such circumstances, the manufacturers resorted to forcing the contract upon peasants and manipulated the advances and the account books to reduce them to

91 F.E.C. Linde, *Indigo: A short sketch of the Cultivation, Manufacture & Trade of Indigo* (Calcutta: Central Press, 1882), 2.

92 In the first quarter of the nineteenth century, they were made to sell their crop to European manufacturers at the rate of 6–10 bundles per rupee depending upon prevailing circumstances and prices. At the average rate of 8 bundles per rupee, the cultivators earned Rs 2 or less per *bigha*, which was not sufficient to cover the costs of growing indigo. In the early 1830s, some planters raised the price to 5 bundles a rupee. This may have provided some relief, but the contract system under which the cultivators produced indigo remained exploitative.

93 The testimony of the company's civil servants in Bengal, Christian missionary activists, and the native peasants before the indigo commission clearly shows that indigo cultivation was not profitable for peasants. J. Long, *Strike, But Hear!: Evidence Explanatory of the Indigo System in Lower Bengal* (Calcutta: R.C. Lepage & Co., 1861), 5–6, 16–17, 20–1, 32, 70–1. The Bengal Revenue department noted in 1831 that about nine-tenths of the land under indigo cultivation in Bengal was more or less under water by the end of July and the crop was liable to be lost by the encroachment of early inundation. BL, Board's Collections, 1504 (no. 58997), Agriculture and Horticulture Society, Calcutta, Extract from the proceedings of Government in the Revenue Department, 8 Nov. 1831, p. 105. In 1855, the officiating judge of Rungpore, G.U. Yule, noted that 'the Ryots, reasonably or unreasonably, are averse to Indigo, believing that there are many other crops which yield a more certain as well as a better profit'. Long, *Strike, But Hear!*, 16.

the position of debt-bondage and to coerce them to produce indigo in perpetuity.[94] Those refusing to do so were subjected to physical abuse.

Violence against peasants took various forms, the most common of which were the forcible taking away of land, labour, and cattle, abducting, illegal detention, and corporal punishment. To carry out these, many manufacturers kept armed men (*lathials*)—hundreds in some cases—at their factories. As early as 1810, the Bengal government noticed the prevalence of such abusive activities and initiated administrative measures to stop the abuse.[95] Nothing, however, could ameliorate the conditions of the peasants. On the contrary, government measures, as we will see below, precipitated conflict between the manufacturers and their workers as the former persisted in their efforts to control peasants and force them to cultivate indigo.

What added to the misery of the peasants were the rising prices of agricultural produce in the 1850s and the lack of a corresponding increase in the price of the indigo they raised. As the Reverend J. Long noted in 1861, the prices of agricultural produce had doubled during the preceding few years but the price of indigo paid to the peasants did not increase even a little.[96] Reflecting on the oppression of peasants, Asiaticus wrote that the manufacturers never raised the price they paid to the peasants.

> For some years, the price of the staple crops has risen greatly, while the indigo planters had continued to pay for the indigo plant, which the raiyats cultivated for them under the system of advances, at rates which had been in vogue for thirty years. The poverty of the cultivators left them at the mercy of the European capitalists, and the system of advances ensured in practice compulsory cultivation of the plants.[97]

Since the early nineteenth century, thus, the relationship between the manufacturers and the peasants in Lower Bengal was fraught with violence.

94 Generally, a written contract was signed by both the parties, but in many cases the manufacturers forced the peasants to sign on a blank paper and then they manipulated the accounts in such a way that the peasant signatories remained perpetually indebted. In many cases, even the full amount of the stipulated advance was not paid to the peasants.

95 The Governor-General instructed the civil and police officials to stop the manufacturers from oppressing peasants. *Papers Presented to the House of Commons relating to East India Affairs*, Circular letter of the Governor-General to the Magistrates under the Presidency, Fort William, 13 July 1810, pp. 1–3.

96 Long, *Strike, but Hear!*, 3.

97 Asiaticus, 'The Rise and Fall of the Indigo Industry in India', *The Economic Journal*, vol. 22, no. 86 (1912), 241.

Exploitation and physical abuse against the peasants intensified so much that their position, for many contemporary observers, looked hardly different from that of slaves. Lord Macaulay, for example, remarked in a memorandum that many peasants were 'reduced to a state not far removed from partial slavery'.[98] In 1832, the Court of Directors observed that 'the greatest of evils of which the ryots complain is the almost utter impracticability of being able to free themselves, should they once have the misfortune to receive indigo advances, either by their own free will or compulsion'.[99] Commenting on the exploitative nature of the advance contract system, the judge of Backergunge wrote to the government of Bengal in 1855 that 'no ryot will take an advance unless he is in the last extremety, and that none ever get out of the Planter's books who are once in them'.[100] In the 1880s, similarly, F.E.C. Linde wrote that 'it is not rare to meet with instances in which whole generations are given over, bound hand and foot, to a factory, the grandson still vainly striving to adjust the accounts which his miserable sire opened in an unhappy moment'.[101]

The exploitative nature of indigo cultivation in India caught the attention of the people and government in Britain in 1859–60, when the indigo peasants in Lower Bengal revolted against the planter-manufacturers.[102] The blue mutiny, as it came to be known in the annals of colonial Bengal, certainly forced the government to look into the state of the industry, but it failed to bring about any fundamental improvement in the conditions of the peasantry. All that resulted was the partial relocation of European planters in the 1860s from Bengal to Bihar (mainly in the districts of the Tirhoot division), where the peasants were made to bear the brunt of indigo production and suffer hardships for the next sixty years or more.[103] Many contemporary European observers noted the

---

98 Lord Macaulay, quoted in Asiaticus, 'The Rise and Fall of the Indigo Industry in India'.

99 *Report of the Indigo Commission appointed under act XI of 1860* (Calcutta, 1860), Appendix 16, Letter from the Court of Directors, London, 10 April 1832, p. 328.

100 *Report of the Indigo Commission*, C. Steer, Judge of Backergunge to the Secretary to the Government of Bengal, 7 Feb. 1855, p. 17.

101 Linde, *Indigo: a Short Sketch of Cultivation and Manufacture*, 4.

102 There is a good literature on the peasant revolt of 1859–60 against indigo planters in some districts of Bengal. Deenbandhu Mitra's *Neel Darpan* written and published in 1860, articulated the evils of indigo plantation system and its ill-consequences. Ranajit Guha, 'Neel-Darpan: The Image of a Peasant Revolt in a Liberal Mirror', in David Hardiman (ed.), *Peasant Resistance in India, 1858–1914* (Delhi: OUP, 1992), 60–110; Subhas Bhattacharya, 'The Indigo Revolt of Bengal', *Social Scientist*, vol. 5, no. 12 (1977), 13–23.

103 Soon, the indigo industry in Bengal dwindled as it largely gave way to the production of jute. *Report of the Administration of Bengal, 1871–72* (Calcutta, Bengal Secretariat Press, 1872), 21, 135; Bose, *Peasant Labour and Colonial Capital*, 51–2, 156.

sufferings of indigo cultivators and their families and accepted the adage 'without exploitation, no indigo'.[104] In the 1880s, thus, F.E.C. Linde wrote,

> For, not alone that the ryot pays a sufficiently high rent for the land he occupies, he is forced much against his will to give up so much of it for indigo cultivation, besides having to supply the cattle, the plough, and the labor required for it.... And the process of preparing the land for an indigo crop is by no means an easy one; for, according to the nature of the site and soil, it has to be ploughed from three to eight times, to be harried once or twice before sowing, not to speak of the weeding when plant has made its appearance above the ground, and the cutting and transporting of the plant at a moment's notice by behest of the task-master. Moreover, in case the first sowings should have proved a failure, say through want of rain or owing to bad seed, then the long suffering Aryan has to do the whole work over again without receiving any compensation whatever. If the work be not done at the time appointed, a duffadar (native overseer) is quartered on him at his expense, until the work shall have been completed. How then is it surprising that the ryot is becoming every year more and more impoverished, and that at the slightest failure of his food crop, nothing is left to him but to die of starvation?[105]

Modern scholarship has understood the peasant–planter relationship as inherently exploitative. Such a characterisation is based mainly on the evidence collected by the indigo commission and the reports that were generated in the aftermath of the indigo revolt. The espousal of the indigo peasants' trepidations by the anticolonial nationalism of Gandhi and his followers in the early twentieth century has also contributed to this interpretation. Only a few scholars have questioned the nationalist construal of peasant relationships with planter-manufacturers and have shown that the notion of an excessive exploitation of peasants by the indigo planters is somewhat exaggerated.[106] They

104 *Minute of the Lieutenant-Governor of Bengal on the Report of the Indigo Commission* (Calcutta: Bengal Secretariat Office, 1861), 1–34.

105 Linde, *Indigo: A Short Sketch of Cultivation and Manufacture*, 3.

106 Colin M. Fisher, 'Planters and Peasants: the Ecological Context of Agrarian Unrest on the Indigo Plantations of North Bihar, 1820–1920', in Clive Dewey and A.G. Hopkins (eds), *The Imperial Impact: Studies in the Economic History of Africa and India* (London: The Athlone Press, 1978), 115–31; Peter Robb, 'Peasants' choices? Indian Agriculture and the Limits of Commercialization in Nineteenth-Century Bihar', *Economic History Review*, vol. 45, no. 1 (1992), 97–119; Tirthankar Roy, 'Indigo and Law in Colonial India', *Economic History Review*, vol. 64, Supplement 1 (2011), 60–75.

have argued that the system was less extortionate than generally assumed and that indigo production was not universally un-remunerative. Their views are based on analyses of the place of indigo in the agrarian ecology, social structures of control, and differential peasant landholdings. Tirthankar Roy, for example, has made the interesting observation that the planters' adversaries were not poor peasants but the 'peasants with privileged tenure'.[107] It is important, therefore, to differentiate indigo-producing peasants from ordinary peasants and sharecroppers engaged mainly in subsistence agriculture. Most Bengal peasants appearing before the indigo inquiry commission, and most of those from north Bihar in the late nineteenth century, had large landholdings and, as such, they were better placed to exploit the system of cash advances than the lesser folks in the villages.[108] To understand the agrarian relations in indigo-producing villages in terms of a discordant and adversarial peasant–planter relationship or to interpret it as excessively exploitative and extortionate and attribute it to the British-led capitalist farming and agricultural commercialisation is too simplistic and untenable on at least three counts.

Such a view postulates the existence of antagonistic class categories and assumes that each class was socially and economically undifferentiated. It dispenses with the role that the complex social structures played in shaping agrarian relations of production. And it dismisses the role of the commodity itself and its unique but varying characteristics in the agrarian ecology of colonial India. As Peter Robb has argued, the subjection of peasants to British planters was never absolute, because the latter always depended on a hierarchy of profit-sharing intermediaries and an 'indirect and intermixed' control mechanism.[109] European indigo planter-manufacturers certainly created the conditions in which subordination, abuse, and extortion of peasants could take

107 Roy, 'Indigo and Law in Colonial India', 67.

108 Most peasants who were examined by the indigo commission had a large landholding: Nuffur Das (had 24 *bighas*), Ghani Dafadar (4 *bighas*), Abadi Mandal (48 *bighas*), Ahad Mandal (107 *bighas*), Siraj Biswas (15 *bighas*), Dinu Mundal (32 *bighas*), Jamir Mundal (35 *bighas*), Dukhi Sheikh (60 *bighas*), Haji Mulla (31 *bighas*), Kadamulla (80 *bighas*). *Report on Indigo Commission*, 1860, 57–72. Rajat Datta considers peasant holdings, ranging from 10 to 30 *bighas*, as small on which agricultural production was undertaken mainly by peasants with the labour of their families. Rajat Datta, 'Merchants and Peasants: A Study of the Structure of Local Trade in Grain in late Eighteenth Century Bengal', in Sanjay Subrahmanyam (ed.), *Merchants, Markets and the State in Early Modern India* (Delhi: OUP, 1990), 151. In the Tirhoot division of north Bihar, indigo-producing peasants' landholding varied from 3 to 7 *bighas* (a *bigha* in Bihar was equal to an acre). Fisher, 'Planters and Peasants', 127.

109 Robb, 'Peasants' choices? Indian Agriculture', 97–119.

place, and some were directly involved in such occurrences. But it were the intermediaries—local chiefs, village headmen, clerks and other employees—and their ambitions to secure a share in the profits that perpetrated violence against peasants. In fact, the instances of violence reveal the inability of European capital to directly control peasants and make them subservient to it. Peasants often contested and resisted attempts by indigo planter-manufacturers and intermediaries to reinforce control.

Resistance occurred in many forms. Some peasants accepted monetary advances from a manufacturer and absconded; some did not allocate the best land to indigo as stipulated in the contract; some sold their crop to others who paid a better price; and some even took advances from more than one manufacturer for the same crop.[110] Peasants' non-compliance with contracts and the losses that this caused were endless concerns for the planter-manufacturers who lobbied, without much success, for a legal provision that would render any breach of contract a criminal offense punishable by the magistrate. In 1811, their demand that civil suits be converted into a criminal cases was rejected by the government under Lord Minto. Only after the indigo rebellion did the government accede to the demand and pass a temporary act, in 1860. This applied to that season alone and was designed to afford 'equal and complete protection' to ryots and planters both.[111]

Many peasants resisted the planters by petitioning to the government and complaining about abuses and violence they suffered from the indigo planter-manufacturers. They took full advantage of the state institutions in their localities and reported any oppression and violence that befell them to the local magistrates. The creation of sub-divisions in districts allowed the peasants greater access to the magisterial courts.[112] The evidence presented

110 In the 1820s, James Hay, an indigo planter in Purnia, noted that many peasants, after receiving advances, escaped from the contract, especially in a bad year, when the value of their produce was higher than the average of the contract price. *Memorial of Mr. James Hay, indigo planter, Poorneah, to the Hon. East India Company, appealing against the proceedings of Mr. William Wollen, judge of Poorneah* (London, 1826), p. 2; *Rural Life in Bengal: Illustrative of Anglo-Indian Suburban Life* [anonymous] (London: W. Thacker & Co., 1860), 90–1.

111 *Selections from the Records of the Government of Bengal: Papers related to indigo cultivation in Bengal*, No. XXXIII, Part II (Calcutta, 1860), Lt. Governor of Bengal to A. Sconce, Legislative Member, Calcutta, 23 March 1860, pp. 358–60; Long, *Strike, But Hear!*, 3. The government had rejected the petition on earlier occasions, but acceded to their demand in 1860 through the Act XI. Long, *Strike, But Hear!*, 33.

112 Apprehending this, many planters opposed this reform initiated by the state to improve the administration and law and justice. A European planter of Jessore in Bengal

before the indigo commission in 1860 reinforces the complaints they frequently made to the court and shows that the judges and officials gave favourable hearing to the peasants and took initiatives to resolve disputes.[113] Litigation, however, was an expensive venture and not all peasants could afford access to magistrates and the courts. Moreover, the peasants generally believed that government administrators were complicit in perpetrating violence and coercion in the industry. Some indigo planter-manufacturers developed camaraderie with local officials and judges and sought to force advances and contracts upon the peasants and then coerce them to comply with it. They also had influence in the upper echelons of the bureaucracy and, at times, influenced judges and officials against being on the peasants' side. On many occasions, peasants' complaints fell upon deaf ears, or the remedial measures were not adequate to root out the problem. Many peasants were, therefore, reluctant to seek the government's intercession and generally acquiesced to the circumstances or resorted to one of the modes of resistance mentioned above.

When petitions were impossible or ineffective, direct action was their response to the planter-manufacturers' oppression. In 1832, peasants led by the *Faraizi* leader, Titu Mir, attacked the Barasat factory.[114] This action inspired the peasants, and European manufacturers were petrified of similar attacks on their factories even in the late 1850s. When the rebellion of 1857 broke out against the company, aggrieved peasants actively sided with the rebels.[115] Two years later, the indigo peasants of Bengal rose against the manufacturers. On both occasions, the peasants not only resisted the manufacturers but also challenged the state, which, in their view, had failed to protect them from the manufacturers' tyranny. These were not the only occasions when the peasants resisted the manufacturers. Indigo peasants actively participated in the anti-landlord and anti-British campaigns of the *Faraizi* Movement in Bengal to such a degree that any indigo-growing peasant who resisted the landlords or manufacturers was branded a *Faraizi*.[116]

---

strenuously objected to founding the headquarters of a new Sub-Division near his factory on the ground of proneness of the natives to litigation 'with the means at their doors'. Long, *Strike, But Hear!*, 3.

113 Many officials who had served in indigo districts of Bengal as magistrates or judges testified to the validity of peasants' complaints. Long, *Strike, But Hear!*.

114 Long, *Strike, But Hear!*, 64; Bose, *Peasant Labour and Colonial Capital*, 148–9.

115 NA, Kew, 30/29/18/1, Statement of an indigo planter in respect to the present disturbances in the North Western Provinces, 1857.

116 Bihar State Archives, Patna, *Report of the Administration of Bengal, 1871–72* (Calcutta: Bengal Secretariat Press, 1872), p. 22.

Peasants in other parts of British India such as Awadh, Agra, and Delhi were less oppressed than those in Bengal. The competition among planter-manufacturers was not so intense, the terms of contract were not rigid, and above all, the manufacturers shared the risks with the peasants. In Bihar, for instance, peasants receiving advances were entitled to compensation if their crops failed or were destroyed. Unlike the peasants in Bengal, they did not fall into the debt trap and were not so much coerced to produce indigo by the manufacturers as their counterparts in Bengal.[117] According to Colin Fisher, the system of indigo production in Bihar was based less on coercion than on persuasion. Generally, planters persuaded peasants to grow indigo by extending credit and liquidity facilities and exercising a 'form of seigneurial control' that they were endowed with as leaseholders of the land (*theeka*).[118] The relatively stable position of the local *zamindars* in terms of their proprietary rights over land and their influence among peasants also seemingly contributed to their better condition than their counterparts in Bengal. This changed in the late nineteenth century and the planter-peasant relationship became somewhat discordant. It worsened in the early twentieth century. Three simultaneous processes seem to have contributed to this.

Perhaps most important was the rapid growth in indigo production in Bihar after 1860 and the intense competition among indigo planters that ensued. Second, the native landlords gradually lost their fiscal and political stability. Many large and small *zamindaris* (estates) became insolvent and depended for their survival on the indigo planters' financial support. The planters bailed them out by extending monetary support; but in return, they took control of their land as leaseholders. For example, Betia estate, one of the largest in Bihar, was rescued by the planters but it lost thousands of acres in *theeka* to the Europeans.[119] This altered the balance of power in favour of the planters. The final factor was the successful launching of synthetic indigo on the world market by Germany in the 1890s. As a better and cheaper substitute, this adversely affected the global market for natural indigo.[120] As more and more of it was put on the market, the demand, price, and ultimately the entire indigo

117 Fisher, 'Planters and Peasants', 115. In parts of Bihar, indigo growing peasants received Rs 11 to Rs 14 per *bigha*, and, in case of crop failure, they received at least Rs 5 and 5 annas as compensation. Shukla, *Indigo and the Raj*, 65.

118 Fisher, 'Planters and Peasants', 117.

119 Jacques Pouchepadass, *Land, Power and Market: A Bihar District under Colonial Rule, 1860–1947* (New Delhi: Sage, 2000), chapter 7. In 1888–89, the indigo planter-manufacturers got 417 villages in farm from the *zamindar*. Chaube, *Betia Raj aur Champaran ke Kisan*, 110–11.

120 A.S. Macrae, 'Competition between the Aniline and Madder Dyes', *Science*, vol. 1, no. 6 (1880), 62–3.

commodity chain began to crumble. Under such circumstances, indigo peasants, merchants, and planters lost whatever profits and incentives they had enjoyed until then and had to bear the brunt of the doomed industry.

Peasant-Planter Relationship in a Long-Term Perspective

In an insightful essay, Colin Fisher has rightly argued that the problem of indigo as an agricultural crop needs to be understood in its ecological context. In his opinion, indigo was part of India's traditional pattern of double or triple cropping, and its successful production depended to a great extent on how well indigo was integrated with this annual agricultural pattern.[121] Peasants resisted growing indigo mainly in low-lying rice-growing regions and especially in times when rice prices were high, as they were in Lower Bengal in the 1850s and in north Bihar in the late nineteenth century. In places where peasants could raise and market their own crops of rice or other grains, as in the *doab* region and the Madras Presidency, indigo did not cause any major agrarian disruption. Some planters in those regions allowed them to manure their rice fields with the indigo refuse from steeping vats.[122] From this perspective, peasants' reluctance or refusal to grow indigo was not a rebellion against the planters or against extortion and abuse, but a fight for economic freedom to grow a crop that made more money than indigo.

If we compare the agrarian relations in the indigo industry of Mughal northern India in the early seventeenth-century and of the EIC-ruled colonial state of the late eighteenth-early nineteenth centuries, we find several characteristics in common. The relationships among peasants, planter-manufacturers, and merchants were complex and full of complementarities and contestations. The system of cash advances to peasant-producers and the intermediation by brokers and merchants were crucial in the seventeenth century, and a much more complex system of advance buying and a highly hierarchized form of intermediation were remarkable features of the industry in the colonial period. In neither Mughal nor colonial India could the state dominate indigo production or trade. This was precisely because, as Peter Robb has pointed out, the intermediaries, even though they sometimes reinforced peasants' subjection to their patrons, kept the state, merchants, and planter-manufacturers apart from

121 Fisher, 'Planters and Peasants'.

122 Fisher, 'Planters and Peasants'. Indigo peasants in Coromandel used plant refuse to manure their paddy lands. BL, Madras Revenue Proceedings (P/440), 63, Proceedings of the Revenue Board, Madras, 1870, p. 5834.

primary producers. This allowed peasants to retain their relative autonomy in economic matters. And being rich peasants with large landholdings, they could use their socioeconomic position to benefit from the industry, especially through the cash advances. The above analysis also reveals the constraints and limits within which the East India Company had to pursue its commercial and fiscal ambitions and exercise sovereignty in the colony. The EIC failed to control the indigo market or to keep up its indigo monopoly as private British and European merchants competed with the company in India and in Europe. As a state entity, too, the company could not control indigo planters who often took advantage of, misused, and circumvented or disregarded the provisions of its law and administration.[123]

123 Ranajit Guha has illuminated this aspect very well in his analysis of Dinbandhu Mitra's *Neel Darpan* (indigo mirror), a literary composition that embodies popular imagination of the indigo industry in Bengal in the mid-nineteenth century. Guha, 'Neel-Darpan: The Image of a Peasant Revolt in a Liberal Mirror', 73–4.

Conclusions

In this book, the primary objective has been to present a history in global context of Indian indigo and its manifold fascinating trajectories in a single narrative. This has been a stimulating task because of indigo's convoluted developmental paths, whether from plant to dye, from production to market and to consumers, or from one period and place to another. What has made this task even more fascinating are the diverse regional differences in the methods and modes of indigo production and trade in India and across the world. Such complexities have enabled me to explore and understand the nuances of the political and socioeconomic settings in which indigo commodity chains were deeply embedded, and kept me constantly reminded of the untenability of generalised or simplistic historical interpretations.

In the first instance, this book is about Indian indigo and as such it examines the long-term dynamics of the indigo industry and trade in their local and global contexts. It shows that the development of India's indigo industry from the seventeenth to nineteenth centuries constitutes a complex mix of continuity, change, innovation, and improvisation. Resilient older modes of production endured alongside new and innovative ones. The book examines the diverse approaches people had towards growing and producing indigo and it suggests that the course of development of indigo production techniques and technology represents successive stages of improvement and innovation. It also shows that the many players in the industry were as amenable to adopting changes and improvements in the precolonial period as they were in the colonial period. Instead of looking at the indigo industry through the binaries of precolonial–colonial, native–European, and primitive–modern, we can now see this as a long period of continual technical and technological improvisation.

In the nineteenth century, a major change occurred in the relative position of peasants, who were reduced to mere suppliers of agricultural raw material to indigo manufactories largely owned by European planters. The evidence shows that some peasants were coerced into cultivating indigo. Cash advances forced many into a debt-trap from which they could never emerge, and in some cases their progeny were forced to cultivate indigo for their forebears' creditors. However, this was not a universal phenomenon, and even where coercion took place, there are instances of peasant resistance, ranging from not putting their best efforts or land into indigo cultivation to outright refusal to cultivate indigo and even rebellion.

 | DOI 10.1163/9789004311558_008

The book approaches the subject from a global perspective and shows that the indigo industry in India was closely connected with the world market and that fluctuations in its fortunes must be understood in global historical and commercial contexts. It traces the emergence of the world market in indigo in the early seventeenth century with the European search for alternative sources of indigo supplies, and situates the Indian indigo industry in this evolving world market. It examines the endogenous and exogenous economic and political factors, especially how Europeans' desire to substitute imports from foreign lands with imports from their own colonies influenced indigo production and trade in India, as well as the nature and structure of the world market.

Secondly, this is a study of the indigo commodity chain and its various stages from production to distribution and consumption. It shows how the commodity chain in Indian indigo evolved from a small-scale, indigenous peasant household enterprise in the seventeenth century to a large-scale European capitalist venture in the nineteenth century. In the earlier period, even though indigo cultivation, manufacture, and trade were inter-connected through monetary advances and forward buying, they were not under the direct control of merchants or foreign trading companies. Indigo production then was largely in the hands of peasants, and different groups of merchants or their corporations dominated the trade. In the nineteenth century, European merchants extended their control over several stages of the chain including cultivation and processing of indigo in India and its distribution in Europe. Merchant firms such as John Palmers & Co. took control of the production and trade in the aftermath of the collapse of the indigo market in Europe in the 1830s, and eventually they superseded the planters and agency houses that had financed indigo production. Later, networks of London-based merchants and professional middlemen dominated these stages in the indigo commodity chain.

The book shows that the indigo chain in India, as elsewhere, was linked to competition with other commodity chains. Fluctuations in their relative market values had a profound impact on the indigo industry. The rise of South Carolina indigo and the decline of Central American indigo chains in the mid- and late-eighteenth century and the conditions that led to the indigo disturbances in Bengal in 1860 and an abrupt decline of the industry there can be seen as resulting partly from producers' responses to changes in the values and profitability of indigo via-à-vis rice, coffee, cotton, or cocoa.

Thirdly, this book is about indigo as a commodity and it examines the many important aspects of the industry, such as labour, production relations, and the nature of state-economy relationship. These are examined from the perspectives of the commodity and by keeping it at the centre of the narrative. This study underscores and explains the changes and continuities in these aspects of the indigo trade over the long term as triggered by indigo's distinct characteristics. In the colonial period, indigo production and trade were embedded in the political economy of the British colonial state in India, and exploring this interrelationship by using the analytical framework of commodity chains has enabled me to examine the limits of the colonial state's reach and the nuances of its relationship with the agro-industrial economy of indigo.

From the political-economic perspective of India and Britain, the book underscores the significance of indigo in the trade between India and Europe. It shows that indigo had a fairly significant share in the total exports from Surat and Bengal to Europe in the seventeenth and nineteenth centuries respectively. During 1796–97 and 1855–56, indigo accounted for about one-third of the total value of exports from Bengal to Britain and about one-fifth of the total exports to all places. In the colonial period, Britain was the main beneficiary as it imported indigo almost exclusively from its territorial possession in India. This nearly freed Britain from investing enormous amounts in procuring indigo from other parts of the world. An estimate made in the 1780s projected that if the Bengal Presidency supplied 25,000 *man* of indigo, Britain's average annual consumption during 1773–83, the nation would save about £375,000 every year that it spent on buying indigo from foreign countries.[1] Britain's gain must have increased substantially when by 1815 annual indigo imports from Bengal had more than quadrupled. The large-scale export of indigo from India also helped Britain relieve the balance of payments problem caused by enormous imports of English cotton yarn and textiles into the colony and offset its trade deficit with other European countries and the United States in the nineteenth century.[2]

The book offers some new perspectives on the history of Indian indigo and the history of commodities in general, as well as on the political economy of Mughal and colonial India. It shows the embeddedness of indigo in the imperial political and economic rivalry in Europe and Asia and illustrates the role of indigo in the historical trajectory of colonialism, nationalism, and imperialism. It will, I hope, stimulate further inquiries into the potential role and impact of commodities on economic and political regimes in India and the wider world.

---

1 BL, Home Miscellaneous, 434, Memorandum of measures and means to introduce, improve and enlarge the manufacture of indigo in Bengal and Bahar by C. Blume, Hugli, Bengal, 30 Dec. 1790, p. 608.

2 Blair B. Kling, *Partner in Empire: Dwarkanath Tagore and the Age of Enterprise in India* (Los Angeles: University of California Press, 1976), 55.

Appendices

APPENDIX 1

Annual Volumes (in Dutch pounds) and Values (in guilders) of the VOC's Indigo Exports from Surat, 1619–1742

	Bayana		Sarkhej		Coromandel		Unspecified	Total
Year	Volume	Value	Volume	Value	Volume	Value	Volume	Volume
1618–19	16,757	—	—	—	105,000	—	—	121,757
1620–21	69,000	—	—	—	67,800	28,367	—	136,800
1621–22	111,625	73,956	46,912	19,020	—	—	—	158,537
1622–23	54,400	27,472	—	—	91,950	—	—	146,350
1623–24	150,700	96,500	84,940	35,862	—	—	—	235,640
1624–25	202,564	146,819	438,861	194,952	78,117	37,666	—	719,542
1625–26	198,626	156,133	495,403	248,607	—	—	—	694,029
1626–27	—	—	—	—	21,975	—	—	21,975
1627–28	133,700	119,400	—	—	—	—	—	133,700
1628–29	179,330	147,974	—	—	45,096	14,872	—	224,426
1629–30	72,681	124,773	61,084	142,703	—	—	—	133,765
1630–31	217,433	220,584	116,552	98,332	—	—	—	333,985
1631–32	—	—	—	—	—	—	—	334,206
1633–34	300,000	439,200	—	—	3,363	—	—	303,363
1634–35	149,341	267,599	—	—	26,092	—	—	175,433
1635–36	202,000	237,570	107,838	—	22,880	—	—	332,718
1636–37	278,046	413,167	69,061	—	507	—	—	347,614
1637–38	67,416	97,500	153,050	158,542	15,130	6,811	—	235,596
1638–39	38,584	52,142	276,004	334,900	—	—	—	314,588
1639–40	149,800	145,300	447,300	323,200	12,159	2,289	—	609,259
1640–41	249,948	304,508	2,160	—	—	—	—	252,108
1641–42	422,304	481,889	211,392	156,781	47,877	15,853	—	681,573
1642–43	363,792	—	140,544	—	99,187	—	—	603,523
1643–44	209,868	178,800	117,648	80,064	101,993	—	—	429,509
1644–45	100,900	105,500	—	—	—	—	—	100,900
1645–46	86,700	98,800	—	—	—	—	—	86,700

 | DOI 10.1163/9789004311558_009

	Bayana		Sarkhej		Coromandel		Unspecified	Total
Year	Volume	Value	Volume	Value	Volume	Value	Volume	Volume
1646–47	79,500	95,600	—	—	—	—	—	79,500
1647–48	145,000	179,400	—	—	—	—	—	145,000
1648–49	—	—	—	—	—	—	151,161	151,161
1649–50	180,000	42,000	—	—	—	—	—	180,000
1650–51	25,000	—	53,568	—	—	—	—	78,568
1651–52	25,400	35,100	—	—	—	—	—	25,400
1652–53	103,500	121,900	—	—	25,621	—	—	129,121
1655–56	137,400	148,700	23,874	—	27,360	—	—	188,634
1656–57	93,700	82,600	—	—	—	—	—	93,700
1657–58	13,800	—	—	—	—	—	—	13,800
1658–59	80,000	—	57,600	—	9,720	—	—	147,320
1660–61	44,000	—	11,232	—	—	—	—	55,232
1661–62	23,330	—	—	—	24,840	—	—	48,170
1667–68	—	—	—	—	10,900	—	—	10,900
1670–71	347,784	—	83,520	—	—	—	—	431,304
1674–75	87,768	—	—	—	—	—	—	87,768
1675–76	—	—	—	—	—	219,104	—	—
1676–77	—	—	—	—	26,976	—	50,000	76,976
1682–83	—	—	—	—	20,040	98,071	—	20,040
1684–85	79,883	92,673	83,104	—	15,000	—	—	177,987
1685–86	78,400	—	—	—	—	122,267	—	78,400
1686–87	—	—	—	—	—	—	100,320	100,320
1690–91	100,000	—	—	—	—	—	—	100,000
1691–92	118,400	—	—	—	—	—	—	118,400
1695–96	284,280	—	29,808	—	—	—	—	314,088
1697–98	250,013	—	—	—	—	—	—	250,013
1699–1700	153,406	308,326	—	—	—	—	—	153,406
1700–01	114,608	—	61,733	—	176,342	—	—	352683
1703–04	—	—	—	—	4,657	5,569	—	4,657
1704–05	—	—	—	—	—	—	155,171	155,171
1708–09	—	—	—	—	—	1,576	173,423	173,423
1711–12	—	—	37,013	—	—	—	—	37,013

	Bayana		Sarkhej		Coromandel		Unspecified	Total
Year	Volume	Value	Volume	Value	Volume	Value	Volume	Volume
1715–16	—	—	—	—	—	—	34,262	34,262
1721–22	—	—	—	—	—	—	25,000	25,000
1740–41	78,730	67,954	—	—	—	—	—	78,730
1742–42	113,320	172,057	—	—	4,982	2,404	—	118,302

SOURCE: *DFI 1617–23*, P. 90 *GENERALE MISSIVEN*, VOL. I, 1610–38, P. 266; VOC 1076, FF. 395^r, 396^r; VOC 1097, PP. 434, 451, 474; VOC 1099, F. 301; VOC 1100, P. 182; VOC 1103, PP. 131, 140, F. 121^r; *DAGH-REGISTER, 1640–41*, PP. 375, 418, 443; VOC, 1108; VOC 1117, F. 665^v; VOC 1122, F. 533^r; *DAGH-REGISTER, 1636*, PP. 35, 262, 295; VOC 1127, FF. 33^v, 69^r, 73^r, 137^r; *DAGH-REGISTER, 1637*, PP. 41, 71, 79; COLLECTIE GELEYNSSEN DE JONGH, 110, P. 239; VOC 1134, F. 464^v; VOC 1151, FF. 742^v–743^r, 860^v; VOC 1168, P. 696; *DAGH-REGISTER, 1643–44*, PP. 178, 183, 188, 199; *DAGH-REGISTER, 1644–45*, P. 250; *GENERALE MISSIVEN*, VOL. II, 1639–55, PP. 399, 547; VOC 1215, F. 642^r; *GENERALE MISSIVEN*, VOL. III, 1655–74, PP. 230, 274, 435, 654, 775; VOC 1297, F. 375^r; *GENERALE MISSIVEN*, VOL. IV, 1675–85, PP. 155, 817; VOC 10406, P. 115; *GENERALE MISSIVEN*, VOL. V, 1686–97, PP. 420, 770; VOC 1620, FF. 168^v, 365^v–366^r; VOC 9056, P. 108; BOEKHOUDER-GENERAAL TE BATAVIA, 10811–12; VOC 1635; VOC 1649, P. 529; VOC 8823, PP. 334, 338; *DAGH-REGISTER, 1661*, P. 201; *DAGH-REGISTER, 1682*, PP. 1398, 1402.

APPENDIX 2

Quantities (in Dutch pounds) and Values (in guilders) of Annual Indigo Sales by the VOC: Amsterdam Chamber, 1642–1765

	Quantities						Values					
Year	Bayana	Sarkhej	Jambusar	Coromandel	Unspecified	Total	Bayana	Sarkhej	Jambusar	Coromandel	Unspecified	Total
1642	—	—	—	—	—	—	428,398	147,967	—	—	10,320	586,685
1643	—	—	—	—	—	—	—	—	—	—	1,337,316	1,337,316
1644	—	—	—	—	—	—	—	—	—	—	574,511	574,511
1645	—	—	—	—	—	—	—	—	—	—	177,365	177,365
1646	—	—	—	—	—	—	—	—	—	—	240,636	240,636
1647	—	—	—	—	—	—	—	—	—	—	140,118	140,118
1648	—	—	—	—	—	—	—	—	—	—	133,276	133,276
1649	—	—	—	—	—	—	—	—	—	—	114,767	114,767
1650	—	—	—	—	67,493	67,493	—	—	—	—	160,519	160,519
1651	—	—	—	—	70,246	70,246	—	—	—	—	126,442	126,442
1652	—	—	—	—	98,151	98,151	—	—	—	—	174,782	174,782
1653	—	—	—	—	54,415	54,415	—	—	—	—	82,921	82,921
1654	—	—	—	—	64,661	64,661	—	—	—	—	182,628	182,628

 | DOI 10.1163/9789004311558_010

1655	—	—	—	—	15,494	15,494	—	—	—	—	31,246	31,246
1656	—	—	—	—	27,294	27,294	—	—	—	—	49,236	49,236
1657	—	—	—	—	23,045	23,045	—	—	—	—	46,163	46,163
1658	—	—	—	—	33,126	33,126	—	—	—	—	74,731	74,731
1659	—	—	—	—	40,131	40,131	—	—	—	—	70,445	70,445
1660	—	—	—	—	14,230	14,230	—	—	—	—	21,834	21,834
1661	—	—	—	—	58,848	58,848	—	—	—	—	84,622	84,622
1662	—	—	—	—	39,673	39,673	—	—	—	—	61,857	61,857
1663	—	—	—	—	9,009	9,009	—	—	—	—	14,662	14,662
1664	—	—	—	—	9,802	9,802	—	—	—	—	21,210	21,210
1665	—	—	—	2,992	0	2,992	—	—	—	—	9,613	9,613
1666	—	—	—	—	4,030	4,030	—	—	—	—	11,326	11,326
1667	—	—	—	—	2,450	2,450	—	—	—	—	6,518	6,518
1668	—	—	—	—	31,155	31,155	—	—	—	—	81,391	81,391
1669	—	—	—	—	7,286	7,286	—	—	—	—	18,073	18,073
1670	—	—	—	—	23,991	23,991	—	—	—	—	57,955	57,955
1671	—	—	—	—	44,200	44,200	—	—	—	—	114,382	114,382
1672	—	—	—	—	84,217	84,217	—	—	—	—	199,906	199,906
1673	8,054	21,444	0	5,335	27,289*	62,122	19,838	24,387	0	4,900	57,191*	106,316
1674	16,861	24,522	0	2,226	45,656*	89,265	38,605	24,748	0	2,192	93,683*	159,228
1675	0	32,190	0	16,376	0	48,566	0	37,933	0	27,302	0	65,235
1676	0	0	0	0	0	0	0	0	0	0	0	0
1677	37,463	9,605	0	0	0	47,068	73,032	8,231	0	0	0	81,263
1678	70,485	2,555	0	7,947	0	80,987	125,668	2,508	0	4,867	0	133,043

	Quantities						Values					
Year	Bayana	Sarkhej	Jambusar	Coromandel	Unspecified	Total	Bayana	Sarkhej	Jambusar	Coromandel	Unspecified	Total
1679	29,800	0	0	0	0	29,800	57,663	0	0	0	0	57,663
1680	22,233	0	0	3,116	0	25,349	52,972	0	0	2,320	0	55,292
1681	—	—	—	—	24,682	24,682	—	—	—	—	—	40,617
1682	—	—	—	—	18,627	18,627	—	—	—	—	—	36,851
1683	—	—	—	—	25,521	25,521	—	—	—	—	—	70,795
1684	—	—	—	—	45,837	45,837	—	—	—	—	—	92,486
1685	—	—	—	—	35,773	35,773	—	—	—	—	—	52,873
1686	—	—	—	—	46,385	46,385	—	—	—	—	—	87,914
1687	—	—	—	—	55,780	55,780	—	—	—	—	—	161,208
1688	—	—	—	—	50,001	50,001	—	—	—	—	—	169,906
1689	—	—	—	—	32,123	32,123	—	—	—	—	—	127,849
1690	—	—	—	—	78,053	78,053	—	—	—	—	—	318,393
1691	—	—	—	—	36,948	36,948	—	—	—	—	—	177,751
1692	—	—	—	—	97,082	97,082	—	—	—	—	—	446,232
1693	—	—	—	—	12,351	12,351	—	—	—	—	—	59,972
1694	—	—	—	—	7,488	7,488	—	—	—	—	—	16,661
1695	149,121	80,104	30,015	465	495	260,200	696,043	154,662	44,048	1,784	2,359	898,896
1696	—	—	—	—	91,209	91,209	—	—	—	—	—	301,599
1697	105,671	29,014	4,954	461	0	140,100	330,758	49,960	8,582	967	0	390,267
1698	200,000	0	9,280	1,450	0	210,730	517,188	0	11,732	2,902	0	531,822

1699	89,000	0	2,030	0	0	91,030	331,540	0	3,400	0	0	334,940
1700	176,814	0	2,030	1,070	0	179,914	584,766	0	3,117	2,622	0	590,505
1701	0	20,990	4,060	1,116	0	26166	0	44,951	7,530	2,415	0	54896
1702	30,932	12,006	6,090	3,132	0	52,160	136,101	27,133	13,349	8,417	0	185,000
1703	150,037	6,072	6,090	2,512	0	164,711	765,394	19,720	17,474	9,788	0	812,376
1704	0	0	0	4,340	0	4340	0	0	0	16,710	0	16710
1705	0	0	0	0	0	0	0	0	0	0	0	0
1706	155,170	0	0	3,069	0	158,239	709,559	0	0	10,657	0	720,216
1707	0	0	0	1,804	0	1804	0	0	0	4,492	0	4492
1708	80,463	0	0	0	0	80,463	369,523	0	0	0	0	369,523
1709	163,246	20,010	25,085	1,328	3,382	213,051	546,129	38,775	31,098	2,240	6,510	624,752
1710	0	0	15,080	1,541	0	16621	0	0	17,518	2,669	0	20187
1711	0	24,978	15,080	0	0	40058	0	24,969	12,871	0	0	37840
1712	0	24,978	0	0	0	24978	0	24,726		0	0	24726
1713	0	24,978	12,035	0	0	37013	0	23,033	9,141	0	0	32174
1714	0	24,978	15,080	0	0	40058	0	43,867	19,142	0	0	63009
1715	0	20,008	19,080	0	0	39088	0	23,806	18,803	0	0	42609
1716	0	0	14,352	0	0	14352	0		12,354	0	0	12354
1717	0	9,903	10,005	0	0	19908	0	11,087	8,864	0	0	19951
1718	0	0	12,036	0	0	12036	0	0	10,451	0	0	10451
1719	0	0	0	0	0	0	0	0	0	0	0	0
1720	0	0	0	0	0	0	0	0	0	0	0	0
1721	0	15,000	0	0	0	15000	0	10,095	0	0	0	10095
1722	0	14,871	0	0	0	14871	0	17,368	0	0	0	17368

	Quantities						Values					
Year	Bayana	Sarkhej	Jambusar	Coromandel	Unspecified	Total	Bayana	Sarkhej	Jambusar	Coromandel	Unspecified	Total
1723	0	0	0	0	0	0	0	0	0	0	0	0
1724	0	0	0	0	0	0	0	0	0	0	0	0
1725	0	0	0	0	0	0	0	0	0	0	0	0
1726	0	0	0	0	0	0	0	0	0	0	0	0
1727	0	0	0	0	0	0	0	0	0	0	0	0
1728	0	0	0	0	0	0	0	0	0	0	0	0
1729	0	19,314	0	0	0	19314	0	22,333	0	0	—	22333
1730	0	0	0	0	17,397	17397	0	0	0	0	43,218	43218
1731	0	0	0	430	0	430	0	0	0	355	0	355
1732	0	0	0	411	0	411	0	0	0	345	0	345
1733	0	0	0	236	0	236	0	0	0	566	0	566
1734	0	0	0	0	0	0	0	0	0	0	0	0
1735	0	0	0	0	0	0	0	0	0	0	0	0
1736	0	0	0	94	0	94	0	0	0	213	0	213
1737	0	0	0	190	0	190	0	0	0	289	0	289
1738	0	0	0	0	0	0	0	0	0	0	0	0
1739	0	0	0	0	0	0	0	0	0	0	0	0
1740	0	0	0	0	0	0	0	0	0	0	0	0
1741	0	0	0	0	0	0	0	0	0	0	0	0
1742	0	0	0	2,256	0	2256	0	0	0	1,899	0	1899

1743	0	24,817	24,303	4,683	0	53803	0	31,098	19,679	1,675	0	52452
1744	0	33,604	16,497	0	0	50101	0	32,382	11,724	0	0	44106
1745	0	37,600	23,499	0	0	61099	0	40,442	16,153	0	0	56595
1746	0	0	0	0	0	0	0	0	0	0	0	0
1747	0	37,704	23,608	0	0	61312	0	40,896	14,668	0	0	55564
1748	0	0	0	0	0	0	0	0	0	0	0	0
1749	0	0	0	0	128	128	0	0	0	0	480	480
1750	0	0	0	0	132	132	0	0	0	0	409	409
1751	0	0	0	0	101	101	0	0	0	0	292	292
1752	0	0	0	0	64	64	0	0	0	0	163	163
1753	0	0	0	0	0	0	0	0	0	0	0	0
1754	0	0	0	0	57	57	0	0	0	0	208	208
1755	0	0	0	0	0	0	0	0	0	0	0	0
1756	0	0	0	0	0	0	0	0	0	0	0	0
1757	0	0	0	0	0	0	0	0	0	0	0	0
1758	0	0	0	4,551	0	4551	0	0	0	11,461	0	11461
1759	0	0	0	26,960	0	26960	0	0	0	15,262	0	15262
1760	0	0	0	0	98	98	0	0	0	0	181	181

SOURCE: VOC 4583 GENERALE STAETEN VAN D' OOSTINDISCHE COMPAGNIE, 1642–1676; VOC 4585–87, GENERALE STAETEN VAN VERHANDELDE GOEDEREN ALS ONVERCOGHTE GOEDEREN...1673–1683, 1684–1688, 1689; VOC 6989, BIJEENBRENGING VAN VERKOPINGEN IN DE RESPECTIVE KAMERS [STATEMENT OF SALES IN THE RESPECTIVE CHAMBERS], 1693–1760.

APPENDIX 3

Indigo Sale Prices (stivers/Dutch pound) in Amsterdam, 1695–1760

Years	Bayana	Sarkhej	Jambusar	Coromandel	Java
1695	93	38	29	76.75	4.5
1697	62.6	34.5	34.75	42	—
1698	51.7	—	25.5	42.6	47.5
1699	75	—	33.5	—	65.6
1700	66	—	30.7	49	55.3
1701	—	43	37	43.2	68.6
1702	88	45.5	43.8	53.7	95.7
1703	102	65	57.3	78	127.4
1704	—	—	—	77	123.9
1705	—	—	—	—	140.6
1706	91	—	—	69.4	106.7
1707	—	—	—	49.8	58
1708	91.8	—	—	—	63
1709	67	38.7	25	34	53
1710	—	—	23	35	47
1711	—	20	17	—	63
1712	—	20	—	—	63
1713	—	18.5	15	—	64
1714	—	35	25	—	70
1715	—	24	20	—	58
1716	—	—	17	—	60
1717	—	22	18	—	79
1718	—	—	17	—	88
1719	—	—	—	—	66.5
1720	—	—	—	—	56
1721	—	13.5	—	—	56
1722	—	23	—	—	56
1723	—	—	—	—	57
1724	—	—	—	—	51
1725	—	—	—	—	47

 | DOI 10.1163/9789004311558_011

Years	Bayana	Sarkhej	Jambusar	Coromandel	Java
1726	—	—	—	—	52
1727	—	—	—	—	46
1728	—	—	—	—	45
1729	—	23	—	—	51
1731	—	—	—	16.5	39
1732	—	—	—	17	41
1733	—	—	—	48	48
1734	—	—	—	—	58
1735	—	—	—	—	53
1736	—	—	—	45.5	61
1737	—	—	—	30.5	61
1738	—	—	—	—	59
1739	—	—	—	—	62
1740	—	—	—	—	67
1741	—	—	—	—	53
1742	—	—	19	17	61
1743	—	25	16	7	57
1744	—	19	14	—	56
1745	—	21	14	—	72
1746	—	—	—	—	69
1747	—	22	12	—	60
1748	—	—	—	—	62
1749	—	—	—	—	59
1750	—	—	—	—	54
1751	—	—	—	—	62
1752	—	—	—	—	55
1753	—	—	—	—	61
1754	—	—	—	—	76.5
1755	—	—	—	—	70
1756	—	—	—	—	90
1757	—	—	—	—	103
1758	—	—	—	50	86
1759	—	—	—	11	83
1760	—	—	—	—	65

SOURCE: VOC 6989 BIJEENBRENGING VAN VERKOPINGEN IN DE RESPECTIVE KAMERS [STATEMENT OF SALES IN THE RESPECTIVE CHAMBERS], 1693–1760.

APPENDIX 4

Quantities (in lb.) of Indigo Exported by the EIC from Surat/Bombay, 1615–1729

Year	Bayana	Sarkhej	Unidentified	Total (lb.)
1614–15	—	190,916	—	190,916
1617–18	182,800	195,000	—	377,800
1618–19	180,000	144,000	—	324,000
1621	—	297,000	—	297,000
1622–23	—	450,000	—	450,000
1623–24	—	255,000	—	255,000
1624–25	—	201,600	—	201,600
1627	40,000	103,093	—	143,093
1630	91,200	132,000	—	223,200
1631	121,000	—	—	121,000
1633	119,200	—	—	119,200
1634	322,728	22,784	—	345,512
1636	—	375,000	—	375,000
1637	45,504	45,504	—	91,008
1638	229,392	52,250	22,560	304,202
1639	—	165,150	—	165,150
1640	91,400	71,840	—	163,240
1640–41	151,200	113,155	—	264,355
1743	111,100	84,640	—	195,740
1744	154,000	—	—	154,000
1644–45	20,160	109,604	—	129,764
1645–46	138,600	24,360	—	162,960
1646–47	199,252	24,000	—	223,252
1648–49	66,000	25,200	—	91,200
1649–50	58,080	—	—	58,080
1650–51	23,430	122,000	43,200	188,630
1656–57	17,347	23,250	—	40,597
1665	—	—	—	27,758
1666	—	—	—	1,554
1667	—	—	—	27,942

 | DOI 10.1163/9789004311558_012

Year	Bayana	Sarkhej	Unidentified	Total (lb.)
1668	—	—	—	409
1669	—	—	—	93,552
1670	—	—	—	100,874
1671	—	—	—	120,812
1672	—	—	—	147,917
1673	—	—	—	107,040
1674	—	—	—	86,617
1675	—	—	—	55,451
1676	—	—	—	189,784
1677	—	—	—	101,178
1678	—	—	—	106,252
1679	—	—	—	49,674
1680	—	—	—	40,558
1681	—	—	—	96,045
1682	—	—	—	84,772
1683	—	—	—	110,243
1684	—	—	—	99,580
1685	—	—	—	20,700
1687	—	—	—	33,860
1688	—	—	—	114,970
1689	—	—	—	25,348
1690	—	—	—	10,550
1693	—	—	—	67,500
1697	—	—	—	2,128
1698	—	—	—	896
1699	—	—	—	68,768
1700	—	—	—	106,176
1701	—	—	—	44,688
1703	—	—	—	130
1704	—	—	—	72,176
1706	—	—	—	115,833
1707	—	—	—	27,303
1709	—	—	—	33,983
1710	—	—	—	96,544
1711	—	—	—	38,388
1712	—	—	—	62,603
1723	—	—	—	12,149

Year	Bayana	Sarkhej	Unidentified	Total (lb.)
1724	—	—	—	11,714
1726	—	—	—	4,368
1728	—	—	—	24,899
1729	—	—	—	65,536

SOURCE: BL, EAST INDIA COMPANY CORRESPONDENCE WITH THE EAST, 2, F. 242[a]; *DFI 1617–23*, PP. 62, 83, 236, 186; G/40/24, F. 26[a]; *EFI 1618–21*, PP. 323–24, 329–30; *DFI 1624–27*, P. 185; *EFI 1624–29*, P. 208, *EFI 1630–33*, PP. 20, 127; VOC 1099, (5–600 PACKS); *DAGH-REGISTER, 1631–34*, PP. 171, 265; *DAGH-REGISTER, 1636*, P. 111; VOC 1122, F. 541[v]; VOC 1127, F. 89[r]; L/MAR/C/4, FF. 132[a], 170[b]; *EFI 1737–41*, PP. 292, 378, 490; VOC 1134, FF. 484[r]–485[r]; *EFI 1642–45*, PP. 136, 162; VOC 1151, F. 839[v]; *EFI 1646–50*, PP. 12, 77, 202, 254, 276; *GENERALE MISSIVEN*, VOL. II, 1639–55, P. 547; *EFI 1651–55*, PP. 300, 335; CHAUDHURI, *THE TRADING WORLD OF ASIA*, APPENDIX 5 TABLE C.10.

APPENDIX 5

Values (in rupees) of Annual Indigo Exports from India, 1795/96–1933/34

Exports	To UK	To All
1795–96	6,144,186	6,251,424
1796–97	3,056,592	3,233,797
1797–98	5,373,861	5,459,844
1798–99	2,371,941	2,379,629
1799–1800	3,528,416	3,553,949
1800–01	3,984,744	3,988,293
1801–02	3,771,407	3,848,139
1802–03	2,779,100	2,973,754
1803–04	4,229,921	4,469,930
1804–05	6,028,524	6,477,041
1805–06	4,523,124	5,221,609
1806–07	5,931,390	7,238,288
1807–08	7,207,505	9,369,025
1808–09	5,946,117	6,944,473
1809–10	3,507,753	4,454,222
1810–11	5,136,300	6,268,377
1811–12	5,426,521	6,042,203
1812–13	5,170,082	6,017,691
1813–14	9,132,531	9,779,194
1814–15	6,138,189	7,249,337
1815–16	10,193,934	12,891,953
1816–17	6,305,702	8,874,885
1817–18	6,379,779	8,031,855
1818–19	5,266,111	6,966,405
1819–20	6,724,284	9,949,895
1820–21	5,077,148	7,592,919
1821–22	5,420,123	8,757,907
1822–23	10,026,300	13,121,699
1823–24	7,975,068	8,738,205
1824–25	11,324,763	13,430,269

 | DOI 10.1163/9789004311558_013

Exports	To UK	To All
1825–26	12,945,734	16,330,506
1826–27	9,008,479	10,885,228
1827–28	15,549,593	19,171,606
1828–29	9,440,672	12,192,642
1829–30	14,209,273	16,978,313
1830–31	9,857,216	13,790,441
1831–32	9,239,303	12,638,774
1832–33	10,151,292	13,928,499
1833–34	5,573,477	9,764,925
1834–35	6,113,364	9,082,724
1835–36	9,068,621	13,717,038
1836–37	10,375,288	15,049,063
1837–38	13,475,294	17,208,994
1838–39	9,685,134	17,249,139
1839–40	17,661,253	24,699,874
1840–41	16,426,461	22,555,324
1841–42	16,668,048	23,996,004
1842–43	10,601,285	16,394,237
1843–44	23,263,239	31,916,914
1844–45	17,364,896	25,805,363
1845–46	12,718,773	19,483,586
1846–47	11,761,688	16,088,846
1847–48	11,585,830	14,524,414
1848–49	15,148,919	19,776,777
1849–50	10,464,721	16,753,728
1850–51	12,864,036	17,178,836
1851–52	14,451,450	20,253,130
1852–53	11,368,870	18,096,850
1853–54	13,907,560	20,677,690
1854–55	12,043,600	17,018,250
1855–56	14,795,570	24,243,320
1956–57	12,201,790	19,379,070
1857–58	12,674,600	17,343,390
1858–59	13,779,540	21,180,160
1859–60	15,062,600	20,212,880
1860–61	13,654,940	18,865,250

Exports	To UK	To All
1861–62	11,990,680	16,475,030
1862–63	16,270,830	21,268,700
1863–64	13,466,460	17,561,580
1864–65	12,956,350	18,601,410
1865–66	12,265,360	18,615,010
1866–67	—	18,158,060
1867–68	12,763,400	18,232,260
1868–69	17,824,750	28,939,990
1869–70	20,399,390	31,780,450
1870–71	23,715,240	31,925,030
1871–72	23,923,870	37,054,750
1872–73	21,962,400	34,268,240
1873–74	25,097,150	35,553,000
1874–75	17,405,940	25,763,020
1875–76	18,232,650	28,750,650
1876–77	17,692,242	29,627,850
1877–78	14,943,687	34,943,340
1878–79	14,919,024	29,604,630
1879–80	14,900,854	29,474,340
1880–81	18,868,636	35,715,850
1881–82	24,152,220	45,091,890
1882–83	16,816,690	39,130,010
1883–84	24,908,390	46,409,910
1884–85	18,678,510	40,689,000
1885–86	17,997,265	37,831,600
1886–87	13,923,168	36,916,770
1887–88	15,434,982	38,906,494
1888–89	15,859,716	39,485,945
1889–90	16,171,673	38,630,836
1890–91	13,624,641	30,731,254
1891–92	9,958,233	32,140,853
1892–93	16,578,836	41,412,023
1893–94	15,760,571	41,821,691
1894–95	14,804,951	47,459,549
1895–96	18,676,934	53,547,583
1896–97	16,540,748	43,707,851

Exports	To UK	To All
1897–98	6,532,736	30,574,019
1898–99	7,175,401	29,704,781
1899–1900	5,591,185	26,925,107
1900–01	4,048,141	21,359,808
1901–02	5,548,700	18,522,554
1902–03	2,211,784	12,056,819
1903–04	1,975,681	10,762,026
1904–05	1,902,676	8,346,073
1905–06	1,502,892	5,863,777
1906–07	1,660,369	7,004,773
1907–08	1,903,051	6,372,734
1908–09	2,016,361	4,904,791
1909–10	503,567	3,518,154
1910–11	642,218	—
1911–12	1,243,905	3,758,000
1912–13	229,110	2,201,000
1913–14	639,120	2,129,000
1914–15	8,400,780	8,995,000
1915–16	14,498,055	20,787,000
1916–17	10,476,345	21,126,000
1917–18	3,338,805	15,281,000
1918–19	2,557,039	12,485,000
1919–20	605,500	13,276,000
1920–21	585,000	4,121,000
1921–22	325,000	5,137,000
1922–23	316,000	1,694,000
1923–24	246,000	2,003,000
1924–25	175,000	1,092,000
1925–26	85,000	559,000
1926–27	75,000	424,000
1927–28	126,000	513,000
1928–29	59,000	233,000
1929–30	59,000	241,000
1930–31	37,000	245,000

Exports	To UK	To All
1931–32	50,000	201,000
1932–33	10,000	72,000
1933–34	19,000	97,000

Note: Figures between 1795–96 and 1857–58 represent exports only from Calcutta.

SOURCE: BL, BENGAL COMMERCIAL REPORTS (P/174), 13, 19, 21, 22, 25, 38, 44, 48, 49, 56, 59, 61, 63–69; *MISCELLANEOUS STATISTICS RELATED TO BRITISH INDIA* (CALCUTTA: SUPERINTENDENT OF GOVERNMENT PRINTING, 1876–1880), VOL. 1, PP. 28–9; *STATISTICAL TABLES FOR BRITISH INDIA* (CALCUTTA: SUPERINTENDENT OF GOVERNMENT PRINTING, 1881–1893), SEVERAL VOLUMES; *STATISTICS OF BRITISH INDIA*, VOL. 1 COMMERCIAL STATISTICS (CALCUTTA: SUPERINTENDENT OF GOVERNMENT PRINTING, 1919), PP. 132, 137–8, 142, 150; *STATISTICS OF BRITISH INDIA FOR 1906–07 AND PRECEDING YEARS, PART II: COMMERCIAL* (CALCUTTA: SUPERINTENDENT OF GOVERNMENT PRINTING, 1908), P. 35; *STATISTICS OF BRITISH INDIA FOR 1909–10 AND PRECEDING YEARS, PART II: COMMERCIAL* (CALCUTTA: SUPERINTENDENT OF GOVERNMENT PRINTING, 1911), PP. 16–17, 26; *STATISTICAL ABSTRACT FOR BRITISH INDIA, 1911–12 TO 1920–21* (CALCUTTA: SUPERINTENDENT OF GOVERNMENT PRINTING, 1922), PP. 474–77, 542–43; *STATISTICAL ABSTRACT FOR BRITISH INDIA, 1920–21 TO 1929–30* (CALCUTTA: SUPERINTENDENT OF GOVERNMENT PRINTING, 1931), P. 623; *STATISTICAL ABSTRACT FOR BRITISH INDIA, 1924–25 TO 1934–35* (CALCUTTA: SUPERINTENDENT OF GOVERNMENT PRINTING, 1936), PP. 656–7, 719.

APPENDIX 6

Quantities (in Dutch pounds) and Values (in guilders) of VOC's Exports of Java Indigo to the Dutch Republic, 1704–1781

Year	Quantities	Values	Year	Quantities	Values
1703–04	6,458	8,012	1742–43	17,528	23,517
1704–05	3,445	4,241	1748–49	21,354	25,260
1708–09	16,458	21,822	1750–51	27,986	34,353
1715–16	23,479	32,418	1753–54	24,006	27,673
1718–19	33,002	47,901	1754–55	21,979	26,511
1721–22	NA	NA	1756–57	28,187	37,504
1723–24	36,585	54,489	1757–58	31,878	43,572
1724–25	33,812	45,560	1758–59	61,446	68,882
1726–27	33,421	45,813	1759–60	131,063	108,759
1727–28	32,231	45,466	1763–64	178,171	125,082
1730–31	29,201	40,634	1764–65	39,218	54,830
1732–33	33,576	47,396	1767–68	23,408	35,306
1733–34	33,516	46,884	1768–69	22,938	29,504
1734–35	38,775	57,839	1769–70	27,903	34,780
1736–37	25,519	37,958	1770–71	21,911	27,829
1737–38	46,638	65,093	1771–72	28,448	35,342
1738–39	36,905	53,102	1773–74	11,389	13,752
1739–40	23,873	37,724	1779–80	21,941	27,243
1740–41	28,789	44,268	1780–81	24,941	31,013

SOURCE: NA, BOEKHOUDER-GENERAAL TE BATAVIA [ACCOUNTANT GENERAL IN BATAVIA], 10810–10837, 10671–10679.

 | DOI 10.1163/9789004311558_014

APPENDIX 7

Values (in guilder) and Volumes (in kilogram) of Indigo Exports from Java, 1824–1873

Year	Values (f.)			Volume (kg.)		
	Private	Government	Total (f.)	Private	Government	Total (kg.)
1824	7,000	0	7,000	—	—	—
1825	37,000	0	37,000	—	—	—
1826	45,000	0	45,000	—	—	—
1827	36,000	0	36,000	—	—	—
1828	94,000	0	94,000	10,000	0	10,000
1829	150,000	0	150,000	20,000	0	20,000
1830	59,000	0	59,000	10,000	0	10,000
1831	99,000	0	99,000	20,000	0	20,000
1832	—	—	339,000	—	—	80,000
1833	—	—	414,000	—	—	110,000
1834	—	—	516,000	—	—	120,000
1835	52,000	992,000	1,044,000	10,000	250,000	260,000
1836	56,000	1,066,000	1,122,000	10,000	190,000	200,000
1837	116,000	2,212,000	2,328,000	20,000	390,000	410,000
1838	160,000	3,010,000	3,170,000	30,000	530,000	560,000
1839	187,000	3,396,000	3,583,000	30,000	40,000	590,000
1840	319,000	6,053,000	6,372,000	50,000	1,000,000	1,050,000
1841	297,000	5,642,000	5,939,000	40,000	86,000	900,000
1842	245,000	4,638,000	4,883,000	40,000	760,000	800,000
1843	567,000	5,104,000	5,671,000	90,000	840,000	930,000
1844	494,000	4,449,000	4,943,000	80,000	730,000	810,000
1845	543,000	4,466,000	5,009,000	90,000	740,000	830,000
1846	438,000	3,942,000	4,380,000	90,000	780,000	870,000
1847	666,000	3,786,000	4,434,000	140,000	740,000	880,000
1848	455,000	2,577,000	3,032,000	100,000	600,000	700,000
1849	595,000	3,369,000	3,964,000	80,000	450,000	530,000
1850	839,000	3,354,000	4,193,000	120,000	500,000	620,000

 | DOI 10.1163/9789004311558_015

Year	Values (f.)			Volume (kg.)		
	Private	Government	Total (f.)	Private	Government	Total (kg.)
1851	576,000	2,304,000	2,880,000	70,000	310,000	380,000
1852	505,000	1,958,000	2,463,000	70,000	270,000	340,000
1853	1,361,000	3,711,000	5,072,000	170,000	480,000	650,000
1854	1,310,000	2,512,000	3,822,000	180,000	350,000	530,000
1855	1,218,000	2,032,000	3,250,000	170,000	290,000	460,000
1856	1,726,000	2,189,000	3,915,000	240,000	300,000	540,000
1857	1,429,000	2,651,000	4,080,000	190,000	340,000	530,000
1858	1,699,000	2,361,000	4,060,000	220,000	310,000	530,000
1859	1,767,000	1,890,000	3,657,000	240,000	260,000	500,000
1860	1,713,000	1,750,000	3,463,000	230,000	210,000	440,000
1861	1,688,000	1,500,000	3,188,000	210,000	170,000	380,000
1862	1,543,000	2,271,000	3,814,000	170,000	220,000	390,000
1863	1,844,000	1,714,000	3,558,000	220,000	200,000	420,000
1864	2,007,000	2,162,000	4,169,000	210,000	220,000	430,000
1865	2,124,000	2,105,000	4,229,000	220,000	200,000	420,000
1866	2,512,000	1,006,000	3,518,000	430,000	110,000	540,000
1867	3,337,000	65,000	3,402,000	690,000	10,000	700,000
1868	2,747,000	0	2,747,000	320,000	0	320,000
1869	3,228,000	0	3,228,000	360,000	0	360,000
1870	3,226,000	0	3,226,000	380,000	0	380,000
1871	2,672,000	0	2,627,000	330,000	0	330,000
1872	2,645,000	0	2,645,000	520,000	0	520,000
1873	2,664,000	0	2,664,000	350,000	0	350,000

SOURCE: PETER BOOMGAARD (ED.), *CHANGING ECONOMY IN INDONESIA: A SELECTION OF STATISTICAL SOURCE MATERIAL FROM THE EARLY 19TH CENTURY UP TO 1940*, VOL. 12A (AMSTERDAM: ROYAL TROPICAL INSTITUTE, 1991), 136–47.

APPENDIX 8

Indigo Prices (rupees per *man* and stivers per Dutch pound) in India, 1609–1757

	Sarkhej	Average price	Bayana	Average price
Year	Rs/*man**	Stivers/lb.	Rs/*man***	Stivers/lb.
1609	10–12	10	16–24	12
1613	14–18	14.5	—	—
1614	10–14.5	11.2	40	24
1615	12	10.9	—	—
1616	13.5–15	13	30–35	19.5
1617	18–22	18.2	32–40	21.6
1618	12–15	12.3	24–25	—
1619	—	—	24–29	15.9
1620	13–15	12.7	28–34	18.6
1621	10	—	—	—
1622	8 to 9	7.7	—	16
1623	—	—	25.25	15.2
1625	12	10.9	27–34	18.3
1627	—	—	33.75–35	20.6
1628	12–15 .5	12.5	24.5–36.5	18.3
1629	12–16	12.7	36–37	21.9
1630	16–18.5	15.7	38	22.8
1632	19–22	18.6	—	—
1633	23–25	21.8	61	36.6
1634	25–30	25	45–62	32.1
1635	18.5–27	20.7	48–50	29.4
1636	26–29	25	42–56	—
1637	20	18.2	—	—
1639	—	—	45	27
1640	16–22	17.5	40	24
1641	16–19	15.9	—	—
1643	—	—	35	21
1644	18 7/8	17.2	26–36	18.6

 | DOI 10.1163/9789004311558_016

	Sarkhej	Average price	Bayana	Average price
Year	Rs/*man**	Stivers/lb.	Rs/*man***	Stivers/lb.
1645	23–25	21.8	37–40	23.1
1646	22 .5–24	21.2	40	24
1647	19–22.5	18.9	39–43	24.6
1648	—	—	36–43.5	23.9
1649	—	—	40–46	25.8
1650	14–15	13.2	35–36	21.3
1654	—	—	48	28.8
1655	13	12	33–38	21.3
1656	13.25	12	33.25	20
1664	—	—	67	40.2
1676	—	—	37	22.2
1713	—	—	70	42
1757	50–60	50	100–110	63

* *man* = 30–37 lbs.

** *man* = 50–53 lbs.

SOURCE: BL, EAST INDIA COMPANY CORRESPONDENCE WITH THE EAST, 1 AND 2, FF. 156[a], 241[b]; G/40/8, P. 13; *LETTERS RECEIVED*, II, P. 152; FRS 84, F. 124[b]; *DFI 1617–23*, PP. 34, 61–2, 138, 287; *EFI 1618–21*, PP. 86, 324; *EFI 1622–23*, P. 109; *DFI 1624–29*, PP. 184, 189, 335, 357; *EFI 1624–29*, PP. 63, 189, 208; *EFI 1630–33*, PP. 59, 127, 131, 215, 225; COLLECTIE GELEYNSSEN DE JONGH, 105; *EFI 1634–36*, PP. 1–2, 138, 142, 292; VOC 1122, F. 515[v]; *EFI 1637–41*, PP. 92, 192, 232; VOC 1134, P. 483; *EFI 1642–45*, PP. 84, 164, 191, 202, 254, 304; *EFI 1646–50*, PP. 31, 77, 114, 143, 202, 219, 276, 305; *EFI 1651–55*, PP. 18, 51, 221, 302; L/MAR/C/4, F. 170[b]; *EFI 1655–60*; CHAUDHURI, *THE TRADING WORLD OF ASIA*, 224.

APPENDIX 9

Indigo Prices in Calcutta (rupees/factory *man*) and London (pence/lb.), 1843–1921

Year	Calcutta	London	Year	Calcutta	London	Year	Calcutta	London	Year	Calcutta	London
1843	150	—	1863	26.8	—	1883	280	80.5	1903	160	45
1844	103.3	—	1864	190	—	1884	307	87	1904	175	42.5
1845	121.6	—	1865	213.7	—	1885	270	77.5	1905	140	41.5
1846	128.7	—	1866	223.7	—	1886	280	79.5	1906	160	42.7
1847	126	—	1867	211.7	—	1887	185	69	1907	170	42.5
1848	110	—	1868	235.5	—	1888	215	73.5	1908	160	44
1849	110	—	1869	263.7	—	1889	245	66	1909	150	43
1850	117.5	—	1870	286.5	—	1890	200	60	1910	155	44.5
1851	158.5	—	1871	270	—	1891	225	67.3	1911	145	43.5
1852	110.6	—	1872	309.7	—	1892	195	52.6	1912	140	38.5
1853	153.5	—	1873	262	63	1893	300	62.5	1913	140	35.7
1854	149	—	1874	NA	75	1894	285	64.5	1914	165	72.5
1855	147.5	—	1875	NA	67.5	1895	275	57	1915	650	166
1856	164.8	—	1876	240	58.5	1896	275	53.2	1916	650	172.5
1857	187.5	—	1877	290	72.5	1897	220	50.2	1917	537.5	144.2
1858	NA	—	1878	230	76	1898	200	43	1918	282.5	120.5
1859	207.2	—	1879	300	75	1899	150	43	1919	372.5	121
1860	201.2	—	1880	317	97	1900	195	47.1	1920	412	172.6
1861	210	—	1881	275	85.5	1901	170	43.6	1921	412	130.5
1862	265	—	1882	305	86.5	1902	170	41.2	—	—	—

SOURCE: *PRICES AND WAGES IN INDIA*, VOL. 8 (CALCUTTA: OFFICE OF THE SUPERINTENDENT OF GOVERNMENT PRINTING, 1891), NO. 13, PRICES IN CALCUTTA OF STAPLE TRADE COMMODITIES FROM 1843–1890, PP. 102–13, NO. 18, PRICES IN LONDON OF CERTAIN STAPLE TRADE COMMODITIES FROM 1873 TO 1890, PP. 122–23; *PRICES AND WAGES IN INDIA*, VOL. 10 (CALCUTTA: OFFICE OF THE SUPERINTENDENT OF GOVERNMENT PRINTING, 1893), PRICES IN CALCUTTA OF STAPLE TRADE COMMODITIES FROM 1843–1893, P. 225; *PRICES AND WAGES IN INDIA*, VOL. 17 (CALCUTTA: OFFICE OF THE SUPERINTENDENT OF GOVERNMENT PRINTING, 1900), PRICES OF STAPLE ARTICLES OF EXPORT FROM 1843 TO 1900, PP. 222–23; *PRICES AND WAGES IN INDIA*, VOL. 27 (CALCUTTA: SUPERINTENDENT OF GOVERNMENT PRINTING, 1910), PRICES OF STAPLE ARTICLES OF EXPORT IN 1873, AND FROM 1885 TO 1910, PP. 110–15; *PRICES AND WAGES IN INDIA*, VOL. 36 (CALCUTTA: SUPERINTENDENT GOVERNMENT PRINTING, 1922), NO. 7, PRICES OF STAPLE ARTICLES OF EXPORT FROM 1896 TO 1921, PP. 38–43.

 | DOI 10.1163/9789004311558_017

Bibliography

1 Primary Sources

1a *Unpublished Primary Sources*

Het Nationaal Archief [the National Archives], *The Hague. The Netherlands*
De archieven van de Verenigde Oost-Indische Compagnie, 1602–1795 [The archives of the United East India Company, 1602–1795]
Overgekomen Brieven en Papieren uit Indië [Letters and Papers received from Asia] Toegangsnummer [Accession number] 1.04.02
1055, 1076, 1097, 1099, 1100, 1103, 1108, 1112, 1113, 1117 1122, 1127, 1134, 1149, 1151, 1157, 1168, 1188, 1215, 1297, 1472, 1474, 1522, 1575, 1599, 1620, 1635, 1649, 1666, 4583, 4585–4587, 4668, 4886, 6989, 7779, 8823, 8854, 9056, 9059, 10406
Boekhoeder-Generaal te Batavia [Accountant General in Batavia] Toegangsnummer [Accession No] 1.04.18.02
10810–10837, 10671–10679, 11830–11831
Collectie Geleynssen de Jongh [the Geleynssen de Jongh Collection] Toegangsnummer [Accession no.] 1.10.30
14, 100, 105, 108, 110, 113, 116, 117, 118, 237, 314
British Library, Oriental and India Office Collection, London, United Kingdom
India Office Home Miscellaneous Series (Home Miscellaneous), c. 1600–1900 [Accession No. H]
57, 406, 393, 434, 449, 499, 737
East India Company Correspondence with the East, 1602–1753 [Accession E/3]
1, East India Company Original Correspondence, doc. no. 117.
2, Original Correspondence from India with Collateral Documents, Vol. II, Anno 1614.
East India Company Correspondence with India, 1703–1858 [Accession No. E/4]
11 Abstract of Letters received from Bengal, 1760–1835
East India Company Draft Despatches submitted to Board of Control, 1784–1834 [Accession no. F/3]
55
Board's Collections: collections of papers in support of East India Company Draft Despatches, 1796–1858 [Accession no. F/4]
60 (doc. no. 1369), 471 (doc. no, 11338), 1504 (doc. no. 58997).
Bengal Commercial Reports [Accession no. P/174]
13, 19, 21, 22, 25, 31, 38, 44, 48, 49, 56, 59, 61–69

Madras Revenue Proceedings [Accession no. P/440]
24, 63
Factory Records [Accession no. G/36]
G/36/84
G/40/8, 24
Miscellaneous
IOR A/2/15, Minutes of Evidence on the East-India Company's Affairs
IOR B/16-18, 20, 29 Court Minutes
IOR P/188, Statement showing the total annual trade of Dye-stuffs exported from Bengal during 1873/4 and 1874/5
L/MAR/C/4
IOR Islamic Manuscripts
Bayaz-i Khushbui [Notebook on Fragrance], by Mirza Mu'tamid Khan, copied by Muhammad Azam, (Shaban 1109 A.H. 42 RR Aurangzeb Alamgir), c. 1698.
Khulasatul Mujarribat [Summary of prescriptions], ed. Sayed Hussain (Rajab 1121 A.H.).
Majmu'at-us Sanaye [A Compendium of artifices] by an anonymous author from Morocco, (*Hakim Philosoph-i magribi*), copied by Sayid Ghulam Murtaza Jafri, 22 RY of Aurangzeb Alamgir (c. 1679).
Nuskha Khulasatul Mujarribat [Manuscript-copy of the summary of prescriptions], copied in 1180 AH by Shaikh Ahmad, c. 1790.
Risala mushtamil bar nuskhahai ataria wa talween-i parcha [Essay based on treatises on perfumes and dyeing of textiles], copied by Sayed Hussain, *Rajab* 1121 A.H. (c. 1709).
The National Archives, Kew, London, UK
[Accession nos. BT, CO, CUST, PC, SP, & T]
BT 13/60 CO 1/27 (doc. no. 52)
CO 5/1265, 1293
CO 137/6 (doc. no. 34), 14
CO 138/7, 11, 16, 1692
CO 153/4
CO 155/1
CO 388/24 (doc. no. 145
CUST 3/5-80
CUST 5/1A, 1B, 1C, 1D, 1E, 2–36, 38, 42, 44, 48, 50, 52, 54, 56, 58, 62, 64, 66, 68,72, 75, 80, 81, 87, 92, 97, 102, 105, 107, 109, 111, 113, 115, 117, 119, 121, 123, 125, 127, 129, 131, 133, 135, 137, 139, 141, 143, 145, 147, 149, 151, 153, 155, 157, and 159
SP 78/271
T 1/516
30/29/18/1

Maharashtra State Archives, Mumbai, India
Surat Factory Diary
16/II (1761–1763)
Returns and Statements: External and Internal Commerce, 1801–02 to 1826–27
3, 4/5, 5/6, 8–16, 20–26
West Bengal State Archive, Kolkata, India
Board of Trade: Commercial, 84, 85, 86
Agriculture, 10C/1, Statement of indigo, p. 94.
Board of Trade, Indigo, 1810–1811
Board of Trade: Indigo 1811–812
Western Cape Archives, Cape Town, South Africa
Inkomende en uitgaande brieven [Incoming and outgoing letters] [Accession no. C]
362, 363, 422, 425, 1466, 1467, 2527
Bibliothèque Nationale, Paris, France
Blochet Supplementary Persan
482, Surat Documents
Chambre de Commerce Archives, Marseille, France
MP 327
J/400-401
Archives Départementales des Bouches-du-Rhône [Departmental archives at Bouches-du-Rhône], Marseille, France
200 E 604
Library, Department of History, Aligarh Muslim University, Aligarh, India
Anonymous, *Sirat-i Firuz Shahi* c. 1370–71 (MS Persian, Rotograph 168)
Archivio di Stato di Venezia, [Venetian State Archives], Venice, Italy
Collegio, Risposte di dentro, filza 10 [Collegio, Risposta di dentro, volume 10]
Peabody Essex Museum Archives, Salem, Massachusetts, USA
Log, 1302

1b *Published Primary Sources*

An Abridgment of Mr. Edward's Civil and Commercial History of the British West Indies, vol. 1, (London: J. Parsons, Paternoster-Row and J. Bell, 1794).

A Treatise on Indigo: containing a succinct account of the proper soil, the culture and preparation of that important article of commerce…, translated from French by Ricard Nowland (Calcutta: James White, 1794).

Abdullah Muhammad bin Omar al-Makki al-Asafi, Ulughkhani, *Zafar ul-Waleh bi Muzaffar al Alih*, vol. I (ed.), Sir E. Denison Ross (London: John Murray, 1910).

Abul Fazl, *Ain-i Akbari* (tr.), H.S. Jarrett, vol. 3 (Calcutta: Baptist Mission Press, 1894).

Asiaticus, 'The Rise and Fall of the Indigo Industry in India', *The Economic Journal*, vol. 22, no. 86 (June 1912), 237–47.

Birdwood, George and William Foster. *The First Letter Book of the East India Company, 1600–1619* (London: Bernard Quaritch, 1893).

Boomgaard, P., ed., *Changing Economy in Indonesia: A Selection of Statistical Source Material from the Early 19th Century up to 1940*, vol. 12a (Amsterdam: Royal Tropical Institute, 1991).

By the King: A Proclamation for the better encouragement, and advancement of the trade of the East India Companie, and for prevention of excesse of private trade (London: R. Barker, 1631).

By the King: A Proclamation for the restraining all his Majesties subjects but the East India Company, to trade to the East Indies (London: R. Barker, 1681).

Chardin, John, *The Travels of Sir John Chardin in Persia* (1643–1713), vol. II (tr.) Edmo Lloyd (London: J. Smith, 1720).

Chadwick, D.T., *Report on Indo-Russian Trade* (Simla: Government Central Press, 1917).

Crawfurd, John., *A View of the Present State and Future Prospects of the Free Trade and Colonisation of India* (London: Ridgway, 1828).

———, 'A Sketch of the Commercial Resources and Monetary and Mercantile System of British India (1837)', in K.N. Chaudhuri, *The Economic Development of India under the East India Company, 1814–58: A Selection of Contemporary Writings* (Cambridge: CUP, 1971), 217–316.

Crokatt, James, *Further observations intended for improving the culture and curing of indigo and c. in South Carolina* (London, 1747).

Crokatt, James and Edward Leigh, *Observations concerning indigo and cochineal* (London, 1746).

Dagh-Register gehouden in't Casteel Batvia van't passerende daer ter plaetse als over geheel Nederlandts-India [Daily register kept in Batavia Castle of events taking place there and in the entire Dutch East-Indies]

1636 (ed.), J.A. van der Chijs ('s-Gravenhage: Martinus Nijhoff, 1899).

1637 (ed.), H.T. Colenbrander ('s-Gravenhage: Martinus Nijhoff, 1899).

1640–1641 (ed.), J.A. van der Chijs ('s-Gravenhage: Martinus Nijhoff, 1887).

1643–1644 (ed.), H.T. Colenbrander ('s-Gravenhage: Martinus Nijhoff, 1903).

1644–1645, (ed.), J.A. van der Chijs ('s-Gravenhage: Martinus Nijhoff, 1903).

1661 (ed.), J.A. van der Chijs ('s-Gravenhage: Martinus Nijhoff, 1889).

1682, part II (ed.), W. Fruin-Mees (Batavia, G Kolff & Co., 1931).

Darrac, Pierre-Paul and Willem van Schendel, *Global Blue: Indigo and Espionage in Colonial Bengal* (Dhaka: The University Press Limited, 2006).

De Cossigny, M. De Palma, *Memoir Containing an Abridged Treatises on the Cultivation and Manufacture of Indigo* (Calcutta: Company's Press, 1789).

De Jongh, W. Geleynssen, *De Remonstrantie van W. Geleynssen de Jongh* [the remonstrance of W. Geleynssen de Jongh], (ed.), W. Caland (s'Gravenhage: Martinus Nijhoff, 1929).

The Dutch Factories in India, 1617–1623: A Collection of Dutch East India Company Documents Pertaining to India (ed.), Om Prakash (New Delhi: Munshiram Manoharlal, 1984).

The Dutch Factories in India, 1624–1627: A Collection of Dutch East India Company Documents Pertaining to India, (ed.), Om Prakash (New Delhi: Manohar, 2007).

'East India Monopoly – Export Trade to India', *The Oriental Herald*, vol. 19, no. 59 (Nov. 1828), 185–203.

'East India Monopoly – Import Trade', *The Oriental Herald*, vol. 19 no. 60 (Dec. 1828), 387–402.

Edward, Bryan, *The History Civil and Commercial of the British Colonies in the West Indies* (London: John Stockdale, 1801).

English Factories in India, (ed.), William Foster, 13 vols. (Oxford: Clarendon Press, 1906–1923).

Fawcett, C.G.H., *A Monograph on Dyes and Dyeing in the Bombay Presidency* (Bombay, 1896).

Finch, William, *Early Travels in India, 1583–1619*, (ed.) William Foster (London: OUP, 1921).

Fryer, John, *A New Account of East India and Persia in Eight Letters Being Nine Years Travels, 1672–1681* (London: R. Chiswell, 1698).

Generale Missiven van Gouverneurs-Generaal en Raden aan Heren XVII der Verenigde Oostindische Compagnie, [General missives of the governors-general and councilors to the Gentlemen XVII of the Dutch East India Company]
Vol. I, 1610–1638, ed., W. Ph. Coolhaas ('s-Gravenhage: Martinus Nijhoff, 1960).
Vol. II, 1639–1655, ed., W. Ph. Coolhaas ('s-Gravenhage: Martinus Nijhoff, 1964).
Vol. III: 1655–1674, ed., W. Ph. Coolhaas ('s-Gravenhage: Martinus Nijhoff, 1968).
Vol. IV: 1675–1685, ed., W. Ph. Coolhaas ('s-Gravenhage: Martinus Nijhoff, 1971).
Vol V: 1686–1697, ed., W. Ph. Coolhaas ('s-Gravenhage: Martinus Nijhoff, 1975).

Havart, Daniel, *Op-En Ondergang van Cormandel* [Rise and decline of Coromandel] (Amsterdam: Jan ten Hoorn, 1693).

Hewatt, Alexander, *An Historical Account of the Rise and Progress of the Colonies of South Carolina and Georgia*, vol. 2 (London: Alexander Donaldson, 1779).

Jourdain, John, *The Journal of John Jourdain, 1608–1617*, (ed.) William Foster (Cambridge: Hakluyt Society, 1905).

Khan, Ali Mohammad *Mira't-i Ahmadi*, part I (ed.), Syed Nawab Ali (Calcutta: Baptist Mission Press, 1928).

Ledyard, John, *Methods for improving the manufacture of indigo: originally submitted to the consideration of the Carolina planters and now published for the benefit of all the British colonies whose situation is favorable to the culture of indigo* (London, 1776).

'Letter from Mrs. Charles Pinckney to Harriott Horry' (10 Sept. 1785), annotated by Joseph W. Barnwell, *The South Carolina Historical and Genealogical Magazine*, vol. 17, no. 3 (1916), 101–2.

Letters Received by the East India Company from its servants in the East transcribed from the 'Original Correspondence' series of the India Office records, 6 vols., eds., Frederick Charles Danvers and William Foster (London, 1896–1902).

Linde, F.E.C., *Indigo: A short sketch of the Cultivation, Manufacture & Trade of Indigo* (Calcutta: Central Press, 1882).

Long, J., *Strike, But Hear!: Evidence Explanatory of the Indigo System in Lower Bengal* (Calcutta: R.C. Lepage and Co., 1861).

Macrae, A.S., 'Competition between the Aniline and Madder Dyes', *Science*, vol. 1, no. 6 (1880), 62–3.

Memorial of Mr. James Hay, indigo planter, Poorneah, to the Hon. East India Company, appealing against the proceedings of Mr. William Wollen, judge of Poorneah (London, 1826).

Minute of the Lieutenant-Governor of Bengal on the Report of the Indigo Commission (Calcutta: Bengal Secretariat Office, 1861).

Miscellaneous Statistics related to British India (Calcutta: Superintendent of Government Printing, 1876–1880), vol. 1.

Osborn, William, *Treatise on the Process and Manufacture of Fine Indigo* (printed in the Indian lithographic press by W. Holland), 1832.

Papers Relating to East India Affairs (Ordered by the House of Commons to be printed, 1811).

Papers Relating to East India Affairs (Ordered by the House of Commons to be printed, 14 April 1813).

Partridge, William, 'On the Manufacturing of Indigo in the United States', *Silliman's Journal*, vol. 6, no. 3 (1830), 193–8.

Pelsaert, Francisco, *De Geschriften van Francisco Pelsaert over Mughal Indië, 1627: Kroniek en Remonstrantie* [The writings of Francisco Pelsaert about Mughal India: chronicle and remonstrance], (eds.), D.H.A. Kolff and H.W. van Santen ('s-Gravenhage: Martinus Nijhoff, 1979).

Phipps, John, *A Series of Treatise on the Principal Products of Bengal: 1 Indigo* (Calcutta: Baptist Mission, 1832).

Prices and wages in India, vols. 8, 10, 17, 27, 36 (Calcutta: Superintendent of Government Printing, 1891, 1893, 1900, 1910, 1922).

Pyrard, Francois, *The Voyage of François Pyrard of Laval to the East Indies, the Maldives, the Moluccas and Brazil* (tr. and ed.), Albert Gray (London: Hakluyt Society, 1887).

Ray, Indrani, 'Of Trade and Traders in Seventeenth-Century India: An Unpublished French Memoir by George Roques', in Lakshmi Subramanian (ed.), *The French East India Company and the Trade of the Indian Ocean: A Collection of Essays by Indrani Ray* (New Delhi: Munshiram Manoharlal, 1999), pp. 1–62.

Rennell, James, *An Account of the Ganges and Burrampooter Rivers* (London: J. Nichols, 1781).

Report of the Indigo Commission appointed under act XI of 1860 (Calcutta, 1860).

Report of the Administration of Bengal, 1871–72 (Calcutta, Bengal Secretariat Press, 1872).

Reports and Documents connected with the Proceedings of the East India Company in regard to the Culture and Manufacture of Cotton-Wool, Raw Silk, and Indigo in India (London: J.L. Cox and Sons, 1836).

Roxburgh, W. and Alexander Anderson, 'Papers in Colonies and Trade', *Transactions of the Society, Instituted at London, for the Encouragement of Arts, Manufactures, and Commerce*, vol. 28 (1810), pp. 249–316.

Rural Life in Bengal: Illustrative of Anglo-Indian Suburban Life [anonymous] (London: W. Thacker & Co., 1860).

Selections from the Records of the Government of Bengal, No. XXXIII, Part II: Papers related to indigo cultivation in Bengal (Calcutta, Military Orphan Press, 1860).

Shortt, John, *An Essay on the Culture and Manufacture of Indigo* (Madras: Fort Saint George Gazette Press, 1860).

Statistical Abstract for British India, 1911–12 to 1920–21 (Calcutta: Government of India Publication, 1922).

Statistical Abstract for British India, 1920–21 to 1929–30 (Calcutta: Superintendent of Government Printing, 1931).

Statistical Abstract for British India, 1924–25 to 1934–35 (Calcutta: Superintendent of Government Printing, 1936).

Statistics of British India for 1906–07 and Preceding Years, part II: Commercial (Calcutta: Superintendent of Government Printing, 1908).

Statistics of British India for 1909–10 and Preceding Years Part II Commercial (Calcutta: Superintendent of Government Printing, 1911).

Statistics of British India, vol. 1 commercial statistics (Calcutta: Superintendent of Government Printing, 1919).

Statistical Tables for British India (Calcutta: Superintendent of Government Printing, 1881–1893).

Strange, G. Le, *The Lands of the Eastern Caliphate: Mesopotamia, Persia, and Central Asia from the Moslem Conquest to the time of Timur* (Cambridge: CUP, 1905).

Symson, William, *A New Voyage to the East Indies: vis. Suratte and the Coast of Arabia* (London, 1720).

Tavernier, Jean-Baptiste, *The Six Voyages of John Baptista Tavernier through Turkey and Persia to the East Indies* (tr.), John Phillips (London, 1678).

———, *Travels in India, 1640–67* (tr.), V. Ball (ed.), W. Crook, vol. 2 (New Delhi, 1977).

The Complete Indigo-Maker, translated from the French of Elias Monnereau, planter in St. Domingo (London: P. Elmsly, 1769).

Thomas, Edward, *The Revenue Resources of the Mughal Empire in India, from A.D. 1593 to A.D. 1707: A Supplement to The Chronicles of the Pathan Kings of Dehli* (London: Trübner & Co., 1871).

Van Dam, Pieter, *Beschryvinge van de Oostindische Compagnie*, vol. 2, part 2 (ed.), F.W. Stapel ('s-Gravenhage: Martinus Nijhoff, 1932).

Van den Broecke, Pieter, *Pieter van den Broecke in Azië* (ed.), W. Ph. Coolhaas, 2 vols. ('s-Gravenhage: Martinus Nijhof, 1962–1963).

Van Linschoten, Jan Huyghen, *The Voyage of John Huyghen van Linschoten to the East Indies*, vol. 1 (ed.), A.C. Burnell (London: Hakluyt Society, 1885).

Weston, Charles H, 'Observations on the Manner of Manufacturing Indigo in the Southern Provinces of India', *Journal of the Franklin Institute*, vol. 8, no. 4 (1829), 233–8.

Wilson, Minden, *History of Behar Indigo Factories (also) Reminiscence of Behar, Tirhoot and its Inhabitants of the Past, History of Behar Light Horse Volunteers* (Calcutta: General Printing Company, 1908).

2 Secondary Sources

Ahmad, Afzal, *Portuguese Trade and Socio-Economic Change on the Western Coast of India*, 1600–1663 (New Delhi: D.K. Publishers, 2000).

Alam, Ishrat, 'New Light on Indigo Production Technology during the Sixteenth and Seventeenth Centuries', in A.J. Qaisar and S.P. Verma (eds), *Art and Culture: Felicitation Volume in the Honour of Professor S. Nurul Hasan* (Jaipur: Publication Scheme, 1993), 119–26.

———, 'Indigo production Technology in Medieval India', in Harbans Mukhiya (ed.), *History of Technology in India vol. II* (New Delhi: Indian National Science Academy, 2012), 367–80.

Alavi, Seema (ed.), *The Eighteenth Century in India: Debates in Indian History and Society* (New Delhi: OUP, 2002).

Arasaratnam, S., 'Monopoly and Free Trade in Dutch-Asian Commercial Policy: Debate and Controversy with the VOC', in idem, *Maritime Trade, Society and European Influence in Southern Asia, 1600–1800* (Aldershot: Ashgate Variorum, 1995), chapter VII.

Bair, Jennifer (ed.), *Frontiers of Commodity Chain Research* (Stanford: Stanford University Press, 2009).

Balfour-Paul, Jenny, *Indigo in the Arab World* (London: Curzon, 1997).

———, *Indigo* (London: British Museum, 1998).

———, 'India's Trade in Indigo: Its Ups and Downs', in Rosemary Crill (ed.), *Textiles from India: The Global Trade* (Calcutta: Seagull Books, 2005), 357–73.

Barendse, R.J., *The Arabian Seas: The Indian Ocean World of the Seventeenth Century* (New York: M.E. Sharpe, 2002).

Bayly, C.A., 'State and Economy in India over Seven Hundred Years', *The Economic History Review*, vol. 38, no. 4 (1985), 583–96.

Bhattacharya, Ananda, *Indigo Rebellion: A Selection (1859–1862)*, (Kolkata: Dey's Publishing, 2012).

Bhattacharya, Subhas, 'Indigo Planters, Ram Mohan Roy and the 1833 Charter Act', *Social Scientist*, vol. 4, no. 3 (1975), 56–65.

———, 'The Indigo Revolt of Bengal', *Social Scientist*, vol. 5, no. 12 (1977), 13–23.

Bose, Sugata, *Peasant Labour and Colonial Capital: Rural Bengal since 1770* (Cambridge: CUP, 1993).

Bowen, H.V., *Elites, Enterprise and the Making of the British Overseas Empire, 1688–1775* (London: Macmillan Press, 1996).

Boxer, C.R., *The Portuguese Seaborne Empire, 1415–1825* (London: Hutchinson & Co., 1969).

Boyajian, James C., *Portuguese Trade in Asia under the Habsburgs, 1580–1640* (Baltimore: Johns Hopkins University Press, 1993).

Chandra, Moti, 'Costumes and Textiles in the Sultante Period', *Journal of Indian Textile History*, vol. 6 (1961), 5–61.

Chaube, Badshaah, *Betia Raj aur Champaran ke Kisan* [Betia Estate and the Peasants of Champaran] (Patna: Impression Publication, 2011).

Chaudhuri, K.N., *The English East India Company: A Study of an Early Joint-Stock Company, 1600–1640* (London: Frank Cass & Co, 1965).

———, *The Economic Development of India under the East India Company 1814–58; a Selection of Contemporary Writings* (Cambridge: CUP, 1971).

———, *The Trading World of Asia and the English East India Company, 1660–1760* (Cambridge: CUP, 1978).

———, *Trade and Civilisation in the Indian Ocean: An Economic History from the Rise of Islam to 1750* (Cambridge: CUP, 1985).

Chaudhury, Sushil, *From Prosperity to Decline: Eighteenth Century Bengal* (New Delhi: Manohar, 1999).

Chowdhury, B.B., *Growth of Commercial Agriculture in Bengal, 1757–1900* (Calcutta: R.K. Maitra, 1964).

Clarence-Smith, William and Steven Topik (eds), *The Global Coffee Economy in Africa, Asia and Latin America, 1500–1989* (New York: CUP, 2003).

Clark, Robin J.H. and Sigrid Mirabaud, 'Identificaion of the pigments on a Sixteenth Century Persian book of poetry by Raman microscopy', *Journal of Raman Spectroscopy*, vol. 37, nos. 1–3 (2006), 235–9.

Commissariat, M.S., *A History of Gujarat, 1297–1573*, vol. I (Bombay: Longmans, Green & Co., 1938).

———, *A History of Gujarat, 1573–1758*, vol. II (Bombay: Orient Longmans, 1957).

Coon, David L., 'Eliza Lucas Pinckney and the Reintroduction of Indigo Culture in South Carolina', *The Journal of Southern History*, vol. 42, no. 1 (1976), 61–76.

Darrac, Pierre-Paul and Willem van Schendel, *Global Blue: Indigo and Espionage in Colonial Bengal* (Dhaka: The University Press Limited, 2006).

Das Gupta, Ashin, *Indian Merchants and the Decline of Surat, 1700–1750* (Wiesbaden: Franz Steiner, 1979).

Datta, Rajat, 'Merchants and Peasants: A Study of the Structure of Local Trade in Grain in late Eighteenth Century Bengal', in Sanjay Subrahmanyam (ed.), *Merchants, Markets and the State in Early Modern India* (Delhi: OUP, 1990), 139–62.

Dauril, Alden, 'The Growth and Decline of Indigo Production in Colonial Brazil: A Study in Comparative Economic History', *Journal of Economic History*, vol. 35 (1965), 35–60.

De, J.C., 'The Earliest Phases of the Company's Indigo Trade', *The Indian Historical Quarterly*, volume XVIII, no. 2 (June 1942), 137–55.

Dirks, Nicholas B., *The Scandal of Empire: India and the Creation of Imperial Britain* (Cambridge, Mass.: Harvard University Press, 2006).

Disney, A.R., *Twilight of the Pepper Empire: Portuguese Trade in Southwest India in the Early Seventeenth Century* (Cambridge, Mass.: Harvard University Press, 1978).

Dmitriyev, G.L., 'From the History of Indian Colony in Central Asia (2nd half of the XIX Century-Beginning of the XX Century)', in Surendra Gopal (ed.), *India and Central Asia: Cultural, Economic and Political Links* (Delhi: Shipra Publications, 2001), 76–98.

Dutta, Abhijit, *Christian Missionaries on the Indigo-Question in Bengal (1855–1861)* (Calcutta: Minerva Publications, 1989).

Edelson, Scott David, 'Colour and Enterprise: South Carolina Indigo and the Atlantic Economy, 1745–1795' (PhD thesis, Lincoln College, University of Oxford, 1994).

Edwards, A. Cecil, *The Persian Carpet: A Survey of the Carpet-Weaving Industry of Persia* (London: Duckworth, 1983).

Enthoven, Victor, 'An Assessment of Dutch Transatlantic Commerce, 1585–1817', in Johannes Postma and Victor Enthoven (eds), *Riches from Atlantic Commerce: Dutch Transatlantic Trade and Shipping, 1585–1817* (Leiden: Brill, 2003), 115–38.

Farmanfarmaian, Fatema Soudavar, '"*Haft Qalam Arayish*": Cosmetics in the Iranian World', *Iranian Studies*, vol. 33, nos. 3–4 (2000), 285–326.

Feeser, Andrea, *Red, White, and Black Make Blue: Indigo in the Fabric of Colonial South Carolina Life* (Athens: University of Georgia Press, 2013).

Fisher, Colin M, 'Planters and Peasants: the Ecological Context of Agrarian Unrest on the Indigo Plantations of North Bihar, 1820–1920', in Clive Dewey and A.G. Hopkins (eds), *The Imperial Impact: Studies in the Economic History of Africa and India* (London: The Athlone Press, 1978), 115–31.

Floor, Willem, *Agriculture in Qajar Iran* (Washington DC: Mage Publishers, 2003).

———, *The Persian Gulf: A Political and Economic History of Five Port Cities, 1500–1730* (Washington: Mage, 2006).

———, 'The importation of indigo into Qajar Iran', *Studia Iranica*, vol. 35, no. 2 (2006), 237–59.

———, *The Persian Gulf: Bandar Abbas, The Natural Trade Gateway of Southeast Iran* (Washington: Mage Publishers, 2011).

Floyd, Troy S., 'The Guatemalan Merchants, the Government, and the Provincianos, 1750–1800', *The Hispanic American Historical Review*, vol. 41, no. 1 (1961), 90–110.

———, 'The Indigo Merchant: Promoter of Central American Economic Development, 1750–1808', *Business History Review*, vol. 39, no. 4 (1965), 466–88.

Furber, Holden, *Rival Empires of Trade in the Orient, 1600–1800* (Minneapolis: University of Minnesota Press, 1976).

Furnivall, J.S., *The Netherlands India: A Study of Plural Economy* (New York: The McMillan Company, 1944).

Garrigus, John, 'Blue and Brown: Contraband Indigo and the Rise of a Free Colored Planter Class in French Saint-Domingue', *The Americas*, vol. 50, no. 2 (1993), 233–63.

Geriffi, Gary and Miguel Korzeniewicz (eds), *Commodity Chains and Global Capitalism* (Westport: Praeger, 1994).

Ghosal, H.R., *Economic Transition in the Bengal Presidency (1793–1833)*, (Calcutta: Firma K.L. Mukhopadhyay, 1950).

Gopal, Surendra, *Commerce and Crafts in Gujarat, 16th and 17th Centuries: A Study in the Impact of European Expansion on Precapitalist Economy* (New Delhi: People's Publishing House, 1975).

———, 'Indian Traders in Uzbekistan in the Eighteenth Century', in idem (ed.), *India and Central Asia*, 19–43.

Goslinga, Cornelis Ch., *The Dutch in the Caribbean and in the Guianas, 1680–1791* (Assen: Van Gorcum, 1985).

Guha, Ranajit, 'Neel-Darpan: The Image of a Peasant Revolt in a Liberal Mirror', *Journal of Peasant Studies*, vol. 2, no. 1 (1974), 1–46, reprinted in David Hardiman, ed., *Peasant Resistance in India, 1858–1914* (Delhi: OUP, 1992), 60–110.

Habib, Irfan, *The Agrarian System of Mughal India, 1557–1705* (New Delhi: OUP, 1999).

———, *Essays in Indian History: Towards a Marxist Perception* (London: Anthem, 2002).

Haider, Najaf, 'Structure and Movement of Wages in the Mughal Empire, 1500–1700', Jan Lucassen (ed.), *Wages and Currency: Global Comparisons from Antiquity to the Twentieth Century* (Bern: Peter Lang, 2007), 293–322.

Haynes, Douglas, 'From Avoidance to Confrontation? A Contestatory History of Merchant-State Relations in Surat, 1600–1924', in Douglas Haynes and Gyan Prakash (eds), *Contesting Power: Resistance and Everyday Social Relations in South Asia* (New Delhi: 1991), 239–89.

Hirsch, Arthur H., 'French Influence on American Agriculture in the Colonial Period with Special Reference to Southern Provinces', *Agricultural History*, vol. 4, no. 1 (1930), 1–9.

Holmes, Jack D.L., 'Indigo in Colonial Louisiana and the Floridas', *Louisiana History: The Journal of the Louisiana Historical Association*, vol. 8, no. 4 (1967), 329–49.

Hopkins, Terence K. and Immanuel Wallerstein, 'Commodity Chains in the World-Economy Prior to 1800', *Review* (Fernand Braudel Center), vol. X, no. 1 (1986), 157–70.

Hurry, Jamieson B., *The Woad Plant and Its Dye* (New Jersey: Augustus M. Kelly, 1973).

Israel, Jonathan, *The Dutch Republic and the Hispanic World, 1606–1661* (Oxford: Clarendon Press, 1982).

———, *Dutch Primacy in World Trade, 1585–1740* (Oxford: Clarendon Press, 1989).

Jurado-Lopez, Alicia, Omela Demko, Robin J.H. Clark, and David Jacobs, 'Analysis of the palette of a precious 16th century illustrated Turkish manuscript by Raman microscopy', *Journal of Raman Spectroscopy*, vol. 35, no. 2 (2004), 119–24.

Kaushik, Devendra, 'Economic Relations between India and Central Asia in the 19th Century', in Gopal (ed.), *India and Central Asia*, 59–75.

Khan, Iqtidar Alam, 'Pre-Modern Indigo Vats of Bayana', in Attilio Petrucioli (ed.), *Environmental Design, Journal of the Islamic Environmental Research Centre* (Rome, 1989), 92–8.

Kling, Blair B., *The Blue Mutiny: The Indigo Disturbances in Bengal, 1859–1862* (Philadelphia: University of Pennsylvania Press, 1966).

———, *Partner in Empire: Dwarkanath Tagore and the Age of Enterprise in Eastern India* (Berkeley: University of California Press, 1976).

Klooster, Wim, 'Curacao and the Caribbean Transit Trade', in Postma and Enthoven (eds), *Riches from Atlantic Commerce*, 203–18.

Knight, Roger G., *Commodities and Colonialism: The Story of Big Sugar in Indonesia, 1880–1942* (Leiden/Boston: Brill, 2013).

Kumar, Dharma (ed.), *The Cambridge Economic History of India*, vol. II, c. 1757–2003 (Delhi: CUP, 1983; New edition, Orient Longman, 2008).

Kumar, Prakash 'Scientific Experiments in British India: Scientists, Indigo Planters and the State, 1890–1930', *The Indian Economic and Social History Review*, vol. 38, no. 3 (2001), 249–70.

———, *Indigo Plantations and Science in Colonial India* (Cambridge: CUP, 2012).

———, 'Planters and Naturalists: Transnational Knowledge on Colonial Indigo Plantations in South Asia', *Modern Asian Studies*, vol. 48, no. 3 (2014), 720–53.

Lemire, Beverly, *Fashion's Favourite: The Cotton Trade and the Consumer in Britain, 1660–1800* (Oxford: OUP, 1991).

Marshall, P.J. 'Economic and Political Expansion: The Case of Oudh', *Modern Asian Studies*, vol. 9, no. 4 (1975), 465–82.

———, *East India Fortunes: The British in Bengal in the Eighteenth Century* (Oxford: Clarendon Press, 1976).

———, 'British Expansion in India in the Eighteenth Century: A Historical Revision', in idem, *Trade and Conquest: Studies on the Rise of British Dominance in India* (Aldershot: Ashgate, 1993), chapter VII.

———, *Problems of Empire: Britain and India, 1757–1813* (London: Routledge, 1998).

———, (ed.) *The Eighteenth Century in Indian History: Evolution or Revolution?* (New Delhi: OUP, 2003).

Martin-Leak, Hugh, 'A Historical Memoir of the Indigo Industry of Bihar', *Economic Botany*, vol. 29, no. 4 (1975), 361–71.

McCreery, David J., 'Indigo Commodity Chains in the Spanish and British Empires, 1560–1860', in Steven Topik, Zephyr Frank and Carlos Marichal (eds), *From Silver to Cocaine: Latin American Commodity Chains and the Building of the World Economy, 1500–2000* (Durham: Duke University Press, 2006), 53–75.

McLachlan, Jean O., *Trade and Peace with Old Spain, 1667–1750* (Cambridge: CUP, 1940).

Mishra, Kamala Prasad, *Banaras in Transition (1738–1795): A Socio-Economic Study* (New Delhi: Munshiram Manoharlal, 1975).

Mittal, S.K., *Peasant Uprisings and Mahatma Gandhi in North Bihar: A Politico-Economic Study of Indigo Industry, 1817–1917 with special reference to Champaran* (Meerut: Anu Prakashan, 1978).

Moosvi, Shireen, *The Economy of Mughal Empire c. 1595: a Statistical Study* (New Delhi: OUP, 1987).

———, *People, Taxation, and Trade in Mughal India* (New Delhi: OUP, 2008).

Moreland, W.H., *From Akbar to Aurangzeb: A Study in Indian Economic History* (London: Macmillan Press, 1923).

Munsi, Sunil Kumar, *Geography of Transportation in Eastern India under the British Raj* (Calcutta: K.P. Bagchi & Company, 1980).

Nadri, Ghulam A. 'Indigo Industry and Trade in Gujarat in the Seventeenth Century' (M.Phil. dissertation, Aligarh Muslim University), 1996.

———, *Eighteenth-Century Gujarat: The Dynamics of Its Political Economy, 1750–1800* (Leiden: Brill, 2009).

———, 'The Trading World of Indian Ocean Merchants in Pre-Colonial Gujarat 1600–1750', in Om Prakash (ed.), *The Trading World of the Indian Ocean, 1500–1800* (New Delhi: Pearson, 2012), 236–9.

———, 'Indigo Processing in Mughal India: 16th–17th Centuries', in Mukhiya (ed.), *History of Technology in India*, 355–66.

———, 'The Indigo Trade of the English East India Company in the Seventeenth Century: Challenges and Opportunities', in Maxine Berg, et al. (eds), *Goods from the East, 1600–1830: Trading Eurasia* (Palgrave Macmillan, 2015), 61–76.

———, Review of Prakash Kumar's *Indigo Plantations and Science in Colonial India* in *Studies in History*, vol. 31, no. 2 (2015), 249–52.

Nagashima, Hiromu, 'The Mughal Dynasty and Markets', in Harada Masami (ed.), *History of the Markets in Japan and Asia* (Osaka: Seibun do Shuppan, 2012), 239–72.

Naqvi, Hamida Khatoon, 'Colour Making and Dyeing of Cotton Textiles in Medieval Hindustan', *Indian Journal of History of Science*, vol. 15, no. 1 (1980), 58–70.

Nash, R.C., 'South Carolina Indigo, European Textiles, and the British Atlantic Economy in the Eighteenth Century', *Economic History Review*, vol. 63, no. 2 (2010), 362–92.

Nierstrasz, Chris, *In the Shadow of the Company: The Dutch East India Company and Its Servants in the Period of Its Decline, 1740–1796* (Brill, Leiden, 2012).

Parry, J.H., *The Age of Reconnaissance: Discovery, Exploration, and Settlement, 1450–1650* (Berkley: University of California Press, 1981).

Parthasarathi, Prasannan, *The Transition to a Colonial Economy: Weavers, Merchants and Kings in South India, 1720–1800* (Cambridge: CUP, 2001).

Pearson, M.N., *Merchants and Rulers in Gujarat: The Response to the Portuguese in the Sixteenth Century* (Berkley: University of California Press, 1976).

———, 'Goa-Based Seaborne Trade: 17th–18th Centuries', in idem, *The World of Indian Ocean, 1500–1800* (Aldershot: Ashgate Variorum, 2005), chapter III, 146–75.

Pouchepadass, Jacques, *Champaran and Gandhi: Planter, Peasants and Gandhian Politics* (New Delhi: OUP, 1999).

———, *Land, Power and Market: A Bihar District under Colonial Rule, 1860–1947* (New Delhi: Sage, 2000).

Prakash, Om, *The Dutch East India Company and the Economy of Bengal, 1630–1720* (Princeton: Princeton University Press, 1985).

———, *European Commercial Enterprise in Pre-Colonial India* (Cambridge: CUP, 1998).

Price, Roger, *An Economic History of Modern France, 1730–1914* (New York: St. Martin's Press, 1981).

Rao, Amiya and Rao, B.G., *The Blue Devil: Indigo and Colonial Bengal—with an English Translation of Neel Darpan by Dinbandhu Mitra* (New Delhi: OUP, 1992).

Ray, Indrajit, 'The indigo dye industry in colonial Bengal: A re-examination', *Indian Economic and Social History Review*, vol. 41, no. 2 (2004), 199–224.

Raychaudhuri, Tapan, *Jan Company in Coromandel, 1605–1690: A Study in the Interrelations of European Commerce and Traditional Economies* ('s-Gravenhage: Martinus Nijhoff, 1962).

Rezavi, Syed Ali Nadeem, 'The Design of Pre-Modern Indigo Vats in North India: A Study of Seventeenth and Eighteenth Century Indigo Vats of Bayana and Kol Indigo Tracts', *Journal of the Asiatic Society*, vol. 61, no. 3 (2009), 71–92.

Riello, Giorgio and Prasannan Parthasarathi (eds), *The Spinning World: A Global History of Cotton Textiles, 1200–1850* (Oxford: OUP, 2009).

Riello, Giorgio and Tirthankar Roy (eds), *How India Clothed the World: The World of South Asian Textiles, 1500–1850* (Leiden/Boston: Brill, 2009).

———, *Cotton: The Fabric that Made the Modern World* (Cambridge: CUP, 2013).

Robb, Peter, 'Peasants' Choices? Indian Agriculture and the Limits of Commercialization in Nineteenth-Century Bihar', *Economic History Review*, vol. 45, no. 1 (1992), 97–119.

———, *Peasants, Political Economy, and Law* (Oxford: OUP, 2007).

Roy, Mira, 'Dyes in Ancient and Medieval India', *Indian Journal of History of Science*, vol. 13/2 (1978), 83–112.

Roy, Tirthankar, 'Sardars, Jobbers, Kanganies: The Labour Contractor and Indian Economic History', *Modern Asian Studies*, vol. 42, no. 5 (2008), 979–80.

———, 'Indigo and Law in Colonial India', *Economic History Review*, vol. 64, Supplement 1 (2011), 60–75.

———, *An Economic History of Early Modern India* (London/New York: Routledge, 2013).

Sah, Raaj, 'Features of British Indigo in India', *Social Scientist*, vol. 9, nos. 2–3 (Sep–Oct., 1980), 67–79.

Samhaber, Ernst, *Merchants Make History: How Trade has Influenced the Course of History Throughout the World* (tr.), E. Osers (London: George G. Harrap & Co., 1963).

Sarkar, Jagdish Narayan, *The Life of Mir Jumla: The General of Aurangzeb* (New Delhi: Rajesh Publications, 1979).

———, *Studies in Economic Life in Mughal India* (Delhi, 1975).

Sen, Sudipta, *Empire of Free Trade: the East India Company and the Making of the Colonial Marketplace* (Philadelphia: University of Pennsylvania Press, 1998).

Sen, Sunil, *Agrarian Relations in India (1793–1947)*, (New Delhi: People's Publishing House, 1979).

Sharrer, G. Terry, 'The Indigo Bonanza in South Carolina, 1740–90', *Technology and Culture*, vol. 12, no. 3 (1971), 447–55.

Shukla, Prabhat Kumar, *Indigo and the Raj: Peasant Protests in Bihar, 1780–1917* (Delhi: Pragati Publications, 1993).

Sidddiqi, Asiya, *Agrarian Change in a Northern Indian State: Uttar Pradesh, 1819–1833* (Oxford: Clarendon Press, 1973).

Smith, Alan K., *Creating a World Economy: Merchant Capital, Colonialism, and World Trade, 1400–1825* (Oxford/Boulder: Westview Press, 1991).

Smith, Robert S., 'Statutes of the Guatemalan Indigo Growers' Society', *The Hispanic American Historical Review*, vol. 30, no. 3 (1950), 336–45.

———, 'Forced Labor in the Guatemalan Indigo Works', *The Hispanic American Historical Review*, vol. 36, no. 3 (1956), 319–28.

———, 'Indigo Production and Trade in Colonial Guatemala', *The Hispanic American Historical Review*, vol. 39, no. 2 (1959), 181–211.

Souza, George Bryan, 'Hinterlands, Commodity Chains, and Circuits in Early Modern Asian History: Sugar in Qing China and Tokugawa Japan', in Tsukasa Mizushima,

George Souza, and Dennis Flynn (eds), *Hinterlands and Commodities: Place, Space, Time and the Political Economic Development of Asia over the Long Eighteenth Century* (Leiden/Boston: Brill, 2014), pp. 15–47.

Steensgaard, Niels, *Carracks, Caravans and Companies: The Structural Crisis in the European-Asian Trade in the Early 17th Century* (Copenhagen: Andelsbogtrykkeriet, 1973).

Subrahmanyam, Sanjay, *The Political Economy of Commerce: Southern India, 1500–1650* (Cambridge: CUP, 1990).

Topik Steven, Zephyr Frank and Carlos Marichal (eds), *From Silver to Cocaine: Latin American Commodity Chains and the Building of the World Economy, 1500–2000* (Durham: Duke University Press, 2006).

Tripathi, Amlesh, *Trade and Finance in the Bengal Presidency, 1793–1833* (Calcutta: OUP, 1979).

Trivedi, K.K., 'Innovation and Change in Indigo Production in Bayana, Eastern Rajasthan', *Studies in History*, vol. 10, no. 1 (1994), 53–80.

Van der Oest, Eric Willem, 'The Forgotten Colonies of Essequibo and Demerara, 1700–1814', in Postma and Enthoven (eds), *Riches from Atlantic Commerce*, 323–61.

Van Eikema Hommes, Margriet, *Changing Pictures: Discolouration in 15th–17th-Century Oil Paintings* (London: Archetype, 2004).

Van Enk, Elly Marie Corrie, 'Britse Kooplieden and de Cultures op Java: Harvey Thomson (1790–1837) en Zijn Financiers' [British merchants and the culture in Java: Harvey Thomson and his Financiers] (PhD dissertation, Vrije Universiteit, Amsterdam, 1999).

Van Santen, H.W., 'De Vereenigde Oost-Indische Compagnie in Gujarat en Hindustan, 1620–1660' [The Dutch East India Company in Gujarat and Hindustan] (PhD dissertation, Leiden University, 1982).

Van Schendel, Willem, 'Asianization of Indigo: Rapid Change in Global Trade around 1800', Peter Boomgaard, Dick Kooiman, and Henk Schulte-Nordholt, *Linking Destinies: Trade, Towns and Kin in Asian History* (Leiden: KITLV Press, 2008), 29–49.

Van Zanden, Jan Luiten, *The Long Road to Industrial Revolution: The European Economy in a Global Perspective, 1000–1800* (Brill: Leiden, 2009).

Wallerstein, Immanuel, *The Modern World-System: Capitalist Agriculture and the European World-Economy in the Sixteenth Century* (New York: Academic Press, 1974).

Watson, Ian Bruce, *Foundation of Empire: English Private Trade in India, 1659–1760* (New Delhi: Vikas Publishing House, 1980).

Watt, George, *The Commercial Products of India: being an abridged version of the Dictionary of Economic Products of India* (London: John Murray, 1908).

Webster, Anthony, 'An Early Global Business in a Colonial Context: The Strategies, Management, and Failure of John Palmer and Company of Calcutta, 1780–1830', *Enterprise & Society: The International Journal of Business History*, vol. 6, no. 1 (2005), 98–133.

———, *The Richest East India Merchant: The Life and Business of Johan Palmer of Calcutta, 1767–1836* (Woodbridge: Boydell Press, 2007).

———, *The Twilight of the East India Company: The Evolution of Anglo-Asian Commerce and Politics, 1790–1860* (Woodbridge: The Boydell Press, 2009).

White, Christopher M., *The History of El Salvador* (Westport: Greenwood Press, 2009).

Winius George and Markus Vink, *The Merchant-Warrior Pacified: The VOC and its Changing Political Economy in India* (Delhi: OUP, 1991).

Wortman, Miles, 'Government Revenue and Economic Trends in Central America, 1787–1819', *The Hispanic American Historical Review*, vol. 55, no. 2 (1975), 251–86.

Yang, Anand A, *Bazaar India: Markets, Society, and the Colonial State in Gangetic Bihar* (New Delhi: Munshiram Manoharlal, 2000).

Index

adulteration 15, 26–30, 166, 137, 137n49, 162–3, 163n30, 172n56
Africa 2, 145
agent 2, 51n129, 61, 63, 82, 83, 83n85, 111, 111n106, 112, 155, 155n3, 157
Agra xvi, xvii, 6, 13, 16, 16n11, 24, 25n35, 27n40, 29, 35–37, 44, 51, 51n128, 54, 62, 63n2, 64, 64n6, 64n7, 68, 69, 70–4, 77, 79, 85, 88, 88n15, 89, 90, 94, 97, 101, 104, 107, 108, 110, 111, 112, 127, 128, 156n6, 159, 159n16, 160n21, 170–5, 177n74, 181, 189
  VOC factory in 106–7, 107n87
agricultural commercialisation 75, 186
Ahmadabad 6, 13n1, 62, 63n2, 64, 67, 68, 68n25, 69, 70, 70n32, 71, 71n34, 72, 73, 94, 97, 98, 101, 104, 111, 112, 119, 156, 158, 162, 162n27, 163n30
Aleppo 68, 91, 92, 92n35, 92n36, 93, 95
Aleppo Merchant 110n97
Ali, Mirza Mir 63n2
Ambon 128
America 175
American colonies 8, 124, 131–138, 147, 147n87, 167, 170n47, 178n80
American indigo 150, 175, 175n69, 180n84, 193
American market 147
Amercian merchants 74, 86, 145n78, 165
American Revolution 135n40, 136, 136n45
amin 51, 51n129
Amsterdam 35, 64n7, 89, 92, 101n74, 102n76, 104n83, 107n87, 125n1, 126, 126n3, 131, 131n22, 206–7
Andrew, Thomas 110, 111, 111n102
Antigua 134, 138
Arakan 88, 88n15
Armenian merchants 64, 64n6, 66, 67, 91, 93–95
Asia vii, ix, 1, 2, 8, 55, 85n1, 86n2, 86n3, 98, 99, 100, 101, 109n94, 111, 112, 124, 145, 153, 165, 179, 194
Asian merchants 13, 33, 61, 66, 86, 89, 91, 93–5, 118, 120
Asiaticus 183
Assada Merchant 110
assamiwar xvii, xviii, 37
Awadh (Oudh) 13, 36, 37, 38n78, 40n87, 44, 49, 77, 79, 85, 170, 171, 171n51, 172n53, 172n56, 173, 173n60, 174, 174n62, 175, 175n68, 189
  indigo production in 49n121, 51n130, 90, 172n56, 177n74, 178n80, 181

Badische Anilin und Soda Fabrik (BASF) 56
bahar xvi, xvii, 63, 68, 98
Baker, Thomas 83, 83n86
Bakhsh, Dawar 156, 156n5
Bakhsh, Murad 162
Bam 93
Banaras 13, 38, 54, 77, 79, 170, 174n62, 181
  indigo production in 177n74, 178n80
  indigo planters in 178n80, 180
Bandar Abbas 92
Bania (merchants) xvii, 64, 88, 88n15, 93
banjaras 162
banker 2, 6n9, 74, 76
Banten 128
Barasat factory 188
Barbados 134
Basawar 13, 89
Basra 89, 92, 93, 95, 155n3
Batavia 35, 101, 103, 126, 127, 127n5, 128
Bayana 8, 12, 13, 13n1, 17, 18n15, 19, 20, 20n16, 21, 22, 24, 25–7, 32, 33, 34, 55, 58, 69, 73, 84, 87, 88, 89, 93, 99, 100–7, 107n87, 111, 111n106, 126, 139, 155, 155n3, 167n39, 197–210
  indigo market in 62–7, 71, 74, 93–5, 97, 156, 159
  prices of indigo from 148–50, 159, 219–20
Bengal xvi, xvii, xviii, 4, 6, 13, 32n59, 35, 64n5, 65n9, 76n58, 77, 78n69, 84, 85, 86, 88, 90, 113, 115n115, 118–20, 122, 133, 136–7, 140n60, 143, 144, 145, 145n79, 164, 164n35, 165, 194
  indigo production in 36–56, 61, 79, 80n77, 81, 113n112, 115, 116–17, 141–2, 147, 147n87, 152, 166–91, 193

prices of indigo from 150–1, 221
Bengal Presidency 7, 33, 36, 49n118, 74, 77, 113, 170, 194
Betia estate 189
Bihar xvii, xviii, 7, 13, 36, 38, 39, 40, 41, 42n94, 48, 49, 50n126, 52n133, 59, 75n54, 79, 80, 80n74, 113n112, 151, 170, 173, 173n59, 180, 181, 184, 186, 186n108, 189, 189n117, 190
Bimlipatam 118n120
blue mutiny 184
Blume, Carl (indigo planter) 75n55, 174
Board of Trade 174, 174n62, 175, 175n66, 175n68, 175n69, 176
Bombay 13n4, 116, 117, 119, 119n122, 120, 121n135, 150
bonded labour 2, 148
Bourgois & Monnie, a merchant firm 95n55
Brahmabad 89
Brazil 143, 143n72, 144n75
Britain/Great Britain 2, 6, 8, 36–38, 52, 56, 76, 76n58, 77n63, 81–84, 86n3, 100, 105, 107, 109, 109n95, 112, 113–115, 115n115, 117, 119, 121, 122, 131–8, 138n55, 140n60, 142, 144, 148, 165, 166, 166n37, 167–8, 170–3, 174n62, 176, 176n72, 178n80, 179, 179n83, 184, 194
British merchants 81–4, 92, 134n33, 165, 174
Broach 13, 72, 89, 93, 156, 156n6
broker(s) 2, 6n9, 61, 63–5, 70, 74, 80, 83, 153, 190
brokerage 64, 83
Bubak 88
Bukhara 120

cake-cutters 50
Calcutta 52, 53, 61, 74, 75, 76, 77, 78, 79, 80, 80n74, 81, 113, 118n120, 119, 122, 145n82, 150, 151, 173–5, 175n68, 176n71, 179n83
Cambay 13, 44, 61, 89, 93, 97, 98, 99, 166n39, 167n39
governor of 156
Cape/Cape of Good Hope vii, 92, 96, 98, 100, 127, 128
Cape Frio 143
caravan xvii, 29, 61, 66, 69–74, 79, 93, 94, 104, 107n87
Caribbean 36, 117, 131, 135
carpenters 50
Carvalho, Tinoco de 97
Central Asia 89, 91, 118, 120
Ceylon 105, 117
chain-men 50
Charter Act (1833) 178
chaukidars 51n129
Cheribon 128–9
China 32n, 121n, 144, 145, 171n50
China pump 43, 43n96, 51
Chinese market 127
Chittagong 88
classies 51
Cochrane, John 82, 154, 171n52, 173n59, 176n71
cocoa 143, 193
coffee 9n, 129, 134, 142–3, 152, 153, 193
colonialism 6, 52n133, 152, 165, 165n36, 194
Colvin and Bazett 75n55, 170n48, 177
commodity chain(s) viii, 1, 9, 9n16, 10, 12, 60, 74, 82, 83, 85, 86, 107, 124, 126, 144, 146, 152, 153, 190, 192, 193
coolie(s) 31, 46, 50, 50n126, 69, 71
Cornwallis, Lord 168, 173
Coromandel 13, 16n10, 16n11, 17n14, 18n15, 19, 21, 22, 22n25, 23n28, 24, 24n30, 28, 28n45, 31, 32, 33, 35, 63, 64n7, 65n9, 67, 68, 69, 69n28, 85, 88, 89, 93, 94, 100, 101, 103, 105, 107, 118, 118n120, 128, 145n81, 160n17, 164
corte 141
cotton 1n1, 9n16, 32n59, 37, 46, 47, 53, 85, 90, 92, 95, 101, 117n118, 119, 119n122, 129, 137, 142, 153, 154n2, 164, 164n35, 166, 166n37, 193, 194
Council of Plantations 134
Court of Directors 30n51, 36, 77, 109, 142, 174, 174n62, 175n66, 176, 177, 180n84, 180n85, 184
Crawfurd, John 4
Crispiana 110n97
cruzados xvi, 99, 99n70
Curaçao 129, 131, 131n

Darrac, Pierre-Paul 41, 118, 145n79
De Cossigny 41
Delhi 36, 54, 69, 73, 77, 86, 88n15, 90, 189
Delhi Sultanate 86, 154n1

Dholka 13, 104n81, 156, 156n5
diwan 156, 156n5, 162
diwani xvii, 166, 167
doab region 13, 190
Douglas, Mr (indigo planter) 180
Dordrecht 103n77
ducats 94
Dutch Republic 100, 101n74, 103–5, 107, 124, 131, 136, 144, 150
dyer(s) 10, 26, 29, 82, 83, 86–89, 91, 91n29, 91n34, 92n38, 93n38, 96, 100, 113, 119, 120, 125, 137, 137n50, 138–140, 147, 148, 163n31

East India Company/EIC xiv, 2n2, 6, 166, 191
  indigo trade of 100–12, 166–79
  trade monopoly of 52, 76, 81, 82, 109–11, 136, 165, 168, 171, 171n50, 179, 191
Egypt 95, 114, 114n114, 122
Eighty Years' War 30
El Salvador 121, 138, 140
England 1, 90n22, 92n35, 92n36, 94n48, 100, 103, 105, 109, 110n100, 111, 124, 132, 132n30, 133, 134n33, 136, 138, 138n54, 140, 140n61, 143, 152n95, 165
Essequibo 129
Estado da India 86, 96–7
European capital 7, 88, 169, 187
European markets 1, 2, 4, 7n13, 8, 10n19, 30, 36, 53, 54n142, 75, 82–4, 85, 86n3, 92, 92n35, 96, 98–101, 107, 112, 114, 117, 122, 124–53, 166, 166n37, 175–8, 179n83, 180n84, 193
European merchants 29, 48, 49n121, 50n130, 61, 62, 66, 74, 96, 109, 118, 120, 122, 137, 165, 172, 174, 176, 178n80, 191, 193

Fairlie 75n55, 170n48, 177
Faraizi xvii, 188
flor 141
Florida 136
Formosa 127
France 1, 83n85, 83n86, 86n3, 105, 113, 115, 116, 117, 117n118, 118, 122, 136, 139, 142, 142n66, 144, 145
Franco-American colonies 175
freight 68, 70, 71, 76, 77, 80n74, 81–2, 136, 152, 161, 171, 171n52, 172n55, 174, 174n62
French colonies 112, 131, 132, 134, 138
French merchants 92
Fryer, John 95
fusts or *fustas* 99

galleys 99
Gandhi (Mohandas K.) 185
Gandi 71
Georgia 136, 137, 176
Germany 2, 83, 136, 139, 142, 189
Ghose, Banarsi 76
Gilchrist & Charters 36, 75n55
globalisation 7
Goa 86n2, 88, 97–99
Gogha 91
gomashta 51n129, 64n5
Gombroon 89, 95, 110, 159n17
Gouden Leeuw 103n77
governor-general xiv, 54, 168, 173, 176, 176n71, 183n95
green-leaf process/method 22, 24, 32, 44, 57
Grenada 134
Guatemala 21, 28, 29, 36, 40, 55, 84, 95, 96, 96n56, 105, 112n110, 121, 121n134, 125, 125n1, 126, 136, 138–42, 144, 146, 148, 150
Gujarat xvii, xviii, 12, 13, 13n1, 15, 15n5, 17, 20, 24, 32n59, 44, 51, 57, 68, 73, 85, 88, 90, 91, 91n30, 93, 95, 96, 97, 98, 99, 100, 101, 103, 104n81, 104n84, 105, 108, 108n93, 111, 116, 156, 158, 161, 163n32, 164, 166, 175
  famine in 126, 148, 158–9
  governor of 29n72, 72n153, 160, 161, 162, 162n28
Gujarati merchants 93
Gurdas (broker) 156n6, 157n7

hackery (cart) 41
Harris, Herbert 75n55, 76
Hawkins, Mr 180
Hindaun 13, 25
Hindustan 41, 88n15
Hollandia 103n77
Honduras 138n56
Hormuz 86n2, 92, 93, 96
Hovhannes, an Armenian merchant 95

Ilbert Bill 167n40
imperialism 194
Indian merchants 6n9, 74, 88, 88n15, 93–5, 120, 155–6, 156n5, 159n16
Indian Ocean 86n2, 96, 97, 155n3

indigo cultivation 15–18, 25–6, 30–3, 36–41, 47–51, 55, 126, 127, 128, 129, 160, 160n20, 166, 166n39, 167n39, 168, 173, 177, 177n74, 178n80, 179–90, 192, 193
indigo industry 1–8, 10, 11, 13, 15, 28–30, 33, 37, 47–9, 49n121, 50n126, 56, 57, 60, 107, 112, 114, 118, 119, 122, 123, 135, 136, 140, 140n63, 144, 146, 147, 154, 159, 164, 165, 169, 175n66, 177–9, 184n103, 190, 191n123, 192, 193
indigo manufacture 4, 5, 12, 18–25, 33–5, 42–7, 50–60
indigo planter(s) xvii, xviii, 7, 11, 17n13, 33, 36, 38n78, 39, 41n90, 47–50, 51n130, 54, 55, 56, 57, 74, 107, 113, 115, 117, 118, 134, 134n33, 135, 137, 138, 139, 142, 145, 145n79, 147n87, 150n93, 169–70, 170n48, 172–174, 176, 177, 177n74, 178, 178n80, 179–93
indigo prices 8, 12, 16n9, 29, 30–1, 34–5, 37, 38, 39, 48n117, 51, 56n147, 57, 60, 62, 64, 66, 67, 72, 75, 76–7, 77n63, 78, 80, 80n77, 81, 82–3, 83n87, 87, 88, 91n30, 92, 93, 94, 94n48, 95, 97, 98, 101, 103, 104, 104n83, 107–10, 112, 115n115, 118, 118n120, 122, 124, 127, 136, 140, 143, 146–52, 154–6, 157, 159, 159n16, 160–2, 162n26, 62n27, 164, 170n49, 171n50, 172, 172n56, 174, 177, 178, 180n85, 182n92, 183, 187n110, 189, 206–7, 219–21
Indigofera tinctoria 1, 15, 15n6
Indigo Growers' Society 140
Indonesia 129
Indo-Russian trade 120
intra-Asian trade 94, 101, 103
intra-Caribbean trade 112n110, 131, 131n21, 133, 134n33
Ireland 133n32, 134
Isatis tinctoria 1
Isfahan 120

Jalali 13, 20n16, 20n18, 20n57–59, 89
jamadar 51n129
Jamaica 105, 107, 112, 132–4, 137, 150
Jambusar 13, 89, 104n81, 105, 107
Janssen, Simon 35
Japan 86n3, 121, 122
Jeddah 91
Jesson, William 110
John Palmers and Co. 52n136, 53, 74, 179n83, 193
Jumla, Mir 159, 159n17, 163, 164

Kabul 91
Kashghar 89
Khan, Afzal 161, 163, 164
Khan, Asaf 91, 161, 163, 164
Khan, Azam 29n48, 162
Khan, Hamid (governor of Broach) 156, 156n6
Khan, Muqarrab (governor of Ahmadabad) 111, 156
Khan, Saif (governor of Cambay) 156
Khatri merchants 88n15
Khiva 120
khud-kasht xvii, 30
Khurja 13, 25, 55, 63n2, 88, 88n11, 89, 104n81, 105, 107, 110
khushki system xvii, 39, 40
Khuzestan 93
King George's War 134
Kirman 92
Kol (Aligarh) 25, 89
Kowahi 59

labour market (*see* market) 52n133, 62, 70
Lancashire 83
lathials xvii, 183
Leeuwaerden 66n14
Leeward Islands 134, 138
Levant 92, 96
Levant Company 100
Levantine trade 91n34
leveraars 62
Lewis and Peat 83
Linde, F.E.C. 12, 15n6, 80n77, 184, 185
Lisbon 92, 92n35, 96–100, 143
Liverpool 83
London 81, 82, 83, 84, 89, 90, 95, 109, 110, 110n97, 111, 113n112, 116, 136, 167, 167n39, 168, 171, 174, 175n66, 175n69
  customs duties in 77, 81n81, 174n62, 174n63
  indigo market in 74, 82, 92, 92n35, 122, 176, 177
  indigo prices in 77, 77n63, 82, 150–1, 170n49, 171n50, 221
  merchants of 83, 193

Long, Reverend J. 183
Lower Bengal 43, 50n126, 181, 182, 183, 184, 190

Macaulay, Lord 184
Madari (broker) 64
Madras 74, 81, 115, 115n115, 118, 118n120, 118n121, 119, 120, 145n81, 166, 167n39
Madras Presidency 13, 44, 45, 49, 151, 178, 190
Mahmud III, Sultan 91
Malabar 105
manager 2, 38n79, 75, 75n54
Manchester 83
Manila 116, 121, 121n135, 144n78, 175n78
Manohardas 112, 157, 160n20
market(s) 1, 9, 10, 11, 12, 26, 28, 29, 30, 33, 35, 47, 51, 56, 57, 60, 61–3, 65, 66, 70, 74, 76–80, 86, 87, 88, 90, 91, 93, 94, 98–9 101, 110, 118–19, 121, 121n135, 147–8, 153, 155, 156–9, 160n21, 163–4, 167, 170, 182, 190, 191, 192
Masih-uz Zaman, Hakim 155n3, 160
Masulipatnam 13, 33, 69, 69n30, 88, 93
Mauritius 127–8, 166n37, 175
Mauritus 103n77
Maya 139
Mecca 91, 91n30
Mediterranean 12, 85, 91, 96, 145
merchant(s) xviii, 2, 9, 11, 12, 26, 28n43, 29, 35, 37, 47, 60, 61, 62–3, 64n5, 65, 65n7, 66, 67, 67n19, 68, 70–8, 80, 81, 88, 97, 101, 108, 109n96, 111, 112, 131, 134n33, 138, 140, 143, 144, 153, 154, 155, 156, 156n5, 157, 159, 159n16, 160–4, 170–2, 172n55, 173n59, 174, 174n62, 176, 178, 179, 190
merchant capital 12, 32, 33, 49, 164–5, 168
mestizo 139
Mewat 13, 20n19, 25, 89
Minto, Lord 187
Mir, Titu 188
Mississippi 136, 176
Mocha 92, 93, 111n106, 155n3
Mohammad, Jan 71
monopoly/monopolies 1, 63, 76, 81, 82, 97–8, 108n93, 109, 109n94, 110, 111, 112, 112n109, 126, 136, 143, 148, 155, 157–65, 168, 171, 171n50, 179, 191
  EIC's loss of 52, 179
Montserrat 134, 137, 137n49
Moran, Mr (indigo planter) 180
Moreland, W.H. 26, 148, 154n2
Mughal India 3n3, 4, 8, 10, 11, 15, 30n52, 53, 62, 96, 163, 164, 190, 194
Mughal merchants 63, 63n2, 67, 155n3
muharrir 51n129
Mukherji, Durgacharan 76
mulatto 139
Multan 88, 88n11
Musa, Mir (Muizzul Mulk) 72, 159
Muslim merchants 88, 94

Nadiad 13
Nagapatnam 13, 18n15
Napoleonic Wars 144
Nasarpur 88
Navigation Acts 107
Netherlands 30, 83
New England 134
New Spain 138n56
Nieuwland 128
nij (cultivation system) xvii, 39, 39n80, 41n90, 47, 181, 181n89
North America 86n3
North American colonies 178n80
North American indigo 175
North American market 147
Nowell, Alexander 177, 178

Oranje 103n77
Ostend Company 172n55
overseer 51, 51n129, 185

peasants 2, 7, 9, 11, 12, 17, 17n12, 27, 29, 30, 31, 31n53, 32, 32n57, 32n59, 33, 34, 35, 37–40, 41, 47, 47n114, 48–9, 50, 52, 60, 74, 112n109, 115, 127, 158, 160, 160n20, 162n28, 164, 169–70, 177, 180, 180–91, 192, 193
  resistance by 184n102, 187–8, 192
peasantry 5, 30, 30n52, 48, 169
Pedder, Robert 83, 83n86
Pelle, Gijsbert 33
Pelsaert, Francisco 13n1, 18n15, 20n19, 25, 25n34, 27, 29, 33, 99
Penang (Malaysia) 122
Penning, Gijsbert 128
peons 69–71

pepper 96–98, 100, 101, 129
Persia 69, 91, 92, 92n37, 92n38, 93, 95, 118, 119, 120, 159n16, 150n17, 160
Persian dyers 92n38, 120
Persian Gulf 85, 89, 93–95, 119, 119n123
Persian merchants 66, 93, 95
Persian wheel 17
Philippines 144, 175
Phipps, John 41, 45n106, 51n129, 54, 115n115, 121n134
Piri, Agha 64, 64n6
Pondicherry 118, 118n120, 145, 145n81
Portuguese colonies 143n72, 143–4
Portuguese merchants 97–8, 156
Portuguese trade in indigo 33, 57, 86, 91n30, 92, 92n35, 96–100, 103, 156
press box 46, 47, 51 56
press-*mistiry* (mechanic) 50
Priangan 128
private trade 52, 84, 109, 109n94, 110, 111, 111n102, 171n50
Privy Council 6, 83, 83n86, 168
Pulicat 13, 63
Purnea District 180
Pyrard, Francois 88

rahdari xviii, 70
raiyyati cultivation xviii, 47–8, 47n114
raiyyati system xviii, 37, 39, 39n80, 40, 41n90, 181n89
raiyyats xviii, 39
Rajasthan 12
rebellion 115, 143, 187, 188, 190, 192
Red Sea 85, 93, 95
Regulating Act 167n40
Rennell, James 79
revolt 2, 184n102, 185
rice 37, 127, 134, 135, 153, 182, 190, 193
Rio de la Goa 127
Rondebosje 128
Roques, George 28n43, 66
Russia 114, 120–121, 122, 136

Saint-Domingue 84, 96, 105, 112n110, 117, 131, 133n32, 142–3, 143n71, 145
Salvador & Ishac Cardeso 96n55
Samarqand 89
Sann 88
Sarkhej 3, 8, 12, 13, 13n1, 15n7, 65–66, 72n39, 73, 74, 87–9, 89n17, 91, 95–6, 97, 99–102, 104, 105, 107, 111, 139, 148
  EIC's attempt to manufacture indigo in 35
  indigo market in 62–7, 70n32, 93–4, 148–50, 155–6
  indigo production in 15–22, 24–9, 32–3, 35, 57, 58n152, 67, 158–9
Semarang 128
Senegal 126, 145, 145n79
Seven Years' War 134
Shahjahan 72, 112, 153
  indigo monopoly of 63, 112n109, 126, 148, 157–161, 163
Shahpur 43, 58, 59
Shah, Sultan Firuz 86, 154n1
Shortt, John 45
Siam (Thailand) 126, 126n3, 127, 127n5, 127n6, 144, 147n87
sikka rupees 37
silk 1n, 37, 90, 92, 94, 95, 119, 137, 160, 164, 164n35, 166
Sind 13, 13n4, 25, 85, 88, 89, 116, 119, 120, 155n3
slave 2, 40, 48, 132, 135, 139, 142, 143, 147n87, 148, 184
slavery 135n38, 184
Smyrna 95, 95n55, 96n56
sobrestiente 141
Sonnemans, Arent 128
South America 2, 143, 175
South Asia viii, 6n9, 166
South Carolina 36, 105, 112, 113, 131, 133–138, 150n93, 193
South-east Asia 87, 112, 129
Spain 30, 133, 136, 138n56, 139, 140, 140n60, 140n61, 141, 143, 144
Spanish-American indigo 138n55, 167
Spanish colonies (in America) 30, 112, 131, 133, 143n71
spice trade 66n15, 97
spices 63n2, 88n15, 96, 97n61, 98, 101, 103, 154n2
Suez 145n82
Suez Canal 82
sugar 9n16, 37, 129, 134, 134n33, 134n36, 142, 152, 162, 166, 166n37

sugarcane 31n54
Sukhram 71
Surat 16n9, 25n35, 29, 61, 62, 63, 66, 68, 69, 70, 70n32, 71, 72, 73, 74, 79, 93, 94, 95, 98, 99, 100, 101, 102, 103, 104, 107, 108, 112, 119, 156, 159, 167n39, 194, 197, 208, 209
  governor of 159, 160, 161, 163
Surinam 129, 131
Symson, William 69
synthetic indigo 2, 56, 113, 114, 119, 121, 123, 146n83, 189

Tack, John 34
Taiwan 126n3, 127, 127n6
Tanjungpura 128
Taqi, Mohammad 156, 156n5, 156n6, 160
Taradas 71
Tavernier, Jean Baptiste 18n15, 67
technology 3n3, 5, 10, 14, 15, 24, 53, 56, 57, 60, 126, 192
textile(s) 1n1, 9n16, 10, 13, 19, 23, 24n30, 28, 29, 32, 32n59, 34n64, 52, 64n5, 70, 82, 83, 85, 86, 87, 89, 89n22, 90, 90n27, 91, 91n34, 92, 92n38, 94, 98, 100, 101, 103, 105, 117, 119, 119n122, 120, 129, 137, 137n50, 158, 163n31, 164n35, 166, 194
  production of 82, 85, 86, 87, 88–90, 92, 113, 140n61
textile industry 86, 86n3, 90, 117–18, 135, 164, 166
theeka system xviii, 48, 181
Thirty Years' War 100, 105, 125, 148
Thomas Andrew 110–11
Tirhoot 38, 42n94, 184, 186
Tirhoot Indigo Association 75n54
Tob, Arij 128
transatlantic indigo 36, 105, 170n47
transportation 1, 12, 67, 67–73, 76, 78–82, 159n16, 171
  cost of 70–2, 71n34, 104, 108, 140, 147–50
  mode of (carts, camel, dromedaries, and asses) 61, 67–70, 79, 88, 108
Trope 69
Turkey 85, 91, 92n37, 95, 155n3
Turkistan 120

United States 14, 52, 113, 114n114, 116, 122, 137, 144, 194
Upper Provinces 17n13, 50, 80n77

Van den Broecke, Pieter 99
Van Linschoten, John Huyghen 88, 97
Van Mitsky, David 128
voorkoper xviii, 62–63, 74

wage workers 2, 148
wakil 51
Warner, George 83
Warner, Mr 180
War of Jenkins' Ear 131, 134
Weesp 103n77
West Africa 118, 126, 145
West Asia 1, 8, 10, 12, 13, 66, 85, 87, 89, 90–96, 110, 111, 114, 116, 118, 119, 144, 155, 159, 161, 167n39
  markets of 94–6, 111, 121n135, 155
  merchants of 13, 33, 66, 89, 91, 93–95
West Indies 8, 36, 129–131, 131n21, 133, 134, 166n37, 175
Wissendas (broker) 64
woad 1, 96, 97, 100, 105, 105n86, 139, 148n88
world market 1, 1n1, 2, 5, 7, 12, 13, 15, 75, 85, 86, 112n111, 118, 121, 122, 124–47, 153, 179, 189, 193
World War 2, 83, 121, 151

xeraphins xvi, 99, 99n70

yarn 90n27, 92, 93n38, 95, 119, 120, 194
Yezd 120
Yorkshire 83

zamindar xviii, 38, 38n79, 39, 49n121, 51n130, 72, 181, 189, 189n119
zera'ati system xvii, 39

www.ingramcontent.com/pod-product-compliance
Lightning Source LLC
LaVergne TN
LVHW010545300926
849162LV00002B/238

* 9 7 8 9 0 0 4 3 1 1 5 4 1 *